WHITE
NATIONALISM

BLACK
INTERESTS

WHITE
NATIONALISM

BLACK
INTERESTS

CONSERVATIVE PUBLIC POLICY
AND THE BLACK COMMUNITY

RONALD W. WALTERS

Wayne State University Press
Detroit

African American Life Series

A complete listing of the books in this series can be found at the back of this volume.

Series Editors:

MELBA JOYCE BOYD

Department of Africana Studies, Wayne State University

RON BROWN

Department of Political Science, Wayne State University

Copyright © 2003 by Ronald W. Walters.
Published by Wayne State University Press,
Detroit, Michigan 48201. All rights are reserved.

Library of Congress Cataloging-in-Publication Data

Walters, Ronald W.
White nationalism, Black interests : conservative public policy
and the Black community / Ronald W. Walters.
p. cm. — (African American life)
Includes bibliographical references and index.
ISBN 0-8143-3019-3 (cloth : alk. paper)—ISBN 0-8143-3020-7 (paper : alk. paper)
1. United States—Race relations—Political aspects. 2. African Americans—Civil
rights. 3. African Americans—Social conditions—1975– 4. Whites—United
States—Politics and government. 5. Conservatism—United States. 6. Political
planning—United States. 7. Nationalism—United States. 8. Racism—United
States—Political aspects. 9. United States—Politics and government—1945–1989.
10. United States—Politics and government—1989– I. Title. II. Series.
E185.615.W3146 2003
323.1′196073—dc21
2003001517

To the Rev. Jesse L. Jackson, Sr.,
*founder and president of the National Rainbow Push
Coalition and a friend and compatriot who
throughout his career has courageously and
consistently challenged the negative effects
of White Nationalist public policy upon all Americans*

Contents

Preface

I have written this book in an attempt to call attention to an important political phenomenon. In that pursuit, I have sought to fashion a theory of nationalism and link it to public policy and its impact on the Black community over the past two decades. My intention has been not only to establish a historical record, but to analyze the meaning of that record in relation to Black Americans' expectations regarding the role government in the long project of eliminating the barriers to their social, economic and political progress. These expectations for social progress have always been linked to two goals: one, the broader path of individuals seeking personal equality and opportunity, and two, the group struggle to achieve a collection of specific goals that contribute to the Black community's self-determination.

It has been striking to me that, despite the fact that Blacks have borne much of the brunt of the new radical Conservative politics, during the period under consideration in this book neither the media nor academia has found a consistent language to describe the movement or its role in tilting the balance away from the larger project of an inclusive American Democracy. In the 1980s, this led me to engage in a brief analysis of the subject of White Nationalist politics ("A White Racial Nationalism in the United States," *Without Prejudice: Journal of The International Organization for the Elimination of All Forms of Racial Discrimination* [Geneva, Switzerland] 1, no. 1 [Fall 1987]). The response was so positive that the article was reprinted and a book became an inevitable consideration.

Therefore, I want to thank those who have helped this book make the transition from a theoretical consideration to reality, such as the Howard University Faculty Research Program and the College of Behavioral and Social Sciences at the University of Maryland, both of which gave me successive periods of release time. While my work progressed, however, two other books intervened that were compatible with my growing interest in leadership: *African American Leadership*, with Dr. Robert

Smith; and *Bibliography of African American Leadership*, with Dr. Cedric Johnson. When I returned to this subject in the late 1990s, graduate research assistants Ester Carr and Adolphus Belk helped with editing and sources, and my brother Kevin Walters's expert knowledge of computers provided me with the necessary technology to produce the manuscript. Greg Mott, a freelance editor, made it possible for me to present a readable copy to my publisher. As well, I am greatly indebted to Dr. Hanes Walton of the University of Michigan, Dr. Robert Smith of San Francisco State University, and Dr. Ron Brown at Wayne State University for their critical reads. But, most especially, I want to thank Arthur Evans, former director of Wayne State University Press, who took a chance on this work when no other publisher would. Finally, I want to thank my wife Patricia, who in her own way makes space for me to address challenges and who helped me to complete this work, especially since it came to maturity as we were moving from our residence of twenty-five years to a new home.

This will not be an easy work to read. Nevertheless, underlying the exploration of this thesis is a vein of hope that evidence of the valence and negative impact of the current policies will lead to a change in course and re-engage a positive, progressive vision for all of our sakes.

Introduction

Ronald Reagan saw the need for a kind of nationalism, as indicated by the documentation that he left, that was necessary at that time.

Professor Douglass Brinkley,
"Presidential Reputations," conference, the Center
for Democracy, Society of American Historians
and the U.S. National Archives, September 11, 2000

A striking feature of the 2000 presidential election, among the many associated with that historic event, was that it completed the capture of the American political system by the radical Conservative wing of the Republican party, a project begun when Ronald Reagan was elected to the White House in 1980. In this work I argue that race has had much to do with the evolution of this politics and that, as a consequence, Blacks have constituted the base target of a set of public policies initiated by the Reagan regime. Thus I will discuss the development of the Conservative movement and its influence on public policy from the perspective of its focus on the Black community.

The force of this politics has caught the Black community off guard, since it deviates substantially from the Liberal vision that resulted in the civil rights laws of the 1960s and 1970s. Now, at the beginning of the twenty-first century, we appear to be living in an era when a dominant sector of the White majority seems to have lost confidence in the promise of America as a liberal democratic state and has been recoiling from this vision, which implies shared power based upon racial equity. Instead, the White majority is proceeding to concentrate economic and social power within its own group, using its control over the political institutions of the state to punish presumptive enemies. The targets of this punishment have been Black, Hispanic and other non-White communities. Here I use the term "target" with the connotation Helen Schneider and Anne Ingram assign it: "The social construction of target population refers to the cultural characterization or popular images of the persons or groups whose behavior and well-being are affected by public policy. These characterizations are normative and evaluative, portraying groups in positive or negative terms through symbolic language, metaphors, and stories."[1] In many ways this work activates the Schneider/Ingram thesis, extending the "targeting" phenomenon to the supposed "ally" of Blacks—the U.S. government—which is also presumed to constitute a threat to the interests of the White Conservative sector. Perceiving itself under threat, this sector mobilized, pursuing a politics that dictates institutional resources should be withdrawn from the target group and rules eliminated which are in any way conceived to disadvantage Whites. I argue that this was accomplished through the fomentation of a nationalist movement by a substantial sector of the White majority.

The case made in this work for the existence of "White Nationalism" as a sociopolitical phenomenon is based on substantial evidence which suggests the proposition that if a race is dominant to the extent that it controls the government of the state—defined as the authoritative institutions of decision making—it is able to utilize those institutions and the policy outcomes they produce as instruments through which it also structures its racial interests. In short, it may reward, punish and so structure outcomes as to protect and enhance racial interests.

The problem in recognizing the purely racial interests of the majority is different from discerning those of a minority group seeking equality. In the case of the Black minority, this group often seeks parity through movements that explicitly espouse "Black power" or other forms of Black Nationalism, practically elaborated as economic, political and group self-determination, and equality with Whites.

Given a condition where one race is dominant in all political institutions, most policy actions appear to take on an objective quality, where policy makers argue that they are acting on the basis of "national interests" rather than racial ones. In fact, how to separate the objective civil interests of the state from the subjective racial interests of those who manage it constitutes a critical problem, posing an impediment to the achievement of democracy—partially defined as racial equality—within the context of a multiracial state. How does one recognize the racial interests of the majority in policy making, since policy is rarely articulated in terms that directly imply favoring the dominant group? Often the straightforward articulation of racial interests is not only difficult to discover but generally absent from public discourse.

The discovery of racial interests under such conditions, then, must be inferential. Policy actions and outcomes must be examined in order to understand which group's interests are advantaged or disadvantaged. For

example, I argue here that the detection of national White-majority interests can be achieved by understanding the sources of White racial alienation that led to the development of an intellectual rationale of policy
"failure." Together with the notion that government actions were detri-
mental to Whites in the social arena, this rationale was used as the pretext for attacks upon policies oriented toward Black group interests and
on the federal government which supported them. Policies oriented
toward Blacks, it was argued, must be devalued of their perceived advantages, and the federal government must be weakened. This could be
accomplished through policies which redistribute power to states and
localities and promote flexible regulation of programs, thus permitting
resources to be utilized in the interests of White-majority communities.

The consequence of this new set of policies is that Black advancement in society is defined as a threat to White national interests in the
competitive context of the "zero-sum" concept. If Blacks are empowered,
then White interests suffer. This interpretation is reflected in the new
definition of "racial discrimination," whereby courts have reversed policies designed to provide fairness to Blacks because they are seen as unfair
to Whites. Indeed, this view has been constitutionalized, resulting in the
decimation of large areas of civil rights and the devaluation of Black
social mobility. Moreover, this logic promotes government actions which
have had the consequence of punishing Blacks by withdrawing resources
and subordinating them by such practices as racial profiling and high
rates of incarceration and execution.

I will also argue that the racial character of White Nationalism has
been further confused by the use of Blacks to promote aspects of White
policy interests. Blacks, especially Black Conservatives, serve as proxy
agents to legitimize the strategies that further White interests. Blacks
have assumed prominent roles in support of policies such as school
choice, which promotes the use of vouchers for students to attend private schools, or the "faith-based" administration of social programs.

Identifying White interests and examining their impact upon the
Black community, this work attempts to describe why a new White
Nationalist movement has emerged, the nature of its politics and the
characteristics of the resulting policies affecting Blacks.

TWO RECONSTRUCTIONS

This new Conservative movement has a historical parallel in the backlash
to the nineteenth-century Reconstruction program, when Whites fostered
a political revolution that overthrew a Liberal regime which they perceived

as a threat to their national unity. This new "White Nationalist movement" presages the return of an era most Blacks believed could never come again, but the full force of its impact has persuaded many even beyond the Black community that this is an alarming phenomenon, with critical consequences for American democracy. Indeed, there is such a strong historical predicate for what has been occurring in the past two decades that some have described the current period as "the second Reconstruction."

In the election of 1880, Republican James Garfield won the presidency with no southern electoral votes. But in 1884, in a scenario reminiscent of Bill Clinton's election in 1992, Democratic party "centrist" Grover Cleveland gained the White House after a campaign in which he claimed he had broken with his sectional allies in the South; he pledged to "support the rights of all citizens." Four years later, with the majority of Blacks voting for him, Republican Benjamin Harrison won a narrow victory over Cleveland. Yet the 1888 election showed Blacks that there was little difference between the two parties, since Harrison calculated that his slim margin meant he needed to strengthen his appeal to southerners, which he promptly did by excluding Blacks from his administration.

Those who were convinced that Reconstruction constituted an "immoral" attempt to raise the status of inferior Blacks to that of Whites set about the political disenfranchisement of Blacks, which had begun as early as 1880. This was undertaken with ferocious vigor and largely completed by 1900. In many ways, the 1896 decision of the Supreme Court in *Plessy v. Ferguson* represented the icing on the cake.

In his seminal work, *The Black Image in the White Mind,* George Frederickson included a chapter on "White Nationalism" which describes the efforts in the mid-nineteenth century of a group of White intellectuals and civic leaders—led by Dutch sociologist H. Hoetink—to effect the racial purification of America and achieve a "homogeneity that allegedly would result from the narrow localization or complete disappearance of an 'inferior' and undesirable Negro population."[2] Frederickson notes that one objective of this group was the containment of the Black population; this project involved antislavery activists who believed that the geographic dispersal of Blacks would make it more difficult for them to achieve social accommodation with Whites as well as Conservatives who believed deeply in Black inferiority. The group's efforts led to such activities as agitation to stop the expansion of slavery and the limitation of Blacks to a southern "Black Belt" that still exists today.

Another group of nineteenth-century White Nationalists attempted to construct "a 'pseudo-homogeneity' that could be attained by the exclusion of the Negro from the community of citizens."[3] Their influence generated the idea that particular areas of the country would be reserved for Whites, and it led to the vicious suppression of Blacks, through such means as deportation and even sanctioned violence. Another result of this movement, Frederickson suggests, was "the rise of a new sense of American nationalism that had clear racial overtones." By the 1850s, the destiny of America had been racialized as a White project; this helps explain the 1854 Supreme Court decision which voided Dred Scott's claim to citizenship on nationalist grounds.

Against the backdrop of this movement, the politics of the last decades of the nineteenth century could be conceptualized as an attempt to re-invoke the White supremacy that was temporarily shattered by the Civil War and forestall the emergence of Blacks as a substantial civic and political force. This was effected by a return to Black subordination through the reinterpretation of the Constitution and the perpetuation of a reign of terror. And it was paralleled by a series of electoral events remarkably suggestive of the politics of the last decades of the twentieth century.

In racial terms, the dominant intent of the first Reconstruction was that peace between North and South would be constructed by the convergence of the interests of Whites in both regions with regard to "the Negro question," effectuating a unity that was, implicitly, of demonstrably greater priority than the freedom of Blacks. Although radical reconstructionists purportedly upheld the logic of the Civil War in their attempt to construct a regime of rights that would ensure Black equality, the greater lesson of the Civil War came to be the domination of the state by Whites who instituted a Conservative regime that virtually eliminated Blacks from political participation and limited their access to national resources until the coming of New Deal politics in the 1930s and 1940s.

Both the first and second Reconstructions suggest the kernel of a theoretical proposition designed to answer several questions. Among these is: What processes initiate the kind of White Nationalist movements that have had such disastrous consequences for Blacks? Within the context of the maintenance of White supremacy, nationalist ideology historically took one of two forms: paternalism, whose adherents considered Blacks childlike, or autocratic engagement, a policy based on the conception of Blacks as beasts. Frederickson has suggested that White paternalistic engagement with Blacks during the late nineteenth century was accompanied by a considerable degree of Liberal noblesse oblige, which encouraged a moderate form of engagement and quasi-democratic forms of equality.[4] These would be allowed in situations where Blacks' engagement with Whites was considered to be appropriate, as in political activity, and most often this happened under the direction of radicals within the Republican party.

By contrast, autocracy was a harsher version of racial relations. In this formulation, individuals who held that Blacks were "beasts" sought forms of social engagement designed to subordinate, punish or eliminate them altogether. John Cell describes this phenomenon vividly: "The extremists left no room for ambiguity. In speech after speech they proclaimed their harsh, violent, nasty views. God had placed blacks only a little higher than the apes—and there was apparently some doubt about that. Intending them for severity, He had marked them with His curse. Anything that might raise blacks from their naturally inferior status they denounced and, when in office, vetoed. As a corollary, anything that the white man might do to defend his supremacy was fully justified."[5]

WHITE CONVERGENCE

What the two perspectives, one Liberal and one Conservative, have in common is that they both affirm the subordinate status of Blacks in relation to Whites as a basic value, a paradigm that, if challenged or changed, would activate both Liberals and Conservatives alike to seek to protect their status and reimpose subordination upon Blacks. This paradigm is so powerful that it has the capacity to energize Whites to invoke common interests and come together regardless of differences of political ideology or party.

The convergence of White political interests also helps explain why, historically, Blacks who have been engaged in political coalitions with one party or the other were abandoned when historical circumstances appeared to threaten White interests from either the Left or Right. What this seems to suggest is that temporary coalitions between Blacks and the Republican party or the Democratic party violated the racial order of unity among Whites but were tolerated as long as these coalitions served a greater value, such as economic growth.

The prime example of this would be the Civil Rights–era coalition of the 1960s between Democrats (including some southern Democrats) and Blacks that existed so long as Blacks were still clearly subordinate in the South and economic growth was occurring in the rest of the country. In the late 1970s and 1980s, when Whites began to perceive that their dominant status was threatened, White racial convergence acted to maintain the racial hierarchy by effecting policies that began to dismantle the civil rights protections.

The political behavior described above classically fits that noted by Professor Clarence Y. H. Lo, who, in his analysis of busing as a "countermovement" motivating force, confirmed the reports of other observers such as Michael Unseem, Gary Orfield and David Sears that there was a strong correlation between antibusing sentiment and the perception that Blacks were making social gains faster than Whites.[6] Lo further argued that the federal government did not operate as a passive judge of competing interests but responded by providing resources, legitimacy and leadership to the developing White Conservative movement.

Such appraisals are consistent with those of "status crystalization" theorists, who assume that class plays a role in building alienation and, therefore, in the types of manifestations of activity perpetrated by alienated groups.[7] However, I will argue here that race also plays a role in the process of White alienation, since it has the capacity to motivate groups across class lines. Social psychologist Johann Galtung suggested that culture was an important intervening variable in disrupting the structural dimensions of status, and that the improvement of economic and educational opportunities for Blacks promoted conflict between Blacks and Whites.[8] Thus, the manifestation of alienated behavior may be expressed differently according to class, with lower-income alienated groups expressing more violent, socially aggressive behavior and higher-income groups utilizing institutional processes aggressively.

I will also argue here that just as the first Reconstruction was driven by a convergence of interests on the part of a critical mass of Whites, the second Reconstruction has replicated this convergence through a political movement led and joined by radical Conservatives. Though public discourse neither recognizes nor names this as a nationalist era in American history, Faye Harrison has argued that "historicized analyses of whiteness go against the convention of ignoring yet universalizing whiteness as an unspoken but naturalized norm presumed to be unaffected by racism."[9] This characteristic of "unspokenness" and the presumption of being unaffected by race allow and promote the reluctance of intellectuals to evaluate Whites in terms of the same racial dynamics accorded other groups. This study seeks to unearth the determinants of White Nationalism through an examination of its impact on the politics of public policy where African Americans are the target population.

THE POLICY IMPACT OF WHITE CONVERGENCE

Since the policy manifestations of White Nationalism in the first Reconstruction were measures that opposed Blacks as part of the process of advancing the restoration of White power in the South and White reconciliation in the nation, the major reason for engaging in such a study is to deepen understanding of a growing impediment to modern Black progress. By the end of the *Plessy* era, a series of Conservative public policies were in place that mandated racial containment, and these will be characterized here as "policy racism." More recently, what has become mainstream politics also fosters the reconsolidation of White power, largely by attempting, and in some cases succeeding, to weaken the civil rights policy legacy that advanced the status of Blacks in American society.

A poignant example of the racially divisive and oppressive strains in modern public policy reside in an example taken from a congressional debate in 1997 over public housing legislation. In this debate, the central issue was an amendment sponsored by Rep. Jesse Jackson, Jr. (D-Ill.). Jackson wanted to eliminate mothers with children under the age of five from the requirement—sponsored by the Republican majority—that all inhabitants of public housing be subject to a mandatory, uncompensated, community service work requirement of eight hours per month. Jackson maintained that: "Forced voluntarism under penalty of eviction demeans residents by saying they are lazy. It tells them that we do not trust them to take part in their own communities, so we must force them to do so. There is no pride in community service when it is mandated as if residents have done something wrong."[10]

Republican House members responded. Rep. Richard Baker (R-La.) asked: "Are we invoking some sort of slavery, as some have suggested, on these individuals? No, there is another purpose behind this. It is to let that individual who stayed within the walls of public housing get out into the community and learn what skills are necessary to get a real job."[11] Rep. Merrill Cook (R-Utah) added: "The overwhelming majority of my constituents tell me that they are troubled by government handouts. We have seen time and time again that handout programs do not work. Public housing was intended to be a helping hand toward self-sufficiency, not another handout. I urge my colleagues to defeat any attempt to remove the work requirement."[12] Next Rep. Curt Weldon (R-Pa.) said: "We have got people who are getting apartments with several bedrooms and a kitchen. They are getting free electricity, free heat, and the gentleman is saying they cannot work 2 hours a week. Come on. Give me a break. That is one Oprah Winfrey show, that they cannot find somebody to mind their kids for 2 hours within the authority."[13]

The Democrats counterattacked. Rep. Joseph Kennedy (D-Mass.) argued:

> [Speaking to Rep. Jim Leach] It seems to me that it is eminently reasonable for us to characterize the way your party has acted towards the poorest and most vulnerable as insensitive to their needs.

I would just point out to the gentleman that another gentleman on your side of the aisle suggested that what the poor in public housing do is sit around and watch Oprah Winfrey. I believe, Mr. Chairman, that that has racist characteristics that ought to be dealt with by the gentleman's side. That is a mean-spirited comment.[14]

Next, Rep. Bernard Sanders (I-Vt.) said: "I would suggest that what this entire process is really about is scapegoating; is having the middle class and the working people think that their problems are because of the poor, rather than looking at what the wealthy and the powerful are doing."[15] Finally, Rep. Patrick Kennedy (D-R.I.) declared:

We all know what is going on here. We should know what is going on here. It is nothing different from the welfare bashing that we saw in the last Congress.

What I am saying, Mr. Chairman, is they are going to pass a policy here that says make the poor pay, because we know what the poor are. We are talking minorities here. Make the poor pay. OK? What they should be doing, if they really thought that the people, the federal government, ought to be getting a little bit of return on its investment, which is what they are trying to cloak this argument as, then why not apply it to every other federal contract and federal program that is out there? They are receiving taxpayers' money. Why are they not volunteering? Because they know and I know what we are talking about. They're talking about the perception out there of the poor being minorities, and they are thinking, they ought to go out and work, because my taxpayers back home are sick and tired of this welfare state.[16]

The ideas expressed by proponents of the community service requirement in this debate—with their vivid racial stereotyping of the poor, racial scapegoating and racist innuendo—are commonplace in the radical Conservative political discourse of the 1990s and beyond. The point, however, is that the policies on which such ideas are based have had real and negative consequences upon the socioeconomic status of a significant sector of the Black community.

Political discourse exhibiting the dominant public attitudes in support of the devolution of governmental power has grown so pervasive that spokespersons for both major parties have formulated and learned to speak in the new coded public language of class and race when discussing public policy. They value being "tough on crime" and enacting "welfare reform." They express support for "the middle class" and for "the future of our children." They espouse "family values" and "individual responsibility."

How to deconstruct this language, uncover its hidden meanings and demonstrate how it is used to define new principles and policies for society is a subsidiary task of this book. Its principal aim is to describe the phenomenon of White Nationalism in the politics of public policy, which has had little direct exposure either in the public arena or in academia.

CONCLUSION

In this work, I seek to represent aspects of the more radical sector of the Conservative movement in national politics, its use of a reawakened nationalist ideology and the impact of this upon issues of interest to the Black community. It is an attempt to understand this movement more clearly by discussing the subject in terms of a series of broad stages: the evolution of the White Nationalist movement and its causes; the impact of the movement on the political culture; the movement's subsequent seizure of the political system; and its promulgation of policy racism.

The Making of White Nationalism

INTRODUCTION:
UPSETTING THE BALANCE OF ATTENTION

Since at least the late 1970s, America has been in the throes of a Conservative social change politics, which has manifested some of the classic features of other such movements: the heightened consciousness of its members, the promulgation of an ideology of alienation and redemption, members' tendency to mobilize around their grievances and their use of various tactics and strategies to effect the objectives of the movement.

Investigations of the motivations of groups which mount movements for social change have yielded studies that now comprise a formidable research literature.[1] There is a rough consensus that among the most powerful motivations are the perception of relative deprivation or the perception of opportunities for change based on actual social progress. In the history of America, however, it appears that aggrieved groups that mobilize to influence the political system for one social reason or another are more typical than those that seek change as a result of their increasing social status. While the former situation might be recognized as the normal one, historical epochs are characterized by "large changes" effected by substantial majorities of the American population responding to events or to their real or perceived social conditions. We appear to be in such an era today, and thus the search for the reasons groups attempt such changes must undertake a more deductive mode of reasoning.

Within American society, which includes contending social groups, there exists a balance of power that conforms to that society's racial composition, and the "balance of attention" or "wish for recognition" by various groups must also conform to that normal distribution of power if society is to remain in equilibrium. It is possible to interpret the grievance of some Whites to mean that insofar as other groups have been accorded public recognition or attention to their claims, these Whites have, as a result, experienced "power deflation" or what they perceive as a disequilibrium that puts them on the losing side of the power equation. Thus they wish to restore the equilibrium and the attendant balance of attention to their social claims for status and to the satisfaction of their needs.

This view is supported by scholars who have studied dominant-subordinate relations. The noted Brazilian philosopher, Paulo Freire, who observes that the achievement of true liberation cannot come solely from reversing the positions of the oppressor and the oppressed. This will merely establish, Freire argues, a new contradiction that foments another cycle of alienation, because the former oppressor perceives that a theft of power has occurred. Writing of the elite class, Freire says:

> Conditioned by the experience of oppressing others, any situation other than their former [one] seems to them like oppression. Formerly, they could eat, dress, wear shoes, be educated, travel, and hear Beethoven; while millions did not eat, had no clothes or shoes, neither studied nor traveled, much less listened to Beethoven. Any restriction on this way of life, in the name of the rights of the community, appears to the former oppressors as a profound violation of their individual rights.[2]

Whites are not homogenous with respect to their interests or racial and ethnic consciousness, and thus there is often societal conflict over issues involving the distribution of benefit among factions, a tension that defines the national power equilibrium existing in American society at any given time. Theoretically, in a collection of essays edited by Seymour Martin Lipset, Mancur Olson explained "equilibrium" concept this way: "If there is some step or combination of steps that will make one or more individuals better off, without making anyone worse off, there is always the possibility some political or administrative entrepreneur will respond to the incentive inherent in the situation and organize a change in policy. This . . . is only one of a vast variety of necessary conditions of political equilibrium."[3] Yet there are ideological tendencies within America's

White population with regard to issues of race or ethnicity that forestall the kind of political equilibrium Olson described.

It is apparent that Black demands (including both nonviolent and violent articulations) for social justice created substantial disequilibrium in the 1960s. Much of the contested terrain of race relations in the 1990s was related to the difference between Blacks and many Whites with respect to the fairness of Blacks' demands, the magnitude of the attempts of the political system to dispense recompense and the meaning of the outcome. Yet it is clear that a Conservative reaction to Black demands was initiated and developed, and with steady growth it has matured to the point that it is now dismantling the institutionalization of the response to these demands.

Since the federal government sanctioned the institutionalization of civil rights, one way in which the extent of Whites' disaffection has been measured is their alienation from government. In national election surveys conducted by the University of Michigan's Center for Political Research in 1974, Arthur Miller found that serious discontent toward government had increased between 1964 and 1970. Over this period, trust in government went from a level of 76% (trust in government "always" = 14%, "most of the time" = 62%) in 1964 to 53.5% in 1970 (trust in government "always" = 6.4%, "most of the time" = 47.1%).[4] Miller's surveys showed that in 1964, those who were opposed to racial integration were the most cynical and distrustful of government, while those who favored integration were the most supportive.[5] By 1970, however, both groups had grown more cynical, and the differences between them had virtually disappeared.[6] In attempting to explain this, Miller hypothesized that those opposed to racial integration were consistently more resentful of civil rights and more cynical and distrustful of government, while those who favored integration grew cynical because of the laggard pace of change.

By contrast, levels of trust in government were at 15% in 1995, but a national survey of trust in government by the Council for Excellence in Government found that this rose to 32% by 1997. In his interpretation of the 1997 survey, Robert Teeter said: "Washington is seen as least successful in 'non-economic issues'—public education, poverty, crime, moral values, drug abuse, and illegal immigration—'that are perennial problems for the country.'"[7] These non-economic issues all have a strong racial or ethnic subtext, reinforcing the notion that racial or ethnic issues comprise a critical dimension of the alienation of Whites, especially with regard to the government's promotion of policy issues that ostensibly favor Blacks.

In the politics of resentment that fueled the first and now the second Reconstruction, a similar ideology obtains: Blacks are an inferior group making a claim to equality with the dominant class to which they are not entitled. This notion of Black inferiority is present both in the older, cruder claims of racists—that Blacks are a subhuman species—and in the more sophisticated claims of postmodern "Bell Curve" intellectual elite theorists such as Charles Murray and Richard Herrnstein, who argue that Blacks lack the intelligence of Whites and are, therefore, not entitled to special consideration in employment or other areas of opportunity, for they will inevitably fail.[8]

The idea of Black inferiority drives resentment in two ways. The first is that some middle-class Blacks, who have in many cases achieved actual equality with some Whites in terms of qualifications and accomplishments, are now in serious competition with them for a variety of resources. Such competition was never envisioned by crude racists, Conservatives or even paternalistic Liberals. Second, the forward progress of many Blacks, in real and popular terms, became part of an antithetical calculus on the part of many Whites who experienced personal economic stagnation. In racial terms, this enhanced the status conflict and fueled White resentment of the presumed advantages of Blacks, which Whites now regard as "preferences." I will comment briefly on both sources of resentment, for it is necessary to explore the roots of the politics of resentment as the driving force behind the White Nationalist movement.

THE ROOTS OF WHITE NATIONALISM

The idea of nationalism, with its corresponding conception of the nation-state, seems to have first emerged in Western Europe. It found its fullest flower in England and France, where "just as the king had required undivided allegiance in the days of royal supremacy, so managers of the sovereign nation-state of the nineteenth century expected not only loyalty to the state but also identification with the language, culture and mores of those who controlled it."[9] Other writers have observed that the "nationalization of race and the racialization of nationhood" extended to the zeal with which "Anglo-Saxon" nations approached their expansion into the United States.[10] As Rogers Brubacker has remarked: "At the heart of Anglo-Saxonism lay the conviction that the Anglo-Saxon (British) race possessed a special capacity for governing itself (and others) through a constitutional system which combined liberty, justice and efficiency. It was a gift that could not be transferred to lesser peoples."[11]

Thus the idea that the racial/ethnic majority would dominate the state was an integral part of the context from which European ethnicities emerged to establish control over America. The various White ethnicities coalesced into a "White" majority group that proceeded to establish a privileged social status which has expressed its dominance over non-White groups and over the major institutions of American society. Tom Nairn has described this as the practice of "civic nationalism," wherein the state mediates the "civil social order" and its underpinnings of decency, privacy, individual and group rights, freedom, enterprise and other "privileges and immunities."[12] And although Nairn would disagree that this civic identity may be regarded as the same as nationalism, I believe that it is, in fact, the ethnic nation, working through the instrumentality of the state, that performs this function.

But what happens when the state becomes disconnected from the nation or is viewed as the instrument of the disempowerment of the cultural majority? In 1974, Seyom Brown of the Brookings Institution predicted that despite speculation that the counterculture of the 1960s would become the dominant culture and erode the basis of the state, such a challenge would be met by the rise of a Conservative reaction, "demanding re-education of all citizens in their social responsibilities and insisting on enhanced rewards for middle-class virtues through changes in taxation and welfare programs."[13]

Such a movement has occurred in the U.S., but rather than being focused upon the citizenry alone it has also expressed itself against the state. Michael Omi and Howard Winant suggest the reason for this is that America is a "racial state" in the sense that its major dynamics of social change have revolved around racial insurgency, reform and reaction. This constitutes, they argue, an unstable equilibrium. Omi and Winant postulate that what happens when the equilibrium is disrupted is a "war of position," where a racial movement seeks to transform the dominant racial ideology and thereby challenge the state and change its behavior. They contend that: "Opposition groups may resort to 'direct action' and explicitly seek to politicize racial identities further; challenge will also take the route of 'normal politics' (legislation, legal action, electoral activity, etc.), assuming this possibility is open to racially identified minorities. Strategic unity will therefore become more necessary for the governing forces or bloc."[14] One answer to the question of motivation posed above and responded to in part by Omi and Winant is that when a significant part of the nation becomes—or feels that it has become—disconnected from the state, it also becomes conservative in the sense that it adopts an interest directed to the reclamation of its traditional role.

This kind of response is fully consistent with the view of Karl Mannheim, who argued that although the content of conservatism is oriented toward tradition, the dynamics of the modern state have often given it a progressive character.[15] This is not the same as liberal progressivism, which wants to reform the entire system. Rather it is a brand of conservative progressivism that desires to keep the state framework but change the offending elements that prevent tradition from becoming prominent once again. Thus conservatism has the ability to become not only progressive but radical in the pursuit of its objectives, and the form of that radicalism is nationalism. We will explore the racial connotations of this later.

The radicalism in this model is typified by the National Socialist movement in Germany. Alfred Rosenberg, one of its major ideologists, thought that the state should be "placed at the disposal of the movement, and its life-strength and powers . . . continuously renewed by the movement in order that it remain flexible and capable of resistance while avoiding the dangers of bureaucratization, petrification and estrangement from the Volk."[16] Rosenberg believed that the National Socialist movement, as the embodiment of the interests of the dominant ethnic/racial group, ought to utilize the state as the instrument of achieving those interests; indeed, the movement acted to manage the state so as to avoid the development of bureaucratic impediments to its cause. The clear implication here is that the "estrangement" of the state from the *Volk* (people) would cause alienation; in turn, this would lead to a purification movement aimed at disciplining the state to once again serve the interests of the dominant cultural group.

A similar phenomenon is observable in America today. A significant segment of the White majority is articulating in various ways that it has become disconnected from the state—that it has become estranged and alienated from the state and wants to discipline the state to serve its interests again. In 1978, Dartmouth sociologist Raymond Hall surmised that it would probably only take a "small increase in equal opportunity . . . resulting from equal opportunity programs . . . [to] prompt whites to escalate their resistance to the recent small gains made by blacks."[17] He noted that the Nazi "final solution" was not aimed at the unskilled and uneducated but at a relatively small, highly skilled and educated Jewish population. Yet the engine of the emergence of the nationalist movement in Germany—and in other societies—has been the alienation of a significant group that has formed an ideology out of its grievance with the state that demands change and promotes a movement to effect it.

Conceptualizing White Nationalism

At the outset, it is perhaps necessary to attempt a definition of this term in a standard form before discussing its elements. I suggested above that the form of nationalism that is the subject of this work begins with the notion of a "nation" or a group of people who share a common cultural framework of ancestry, physical distinctiveness and beliefs. These people are distinct from the state, but they seek to control it in pursuit of implementing their sense of self-determination. This is very close to Lowell Barrington's definition of nationalism: "What makes nations unique is that they are collectives united by shared cultural features (myths, values, etc.) and the belief in the right to territorial self-determination."[18]

The issue of territoriality raised in Barrington's article is important, since self-determination is expressed through the instrumental power of the state with the intention of impacting both the land and the people—in short, the "territory" of the state. Thus if the dominant group controls the territory, the difference between the ethnic group politics of the majority and that exercised by other ethnic groups (or "races") is that the latter are relegated to a much narrower sense of self-determination that rarely involves control over territory, only over culture. In this sense, the politicization of the minority ethnicity is not the same as the politicization of the ethnicity of the dominant cultural group.

Moreover, the issue of process is that nationalism is an organized endeavor to effect the objectives cited above. Thus the politics of White Nationalism is the means by which the White majority maintains its control over the state, through the forms of politics and the issues involved. Robert Kaiser defines nationalism as "the pursuit—through argument or other activity—of a set of rights for the self-defined members of the nation, including, at a minimum, territorial autonomy or sovereignty."[19] Thus the theorized activity involves not only the amorphous concept of the "exercise of power" in its various forms but also the maintenance of the public legitimacy of the group to exercise this power by establishing and maintaining a set of rights congruent with this objective. We will discuss this later with respect to the concept of "reverse racism," but it is important to note that the nationalist proposition is not only the establishment of such rights but the delineation, through this process, of who does not share them.[20]

Some of those who have conceptualized the meaning of nationalism have done so from the perspective which emphasizes the state, the country and its territorial boundaries. Within this framework, the "nation" is the cultural group that either has effective control over the territory or is seeking self-determination in the form of territorial control or sharing. Nevertheless, this is a useful perspective for the task of analyzing the emergence of White Nationalism within the United States.

Certainly there is debate in the literature over the extent to which the political mobilization of ethnic groups within the nation may be equated with a form of nationalism. Anthony Richmond believes that while such mobilization may constitute a proto-nationalism, it does not qualify as full nationalism until all the elements are present in the movement.[21] Barrington issues a critical caveat when he observes that "'Ethnic Nationalism' is a legitimate term when the nationalist movement is mainly emphasizing the definition of the membership boundaries of the nation and is basing this definition on an existing ethnic identity."[22] My contention is that the process through which White Nationalism has articulated its view of the definition of the nation—its rights, its membership within these boundaries—is a brand of radical Conservatism that is nativistic and espouses community violence as well as the making of authoritative choices with respect to public policy. I will argue that radical Conservatism has expressed its nationalism in such a way as to clearly consider the question of racial advantage and to propagate actions which have had a deleterious impact upon Blacks and an empowering impact upon Whites.

In conceptualizing White Nationalism, one must confront the "White nation" and its prevalence. Just as every Jewish person is not a Zionist and every Black person is not a Black Nationalist, every White person is not a White Nationalist. Nationalists have in common the fact that they are concerned with utilizing power to effect the objectives of their cultural nation. Yet it may often be difficult for a White person to be conscious of the ways in which both cultural and political "Whiteness" operate. Functioning as an individual in society, one may often not be sure of the consequences of one's White identity and the power process of domination. Ruth Frankenberg suggests that "Whiteness" is "a location of structural advantage, of race privilege. . . . [A] 'standpoint,' a place from which white people look at ourselves, at others and at society . . . a set of cultural practices that are usually unmarked and unnamed."[23] Yet the interrelationships among White ethnic minority groups lead to a coalition that results in the concept of group "Whiteness" and provide the collective as a majority with the ability to exercise effective national power. This makes any White person potentially powerful in relation to non-Whites. He or she is a representative of the White group power system which dispenses both micro and macro White race privileges.[24]

However, in the competition among ethnic and racial groups, alienation from one another has increased. Consider the sentiments of Paul Deau, head of a confederation of White ethnic groups, expressed in 1971 and cited by Robert Lemon in *The Troubled American:*

> Right now, the ethnic vote is up for grabs. . . . New York liberals are dogs. The burning of cities, lawlessness, permissiveness in our colleagues, is pushed as a weapon by progressive liberals to bring the nation to its knees so they can rule. Nixon has said he would be the champion of the forgotten man. We're still waiting. . . . We're not going back to the liberal Democrats. They took our vote and shut us off from the benefits. Unless the GOP gives due consideration, they can't make any headway. We're not going to exchange one master for another. So Wallace may be the only answer.[25]

It is now well known that in the 1960s and '70s the Republican party did make overtures to disaffected ethnic groups, and their support contributed to Nixon's election victories in 1968 and 1972.

My initial rationalization of the approach of this work—that there is presently an essential unity among the White majority analogous to that which arose during the first Reconstruction—is supported by historian David Blight. Blight aptly chronicles how, in the painful attempt to reconstruct the nation after the war, a mythical culture was constructed that helped rehabilitate the South and deny the original reasons for the conflict; this process also helped give collective force to the re-subordination of blacks.[26] George Frederickson, a leading student of White Supremacy, explains the cultural coherence of Whites during Reconstruction in terms of the acquiescence of northern elites to southern racial segregationist policies to consolidate "a new national consensus on race policy." He cites Paul Buck, author of the work *Road to Reunion,* *(1860–1900)*, who concluded: "The Negro paid a heavy price [so that] whites could be reunited in a common nationality."[27]

In fact, one of the most significant features of American society is that ethnic nationalism has been relatively quiescent, despite the existence of obvious ties between domestic ethnic groups and those abroad. The forces responsible for this, such as a strong Anglo-conformity doctrine and the attraction of the American model of economic progress, promoted an integration of White ethnic groups that produced a collective which uses race—either consciously or unconsciously—as a currency of privilege, mediating the exercise of social mobility and various forms of political power. This reality makes it possible, for example, for a recently arrived White person from Russia, a former cold war opponent of the United States, to enjoy the race privileges of Whiteness, even to the point of participating in the dominance of Blacks whose families have lived in this country for generations.

Daniel Bell asserts that in a plural society with distinct ethnicities, the fact that social groups often compete on the basis of ethnicity allows each group to forge a common set of cultural elements of identification that are used to claim cultural space or status in society. He further contends that the intensity of interest-group rivalry makes it certain that the political system becomes the most salient arena "in the competition for the chief values of society."[28]

It will be recognized, of course, that racial competition has an interchangeable dynamic. For example, if one consults any standard work on the subject of Black Nationalism, one will find the equivalent of Raymond Hall's view, that Black Nationalism may be defined by themes such as:

racial integrity, which means that the group was distinctive and different
from others with its own cultural determinants;
racial separatism as an objective to protect the integrity of the group;
racial solidarity, which furthered the coherence and unity of the group in
the pursuit of its survival and other objectives such as politics;
interest in control of the space within which the group functioned in
order to further its destiny and effective participation in the national
society.[29]

My description of White Nationalism is unique only to the extent that there are few overt assertions of White racial interests, especially with respect to the diffusion of nationalist impulses into the mainstream. In the eighteenth and nineteenth centuries, it was not uncommon to find straightforward expositions of the rights of Whites, especially Anglo-Saxons, based upon a notion of their right to self-determination—which included the right to a superior status. However, as the objective status of Whites as the majority group that wields effective social power over all institutions was achieved, it became unnecessary to articulate such overt nationalist claims in racial terms. So we might use the operational device of identifying overt racial claims as the basis of a collective ideology of White Nationalism, parallel to those projected by Black Nationalists. For example, it may be possible to identify nationalism by discerning which group is the target of the intended action and which group is the major beneficiary of such action.

Thus, if Blacks are substantially identified as negatively implicated in policy related to welfare, or crime, or affirmative action or other such race-loaded areas, then it is fair to assume that they are the social target of White Nationalism—unless, that is, one holds the position that the consistency of such effects was accidental. The other side of the coin is that the purported injury to Whites resulting from such policies may serve as a manifestation of the existence of a collective consciousness and sense of injury; thus the assertion of collective counter-rights has a nationalist intent.

It is possible to identify some dominant tendencies within the White majority which conform to the criteria of nationalism, although by no means do these apply to all Whites.

On the basis of a common European heritage, Whites have a sense of racial consciousness that defines them as distinctive within American society;

Whites practice racial separation from other groups within American society through a massive movement away from Black populations in cities, resulting in the creation of many thoroughly White or mostly White areas;

Whites have a cultural notion of Whiteness which brings about a strikingly similar (unified) set of racial attitudes toward non-White groups that persist as stereotypes and establish a unified self-perception;

Whites maintain control over the principal institutions of American society through dominance of numbers and through subordination of other groups, such as Blacks and other non-White minorities, and this has led to economic and political power.

There is, of course, a difference in this description between Whites who are overtly nationalist and those who are not. Many Whites have ceded their race privilege in order to advocate or support equality and attempt to achieve a society that does not function as a racial hierarchy. There is a clear distinction between these Whites and those who objectively manage the state interests in pursuit of "the national interest"—meaning that the theoretical interest of all citizens must be consistent with the objective interests of the White majority.

Nevertheless, one begins to analyze White Nationalist behavior with the observation that a critical aspect of its expression of nationalism—where alienation is the driving force—is that this movement is directed not only against the state but also *against the presumed clients of the state who are perceived to constitute the "offending culture."*[30] That is why the nativistic Nationalist movement within the aggrieved segment of the White majority population expresses itself violently toward a particular group. Blacks have become a main aspect of the "offending culture," and some Nationalist Whites have come to feel that it is legitimate to express their views by physical, verbal and policy attacks on Blacks—or on symbols of Black progress and community well-being—as a mechanism for restoring their own self-esteem.

WHITE SUPREMACY, WHITE NATIONALISM AND RACISM

Since the dawn of the republic, the agents of White Supremacy have been nationalists who have manipulated the way in which racism was expressed in society—the shape of it and the extent to which it has limited opportunities for Blacks and other people of color. As such, the task of the management of White Supremacy by White Nationalists has been inculcated in the challenge of using power, both violently and nonviolently, to promote the interests of Whites and their domination of Blacks and others. Indeed, it would be illogical to assume that a powerful phenomenon such as White racism has only a social or cultural impact and does not have political manifestations.

Yet the phenomenon of elite White Nationalism has been excused as episodic and uncommon. It has been largely ignored as a distinct fact or occurrence. Journalists, social analysts, politicians and other opinion leaders have focused on the discrete manifestations of the racism of working-class White Nationalist fringe groups rather than the ideology that produced them. For example, these opinion leaders have dealt with the rise of the skinheads, the reformation of the Ku Klux Klan and the Aryan Nation, the emergence of militias, police brutality captured on videotape and the burning of Black churches. They treat these as separate incidents, unconnected to a social climate that has nurtured a formidable political force. And where they have admitted that this has been a period of considerable "discontent," they have not gone on to characterize the nature of that political discontent as having taken on a form that is so virulent it has the capacity to capsize the very institution of democracy itself.

The acceptable civic form of the White Nationalist political ideology within American politics has been Conservatism.[31] In the 1990s so many Whites found it fashionable to be Conservative and anti-Liberal that this has become the dominant norm in American politics. Conservatism, however, has always contained a healthy strain of the nationalism which fosters the concept of White Supremacy. It was nineteenth-century White Conservatives who overthrew the "Radical Republicans" who fashioned the liberal Reconstruction that assisted freed black slaves in entering society. They reinterpreted the Fourteenth Amendment to the Constitution and the civil rights laws of the nineteenth century to re-empower White southerners at the expense of Blacks. The crowning achievements of this movement were *Plessy v. Ferguson,* the near elimination of Blacks from the franchise and their social re-subordination in the South through a campaign of intimidation, terror and violence. Yet as "radical" as these Conservatives were, they were not viewed as such by the majority of Americans.

These same Conservatives constructed an ideology of Black inferiority as the basis of Black social disorganization, but W. E. B. Du Bois sought to show, through works like *The Philadelphia Negro,* that this disorganization was the product of slavery and its legacy of poverty, cultural difference and denial of education and social skills. In 1860 William Yancey, an Alabama politician, addressed an audience with these words: "Your fathers and my fathers built this government on two ideas; the first is that the white race is the citizen and the master race, and the white man is the equal of every other white man. The second idea is that the Negro is the inferior race."[32] John Cell, another student of White Supremacy, notes that southern Whites, temporarily disempowered by Reconstruction, were more angered by that than by the Civil War. When Blacks in the South briefly held institutionalized roles as voters, officeholders and wielders of some power, Whites were angered and demoralized and this made them determined to reclaim their "rightful" place. (Cell says that Lord Bryce, in his essay on "The Negro Question," blamed the deterioration of race relations in the South at the turn of the century and afterward on "the mean whites."[33])

This ideology of Black inferiority spawned an attack on Black intelligence through an early twentieth-century version of the "Bell Curve" science known as eugenics. For more than a half century this ideology was the rationale for racial segregation and unequal treatment in both the private and public sectors. Conservative racists were the first to condemn the 1954 Supreme Court decision in *Brown v. Board of Education,* on the grounds of fundamental racial incompatibility because of Black mental inferiority.

Professor Alphonso Pinkney believes that "conservatism is, by its very nature, racist."[34] Yet to some extent it is important to divorce Conservatism from White Nationalism, at least where race is concerned, because in different eras some Conservatives have also supported Liberal programs expanding human rights. Here one thinks of Franklin Delano Roosevelt, the patrician father of the New Deal, or the pro-civil rights actions of Sen. Everett Dirksen of Illinois. Barry Goldwater, a federalist Conservative, voted against the Civil Rights Act of 1964, believing that such an issue was not the purview of the national government but should have been resolved by the states.[35] Neither Dirksen nor Goldwater sided with George Wallace in 1968, when he championed a Conservatism rooted in the racial politics of the old South as the underlying basis of his "populism."

This raises the question, however, of the issues axis of Conservatism in deciding what it has supported and opposed in cultural and policy terms. For the past 30 years at least, one of the most important defining aspects of American Liberalism has been racial tolerance and support for racial justice in both private and public social policy. This means that one of the ways we are able to understand the degree of White Nationalism within Conservatism is by examining the changes in nature and degree of support for oppositional social policy affecting Blacks and other non-Whites negatively and the groups which sponsor such changes.

While overt White Nationalists or Supremacists have generally been extremists and thus social pariahs, these White Nationalists and mainstream Conservatives have always maintained a symbiotic relationship. Lower-class White Nationalists have traditionally exercised the kinds of harsh means of social control from which mainstream Whites and the Conservative upper class benefited. For example, in southern towns members of the Ku Klux Klan and the police were often one and the same. These organizations maintained strong linkages, joining together to retain the control of Blacks that was necessary to legitimize social and economic codes which advantaged the southern upper-class planters and aristocrats. Without enforcement of the decisions made by the mainstream Conservatives who were part of the comprehensive White social consensus, Blacks could not have been kept from participating in the social, economic and political life of the South. And aggressive policing enabled White landowners, for example, to cheat Black sharecroppers out of wages and enforced White cultural standards upon the social behavior of Blacks.

Even in twentieth-century northern and western cities, there have been long-established linkages between police departments, the military and hard-core racists such as the Ku Klux Klan or neo-Nazi groups. Racist police have been tolerated in many cities because they have been regarded as the first line of defense against Black or Hispanic violence.

Thus people who themselves may never have joined a racist group or carried out racist acts have benefited from the social control exacted by police and racist organizations. In a dominantly Liberal culture, violence and aggressiveness of racial policing are not tolerated, but they are promoted in a Conservative culture. Indeed, this is what binds those who participate in the institution of Black subordination and those who, though they do not, are its direct beneficiaries.

Today it is considered unfashionable to be openly racist, and the fact that racists have adopted the convenient cloak of Conservatism often makes it difficult to separate the two. The result is that White Nationalism has permeated the highest political institutions in the country and begun to affect the formation of public policy in important ways. The link between White racism and White Nationalism is that Whites who have attempted to utilize the political system to enact a new regime of social control over Blacks and other people of color employ the ethos of White Nationalism as a subtext of their policy "reform." Politics and policy are the new instruments of social change, although open racism is still practiced both officially and unofficially. Mainstream White Nationalists have become accustomed to using White control over institutions to dispense certain outcomes in order to punish the offending culture. The operation of White Nationalists is evident in the rearrangement of the underlying tenets of civil rights and social resources in ways that re-empower Whites.

Are White Nationalists always racist? How credible is the claim that being pro-White is not the same as being anti-Black? To answer the first question: It depends upon one's definition of racism, which in modern usage is often confused with race prejudice. Racism combines race prejudice with the intention to bring about racial harm through the use of personal and institutionalized power. The problem is that because of the objective function of Whiteness as the default majority class position in society and the consolidation of White control over the state, the ideology racism promotes may be deployed without overt public articulation. The intentional motivation to exclude and subordinate Blacks and other people of color may go undetected. In fact, it can be denied.

Again, it is inevitable that in describing an ideology one encounters the problem of what definition to use to determine the practitioners—that is, defining not only what but who. I will not attempt the impossible task of delineating just how many Americans are White Nationalists or precisely who they are, but I will argue that those who support measures that have a negative impact upon the quality of Black life are, either intentionally or unintentionally, White Nationalists by definition. Nor will I claim that White Conservatives and White Nationalists are always the same, yet the overlap between them is such that the effects of Conservatism may often yield the same outcome as those of White Nationalism. For example, when fiscal Conservatives support government budgets that severely reduce or eliminate social programs, the result may be the same as the one desired by those who *intended* to deprive certain groups of resources. This makes possible a coalition of interests in which an explicit ideology of subordination does not have to be made manifest.

It is certainly easier to suggest that those whose activities are more directly designed to have a specific effect may be defined as White Nationalists, particularly if these activities produce racial subordination. This issue was addressed by John Cell who, in his study of White Supremacy in the South at the turn of the century, made a distinction between White southerners who were segregationists (a term covering a wide variety of attitudes toward Blacks) and generally wanted—for economic, social or other reasons—to maintain separation from Blacks and White southerners who "intended to 'keep the niggers down' for all time and in every conceivable way, and that was that."[36] Cell cites the author Howard Rabinowitz, who suggests that at the turn of the century segregationists were in the majority, since many Whites, though wanting to retain racial separation, also believed in a degree of social uplift for Blacks, through education, the inculcation of habits of thrift and other means that would enable them to develop their own society.[37] This was the main reason the words of Booker T. Washington's 1895 Atlanta Exposition speech were so widely heralded by southern Whites.

In summary, *White Nationalism might be defined as that radical aspect of the Conservative movement that intends to use both unofficial power and the official power of the state to maintain White Supremacy by subordinating Blacks and other non-Whites.*

THE DISTINCT SOUTHERN ELEMENT

Southern politicians have traditionally served as spokespersons for an overt form of White Nationalism that has had negative consequences for Blacks, and in modern times they are overrepresented in the Conservative movement. It is important to note with respect to the issue of membership in the White Nationalist movement that traditionally the most racist, supremacist and nationalist activities have occurred in the South. As a consequence, there is the perception that racial animus has been strongest in that region. With regard to the preoccupation of the southern wing of the Republican party, Wilson McWilliams declared: "Racism, not conservatism, was the key to the Southern strategy." V. O. Key argued that attendant to this was the emergence of an "orgy of violence" directed at Blacks, just as happened at the turn of the century when southern politics began its reascendence.[38] Moreover, Ira Katznelson, Kim Geiger and Daniel Kryder have remarked that in the period 1933–1950 the southern bloc in both the House and Senate frequently exercised what they call "the Southern Veto," a blocking vote that severely limited the passage of Liberal legislation.[39]

One expression of the depth of the distinct White southern viewpoint came from George Washington Cable. Cable, a self-identified "Southern White Man," wrote a letter to the *New Orleans Bulletin* in 1875 complaining about the expulsion of a mulatto mathematics teacher (who had been educated at École Polytechnique in Paris) from his teaching position at Central Boys High School in that city. Cable's letter to the editors drew this reply from them:

> Between whites and Africans there is now and has always been an antipathy of instincts. These instincts appear under all conditions, and no familiarity or racial blending, or unnatural hybridity, can conquer the in born, centrifugal, and mutually repellent propensity which causes the two races to shun each other. The only condition under which the two races can co-exist peacefully is that in which the superior race shall control and the inferior race shall obey. . . . For our part we hope never to see the white boys and girls of America forgetful of the fact that Negroes are their inferiors.[40]

Most observers believe that such harsh racist attitudes have passed into history and that southern views of race have moderated. However, it takes such attitudes a long time to die, and many events cause one to question whether they have disappeared entirely from southern consciousness. The Confederate flag and other symbols of southern White Supremacy have reemerged as legitimate cultural icons to accompany a more Conservative ideological attitude. In 1986 there were only 500 members in 12 chapters of the North Carolina Sons of the Confederacy, but ten years later there were 71 chapters and nearly 3,000 members.[41] One expert on southern history reported in 1966 that "virtually no one is willing to say 'I am a racist' anymore, not even the Klan. Now they cling to the [Confederate] flag and say they're protecting the memory of their great-grandaddy. They are protecting the history of the South."[42] However, Harry Watson, a professor at the University of North Carolina, explained that the recent increase in membership of groups such as the Sons of the Confederacy "has not been driven by a love of history. It's a way to express dissatisfaction and anger, and that's something that we should pay attention to."[43]

Notably, references to Jefferson Davis are current in the political speech of southern politicians such as Senate Majority Leader Trent Lott, who, in a 1984 interview with *Southern Partisan* magazine, said: "I think that a lot of the fundamental principles that Jefferson Davis believed in are very important to people across the country, and they apply to the Republican party, from tax policy to foreign policy, from individual rights to neighborhood security. These are things that Jefferson Davis and his people believed in."[44] It is also fair to note that Davis's policies were shaped within the context of slavery and the struggle to make the southern White oligarchy secure in its domination of an agricultural region and of a people they considered inferior to themselves. Is this the same paradigm that undergirds the linkage between the South and the Republican party today?

It may be confidently asserted that one strain of White Nationalism continues to be promoted by southern political leaders in both the private and public sectors as it has been historically. In fact, at the fall 1997 meeting of the Sons of Confederate Veterans, Ron Wilson, Commander of the Army of Northern Virginia unit, remarked: "Jefferson Davis said, 'The battle sounds of this war may have subsided, but this war is not over. It will be decided in another generation at another time.' I believe that we're that generation and the time is now."[45] I suggest that the impact of these attitudes upon Blacks has been profound.

THE BLACK THREAT

Black Competition

Building upon the discussion above with regard to group competition, I argue here that the mobilization of at least two forms of Black social capital, political and economic, have acted to create the perception of a threat to White interests.

Political. A substantial body of informed opinion has concluded that one major impact of the Voting Rights Act of 1965, which made possible a significant increase in Black political participation, was the development of a large cadre of Black elected officials whose influence within the Democratic party threatened White dominance of the party.[46] In fact, since 1964 the strength of Black voting for Democratic candidates has historically been above 80%. This margin of Black support was a central factor in the election of Democratic officials at local and national levels, and it culminated in the formidable candidacy of Rev. Jesse Jackson for president in 1984 and 1988. Yet Robert Huckfeldt and Carol Kohfeld argued that the Jackson campaign contributed to the racial "threat effect."[47] Using a "power theory" of intergroup relations, they concluded that "where the threat posed by a minority group is high, the dominant group's response is predicted to be more hostile than in a context where that threat is low."[48] Their analysis of areas in the South where Blacks registered to vote in large numbers revealed that the response of White politicians to this phenomenon was mostly hostile.

The combination of increasing Black political participation in the Democratic party and government policies that appeared to stimulate Black social advancement enhanced the notion of competition. This occurred even though Blacks were only 11% of the population in the 1970s and the competitive part of the population even smaller: by the mid-1970s less than 20% of Black families earned an average income, and 40% were officially classified as poor.

Economic. When analyzing the economic basis of the rise of White Nationalism, one must consider that White alienation from both government and civil society has been accompanied by a simultaneous rise in the Black and Brown middle classes. Since White Nationalists believe that persons of color, particularly Blacks, are inferior, what logically follows is that they must believe Blacks should not have equal access to certain social resources and social status. In turn, this means that Whites resent the fact that Blacks are accorded access to social resources or that they appear to have achieved equal status. In attempting to understand the upsurge of Conservative voting in the 1994 election, one observer, Dr. Jean Hardisty, mentioned such factors as the Conservative religious revival, economic contraction and restructuring, backlash and social stress, and a well-funded network of Right-wing organizations. However, she also argued, as I do, that race is a significant factor in White resentment and that it is stimulated, in part, by economic considerations:

> The theme of white resentment of a perceived increase in the power of racial/ethnic minority groups plays heavily in the agenda of the right. That resentment is fanned and augmented by the decreased sense of economic security of many working and middle-class white people (such as suburban, white Republican males, white rural males, or women whose status is attached to those men) as a result of economic restructuring. There is no doubt that racial resentment and racial bigotry are major factors in the current resurgence of the right.[49]

The resentment appears to arise from a number of sources. On the one hand, positive sources are in evidence, such as various indices of progress by Blacks in professional occupations, education, sports and so on. With respect to negative elements, there is the continuing presence of deep and entrenched poverty in Black communities; the dissolution of poor Black families and the claims this makes on public resources; high levels of crime in Black neighborhoods; and the nature of the mass media, driven, in part, by Black underground behavior. Of all these, the most significant source of resentment has been Black economic progress, which threatens to challenge the superior social status of Whites and release Blacks from their subordinate position in society.

Conservatives have labored mightily to emphasize the progress that Blacks made from 1960 to the 1990s, largely to support their position that Blacks do not need further so-called "preferential treatment" in public policy.[50] For example, Abigail and Stephan Thernstrom assert that: "The number of blacks practicing . . . law . . . is eighteen times what it was [in 1949]. There are nineteen times as many African-American editors and reporters as there were in 1950, and 33 times as many black engineers. In 1949 no sizable city in the entire country had a black mayor, and just two African Americans were members of the U.S. Congress. Today most of our largest cities have—or have had—a black chief executive, and more than forty blacks hold seats in the House of Representatives."[51] They go on to cite other instances of Black middle-class progress: "The number of black college and university professors more than doubled between 1970 and 1990. . . . The number of physicians tripled, the number of engineers almost quadrupled, and the number of attorneys has increased more than sixfold."[52] But, citing the fact that "[h]alf of all black professionals are employed by government," they acknowledge the fact that "black entrepreneurship remains underdeveloped."[53]

Professor Andrew Hacker presents a more Liberal view of Black progress than the Thernstroms, suggesting that how one evaluates it depends upon how one interprets the percentages of loss and gain in various fields.[54] He agrees that the number of Black college professors grew substantially between 1960 and 1980, but he points out that the proportion has stagnated for twenty-five years; the same is true, he noted, for Black physicians, the number of whom has actually declined in recent years. Hacker's presentation of census data shows that the number of Black telephone operators, firefighters, electricians and health care professionals has increased dramatically, largely due to the fact that White women have left these fields for other jobs, thus creating opportunities

TABLE 1.1	Black Occupational Gains, 1970–1990	
Occupation	*1970*	*1990*
Police officers	23,796	63,855
Electricians	14,145	43,276
Bank tellers	10,733	46,332
Health officials	3,914	13,125

Source: Andrew Hacker, *Two Nations: Black and White, Separate, Hostile, Unequal* (New York: Charles Scribner's Sons, 1992), p. 121.

for Blacks. Hacker's summary of the most significant job increases by Blacks is presented in Table 1.1.

Hacker's figures and those cited by the Thernstroms were developed in the context of arguments for and against affirmative action. The Thernstroms paint a picture of Black occupational progress designed to validate White opposition to affirmative action. However, one must ask: why the angst? Perhaps one reason is that the increasing number of Blacks in certain professions has put them into direct competition with Whites—a position they were not perceived to be able to achieve—and despite the fact that the actual number of Blacks in these professions is still exceedingly small.[55]

In attempting to account for the relatively low proportion of Blacks serving as waiters, bartenders, hairdressers, chefs and so on in the hotel and restaurant industries, Hacker suggests: "Sad to say, many white Americans feel uncomfortable in establishments that have a pronounced number of Black employees."[56] According to him, it is no accident that Black women hold 64% of all Black professional positions and have expanded into the private sector in greater numbers than Black males, since they are considered less resentful, less hostile and thus less threatening to Whites—especially to the White males who dominate the occupations in this sector.[57]

In a book assessing the failure of racial integration, Tom Wicker recounts a conversation between the distinguished Black historian John Hope Franklin, who in his youth worked at North Carolina College, and a White professor who worked nearby at Duke University. The latter was incredulous that Franklin would favor ending segregation, lest he, like other Blacks, lose whatever advantages it offered, including jobs at Black institutions. More importantly, the White professor asserted that his own status would not be threatened by desegregation. However, Franklin assured him that if integration came and if Black professors transferred from NCC to Duke, his job would indeed be in jeopardy.[58]

In actuality, the fact of interracial competition may be the cause of much tension within higher education. More than any other American institution, higher education has experienced substantial change in its inclusion of Blacks, both in student bodies and in the professoriat (though in many cases the numbers are still exceedingly small: in predominantly White institutions of higher learning, Blacks comprise about 5% of students and 2% of professors). Perhaps it is thus no surprise that academics have been in the forefront of the Neoconservative movement, creating the National Association of Scholars, helping promote California's Proposition 209 and writing books and articles opposing affirmative action—even from positions at prestigious institutions with a Liberal bent, such as Harvard University.

White Economic Stagnation

A primary stimulus of White resentment is the combination of Black progress and White decline, which is nowhere more evident than in the changes in the economic fortunes of the average White family over the past twenty years. The slowly emerging, often unarticulated message of the stagnation of White economic status is matched by Whites' perception of a government-led Black renaissance. This perception has been confirmed by Blacks serving variously as high-profile mayors of America's largest cities, heads of its largest foundations, members of presidential cabinets, occupants of prestigious academic chairs, college presidents and the like. These have all helped create the stereotype of a level of Black progress greater than that enjoyed by Whites.

Soon after the dramatic Republican congressional victory in 1994, Secretary of Labor Robert Reich delivered a speech to the Democratic Leadership Council that sought to explain why White economic stagnation had occurred:

> The old middle class has become an anxious class—worried not only about sustaining their incomes but also about keeping their jobs and their health insurance. Our large corporations continue to improve productivity by investing in technology and cutting payrolls. In a recent survey, three out of four employers say their own employees fear losing their jobs. Meanwhile, 1994 is on track to become history's biggest year for mergers and acquisitions. But who wins in this

$300 billion derby? Certainly not the average worker. When two industry giants merge, the advantages of the deal often come from layoffs. Across America, I hear the same refrain: "I've given this company the best years of my life and now they dispose of me like a piece of rusty machinery."[59]

Reich asserted that this pattern of "downward mobility" had begun about 15 years earlier and had created a "divergence" in incomes between the middle class and the "over-class" that was enhanced by the economic policies of the 1980s. He noted that in 1993 the top fifth of American households received 48% of the total income and 72% of the growth in income from the preceding year. Meanwhile, the top 5% of income earners were taking home 20% of all income and 40% of the growth in income.

Reich had observed these trends before entering government service. In a 1989 article in the *New Republic,* he reported that between 1978 and 1987 "the poorest fifth of American families became 8% poorer, and the richest fifth became 13% richer. That left the poorest fifth with less than 5% of the nation's income, and the richest fifth with more than 40%."[60] He noted further that during this period, as the real earnings of unskilled workers were declining, the real incomes of workers on Wall Street in the securities trade increased 21% and the number of poor increased by 23%.

One reason for wage divergence was the pressure on employment in the 1970s and 1980s. The new pattern of layoffs and "downsizing" played an important role in shattering the traditional pattern of high education/high wage employment. A *New York Times* analysis of Labor Department data that was part of the newspaper's wide-ranging study of the phenomenon of "downsizing" concluded: "In a reversal from the early 1980s, workers with at least some college education make up the majority of people whose jobs were eliminated, outnumbering those with no more than high school educations. And better-paid workers—those earning at least $50,000—account for twice the share of the lost jobs that they did in the 1980s."[61] Moreover, of those fired, data indicate that only 35% acquired better-paying employment.[62]

Mergers and Downsizing: In crude terms, "downsizing" meant the mass firing of American workers, a practice that became a pervasive threat to the American dream, enhancing the sense of social anxiety to a degree not seen since the Great Depression. Between June 1992 and June 1995, the largest layoffs occurred in IBM, AT&T, General Motors, Boeing, the U.S. Postal Service, Sears, Hughes Aircraft, Bell South,

TABLE 1.2	Workforce Layoffs, June 1992–June 1995	
Firm	*% of workforce affected*	*Number (thousands)*
IBM	30%	122
AT&T	25%	83
General Motors	20%	74
Boeing	37%	31
Sears	15%	50
Hughes Aircraft	32%	25.4
Bell South	23%	21.2
McDonnell Douglas	20%	21
Digital Equipment	22%	20

Source: People Trends Newsletter; cited in Margaret O. Kirk, "When Surviving Just Isn't Enough," *New York Times,* June 25, 1995, p. 11.

McDonnell Douglas and Digital Equipment, as shown in Table 1.2. This was only the leading edge of a trend in both the private sector and government. Downsizing in government at all levels affected 475,000 workers between 1980 and 1995. And in the first quarter of 1996 alone over 250,000 workers were laid off in the private sector, perhaps one-half million for the year as a whole.[63] Most important, in recent years the following type of headline has led stories about increasing gains in the stock market: "Productivity Increases 4% in a Surge without Hiring."[64]

Decline of Organized Labor: Another significant cause of White economic stagnation is the decline in the effectiveness of organized labor. Traditionally it was the role of organized labor to distribute the fruits of American industrial production among workers by collective bargaining and the enforcement of contracts through strikes and other job actions. Professor Richard Freeman, an economist at Harvard University, suggests that the decline of organized labor may help to explain as much as one-half of the decline in wages, since the pressure to reduce wages has not been as effectively rebuffed by organized labor as it was in the past.[65] In fact, the downward spiral of the influence of organized labor matches the two-decade parallel decline in the wages of workers. Whereas in the 1950s as much as one-third of the entire labor force was unionized, this figure declined to about 11% in 1994.[66] The stronger position of labor unions in Western European countries and the relative stability and expanse of the social safety net in Europe testify to the significant role of labor in maintaining workers' economic viability.

Alienation and Racism

All the factors outlined above have contributed to the economic instability faced by the White middle class. The new pattern of massive employee firings has created a sense of precariousness among the most educated, economically mobile and politically sensitive class of Americans. Nowhere is this better illustrated than in the *New York Times* study entitled National Economic Insecurity Survey, which was conducted in December of 1995. Respondents in the sample of 1,265 were divided into self-identified categories: crisis layoff, non-crisis layoff, friend layoff, no layoff, worried and extra job. Because of the high degree of agreement among categories, and for the sake of simplicity, I have established in Table 1.3 a mean of these categories with respect to several critical questions as they appeared in the survey.

These selected results from the *Times* survey suggest several important considerations, one of which is that while respondents rejected job preferences for women, they rejected preferences for Blacks by an even larger margin. Upon further analysis, this suggestive result reveals a substantial correlation between those in the combined group who felt that obtaining work was difficult in their neighborhood and those who were angriest at political parties. Also, those who were angriest at political parties showed the strongest affinity to particular characteristics, such as rejecting preferences for women and Blacks.[67] Surprisingly, however, this angry group also believed that it was the responsibility of government to take care of citizens who could not take care of themselves—a finding which runs contrary to the ideology adopted by the dominant political class.

Nevertheless, a broad discussion of the nature of White privilege as the anchor of racism in various aspects of American life has begun amid clear evidence that the perception of a threat to White dominance has produced growing anxiety among Whites, especially White males. For a wide-ranging presentation of this issue in the *Washington Post*, Lynne Duke interviewed several White males who reported feeling the stigma that recently accrued to their identity in a newly diverse workplace.[68] What is most striking in this reportage is the view that the threat must be ended. One of Duke's respondents—clearly intimidated by the presence of an increasing number of Blacks, Hispanics and women in his workplace and by the decline of White males attending staff meetings— asked: "What happens when I'm the only one? Should I just offer them my position and leave? I know it sounds ridiculous. But my point is: There's got to be some point where we say enough is enough."[69] Although

TABLE 1.3 Selected Responses from the National Economic Insecurity Survey

Question #6: In your community these days, how easy is it for someone who is trying to find a job to get a good job at good wages — very easy, somewhat easy, somewhat hard, very hard?

Very easy	Somewhat easy	Somewhat hard	Very hard	DK/NA
2.0%	9.8%	38.1%	45.5%	4.6%

Question #9: Would you agree or disagree with the following statement: "I'm angry at both political parties"?

Agree	Disagree	DK/NA
62.3%	33.3%	4.4%

Question #18: Do you believe that where there has been job discrimination against women in the past, preference in hiring or promotion should be given to women today?

Yes	No	DK/NA
36.2%	59.0%	4.8%

Question #19: Do you believe that where there has been job discrimination against blacks in the past, preference in hiring or promotion should be given to blacks today?

Yes	No	DK/NA
32.5%	62.5%	5.0%

Question #20: Would you agree or disagree that it is the responsibility of government to take care of people who can't take care of themselves?

Agree	Disagree	DK/NA
63.8%	29.9%	6.3%

Source: "The Downsizing of America," Special Report, *New York Times* (New York: Random House/Times Books, 1996), pp. 278, 280, 283.

the blame for this anxiety is most often directed against both women and minorities, actions to eliminate the stigma and the condition of feeling unprivileged most often targets non-White minorities. Witness the fact that the Supreme Court has upheld Title IX, a form of affirmative action in athletics that privileges women—mostly White women—while at the same time striking down affirmative action measures intended to enhance the status of Blacks.

Could this attitude be a modern version of the "racial democracy" thesis, that democracy can only exist among privileged White Americans—with the residual thought that it should not be fully extended to others? It is altogether possible, since the factors described above clearly demonstrate that Whites may be angry both at the way in which certain factors limit their opportunities as well as at minorities and the legal regime which supports them. But it is more likely that in seeking a rationale for their misfortune, Whites practice the "symbolic racism" of using Blacks and other disadvantaged groups to explain their misfortune while failing to fully acknowledge the dominant impact of these factors. Therefore, it is reasonable to assume that the force of the ideology which exceeds the moderate temper in the public at large and which pushes public policy in the direction of attacking government is derived from a nationalist core belief system rather than merely from public opinion.

CONCLUSION

We find today, as George Frederickson found in an earlier period of history, that Black Americans appear to be paying a heavy price for the reconsolidation of White national power. The formation of a new consensus about Black rights is being reshaped to the advantage of the White majority. So far have some nationalist politicians succeeded in nationalizing negative attitudes and policies toward Blacks that today we are close to the abolition of several notions: that there exists an oppressed class in America defined by race; that no one now living had anything to do with oppressing Blacks, Hispanics, Asians, women, the disabled, or the aged; and that in any event the oppressed classes have obtained such extensive protection under the law that the White majority is now oppressed as a result.

The problem with this widely shared viewpoint, which is frequently expressed in public opinion polls, is that very little of the institutional leadership or the benefits distributed by major institutions can be shown to have changed markedly over time. So we have arrived at another era where what is racially down is up and up is down, where the social disadvantage of important segments of society can be changed at the whim of the majority to re-advantage themselves. But then, that is the clearest expression of the existence of White power.

The Formation
of a Policy Rationale

INTRODUCTION

This chapter comments upon the evolutionary impact of a set of policy concepts that grew out of the grievances that motivated the movement of White Nationalism. The rise of this movement, which has found its most shocking manifestation in public forms of violence, signaled a profound mood shift within the American body politic and stimulated a concomitant movement of a group of intellectuals to shift their stance from Liberalism to Neoconservatism. In this new posture, they rejected the prevailing political emphasis on civil rights, developing in its place a counter ideal of stability and order based on such issues as morality, family, community and the failure of Liberal social policy. These issues became the intellectual capital for public policy conflicts aimed at devolving government power and weakening the civil rights infrastructure, which Neoconservatives saw as a threat to their control of civic space. From the beginning, the intention of the White Nationalist policy agenda was to supplant the Liberal agenda and thereby re-empower its own constituency in American politics. However, insofar as this has been accomplished at the expense of Blacks, the phenomenon is treated here as the development of "policy racism."

The Nationalist Ethos of "American Exceptionalism"

One of the most corrosive impediments to the continuing attempt to achieve social equality in America is the heightening and reemphasis of White Supremacy through a White Nationalist movement fostered, in part, by the doctrine of "American exceptionalism." In the most nationalist eras of American history, rhetoricians commonly invoked the doctrine of the special destiny of America, preordained by God himself, in an effort to rationalize the dehumanization of Blacks and other people. In those times, jingoistic internationalism was often practiced by the state and its dominant actors in parallel with the domestic version of nationalism.

Today, in the tradition of previous nationalist eras, one can observe, as Seymour Martin Lipset did in his work *American Exceptionalism,* that "a majority of people . . . tell pollsters that God is the moral guiding force of American democracy."[1] This belief has evoked a "super-patriotic" attitude among many Conservatives and gives weight to their view of the rightness of adopting certain principles. It has also stimulated religious conservatives to enter the political arena.

Religious conservatives have given a powerful legitimacy not only to Conservative ideology but to its policy agenda as well. Irving Kristol asserts that there can be no significant movement without a moral core and that "exceptional Conservatism" is a movement.[2] Ronald Reagan's trade in the doctrine of American exceptionalism was fundamentally useful in repairing the damage done to the American psyche by the loss of the Vietnam War (the sense of national shame came to a boil when Americans were held hostage in Iran in 1980). To rekindle Americans' sense of pride, Reagan traded effectively on the symbolics of American power and glory in past victories, conjuring up sentiments consistent with the feeling that the continuing erosion of American power must be stopped and the nation's honor vindicated.

Many observers have noticed that once it is unleashed, the power of this ideology of nationalism cannot be contained within one particular sphere. George Frederickson has suggested that in the late nineteenth century the emergence of American nationalism had a double effect: the first in the international arena, the second in the domestic one, where American nationalism gave rise to hyper-ethnocentric attitudes and shaped the manner in which those who controlled the state treated "inferiors."[3] Once directed toward external enemies, nationalism may eventually bleed into the domestic culture, and vice-versa. Indeed, the McCarthy era after World War II may be interpreted as an attempt to effect an internal purge of America's perceived enemies as part of the victory over external foes. Of course, analysts have pointed out that German internal nationalism was a primary motivation for the external manifestations that led to the Second World War.

Reagan's latent assertion that his presidency would put things right both at home and abroad forged a tremendous connection not only with those who felt the shame of Vietnam and wanted to reverse the public verdict of the 1970s on the error of American involvement there, but also with those who felt dispossessed by the attention given to Blacks in the era of the Civil Rights movement and the implementation of its policy legacy. The result was an explosion of patriotism not seen since the Second World War, and this acted as a potent weapon of political judgment against the Democratic party and Liberals who opposed the Vietnam War and were sympathetic to civil rights. From that point on, Liberalism experienced a slow decline as a political ideology of any consequence.

Yet Professor Lipset says that "Americanism" has taken on a utopian character, utilized as an ideology by both Liberals and Conservatives.[4] For example, in the modern struggle over the distribution of benefits among various sectors of society, both Liberals and Conservatives repair to the American creed's emphasis on individual rights. However, Lipset suggests that "the complementary egalitarian and individualistic elements in the American creed" now conflict with the group equality quest of Blacks. The lesson of the Civil Rights movement is that Blacks, because of the American history of slavery and post-slavery exclusion, have had to fight for rights and resources as a group. However, the utopian character of the American exceptionalist legal myth frequently obscures the fact that the individualistic concepts enshrined in the American Constitution were meant to apply within the egalitarian framework of White male citizenship. Between Blacks and Whites, the *group* character of their histories was, indeed, the defining feature both in law and in practice.

Ultimately, the notion of American exceptionalism tries to paint a normative picture which suggests that the reason for America's global achievements is rooted in its domestic value system. This formulation, then, is supposed to provide domestic legitimacy not only to the dominant values of the state but, by inference, to measures taken against groups whose actions appear to threaten the dominant group's conception of "the national interest."

SHIFTING IDEAS AND ALLEGIANCES

The Neoconservative Shift

Without attempting to provide a history of the emergence of the Neo-conservative movement here, I would suggest that its intellectual manifestations originated in the split within the Liberal movement of the 1960s over a number of issues. These included control of the Civil Rights/Black Power movement, the Arab-Israeli conflict, disorder in urban areas and the movement against U.S. military involvement in Vietnam. John Ehrman says that reformist Liberals were caught in a contradiction: having helped foster a substantial change in the social order, they abhorred what they felt was the runaway radicalism that ensued.[5]

Because government failed to eliminate poverty and ameliorate other conditions through the morally charged apparatus of the Liberal state, skeptical Neoconservatives gravitated toward stronger conceptual instrumentalities such as religion and nationalism to achieve both order and the protection of their status.

> When political opponents are demonized, simple ambition is reinforced and politicians are tempted to overstep the bounds of law. When domestic politics is turned into a contest between the forces of good and the forces of evil, when political opponents are regarded as the enemies of civilization, the results are dishonest political tactics, corruption and conflict.[6] Shadia Drury paints a remarkable picture of many of the leaders of the Neoconservative movement as both disciples of Leo Strauss [and] of Neoconservatism as divorced from the broader [strain of] conservatism in its radical and reactionary character.[7]

Thus in weighing the balance between change and stability many intellectuals come to feel what Daniel Patrick Moynihan expressed to the 1967 convention of the Americans for Democratic Action: Liberals needed to see social stability as an "essential interest." Thus a new emphasis on both patriotism and order led many liberals to break with the politics of the 1960s as well as with the more radical views of its progenitors such as George McGovern, whose 1972 presidential campaign came to be viewed by the emerging Neoconservatives as a threat to the state itself.

This was an important split in that it set free from the progressive project of the 1960s a powerful chorus of intellectual voices. Irving Kristol,

Aaron Wildavsky, Midge Decter, Nathan Glazer, Lionel Trilling, Seymour Martin Lipset, Norman Podhoretz, Benjamin Wattenberg and others employed organs such as *Commentary,* the *New Republic,* the *National Review* and *Encounter* to help shape the new Conservative orthodoxy in opposition to many of the objectives of the Civil Rights movement.[8]

At the same time, the modern intellectual infrastructure of the traditional Conservative movement was slowly being created: Melvin Laird and David Packard raised funds for the creation of the American Enterprise Institute, the Hoover Institution at Stanford University and Georgetown University's Center for International and Strategic Studies. The influential Heritage Foundation was created in 1973 by Paul Weyrich and Edwin Fuelner with funds provided by Joseph Coors, and by the late 1970s many other Conservative organizations had been created.

As a result of this Conservative mobilization, a veritable rush of journals and magazines appeared in the mid-1970s, including *Conservative Digest,* founded in 1975 by Richard Viguerie; the American Enterprise Institute's *Public Opinion,* which first appeared in 1977; and the Republican National Committee's *Common Sense,* which began publication in 1978. In his book, *A Time For Truth* (1979), William Simon, a Conservative financier and later Ronald Reagan's Treasury secretary, boldly announced that there should be created a "conservative counter-intelligentsia" to confront the so-called Liberal bias of the media, think tanks and universities. He said: "Funds generated by business must rush by multimillions to the aid of liberty . . . to funnel desperately needed funds to scholars, social scientists, writers, and journalists who understand the relationship between political and economic liberty."[9] In response to his call, donations poured in to help establish periodicals and create a communications media network of television and radio stations all over the country. With these instruments in hand, the Conservative movement was in a position in the late 1970s to create a more consistent philosophy and to have a serious public influence upon politics and public policy.

Social Issues Reinterpreted as Moral Issues

One of the tenets of the emerging Neoconservative philosophy was that a major crisis in American life had been created by the fact that popular culture acts in an antithetical fashion to the presumptive moral foundation which has been responsible for the nation's "exceptionalism" and stability. Professor James Q. Wilson, a well-known Neoconservative political scientist, puts it thusly: "Many Americans worry that the moral order that once held the nation together has come unraveled. Despite freedom and prosperity—or worse, perhaps because of freedom and prosperity—a crucial part of the moral order, a sense of personal responsibility, has withered under the attack of personal self-indulgence."[10] Wilson goes on to cite some examples of "selfish" personal behavior, such as "high rates of crime, the prevalence of drug abuse, and the large number of fathers who desert children and [the] women who bore them."[11]

Wilson's examples imply "selfishness" as a motive for actions that are also rooted in systemic poverty. Yet other Conservatives agree with him, and even expand the list of examples to include sexual permissiveness, antiauthoritarian behavior and gender role substitution. Moreover, cultural minority domination of modern music and non-mainstream art and literature has touched off a war with mainline institutions of culture and politics. Conservative politicians have attempted to discipline the creators of visual arts, music lyrics, movies and the like by proposing various forms of sanctions, from the withdrawal of federal funds to boycotts of record companies that produce rap music.

In this conflict, Blacks have also been targeted as the progenitors of the dangerous underclass culture of drugs, gangs, openly promiscuous sexual behavior and stylistic expressions in speech, dress and social mannerisms.[12] Newt Gingrich has repeatedly cast aspersions on what he calls the "counterculture" and targeted it for either reform or elimination. Although this term has an association with the "counterculture" of the 1960s' pot-smoking hippies, political revolutionaries and antiauthoritarians, the current use of the word clearly alludes to the urban underclass culture. When White parents observe their children adopting the cultural style known as "Wiggers" (White Niggers), using drugs or condoning their use, or consuming rap or reggae music, they want to discipline the perpetrators of this counterculture through the power of public policy.

Gingrich's demands for the enforcement of Anglo-conformity cultural standards and the moral movement headed by the Christian Coalition and other such groups both focus on the behavior of American citizens which they find reprehensible. This issue is being fought out on the floor of Congress and in state legislatures, as evident in the demands there for such measures as welfare reform, the imposition of youth curfews, the sentencing of youth as adults, pressure on the movie industry to adopt new labeling standards and the elimination of the National Endowment for the Arts.

Nevertheless, the counterculture system has strong support among many people, especially young ones, and the commercialization of this culture has produced a general acceptance of different (whether "lower" or "higher" depends upon one's orientation) cultural behaviors. Thus a more fundamental fissure has opened between the political and cultural sectors of society, illustrated by the attempt of the political sectors to discipline aspects of cultural behavior. The ineffectiveness of much of this "V-chip" politics has only added fuel to the fire. Every major newspaper regularly contains entertainment promotions that feature photos of major movie stars with pistols or other weapons pointed at the reader, as well as advertisements with strong sexual content. Lurid aspects of the culture to which Conservatives and others object are protected by wider aspects of capitalistic commercialization, by First Amendment guarantees of free speech and by the widespread acceptance of these aspects of American popular culture both at home and increasingly abroad. Yet the targets of the rage felt by some Whites and some Blacks as well appear to be the youthful Black purveyors of the culture rather than those who control the products and reap great economic benefits from them.

Social and economic amelioration policies that might have reduced the differences between the racial aspects of the counterculture and the majority of American Whites have been rendered morally suspect because of the implicit and explicit imputation of immorality to the poor and dependent and because of the perception of these policies' "unfairness" toward Whites. This judgment is ideologically important in that it has helped political Conservatism break loose from its moorings in institutionalized religion and become a political constituency within the radical Right. Political Conservatives use immorality as the central justification for their attacks upon not only "liberal" public policy but also any other measures deemed to benefit members of the offending culture.

Politics and the Moral Instrument

As with the proponents of the Civil Rights movement in the 1960s, Conservative Christians who wanted to pursue their values to the point of ultimate legitimation had to move into politics. As this was happening, old familiar racist concepts—such as the idea that the Bible sanctions slavery—began to reappear, except that this time the sentiments issued forth from the mouths of public officials such as Charles Davidson.[13] Even though Davidson—a first-term state legislator from Jasper, Alabama, who ran for a seat in the U.S. House of Representatives in 1996—eventually abandoned his campaign, his remarks are symptomatic of the confidence some individuals have had that they could voice such sentiments publicly again. The difference is that whereas in the past this view would be justified on the grounds of racial superiority, Davidson asserted: "The issue is not race, it's Southern heritage."[14]

Professor Michael Johnson's analysis of the "New Christian Right" suggests that there were two predominant phases in its development. From the Moral Majority of the 1970s and early 1980s to the Christian Coalition of the 1990s, this period has seen an intensive mobilization of religious activists into the policy arena. Johnson's study shows that while in the 1970s most of the Moral Majority supporters identified themselves as Conservatives and either sympathizers or members of the Republican party, the nature of the movement is far more complex because of the tendency of fundamentalist ministers, especially in the South, to eschew participation in politics. Nevertheless, the modern base of the New Right movement as it has evolved from the 1970s has become distinctly rooted in both Southern Baptist and "born again" churches in other parts of the country.[15]

The character of the movement has changed as its theological emphasis in the 1960s and 1970s gave way to a more explicitly political character in the 1980s and 1990s. Pat Robertson and Jerry Falwell were the leading forces in a coalition of Conservative Christian organizations that lobbied Congress in the 1970s on issues related to their "moral" perspective: the SALT II treaty, abortion, school prayer, domestic violence, IRS treatment of federal aid to Christian schools, the Department of Education, economic sanctions against Rhodesia, school busing and "parental rights legislation."[16] However, the strong support of many in the religious establishment for the traditional principle of "separation of church and state," together with the lack of professionalism in its lobbying operation, prevented the fulfillment of the coalition's agenda. Nevertheless, the newly energized Christian activists would be important in electing Ronald Reagan to the presidency in 1980, and Falwell would describe him as "the best Christian who ever walked the face of the earth."[17]

In any case, the groundwork for the entry of Christian activists into the Republican political infrastructure was laid in this period, and their efforts culminated in Pat Robertson's 1988 presidential bid. Robertson's campaign used political action committees and direct-mail fund-raising databases targeted toward the Christian constituency as well as a professional political staff led by Ralph Reed, a political scientist with a Ph.D. degree. Reed brought a high degree of order and political organization to the Christian Coalition and helped establish individual chapters that collectively played a significant role in local politics. This grassroots army coalesced in the 1980s, and by the 1990s it had essentially captured a large share of the control of the national Republican party. In the 1994 elections, 15% of the White male electorate belonged to the "born again" category, and in 1996, 17% of White voters claimed membership in the Religious Right; most of these cast votes for Bob Dole in a losing cause, yet they played a significant role in Republican victories in U.S. Senate races in Kansas, Arkansas and Colorado.

"Community": The Moral Objective

Armed with the certitude that government not only has failed to address major social problems but has actually made them worse, some intellectuals have proceeded to propose the moral argument as the primary corrective. Along with James Wilson, they assert that individual moral failing on the part of the poor and the racially disadvantaged, not their lack of group power, accounts for their misfortune, and thus problems can be solved by individuals making correct moral choices. Philip Selznick, for example, asserts that: "At bottom, the communitarian challenge is a demand for more extensive responsibility in every aspect of personal experience and social life. It calls for a doctrine that builds on the continuities of personal and social responsibility, personal and social integrity, individual and collective judgment."[18]

Selznick and Amitai Etzioni, founders of the modern Communitarian movement, and others hold the Communitarian solution in high regard because it involves the least governmental intervention. The idea is that the community and its private institutions, not primarily the government, should be responsible for the poor or the otherwise dependent, much in the way that private almshouses and other neighborhood social organizations meted out charity to the poor in nineteenth-century America and England. They also favor the Communitarian response because of its emphasis on individual responsibility to the community as the prerequisite for any assistance.

Communitarian views manifest no understanding of the depth of the causes of modern poverty, the relative responsibilities of individuals and groups, or the proper role of a modern—and, not incidentally, rich government—in national affairs as a concomitant moral issue. In part, the failure of Communitarians is their lack of understanding that the community impulse to respond to human needs arose not from the failure of government but from the socioeconomic character of the modern community itself, which has been shaped by in part by persistent crises of collective survival—such as unemployment and massive levels of poverty—which often are related to race and ethnicity. This is why communities have not been oases of mutual human interdependence across racial lines, but instead contested terrain, where turf succession and control are the stuff of relationships.

Communities are not presently constructed as they were in the past. In fact, it is an open question whether suburban communities are communities at all. They have created an opportunity for the privatization of values such as anonymity, privacy itself, affluent indulgence, class mobilization and so forth, as a result of families having achieved a level of affluence and the desire to utilize it for largely private ends. As a result, today many Americans live in communities but are not of them. They do not experience integral human relationships with their neighbors. In fact, they often do not even know their neighbors' names.

Communitarians, however, often have a mythically harmonious vision of community, which fits the culturally homogenous model and is therefore specious when it comes to challenging people—in general—to assume responsibility for strangers who belong to another group. In fact, in their definition of community, Communitarians often deprecate the force of culture and thus miss the fact that the repression of a specific culture within the "community" represents an impediment to the ability of its members to exercise "personal responsibility."

Beyond this, the notion of community response to human needs as the dominant solution is specious when it is understood that charitable civic groups themselves have repeatedly indicated that the limited scale of their operations affords an insufficient level of resources to respond to the growing magnitude of social problems. Indeed, many groups with large-scale operations, such as Catholic Charities, obtain from the government a substantial share of the economic resources they use to serve the poor and disadvantaged. Rather than being independent agents of an autonomous organization, they are part of the social service network that depends upon government for resources.

Black people have a strong notion of "community" that is unique yet includes elements derived from the wider political and moral consensus with respect to individual liberty and autonomy, democratic decision making, and so on. Racial "community" implies sharing a common heritage with individuals who originated from the same people and who are of a similar culture. It is also associated with neighborhood location or a local place where originally a similar people were segregated and where their social organizations developed and their network of associations were nurtured. Moreover, it is what Selznick has described as a "community of principle," not merely a community of observance, for it is held together by a principle which requires adherence to a set of legal norms.[19] In this sense, Blacks share the potential democratic ideal as embedded in the principles of the Constitution, the Declaration of Independence and other legal norms.

Blacks also have a threshold for entrance into their own conception of moral community: the obliteration of impediments to their access to the wider community of opportunities, especially the stumbling block of racism. And this threshold rises with the acknowledgment of the need to eliminate other impediments, such as classism and sexism. Whites, however, led by a White Nationalist ethos, appear to be diverging from the national consensus regarding the importance of eliminating racism; many declare that racism no longer exists and thus remedies are no longer necessary. These divergent views only make the entire democratic consensus more contentious, not only for Blacks but for everyone else in society as well.

Both within and outside the Communitarian context, the family has become a symbolic corrective as an agent for solving many of the social problems of poor and urban America. Policy makers have resurrected the 1969 Moynihan Report to emphasize his perspicaciousness on the contribution of teenage pregnancy to poverty, when in fact subsequent researchers have evolved a more sophisticated analysis which establishes that poverty is likely to promote teenage pregnancy. Indeed, Professor Thomas Boston, like other economists, shows that the diminution of fertility rates is a natural consequence of rising income, and thus an increase in those rates is not necessarily the result of inherent immorality.[20]

The family-based corrective to teenage pregnancy, inferior educational systems, school violence or any number of maladies is couched in a time-warped notion of the nature of the family in the late 1990s and early 2000s. The idea of the nuclear family as a norm has eroded in the face of rapid increases in both divorce and teenage pregnancies in the White community. This has created a minority status for the nuclear family and constructed a complicated mosaic of different types of family circumstances, with none having the distinction of being "normative." Unfortunately, there appears to be little understanding that the dissolution of the traditional family is a phenomenon whose causes are beyond mere racial or economic class analyses and possibly include gender competition and other salient dynamics.

Failing to take such considerations into account, Stephan and Abigail Thernstrom assert that despite equivalent growth in the rate of teenage pregnancies in Black and White communities, the disproportional existence of poverty among Blacks should lead Blacks to adopt behavior which tempers this growth.[21] The Thernstroms do not, however, indicate which resources the poor might use to alter such behavior, nor how these resources will be delivered. The extent to which "family values" represent a normative solution for all cultures and models is highly questionable, yet many members of the Conservative movement act as though the hegemony of the traditional nuclear family is still so powerfully operative as to constitute a general corrective to social problems.

RATIONALES FOR THE POLICY SHIFT

The Pretext of Social Policy Failure

Immorality was one important pretext for the formulation of the White Nationalist movement, but governmental waste, corruption and policy failures were also set forth as reasons to devalue government and its products. This perspective led to the dictum that has been utilized in the 1980s and 1990s Conservative approach to government with regard to social policy toward the poor: "everything is broke; nothing has worked."

This rationale for an attack upon the Black community is not new. One southern Democrat, writing in 1900 about the reasons for excluding Blacks from the franchise, said that: "Southern men of enlightenment and great ability affiliated with the Republican party of the South in an effort to direct the new-made [black] citizen to a use of the power placed in his hands for the good of the state and its people, but only to meet with *failure after failure.*"[22] When Liberal Republicans tired of Reconstruction even they could be heard to say that the Freedmen's Bureau, set up as a mechanism to put an economic floor under freed slaves, had failed and was a waste of taxpayer funds.

All of this sounds uneasily like the Conservative Republicans of today who rail at the failure of government policies designed to improve the living standards of Blacks and the poor. The modern viewpoint is that government "over-promised" in setting out to eliminate poverty and sponsored many social programs that "have not worked." Indeed, government coddled the poor and made them "dependent"; people should be forced to become independent, and this will happen only when government support programs are eliminated.

Conservative Republicans hold that in an attempt to fulfill all its social promises, government has grown too big, intruding into every aspect of American life and taking larger and larger portions of the taxable income of citizens to give to the "unworthy." The proposed remedy is to reduce the size of the federal government significantly, greatly reduce and balance its budget, and in so doing redirect its responsibilities away from the social sector. Indeed, it is surprising how easily the rhetoric often repeated by public officials that "nothing has worked" in social policy has been broadly accepted, especially when the beneficiaries (Black and White) of a generation of such policies can be easily identified.

George Gilder's book, *Wealth and Poverty,* must have been a welcome addition to the pantheon of rationalizations for establishing "tough love" policies to replace the "welfare state."[23] Gilder argued that America's "neurotic" preoccupation with Blacks was misplaced and was the product of the Liberal imagination, which made every conceivable excuse for Black poverty. Using examples of accomplished Blacks such as Franklin Thomas, former head of the Ford Foundation, and the increasing number of Black elected officials, Gilder excoriated White Liberals for their failure to "tell the truth about blacks": that instead of their theorized victimization due to racism and discrimination, they have the chance to achieve anything they wish. The charge of American racism, which Gilder considered to be overly provocative, "slanders whites" and "deceives and demoralizes blacks" since it would have been possible for Blacks to achieve except for the construction of a governmental regime based on compensation for personal failure.

Gilder's opposition to the entire panoply of government assistance programs was consistent with his general analysis. He suggested flatly that "the ONLY dependable route from poverty is always work, family and faith."[24] Gilder effectively set the stage for the proposal that because of the "coming welfare boom," Conservatives should prepare to ruthlessly crack down on the system because of the inherent human deficiencies it has fostered. Ironically, he would make Black economic fortunes dependent upon another government project, "supply-side economics," which, he argues forcefully, would generate the economic growth that alone can lead to prosperity for Blacks and greater freedom for Whites.

Perhaps more than any other intellectual, Charles Murray, a Conservative policy analyst, has sought to destroy the foundations of the Liberal approach to social policy. In his *Losing Ground* (1984), Murray cleverly exploited the theme of policy failure, arguing that the Great Society programs of Lyndon Johnson's era had worked to the *disadvantage* of Blacks.[25] This startling assertion, taken at face value by many leading opinion makers, became a standard of the media construct of the movement, undergirding the Reagan administration's dismantling of many social programs, including the Comprehensive Education and Training Act. Murray continued this theme in the controversial *Bell Curve,* co-authored with Richard Herrnstein. Here they transparently argued for the dismantling of affirmative action programs on the basis that since Blacks were intellectually inferior and could not perform at a level equal to Whites, affirmative action programs would have no chance of success.[26]

Another attempt to convince the public of the failure of affirmative action found Ward Connerly and Newt Gingrich co-authoring an op-ed article that framed the issue by erecting a standard of "racelessness" (a word they attribute to Martin Luther King, Jr.), then proceeding, in the traditional way, to suggest that after four trillion dollars in government spending, "government has brought about as much discrimination as it has eliminated."[27] They suggested that "failed social policies have not educated our children," offering as proof declining SAT scores and other maladies. They declared that increased government spending is not the answer, that radical reform—specifically, a program of school vouchers—is the only way to improve public education.

Such attacks on government, formulated in terms of the national government's "failure" to make the American social fabric more equitable, are also evident in the work of authors such as Marvin Olasky. Writing in a Communitarian vein, Olasky argues that with respect to the so-called underclass, social policy bureaucrats forgot that the culture of voluntarism was essentially the safety net upon which Americans relied between 1840 and 1940.[28] This culture was established and sustained by the efforts of many community and city-wide organizations that took responsibility for the poor and less fortunate in a way which Murray, for example, has suggested was historically effective and could work today, through private support of such agencies as orphanages.

Tom Wicker, a prominent Liberal journalist, responds to the failure thesis from his own perspective. He argues that what has failed is not government policy but the national consensus in society about the role of race: the national consensus was demolished by the emergence of a new Conservative movement and an attendant stream of racism.[29]

Whether one believes Connerly and Gingrich, Olasky or Wicker, it is striking that all have grasped the sense of the failure of America to come to grips with the existence of Black people and their issues. This is another way of saying that America refuses to confront the past legacy of slavery and its manifestations in our present lives. In a way, both sides hint at the failure of Black people to become assimilated into the mainstream of American life. Conservatives say this is because Blacks and other groups have not exercised enough personal responsibility, and Liberals say that not enough resources have been applied to the problems faced by Blacks. They also feel that regardless of the extent of Black assimilation, the personal situation of Blacks has declined to the point that society cannot afford the means to achieve social justice and equality without further disadvantaging Whites. In this sense, the issue may have become whether White Americans can tolerate social (racial) equality projects any longer.

The rhetoric that government has failed leads to the question of *whom* it has failed as well as to another question, one that is seldom asked: Would Blacks have been better off without the publicly sponsored social programs of the 1960s? The generally received wisdom—that all the Great Society programs have failed Blacks, other minorities and women—is demonstrably false. It is also the surest sign that a powerful ideology is at work which will not yield to mountains of facts to the contrary. Perhaps another question would illuminate this further: If nothing worked, then where did the Black middle class come from? Profound misunderstanding serving as the basis for politics and public policy has led writers such as Wilson Carey McWilliams to characterize the era between 1976 and 1994 as "the Politics of Disappointment." Yet Blacks, the elderly and women did relatively well in that period. The fact that the programs of the 1960s did not cure poverty is not the fault of the programs but of misplaced expectations and, ultimately, the failure of the managers of the economic system.

By the late 1990s, the concept of social policy failure, surprisingly not refuted by Liberal and Progressive social policy analysts, had become a staple of the White Nationalist claim that its more Conservative policies would be successful both for Blacks and for other disadvantaged minorities as well.

The Tax Revolt: Opposition to the Rights/Welfare State

Examining the application of a moral argument for economic policy in opposition to Neoclassical economists, Etzioni noted that studies had found "a relatively close association between the sense that taxes are fairly imposed, the sense of the legitimacy of the government, the purposes for which revenues are used, and the extent of tax evasion."[30] This would indeed appear to be true, since the growth of the perception of the illegitimacy of government in the late 1980s was parallel to—or perhaps was fueled by—the feeling on the part of many Whites that their taxes were being misused. Not all tax revolts have had a direct or indirect racial referent, since taxes have never been popular, but the tax revolt within the context of the Conservative movement has carried a distinct though indirect racial connotation.

As early as the rise of George Wallace's American Independence party in 1968, the ideology of the lower-middle, blue-collar stratum of American society—called by Robert Hoy the Middle American Radicals (MARs) movement—expressed a growing resentment against "the establishment," and this grew into an antigovernment stance. Another observer remarked that if one statement, gleaned from a focus group of MARs in the 1970s, summed up this ideology, it was: "The rich give in to the demands of the poor, and the middle income people have to pay the bill."[31] The MARs were not yet a political class in the '70s, but they had begun to feel the effects of the increasing economic instability that would shape the motivations of the Conservatives who led the California tax revolt in the 1980s and 1990s.

Thomas and Mary Edsall accurately describe "race, rights and taxes" as the critical forces which contributed to the alienation of the White majority.[32] Their theme is that alienation fostered by a perception of comparative racial advantages led Whites to attack racial rights programs and reevaluate their economic contribution to and return from the federal government. Like other writers, the Edsalls associate the American electorate's positive attitude toward Republican-led government with the emergence of Conservatism and a profound reaction against the Civil Rights movement, the urban revolt (defined by many simply as crime) and the continuing growth of poverty. The manifestations of this attitude were racial polarization and White opposition to social expenditures such as welfare, which reached its highest level in 1976 and remained there throughout the 1980s.[33] The tension between the perceptions of high tax rates and illegitimate expenditures helped fuel the movement of many blue-collar Whites into the Conservative Republican camp in the 1980s.

The Edsalls present findings from 1985 focus group sessions conducted by Democratic pollster Stanley Greenberg on the attitudes of "Reagan Democrats," those White, working-class voters who were traditionally part of the Democratic base yet voted for Reagan in 1980 and 1984. Among other things, Greenberg found that "these white Democratic defectors express a profound distaste for blacks, a sentiment that pervades almost everything they think about government and politics. Blacks constitute the explanation for [white defectors'] vulnerability and for almost everything that has gone wrong in their lives; not being black is what constitutes being middle class; not living with blacks is what makes a neighborhood a decent place to live."[34] The Edsalls relate a subsequent study by the Democratic National Committee which also found deeply polarizing attitudes toward Blacks by Whites. White voters felt threatened by the Black underclass, whom they believed consumed their taxes and used affirmative action to bar them from jobs, and they felt that the culture of the underclass threatened to corrupt their children.[35]

The profound sense of betrayal by and consequent mistrust of government is clearly related to some Conservatives' sentiments about the extent to which government favored Blacks. These sentiments prompted them to initiate a "fairness" movement devoted to bolstering the "white

| TABLE 2.1 | White Attitudes on Policy Issues by Level of Information |

Issue	*Most informed*	*Least informed*
Favor cutting aid to cities	48%	58%
Willing to pay more in taxes to help low-income minorities	68%	34%
Believe that minorities can overcome prejudice and work their way up without special help from government	41%	82%
Believe that affirmative action should be limited	43%	63%
Believe that reverse discrimination is a bigger national problem than discrimination against minorities	13%	48%

Source: "A Distorted Image of Minorities in America," *Washington Post*/Kaiser Family Foundation/Harvard University survey, *Washington Post,* October 8, 1995, p. A27. Survey sample of 1,970. "Most informed" respondents gave correct answers to five or more questions designed to determine knowledge of issues, while "least informed" respondents gave incorrect answers to five or more such questions; 22% of respondents fell into the "most informed" category, and 38% fell into the "least informed" category.

middle class," a euphemism for Whites in general. Table 2.1 shows the results of a survey that looked at the relation between Whites' views of policy issues and the degree to which they were well informed about these issues. Although the figures in this table illustrate that attitudes moderate within the White population depending on whether Whites are either "most" or "least" informed, the degree of support among the informed for government programs that serve minorities is also noteworthy. However, the point of the survey was not only to discern differences among Whites with respect to racial information, but whether existing racial perceptions also influenced views of public issues. The researchers concluded that they do.

Negative attitudes toward social policies directed toward Blacks and other minorities were apparently colored by respondents' negative views of minorities. They manifested the classic symptoms of White Nationalism, such as the perception of Blacks as inferior, resentment based on the belief that Blacks are more advantaged by affirmative action and other government programs, and a willingness to support radical—even punitive—

measures to reverse the flow of public financial resources and other benefits to them. As Professor Robert Blendon of Harvard University said, the survey shows that "blacks and whites may as well be on two different planets," but its most significant implication is that Whites holding such divergent views have the enormous advantage, by virtue of their superior position in society, of using the policy system to effect negative outcomes for Blacks consistent with their racial attitudes.[36]

THE WAR ON GOVERNMENT

Once it became accepted wisdom among Conservatives, the philosophy of policy failure led to an attack on the political system regarded as responsible for it. It is now an article of faith that Americans have adopted a decidedly negative attitude toward the state or "big government." This attitude became so prevalent—moving beyond party and ideology to become a general norm—that during the 1996 presidential campaign Bill Clinton was led to announce that "the era of big government is over."

Indeed, so personal has this antipathy toward government become that members of Congress have been physically threatened; in recent years the FBI has investigated an unprecedented number of threats, which are said to have increased "quite dramatically."[37] A virtual state of war has existed between White Liberal and Conservative politicians with respect to which side can "reform" government more drastically in order to comport with, and thereby benefit from, the politics of this antigovernment mood. With respect to the Clinton era, as we shall see in chapter 4, it led to the policy, complete with a vice-presidential portfolio, known as "Reinventing Government."

This debate began in the 1970s, when the discontented working class found in government an new enemy to their social progress but lacked the sophistication necessary to craft complex and persuasive reasons for their perception of government's failure. In the mid-1970s, intellectuals like Willard Gaylin, Ira Glasser, Steven Marcus and David Rothman sought to understand more clearly whether those who were dependent upon government were truly being served by existing social policy.[38] They concluded that the "state as parent" (or biological) model of top-down intervention—that is, efforts to affect paternalistic direction in improving the lives of the dependent based on authoritative prescriptions of government—was misguided. Their goal, which was described as "progressive," was "to test the minimum limits for the exercise of state power in order to enhance autonomy."[39]

Indeed, Glasser and his colleagues asserted that the rise of the social services regime with all its good intentions led instead to the ravaging of liberty through a set of paternalistic institutions—such as public schools and institutions to care for the elderly, the poor, the young and the disabled—managed by professional service providers armed with vast grants of discretionary power.[40] The Progressive struggle partly involves an attempt to endow the poor with a voice against these agents of the state; to weaken the ability of, for example, the welfare system to control individuals' private lives; to support the elderly against care institutions' mismanagement of their money and personal property; and to bolster other rights of free speech, movement, access to information and due process.

Thus, in a very interesting way, such "Progressive intellectuals," who began to sour on the role of government in helping the less fortunate, aligned themselves with alienated members of the working class who had begun to oppose government policies because they believed these policies *favored* the less fortunate. By the late 1980s, this had become a powerful, if unintended, coalition that eventually included other intellectuals—for example, economic conservatives and those who opposed the role of government in civil rights.

Still an integral segment of the revolt against government was opposition to its role as a protector of those interests and rights that Blacks have traditionally regarded as important, such as the right to vote and hold office, to have access to public accommodations, to be treated fairly in the workplace and in education and to have a decent job. To the extent that the federal government assisted in these projects, it became a target, especially of southerners, some of whom have sought public office with the specific objective of changing the policy system.

The Devolution Resolution

One result of the opposition to the federal government was that by the 1990s, proposals for the devolution of more economic resources and responsibility for national programs to the state level became accepted features of the policy environment. Some analysts transformed the popularity of the "failed policy" thesis into a motivation for devolving power, suggesting that this was the consequence of government spending on social programs that yielded no results. For instance, Martha Derthic said: "More than anything else, it was the costly outpouring of federal Medicaid mandates between 1984 and 1990 that led to today's heightened interest in recasting intergovernmental relations."[41] She noted that congressional expansion of states' role in administering Medicaid continued even after governors from both political parties objected to such expansion in the summer of 1989. The governors' reaction was rather late in coming, however, and it coincided with the states' opposition to so-called "unfunded mandates."

It is sometimes forgotten that all the programs of the so-called New Federalism, including the version initiated by Lyndon Johnson in 1965, were based on some form of revenue sharing between national and local governments. Indeed, since that time states have come to expect federal support for local programs, to the point that their planning routinely incorporates such assistance in funding the expansion of their local social responsibility. The more recent motivation for the historical shift in the balance of federalism toward the states, however, has deep roots in the crucible of race relations. It is linked to the legacy of other eras, when those who rejected the authority of a strong central government consistently asserted the rights of states in order to prevent the integration of schools and public accommodations, and to forestall federal oversight of the voting process and other basic citizenship rights.[42]

Yet while the newest effort at devolution uses the rationale that local government is more efficient, a Brookings Institution study finds that this conclusion is not necessarily warranted.[43] Moreover, Richard Nathan, a distinguished analyst of government policy, assessed the Reagan era devolution of block grants and found that state governments did not retrench spending as a result. Instead, with increased levels of funding and responsibility, they expanded government, achieving "higher service levels than otherwise would have been the case."[44] Even conservative economist Lawrence Mead concluded, in an analysis of the Wisconsin AFDC program, that if the goal of efficiency—that is, promoting self-sufficient clients who need less government assistance—is to be achieved, this would require *greater* social (government) infrastructure expenditures, not less.[45]

(The search for program efficiency is generally based on "cost-benefit" or "cost-efficiency" calculations. Cost-benefit calculations compare costs with normative judgments about alternative approaches to policy on the basis on how they further the national interest. Cost-efficiency analysis compares the degree of program impact at various levels of costs with the objective of gaining the most benefit for the least cost.)

Devolution of power is one ideological answer to the perceived wrongs of government. In more rational times, the general issue of governmental reform would place efficiency above any other single factor thought to solve the problems with government operation. But efficiency has been rejected, or else interpolated with the idea that power should be dispersed to the local level, where issues that affect people can be more effectively approached.

The objective of perfecting the operation of the programs through their administration is consistent with the practices of public adminis-tration and good government. However, approaches to this problem that only counsel a strategy of reflexive reductions in program budgets and functions are inconsistent with either the objectives of good government or efficiency in administration.

It is possible, then, to reach the conclusion that the devolution of the power of the central government has been initiated out of ideology rather than efficiency and that the motivation for this is to deprive the offending group of government protection and weaken the major mech-anism that distributes economic resources. *It is clear that the point of the redistribution of national power and its devolution to local entities is to affect the consolidation of power in the hands of a more dependable cul-tural elite. In effect, this amounts to the "privatization of social power."*

This is a major issue in American politics and society, for if govern-ment actually does not work, or is perceived not to work and, as a con-sequence, is under constant attack, the very idea of the grand American experiment with democracy is severely diminished in the process. This issue comprises much more than the simple question of whether one is liberal or conservative with regard to the use of governmental power, especially in the area of social programming. The cost of devolution could be catastrophic, because measures targeting Blacks and other disadvan-taged groups which are perceived as threatening the advantages of the alienated segment of the White majority may themselves destroy the entire experiment of liberal democratic government.

GINGRICHISM IN THE POLITICAL SYSTEM

The relatively positive reaction to the strong rhetoric that accompanied the Conservative movement caused many politicians at all levels of gov-ernment to give its adherents even greater legitimacy, both in public speeches and in legislation. In fact, Newt Gingrich, a leader of this move-ment, skillfully used it to craft both a mobilizing ideology and a Con-gressional legislative policy agenda. Although he had campaigned on Conservative issues for nearly a decade before, from the moment he became Speaker of the House. Marrying ideological leadership to leg-islative power, he became arguably the most important Conservative leader since Ronald Reagan. Thus, it is important that Gingrich's ideas be considered here, since they formed much of the policy framework of the Republican party between 1994 and 1998.

The Cultural Crisis

In many of his presentations in the 1980s and 1990s, Gingrich referred to himself as a "revolutionary," as the leader of a "revolution." He formulated the notion of a "cultural crisis" as the root source of the "trouble" he saw in society, and he indirectly indicted urban residents, many of whom were Black. (The nature of the cultural crisis as it is perceived by Conservatives might be described in terms of the issues which have become targets of the Conservative agenda. Among these are the rise in out-of-wedlock births, violence in the streets, gang involvement in drug murders and sales, rap music with sexually explicit and violent lyrics, a dress code derived from "hip-hop" culture, multicultural education, steadily increasing Hispanic immigration and affirmative action/racial preferences.)

Proof of Gingrich's conceptual intent may be found in a revealing interview he gave in June of 1995, in which he revealed his racial views when he suggested that the economic plight of poor Blacks was partly a result of their "habits" and that the Civil Rights movement was more focused on grievances than on economic development. His attribution of certain "habits" to Black people extended to the Black middle class; he remarked that "the habits of the church and the habits of the lawsuit have become more powerful than the habits of acquisition and the habits of job creation."[46] Gingrich appeared to deprecate the objective of school integration when he proposed that all the money spent on school busing should have been spent on "intensive education" for Black children—though presumably in segregated settings.[47] Gingrich's "habit" or negative-behavior-based view of the reason for Blacks' status in America was typically Conservative and narrow in that it made no reference to how majority control of the American opportunity structure maintains the subordinate status of out-groups.

For Gingrich, the remedy is a nationalist project, the reclamation of undisputed cultural dominance by the majority, who should set about "Reasserting and Renewing American Civilization"—which is the title of the second chapter of his *To Renew America*. Like Liberal historian Arthur Schlesinger in *The Disuniting of America*, Gingrich claims that the rise of multiculturalism has obliterated allegiance to a common culture and led to the collapse of society's ability to teach ethical behavior. And like other prominent Conservatives, such as William Bennett, Gingrich ties ethics to the Conservative version of American culture or "civilization." Moreover, he arrogantly asks, "[I]f we don't teach ourselves how to be Americans how do we teach other people?"[48] The Gingrich/Bennett view of "ethics" offers a specific form of authoritarian socialization, the content of which is a regimen that hews to the historical line of Anglo-conformism: one learns how to be an American by modeling oneself after members of the ruling class.

This would perhaps not be arrogant or dangerous if Gingrich's vision of America was at all balanced or inclusive. However, his notion of America follows the romantic nationalism of Ronald Reagan, as demonstrated by his assertion that "America is a series of romantic folktales that just happen to be true."[49] Moreover, this vision does not stop at the borders of America. In his unabashed nationalism, Gingrich wants America to "lead the world," and in that respect his nationalism is consistent with the version of American exceptionalism that constructs a coherent attitude and set of actions which encompass the entire world.[50]

The Individual and the Opportunity Society

The Gingrich view of America is that it is a culture of fully integrated people who pursue a common system of shared opportunity and happiness. This absolutist characterization is close to the "sleeping beauty" concept of a perfect America and to Ronald Reagan's "shining city set on a hill"— metaphors for America that are at the core of Gingrich's messianic thinking. Gingrich asserts of America: "We have no caste system, no class requirements, no regulated professions, no barriers to entry. Despite the best efforts of modern elites to discount upward mobility and to argue that America is no different than Europe or other class-dominated cultures, the fact remains that we are an extraordinarily fluid society."[51] In this as in other such comments, and in his description of a mythically perfect America, Gingrich betrays either a devastating naivete with respect to the impediments to upward mobility faced by most citizens of color, women, the disabled and the elderly, or a willingness to indulge in a crass and cynical distortion of the truth.

Additionally, Gingrich grossly misconstrues the social process of mobility by confusing *legal* individualism with *social* individualism. That is to say, when one extrapolates a notion of legal individualism from the Constitutional structure of the country and its grant of individual rights—and, by extension, its emphasis on the individual personality—that is not the same concept as social individualism. Certainly, the rights of individuals are protected in the social setting within which they operate. But more often than not, people operate as individuals *within a group setting,* using group-based resources derived from the primary family, neighborhood groups and social and professional groups. These groups are critical because their relative status and the extent of their resources often determine the limits of the mobility process for individuals. In fact, the maintenance of the rights and integrity of the individual under law and society is the raison d'être for the mobilization of many group resources. As economic and social group mobilization take place, individuals acquire support from their group structure and thus gain the individual freedom to exploit their personal resources.

Finding a Policy Language

Like George Wallace, Newt Gingrich helped introduce nativistic nationalist sentiments about race into the public discourse by developing euphemisms. In particular, he helped popularize the notion that the "middle class" are "the taxpayers," a subtle but nonetheless meaningful construction in which the middle class symbolizes Whites. Since Blacks are presumably not predominantly middle class, they also are not predominantly taxpayers. This status devalues their policy-making claims, since the underlying assumption is that only taxpayers have the moral right to set public policy priorities.

Gingrich's nomenclature was quickly adopted by the general public, for his views fed the popular stereotype that urban neighborhoods contained few taxpayers, as his reference to the importance of enterprise zones might suggest: "These [poor] neighborhoods pay almost no taxes anyway and since they drain the public treasury through welfare payments, the cost of giving them tax breaks would be relatively small."[52] However, Dr. Andrew Brimmer, an economist and former member of the Federal Reserve Board, found that Blacks pay $5.3 billion in taxes annually, and that most of them are part of the working poor.[53]

The Gingrich language helped buttress the Conservative view that moral failure is the basis of such problems as crime, drugs, teenage pregnancy, family breakdown, welfare abuse and joblessness. This, too, follows an old but consistent line of Conservative attitudes that regard the poor as immoral people or persons who reject personal responsibility for their own lives. The issue of responsibility takes on a clear racial cast in the assessment by Nationalist Whites of who is responsible for the plight of the less fortunate (including Blacks), and how to resolve the problem of responsibility. More personal responsibility and less government aid are perceived to be the solutions to the problems of poverty and racism, and this view has become a basic tenet of the Conservative movement.

Its popularity is clearly evident in a 1996 poll which found that respondents considered crime and drugs the two most important social issues, and the moral crisis third most important.[54] But when respondents were asked whether the bigger problem was that government was not working well or that people were not assuming responsibility for themselves, those surveyed overwhelmingly chose the responsibility answer (49% to 26%).[55] Moreover, more respondents thought the country's main problem was morality (59%) rather than lack of economic opportunity (27%), and nearly half of them (48%) agreed that the reason immorality was high was that people "did not care to act responsibly."

When one combines negative views about minorities with the priorities expressed in this survey, one senses the content of the ideology driving political institutions to shape specific policies at this era in American history. This ideology maintains that Blacks and other minorities are major producers of the problems that face this country and that the principal source of these problems is the growing immorality of personal behavior. The problems would be resolved if only Blacks and other similarly situated individuals would merely exercise more personal responsibility. Further, this ideology regards government support and the availability of greater economic opportunity as less important contributors to the solution of social and economic problems than a long-term strategy of education that would provide increased income and encourage socialization to mainstream norms of behavior.

If one looks carefully, then, at many of the social policies constructed in the 1980s and 1990s, one sees that the underlying themes of correcting flaws in personal behavior by promoting more personal responsibility and blaming the victims for their circumstance are inherent in the rationale.

Freedom and Governance

Another powerful norm of Conservative thought has been the issue of personal freedom and the threat to it posed by the behavior of the state and its clients—that is, minority groups. Gingrich's answer, like that of other Conservatives since Barry Goldwater, is to restore American civilization by creating as much "freedom" as possible for individuals to control their own lives. It should be understood that by this Gingrich does not mean economic individualism, an activity which produces for each family an individual paycheck, but rather social individualism, a collection of behaviors that define the sum total of how people live their lives.

The central flaw in this thesis is that individuals are presumably disconnected from each other and do not participate in networks of power. Moreover, "freedom" is gained only at the expense of others, and special protection of the rights of the disadvantaged is abrogated. Such a notion of freedom is neither egalitarian nor democratic, for it dispenses freedom disproportionately.

Furthermore, such "freedom" must inevitably be won at the price of the diminution of the power which represents the societal collective in the form of the central government. Gingrich believes in a strong government, but one that has a relatively narrow mandate, with jurisdiction limited to such matters as defense, health, the economy and the environment. He also believes in enlarging the scope of the private social realm and reducing its responsibility for managing equality. However, this would foster an unregulated use of power by private groups in which there is far less non-White participation than in official circles of government.

Historically, the expansion of freedom for a racial elite has invariably resulted in its ability to impose additional controls over the less powerful. In slavery times, such unchecked freedom meant the freedom to possess another human being. So how far does this new concept of "freedom" extend today? The intent of many policies championed by the Conservatives has been described as a "mean-spirited" attempt to do harm and actively punish groups that did not support them.[56] This characterization was made by a *New York Times* journalist after observing a rally of 1,000 people who had gathered on the steps of the Capitol to challenge Republican budget proposals that the protestors believed would reduce resources devoted to poor children. In response to the demonstration, Republicans charged that the protesters represented "special interests." In a follow-up opinion piece, Bob Herbert wrote: "What an accusation from a party that is trying to throw poor children off the welfare rolls; a party that would eliminate federal nutritional standards for school means a party that would cut benefits for *handicapped* children; a party that would reduce protection for abused and neglected children, even though reported cases of abuse and neglect tripled between 1980 and 1992."[57]

It is interesting to note that Conservatives initially used the phrase "special interest" politics with reference to Black proponents of civil rights, but the term took on a larger meaning when they began to routinely apply it to any opposition group. Nevertheless, the pursuit of "freedom" for some often means a policy trade-off of resources for others. Although Conservatives have felt victimized by this practice in the past, their role as leaders of the policy system in the present era has given them the opportunity to engineer trade-offs that heavily favor their supporters.

POLICY RACISM

The Reinterpretation of Racial Disadvantage

One of the major results of the shaping of an intellectual policy rationale for White Nationalism has been the reinterpretation of certain critical concepts. The key concept used for over thirty years in public policy to define the harm that Blacks have experienced because of their subordination by Whites in American society has been racism. A major project of the intellectual wing of the White Nationalist movement has been the reformulation of this concept in order to neutralize it and apply it to Black victimization of Whites. With the concept of White racial victimization thus established, racism acts in its modern context to re-empower Whites. Once this connotation was popularized, the term racism lost much of its particularity to Black victimization. I will briefly describe the path this concept has traveled on its journey to performing its new role for White Nationalism.[58]

The modern concept of racism was defined by Stokeley Carmichael and Charles Hamilton in their book *Black Power*. There they explained that by "racism" they meant "the predication of decisions and policies on considerations of race for the purpose of subordinating a racial group and maintaining control over that group."[59] They described this social phenomenon as one that may be expressed in both covert and overt acts committed either by individuals or by groups, and thus, they argued, there is both individual and institutional racism. A similar definition was developed by the nationally regarded sociologist of race, Joe Feagin, in the early 1980s: "Discrimination refers to actions or practices carried out by members of a dominant group (such as whites) or their representatives, which have a differential and harmful impact on members of a subordinate group (such as blacks)."[60] Feagin added that racial discrimination comprised both overt and subtle acts, practiced by individuals but also "deeply imbedded in large-scale organizations."[61] Such definitions provided the origin and setting of the concept of "institutional racism."

But while sociologists have traditionally utilized the term racial prejudice to describe the psychology of making distinctions based on race and discrimination, Andrew Hacker says that "racism goes beyond prejudice and discrimination and even transcends bigotry," that it is an accu-

mulation of several varieties of prejudice and action based on the perceived race of the individual or group.[62] In a book written with Herman
Vere and published in 1995, Feagin supplemented his earlier definition
of racism: "White racism can be viewed as the socially organized set of
attitudes, ideas, and practices that deny African Americans and other
people of color the dignity, opportunities, freedoms, and rewards that this
nation offers white Americans. The concept of white racism encompasses
the attitudes and ideologies that motivate negative actions against blacks
and other minorities."[63] Feagin's more recent definition encompasses the
key ideas of White Nationalist ideology: White social dominance and
control of activities that produce harm to non-White individuals or
groups.

Yet this definition is at odds with more Conservative formulations.
Symptomatic of the change in conceptualization is a work by Byron Roth,
published in 1994, which questions the extent to which White racism is
implicated in the social problems of Black children. Roth prefers to see
such problems as educational difficulties or illegitimacy as the outcome
of poor behavior. In effect, he questions the existence of a racial stratifi-
cation system that is comprehensive enough to produce White dominance over the lives of Blacks and bring about negative outcomes in most
every area of their existence:

> There can be little doubt that there are people who openly express
> antagonism to blacks, and probably many others who secretly share
> their antagonism. But it is simply not clear how many white Ameri-
> cans are avowed racists. Nor is it clear what proportion of racists
> there are in positions of influence who can in any major way affect
> what happens to blacks. So long as such questions remain unan-
> swered, it is unwise and perhaps counterproductive to accept many
> common assertions as to the sources of black difficulties.[64]

In other words, Roth equates racial antagonism with racism. Moreover, since "it is simply not clear" how many racist Whites there are, he
questions whether they exercise sufficient presumptive dominance over
Blacks to an extent that is great enough to shape outcomes. On the basis
of a presumed lack of clarity, Roth rejects the proposition that most
Whites are linked to each other in a racial network of power and status;
instead he implies that what matters is how many dedicated racists there
are—though he does not define the term racist.

Thus, like many Neoconservative writers of the 1970s, Roth has
challenged, on the most shallow of premises, traditional definitions of

racism and the civil rights policies upon which they are based. Similarly, Dinesh D'Souza, a Conservative intellectual at the Hoover Institution at Stanford University, attempted to "normalize" racism as the natural reaction of Whites to real phenomena they experienced from contact with or information about Blacks. This process, however, of legitimizing racism as "natural" is also based upon legitimizing both racial stereotypes as the real character of groups and the negative reaction of others to those very often mythical and distorted attributes.

CONCLUSION

The question must be raised at this point whether the disadvantages suffered by Blacks because of the shift in political ideology and the resulting impact upon policies especially affecting Blacks amounts to policy racism. As we will see, Ronald Reagan was called a "racist" by some of the most moderate Black political leaders in the country. The same charge has been leveled against other White politicians, such as New York City Mayor Rudolph Giuliani by Black leaders who would normally abjure such labeling but who employed it in this instance because of the harm inflicted on Blacks by Giuliani's policies.[65]

The concept of discrimination has always contained the element of racial harm, especially when perpetrated upon Blacks. The issue of intent is relatively easy to determine in the case of individuals, because they generally announce it or otherwise make it obvious. However, the management of institutions so that they have a racial effect—that is to say, cause harm to a racial group—may be regarded as institutional racism. But how can one argue that no one is to blame for institutional racism, that no one has responsibility or culpability for disparate racial outcomes, when it is a common practice to hold chief executive officers accountable for the behavior of their organizations in other respects? Since policy is the outcome of institutions distributing resources, policy racism in either its intended or unintended effect is a rational characterization. The institution is culpable because it is the system through which resources are distributed, and the managers are culpable because they are in control of the processes by which the institution functions. Therefore, in this study I will be dealing essentially with the way in which the Conservative political movement, through the activity of the most radical segment of White Nationalism, has fostered "policy racism."

CHAPTER 3

The Assumption of Official Power

INTRODUCTION

This chapter will briefly examine the assumption of political power by the Conservative movement in executive and legislative branches of government and the nationalist tendencies that emerged in the approach of each to public policy affecting Blacks. I will emphasize here the restructuring of economic priorities in the context of new political attitudes; subsequent chapters will comment upon specific policy issues such as affirmative action, crime, welfare and Black-majority congressional districts. A major reason for addressing the change in economic priorities is that the ideology of the Nationalist movement is often most clearly delineated by proposals related to the budget and by taxation policies related to social expenditures. I will also address the Republican assumption of congressional power (1994 to 1998) and the influence of White Nationalism upon legislation affecting Blacks as outlined in the "Contract with America." This chapter sets the stage for chapters dealing with deregulation of rights, education, political participation and other subjects.

THE EXECUTIVE BRANCH

The Impact of Reaganism

Few of the standard volumes outlining Ronald Reagan's rise to power have adequately captured the fact that his emergence was the result of

the Conservative movement. Rather, both opponents and proponents
have fostered the view that Reagan himself was responsible for formulating and implementing the Conservative doctrine of his administrations.[1] In fact, Reagan represented a small group of activist New Right
Conservatives from California who were seasoned in their opposition to
civil rights, the Black Panther party and the antiwar movement. In the
late 1950s, the New Right emerged from the Taft wing of the Republican party through the John Birch Society, in opposition to the moderate
Rockefeller wing of the party.[2]

Anthony King and David Sanders admit to "puzzlement" as to the
sources of the policy success of an ex-actor, ex-professional dinner
speaker.[3] In fact, William Raspberry, a senior African American journalist, wrote one day after the 1980 election that it reflected the existence
of a massive resistance movement against civil rights that boded ill
because it had the ability to legitimize "recessive racism" in subtle ways;
Raspberry predicted and that by Reagan's second term, the use of this
political currency would be "hazardous for the aspirations of black people."[4] Two other seasoned observers said of Reagan's election: "Ronald
Reagan was elected to the White House—and the Republican party
gained control of the Senate and scored significant gains in the House—
mainly because the American people agreed with the ideological orientation of leading Republican candidates. Citizens, therefore, expected
Republicans elected to office to be guided by conservative precepts in formulating internal and external policies."[5]

The early nationalist content of Reagan's rationale was manifest in
the ring of his political rhetoric. Reagan viewed America as a "shining city
set on a hill," and he trumpeted American global military strength as the
country's most enduring asset, laying a predicate for budget increases in
defense spending during his administration. His jingoistic rhetoric was
suited to his preoccupation with the cold war, which had, since World
War II, been the Conservatives' central foreign policy focus. Reagan
backed up his rhetoric by championing Right-wing anti-Communist factions involved in civil wars in Asia, Africa and Latin America and in military assaults on Black nations such as Guyana and Panama in pursuit of
ill-defined anticapitalists and drug cartels.

Reagan's antigovernment philosophy reverberated with certain
groups as a liberation movement. He frequently told audiences he wanted
to create conditions that would "loose you to let you take control of your
destiny again." In a blatant pitch to those who felt the balance of attention had shifted to domestic minority groups and women, he promised
inferentially to redress that balance by removing governmental protection

of their status and access to its resources. Employing language that conjured up a mythical past when everything was in order, Reagan appeared to genuinely want to turn the clock back to a time when America's White-dominated political and social structure was unchallenged by the claims of disadvantaged groups, when everyone "knew their place." Few Blacks, however, wanted to return to Reagan's mythical "shining city."[6]

Indeed, Reagan's actions bespoke a deep-seated animus toward Blacks. Not only did he begin his 1980 campaign near Philadelphia, Mississippi—the site of the murder of three civil rights workers in the 1960s—he also visited the Neshoba, Mississippi, fairground that was frequently used as a meeting place by racist groups. His appearance there signaled his compatibility with the southern wing of the Republican party, which contained many politicians who held similarly Conservative views on states' rights, social policy and civil rights.[7] This led to a shouting match between Reagan and Blacks when his campaign reached the Bronx section of New York.

In the course of the campaign, Black leadership gained a sense of Reagan's intent, and six months into his administration, Vernon Jordan, then head of the National Urban league, was quoted as saying that Reagan was "leading a massive march to the rear on race relations." Jordan ridiculed Reagan's rhetoric as "slogans . . . that reinforce the meanest instincts of selfishness."[8] His administration initially opposed the idea of a federal holiday for Martin Luther King, Jr., implying that King had been associated with the Communist movement. Moreover, it began to accuse civil rights leaders of using race conflict to generate support for themselves and their jobs, rather than their constituencies. In his 1982 budget, Reagan proposed eliminating many programs through which civil rights groups had obtained funds. The NAACP and the SCLC had received few federal grants, because, according to the Rev. Joseph Lowery, head of the SCLC, "we jump on government too much to have to depend upon them for survival."[9] But other organizations, such as the National Urban League and Operation PUSH, held millions of dollars in government contracts either to promote social policies or manage social service projects. Rev. Jesse Jackson asserted that Reagan was "going out of his way to punish us because of our support for Carter and our outspokenness on what we consider to be the president's [inadequate economic approach]."[10] Several Black leaders voiced their determination not to be silenced even though their organizations accepted government funds.

Reagan declined to accept an invitation to the NAACP convention in 1980. However, he did attend in June of 1981, when he defended his cuts in social programs as measures made necessary by inflation and a declining economy, and he urged the organization to help end federal "bondage."[11] One month later, Vice President George Bush spoke at the National Urban League convention, where he warned civil rights groups "not to bring us an old agenda that was tied to the status quo."[12] Attendees at both meetings had their views confirmed: the administration was adopting policies that were explicitly opposed to their interests.

In 1982 President Reagan adopted a strategy of symbolic appearances at Black venues such as schools and churches. On one occasion he was challenged to explain a letter sent to him by Sen. Trent Lott (R-Miss.) requesting that he discipline the IRS for initiating a series of court actions against largely White, racially segregated institutions—such as the Bob Jones University—that were receiving federal funds. Reagan's response was that such issues should be settled by legislation rather than by court action.[13]

Reagan's first term stamped an indelible impression upon the minds of civil rights leaders, who became convinced that their relations with the White House were intractably poisoned by the president's deeply Conservative viewpoint. He held no substantive discussions with them and had, in fact, appeared to close off their access to the White House, though in January 1985, on the Martin Luther King, Jr. holiday, he met with a group known as the Council for a Black Economic Agenda.[14] This led John Jacob, the new president of the National Urban League, to observe that the meeting appeared to be a deliberately chosen alternative to one with leaders who represented mainstream Black constituencies.[15] Julian Bond, then a Georgia state senator, concluded that "[Reagan's] constituents are the right-wing fringe, the Ku Klux Klan types, whites who have always hated blacks."[16] Likewise, Benjamin Hooks, then executive director of the NAACP, characterized the president's leadership in conceptualizing affirmative action as "reverse discrimination" because of its efforts to reverse court consent decrees in 50 communities which were designed to foster school integration.[17] William Gibson, board chairman of the NAACP, said that after waiting and hoping that Reagan's views would change, he had determined that the president was a "reactionary racist."[18]

Key Reagan appointees actively enforced policies that were strongly opposed by Blacks. For example, Clarence Pendleton, Jr., a California businessman, was appointed chairman of the U.S. Civil Rights Commission in what many interpreted as an anti-civil rights thrust. Pendleton often attempted to discredit established Black leaders by referring to them publicly as "media-designated" leaders and even "racist."[19] Shortly after joining the administration, he became president of an organization of Blacks known as the Conservative Coalition, which was associated with the Heritage Foundation, a far Right policy think tank.[20]

Pendleton's negative attitude toward the prevailing civil rights policy clearly reflected the administration's approach to affirmative action and to the operation of the Equal Employment Opportunity Commission, one of the most important civil rights agencies. Transition documents of the Reagan administration reveal the policy goal of rescinding Executive Order 12067, which implemented Executive Order 11246—establishing authority for affirmative action in hiring—promulgated in the Carter administration. These documents called for several anti-affirmative action measures, including:

a freeze on new EEOC guidelines for one year;
the appointment of "an individual at EEOC who is a staunch proponent of individual freedom and steadfastly opposed to discrimination as set forth in Title VII of the 1964 Civil Rights Act";
an immediate move by the new chairman of the EEOC to reorganize the agency's components, including the Equal Opportunity Coordinating Council, with a view toward implementing President Reagan's program;
forming a private sector advisory committee to ensure sufficient input for those against whom the EEOC had filed many charges.[21]

By 1985 a draft plan was developed as a substitute for Executive Order 11246 that would abolish regulations requiring numerical goals for minorities and women. The initiative was vigorously contested by the civil rights community, and although it was not formally adopted by the administration, it is another illustration of Reagan's attempt to carry out long-term political objectives.[22]

The person who ultimately came to administer the Reagan administration's anti-civil rights program was Clarence Thomas, a Conservative African American lawyer who was appointed head of the EEOC. William Bradford Reynolds, then assistant attorney general for civil rights, launched a virtual crusade to stop school busing. He set about reversing court orders, challenging minority set-asides in Dade County, Florida, and other places, and attempting to overturn job hiring goals in Indianapolis and other cities.[23] Clarence Pendleton justified the administration's opposition to these policies on the grounds that they "create[d] a kind of animosity and racism that were not there before."[24] This attitude even led Pendleton to challenge the separate caucuses created for Blacks, Hispanics and Asians in the Democratic and Republican national parties.[25]

Urban Decline

The impact of Ronald Reagan's urban policy upon the lives of Black Americans was significant because they comprised the most highly urbanized group in America. In the 1960s, at the height of the Civil Rights movement, the great migration of Blacks from rural southern areas to cities in both the north and the south was culminating. By the time of the 1970 census, Blacks had reached a 70% urbanization rate, and three decades later fully 52% of Blacks still lived in cities.[26] By 1980 America's 153 largest cities had an average Black population of 17%; in the northeast and central regions of the country, this figure was 22%. Several major cities with Black mayors—including Atlanta, Baltimore, Birmingham, Detroit, Gary, Newark, New Orleans and Washington, D.C.—had a majority-Black population. Moreover, a Brookings Institution study found that of the 19 cities which were the most distressed, seven had large Black populations and four were predominantly Black.[27] There is no doubt that national urban policy is material to the quality of Black life.

As the percentage of the American population living in suburbs rose by 5% from 1980 to 1990, the Black middle class joined the movement, and the Black population in suburbs grew from 5.7% to 8.0%.[28] As a result of demographic changes, the tax base of cities was already suffering when Ronald Reagan became president. One analysis of city budgets indicates that the deterioration in the fiscal health of cities was most severe in the 1972–1982 period, to the point that cities would have needed 73% more revenue in 1982 to maintain the 1972 level of service delivery.[29]

Although the overall health of cities improved somewhat in the 1980s, cities with populations over 100,000 did not improve much because of their continued loss of population and hence tax revenues. And the added problem of the decline in federal assistance to cities in the 1980s has been documented: "For the average city over the 1972–1982 period, federal aid fully offset the decline in fiscal health that was not accounted for by state assistance. But for the largest cities (over one million population), federal aid offset only about one-third of the decline. Since federal aid to cities declined substantially during the 1980s, the underlying fiscal position of the largest cities has undoubtedly worsened."[30]

The Reagan/Bush Impact

It is obvious that cities needed more federal assistance in the 1980s. However, when Reagan became president he initiated a substantial decline in such assistance. One of the first things he brought about was a massive shift of economic resources from urban areas. In this he followed the logic of the Laffer curve, a "supply-side" economic theory devised by University of Southern California economist Arthur Laffer, who argued that large tax cuts would free up capital that would be invested and set off an economic boom. His thesis was that government spending to manage social programs depressed incentives for work and savings in the private sector, which in turn slowed economic growth and lowered tax revenue. Thus, both as a matter of anti-social policy ideology and following the logic of the Kemp-Roth tax cuts, the administration effected a substantial reduction in social programs serving "weak clients and weak claimants" to help finance the deficit that resulted from the tax cut and to generate revenue to shift to the defense budget.[31] The Reagan tax cut was designed to help those who controlled capital, on the strength of the feeling that they would invest it more wisely than would the poor, who "tended not to work or not to work efficiently, not to earn beyond sufficiency, [and] not to store money for larger purchases in capital-creating banks."[32] The action satisfied both fiscally conservative Republicans and anti-social policy Republicans at the same time, but for different reasons.

Other Reagan proposals passed by Congress changed eligibility requirements for cash assistance to the poor through Aid to Families with Dependent Children (AFDC), reduced the food stamp budget by 1% and delayed the adjustment for inflation, and severely reduced the low-income housing assistance budget.[33] Both taxes and spending were cut as a result of the Economic Recovery Tax Act of 1982, which slashed tax rates for the rich by 30% and reduced welfare spending as well. An analysis of that act by the Congressional Budget Office clearly showed its regressive nature: people with annual incomes under $10,000 would suffer the most from its implementation. This was consistent with the philosophical predisposition of Laffer-theory economics, and the bill's passage came at a time when the poverty rate for Blacks was 32% and growing.

Indeed, the tax cuts did stimulate economic growth. Between 1980 and 1990 federal revenues grew by $209 billion, an expansion of 26%.[34]

Defense spending increased by 41% or $86 billion in the same decade, but social programs, such as AFDC, declined 1%, and food stamps and school lunch programs by 6% and 4%, respectively. Although spending for Head Start increased by 12% and foster care grew by 15%, reductions in other social programs were striking: social services block grants, 33%; community services block grants, 46%; education block grants, 3%; and training for the disadvantaged, 36%.[35] In late spring 1984, federal aid for youth summer jobs was slashed by $100 million, and in Chicago, where funds were reduced by 47%, 16,000 youth were unable to find summer employment.[36] Other cities suffered similar reductions: Cleveland, 42%; Dallas, 40%; Indianapolis, 39%; Minneapolis, 38%; St. Louis 37%; Birmingham, 32%; Washington, D. C., 25%; and New York City, 20%.[37]

Clearly these policy changes were intended to severely reduce the flow of economic resources from the federal government to the urban poor. The Center on Budget and Policy Priorities, a Liberal Washington, D.C., research organization, issued a report, based on census data, showing that in 1986 far fewer families and children were moving out of poverty as a result of government transfer payments such as AFDC and Social Security contributions than in 1979, primarily because of cuts by the Reagan administration and the attendant failure of states to adjust benefit levels of these programs upward to account for the effect of inflation.[38] The report also found that the combined impact of AFDC, Social Security and Unemployment Insurance payments in 1979 reduced by one-fifth the number of people who would otherwise have fallen under the official poverty line. The center further noted that the Reagan administration's fiscal year 1987 budget proposal contained cuts of nearly 16% in low-income programs, $17 billion less than 1986 levels. The net effect of these cuts, amounting to 4% between 1978 and 1987, was an expansion of poverty, especially for children.[39]

Deepening Poverty

By 1988 the poverty rate for Blacks in urban areas was 31.2%, nearly 9% higher than the suburban Black rate of 22.6% and 13% higher than the Black rate outside metropolitan areas of 19%. Economic decline in urban areas led to increase disparities between Black and White incomes. In 1988 the per capita income of Blacks outside of metro areas nationally was $7,990, in metro areas it was $7,100, and for inner-city Blacks it was $6,754.[40] Poverty rose in both 1990 and 1991, increasing in 1991 alone by a substantial 2.1 million persons to a total of 35.7 million, or 14.2%, up from 31 million in 1989.[41] The 1988 Commission on the Cities concluded that in that year, poverty was worse than it had been in 1969, when 24 million people were officially below the poverty line; indeed, the poverty rate rose from 12.7% in 1969 to 19% in 1985.[42] Between 1975 and 1985, poverty in central city tracts nearly doubled, from 4.1 million persons to 7.8 million. Meanwhile, reductions in federal funds meant that less was being spent on education, job training and other non-insurance programs, where resources fell from 4.2% of GNP in 1980 to 3.7%

in 1988.[43] This decrease in resources served to complicate issues of welfare dependency, crime and other social problems.

The term "welfare state" used as a general description of the role of the federal government in the social policy arena expressed the leading edge of the animus. As David Stockman, Reagan's budget director, said: "The Reagan Revolution required a full-frontal assault on the American welfare state. Accordingly, forty years worth of promises, subventions, entitlements, and safety nets issued by the federal government . . . would have to be scrapped or drastically modified."[44] This sentiment was reflected in Reagan's fiscal year 1981 budget, which proposed $7.2 billion more in defense spending and $41.4 billion less in domestic spending than proposed by Jimmy Carter.[45]

It is interesting to note that since federal government spending as a percent of GNP was 18% in 1980 and 24% in 1986, Reagan did not "rein in" government spending. He did, however, curtail and reduce the growth of selected government programs aimed at specific clients in the body politic. In 1980, 10% of city funding represented federal support, but by 1992 the figure was 4%.[46] Again, the burden of the reduction in federal support of cities fell upon the Black community.

The Reagan Legacy and Bush

Reagan possessed a strategic vision that combined anti-big government Conservatism with an attack on government domestic programs which supported minorities and the less fortunate. His explicit policy priorities exhibited the residue of a nationalism that contained a punitive attitude and policy outcome toward minorities perceived to be government's main beneficiaries. Though it is not at all clear that George Bush had a similar philosophical or strategic approach to Conservative governance, it is evident that he wanted to benefit from, and thus attempted to maintain, the general aura of Reaganism.

The record indicates that the Bush administration maintained and reinforced the framework of social policy that had been set by Reagan. For example, from 1988 to 1991 funding for employment increased by only 4%; since this did not even keep pace with inflation, it amounted to an effective reduction in funding. The housing budget suffered even deeper cuts: throughout Bush's term in office it remained at the rate inherited from Reagan.[47] This occurred despite the efforts of the popular and activist Secretary of Housing and Urban Development Jack Kemp, whose ideas for urban development, even though they were basically Conservative, were not acknowledged by the administration until the presidential campaign of 1992. Mary Brunette, Kemp's assistant at HUD throughout the Bush administration, said that before then it had been nearly impossible for Kemp to engage the attention of top White House officials—that "[i]t was like speaking to a void."[48]

Kemp had wanted to wage a "new war on poverty," one that would be different from the Lyndon Johnson version because it would be motivated by entrepreneurship, which Kemp believed would restore economic growth and jobs to America's inner cities. Speaking to the U.S. Conference of Mayors' annual meeting in June of 1992, Kemp said: "We must embark upon an audacious, dramatic effort to restore economic growth, educational opportunity and home ownership for poor people—not through 'trickle-down government' but through individual empowerment, expanding privatization and tenant ownership of public housing, minority entrepreneurship, and true welfare reform that liberates people instead of entraps them."[49]

Kemp's ideas, however, always suffered from a crisis of credibility. Few, either on the Right or the Left, believed that the goal of poor residents in public housing was to own such units rather than escape them as soon as they were able to obtain better housing in better neighborhoods. (Reflective of this is the massive flight of lower-income housing project residents from Washington, D.C., to better housing in nearby Prince George's County, Maryland, in the 20 years between 1970 and 1990.) Kemp's idiosyncratic vision of welfare reform, couched as "individual empowerment" projects, was only trusted because it ran counter to group-oriented empowerment and income methods proposed by residents of poor Black neighborhoods.

In preparation for the presidential campaign of 1992, George Bush formulated a six-point urban agenda. This amounted to an expansion of the HOPE program, the Weed and Seed program, welfare reform, youth employment and 50 enterprise zones. Congress did pass an enterprise zone plan in the closing days of the Bush administration, as part of a tax bill, but since the bill in its final form was unpalatable to Bush, he vetoed it.[50]

Thus by the end of the Reagan-Bush years, the fiscal strategy of their administrations had created huge federal budget deficits that would—even if cities had not been so out of fashion—inhibit the ability of the federal government to contribute much to the alleviation of the urban crisis. Whether one agrees that this was a deliberate strategy, it is clear that by 1993, as Mayor Sharpe James of Newark, New Jersey, head of the National League of Cities, indicated, "We're at a crisis turning point in our cities." That organization's annual report revealed that cities had experienced virtually no growth in revenue and that urban residents were paying more in taxes and receiving fewer city services.[51]

THE LEGISLATIVE BRANCH

Republican victories in 1994 in both the House and Senate marked a sea-change in what political scientists regard as "party realignment" with respect to the size and scope of change in people and policy positions. Indeed, Michael Barone, a Neoconservative and an author of the *Almanac of American Politics 1996*, said that the 1994 election meant: "We are moving away from, not toward, an ever-larger government; we are at least uneasy about our renunciation of traditional cultural mores, and possibly ready to embrace them again; we cherish an inchoate, *mostly unarticulated American nationalism* that guides our unfocused, seeming contradictory impulses on foreign and defense and trade policies" (my emphasis).[52]

Barone was, of course, mostly correct in that the nationalism of which he spoke was—and has been—largely unarticulated. However, it often was made explicit in actions which had racial connotations, as I argue throughout this work. Its power was illustrated in Pennsylvania, for example, when Democratic Sen. Harris Wofford was unseated by a young two-term Congressman, Rick Santorum, a new Conservative who considered himself to be a right-of-center Progressive. In his debates with Wofford, Santorum espoused the doctrine of the failure of the Great Society, the runaway welfare state and rampant crime in the streets, and he suggested that the cure was less government interference and more fiscal accountability and personal responsibility.[53] Strangely, instead of defending the Great Society, Wofford, a veteran of the Peace Corps who had marched with Martin Luther King, Jr., attempted to adopt a more Conservative posture in the campaign, which he lost. Indeed, the issue for Democrats such as the Speaker of the House in the 103rd Congress Thomas Foley, (D-Wash.), who also lost his seat to a Conservative Republican, was how to defend against the charge that a candidate was not "tough on crime."

In fact, in an election that *Newsweek* magazine called "the Revenge of the Right," few Republican congressional candidates lost in 1994, a striking result which clearly indicated that voters were rejecting the results of Clinton's first two years in office and responding to the Conservative doctrine espoused by Republicans.[54] Charles Krauthammer, a Conservative columnist, remarked that this was the most explicitly ideologically committed group of House Republicans in modern history.

Although this historic change was effected by less than 20,000 votes in an election with a national turnout of only 37%, Speaker Newt Gingrich immediately declared a mandate for the Conservative revolution embodied in the "Contract with America."[55] And the Republicans' assertion that they had received a mandate was reflected in the manner in which they assumed control of the House.

Shortly after the Republicans took office on January 8, 1995, the new Rules Committee chairman Gerald Solomon (R-N.Y.) took down from the committee hearing room wall the portrait of Liberal southern Democrat Claude Pepper (D-Fla.), a previous chairman. In its place he installed a portrait of another former Democratic chairman, "Judge" Howard Smith (D-Va.), an act which angered members of the Congressional Black Caucus. Smith, who served in the House of Representatives from 1931 to 1957, was a key obstructionist of the 1950s and '60s civil rights legislation intended to foster integrated schools; his view was that "racial mixture is abominable to Southerners."[56] Solomon remained adamant about the exchange of portraits, alleging that his action had nothing to do with civil rights, but not long after the public outcry, he removed the portrait of Smith and symbolically hung one of Ronald Reagan in its place. Two years later he reinstated the portrait of Rep. Pepper, in a gesture aimed at restoring some measure of civility to his severely divided committee.[57]

The House

In many instances, the language of Republican candidates in the 1994 congressional campaign encoded a rhetoric which involved an attack not only on Liberal Democratic policies but on government itself. In debate after debate between Republican and Democratic candidates, the phraseology of Conservative ideology linked the Democratic party to support of the failed welfare state which wasted American taxpayer money, fostered teenage out-of-wedlock births, encouraged intergenerational sloth in people who would not work and runaway fathers who would not pay for the children they fathered, and was responsible for crime-and-drug-infested neighborhoods and every other conceivable social malady.

The antidote to this state of affairs was outlined in the collective vision of the "Contract with America," signed by Republican candidates on the steps of the Capitol on September 27, 1994. The contract sought "to renew the American Dream by promoting individual liberty, economic opportunity and personal responsibility, through limited and effective government, high standards of performance, and an America strong enough to defend all her citizens against violence at home or abroad."

The expression of this vision clearly held some coded oppositional messages, including one which, in the words of Seymour Martin Lipset, rejected a concept followed in other administrations that "applied the principle of 'communal rights' to other minorities, as well as to women. This effort was designed to guarantee equal results to groups."[58] Under the terms of the "contract," the legitimacy of the right to call upon public resources would apply only to individuals, not groups—despite a clear history of the disempowerment of Blacks as a group. This new individualism mischievously ignored—and continues to ignore—the pervasive phenomenon of White group rights that are legitimately exercised every day in many different ways.

Another encoded message in the language of the contract is the goal of enhancing the power of government to defend citizens against domestic violence. So-called "street violence" was regarded as a more important domestic "national security" issue than the white-collar violence that is far more destructive of the nation's viability. The contract elevated the kind of violence practiced by the poor—Whites but especially non-Whites—to the level of a national security emergency.

When Congressman Newt Gingrich rose in the House to speak of the unveiling of the "Contract with America" that day on the steps of the Capitol, he said: "I think this country is in trouble. People have talked about the economic recovery and all this stuff. Nonsense. The underlying core pattern of where America is at is real trouble. If you do not believe me, watch any major city local television news, including Washington, for two nights. The child abuse, the rape, the murders, the cocaine dealing, the problems of American life are unbelievable."[59] Gingrich's words betrayed the notion that a narrow social sector of Americans is the source of such problems.

Ronald Reagan bestowed the highest priority on national defense and economic growth, devaluing the domestic woes suffered by the poor and minorities in the inner cities. By contrast, Gingrich characterized family and community disorganization and negative adaptive behavior as the enemy, the foremost crisis of American civilization. The stated objective of the "Contract with America" was to restore "accountability, and the faith and trust that come with it," "the fabric of trust between the American people and their officeholders."[60] The document sought to formulate a common program that would challenge the Democratic order on the basis of the sense of alienation and estrangement from government felt by many Whites. Ten bills were proposed to accomplish this.

Fiscal Responsibility Act (cut the deficit and entitlement programs)
Taking Back Our Streets Act (more resources to fight crime)
Personal Responsibility Act (cut welfare and eliminate entitlements)
Family Reinforcement Act (child support enforcement)
American Dream Restoration Act (middle-class tax relief)
National Security Restoration Act (increased defense funding and
    increased supervision of defense spending)
Senior Citizens Fairness Act (increase Social Security and cut taxes)
Job Creation and Wage Enhancement Act (aid to small businesses,
    capital gains tax cut)
Common Sense Legal Reform Act (decrease product liability awards)
Citizen Legislature Act (term limits)

Fully half of these bills would be punitive in their impact: the Fiscal Responsibility Act, the Taking Back Our Streets Act, the Personal Responsibility Act, the Family Reinforcement Act and the Common Sense Legal Reform Act. Although the other items in this agenda substantially favored the White majority, these five would have a disproportionately negative impact upon Blacks, and they will be addressed in succeeding chapters. Nevertheless, it is important at this point to briefly elucidate the themes of this punitive legislative agenda and their intended audiences.

Balancing the budget through drastic reductions in entitlement programs and additional cuts in taxes deprives future governments of revenues to restore these programs, and this amounts to balancing the budget on the backs of the poor, a disproportionate number of whom are Black. This strategy undergirded the Republican budget proposals of 1995. *U.S. News and World Report* charged that Republicans were "waging war on the poor—on occasion with the acquiescence of Democrats."[61] Another observer pointed out that as a result of these proposals, the poorest fifth of the population would lose the most, $1,521 per year, or 11.4% of their annual income. The same conclusion was reached by the Center on Budget and Policy Priorities with regard to the work of the 104th Congress,[62] and this was confirmed by analysts such as John Charles Boger. In discussing the sources of contemporary racism, Boger said that despite the race-neutral facade of the Republican proposals, "they would have a serious unequal racial impact, since racial and ethnic minorities have disproportionately lower incomes and are disproportionately served by the programs scheduled for revision."[63] He suggested that the racial imbalance was intentional and that the rhetoric of the initiatives "bristled with barely concealed impatience or hostility toward low-income African Americans, Latinos, and recent immigrants to the United States."[64]

This legislative agenda was being pursued even as Democrats and Republicans were working out a framework to balance the budget and eliminate the budget deficit by the year 2002. Battle lines were drawn, and politics in the House became vicious and sharply oppositional. Liberals clashed with Conservatives, often along party lines but just as often along ideological ones. Speaking on the balanced budget issue, Congressman Major Owens, an African American Democrat from New York City, said that if the budget were balanced by 2002, "every economist . . . understands that . . . there will be devastating cuts in Social Security, Medicare, Medicaid, veterans programs, college loans and grant programs, and nutrition programs for hungry children."[65] John Kasich, the Republican chairman of the House Budget Committee, was absolutely determined to secure a balanced budget agreement on Republican terms as a means of redistributing power. He declared: "Our vision for the twenty-first century is taking power and money and control and influence from this city [Washington, D.C.] and giving it back to men and women all across this country. Frankly, the power of bureaucracy and red tape and misplaced compassion . . . in some respects takes away the incentives for the individual to fly."[66]

The budget resolution passed in May of 1995 mirrors the spending reduction strategy of the Republican revolutionists to greatly reduce the power of government. The figures in Table 3.1 illustrate their priorities. It should be pointed out that although Conservatives formulated an ideology that simplistically claimed a mandate for small government, public opinion on this point suggested a more complex, even contrary stance. For example, in a national survey taken in September 1993, Peter Hart found that with respect to national priorities, respondents favored "reinventing government" ahead of either crime, NAFTA or health care. Stan Greenberg, a Democratic pollster, did a national survey for the Democratic Leadership Council in the same year which asked whether people would be more likely to vote for a candidate who wanted to radically change the way government does things—cut bureaucracy, make government more efficient and give ordinary people better service and more choices—or a candidate who wanted to cut the federal bureaucracy by 20 percent. By far, most respondents chose the first alternative, evidence that voters wanted not necessarily a smaller government but certainly a more efficient one. This preference was confirmed by a subsequent Greenberg poll later that year.[67]

Bill Clinton espoused a concept of government that would be both smaller and more efficient, and popular support of this concept was one of the keys to his electoral success. By contrast, candidates who have

TABLE 3.1 House Budget Resolution, Spring 1995	
Program	*Billions of dollars*
Medicare	87
Medicaid	56
Welfare, food stamps, SSI, federal retirement and unemployment insurance	31
Transportation	14
Education and training	13
Foreign aid, peacekeeping	11
Environment, natural resources	8
Defense	7
Justice, crime	7
Other programs	65
Federal employee pensions	2
Eliminating corporate subsidies	8
Revenue from economic growth	8

Source: Steven Pearlstein, "'Hope' is a Number in GOP Math," *Washington Post,* May 17, 1995, p. A1.

proposed eliminating vital functions of government maintained by cabinet agencies have frightened voters who are dependent upon government functions. A broad-brush opposition to government as a means of punishing selected government-dependent communities has been unproductive, and this has forced Conservatives and White Nationalists alike to be more discriminating in their policy choices.

One indication of the force of the Conservative ideology operating within Congress in the mid-1990s is that votes on items in the "Contract with America" in both the House and Senate demonstrate a considerable degree of Republican coherence. In an analysis of 15 votes in the House and six votes in the Senate, the *Almanac of American Politics* found that in the House, nearly two-thirds of Republicans (148 of 230) had a perfect voting record on the contract, while four-fifths of Senate Republicans were united on the measure (44 of 54).[68]

The strongly ideological way in which radical Republicans of this era assumed control of Congress demonstrates the continuing power of the Conservative movement among White voters. That power gave coherence to Republican politics and lent substantial support to the radical leadership of Newt Gingrich on issues not addressed in the contract. In December of 1994, in the first flush of their election victory, White Nationalists proposed the abolition of the Department of Housing and

Urban Development, the Department of Education and other vital agencies of government. Their view of these agencies is indirectly illustrative of the existence of their racial agenda.

By contrast, there was nothing indirect about Gingrich's attack upon the Equal Employment Opportunity Commission, specifically its testing program. Testing had long been used as a tool to determine the extent of discrimination in housing, employment, consumer service and public accommodations, and the Supreme Court had held that "testing" was a valuable tool in this respect. In January of 1998 the EEOC proposed a one-year pilot program that would use "testers" for the first time to discover the extent of employment discrimination in particular industries. As EEOC Chairman Gilbert Casellas said, "hiring discrimination can be difficult to detect" because of subtle methods utilized by some employers.[69] However, the National Federation of Independent Businesses, an organization with strong Republican party ties, objected.[70]

Hearings were held on the "Future Directions of the EEOC," at which Speaker Gingrich alleged that "testing" was unfair. He claimed: "The use of employment testers, frankly undermines the credibility of the EEOC. The government should not sanction applicants' misrepresentation of their credentials to prospective employers. The use of testers not only causes innocent businesses to waste resources interviewing candidates not interested in actual employment, but also puts a government agency in the business of entrapment. It assumes guilt where there has been no indication of discriminatory behavior."[71] The Speaker also indicated that he would support a $37 million budget increase for the EEOC provided that it did not expend any of these funds on testing.[72] Facing this threat, the EEOC pledged not to use this method of determining discrimination.[73] (This episode was rather typical of Gingrich's leadership as Speaker of the House. He often took the floor on important issues that struck at the heart of the "welfare state," such as welfare reform, and testified at hearings regarding the elimination of racial designation on census forms.)

The Senate

As a result of the 1980 elections, Republicans came to power in the Senate, winning 12 seats—their biggest gain since 1958. What was important about this election as a harbinger of things to come and as an indicator of the mood of the country was that the Republican victories were national in scope. The seats that switched from Democrat to Republican were in New Hampshire, Indiana, Iowa, South Dakota, Wisconsin, Alaska, Idaho, Washington, Alabama, Florida, Georgia and North Carolina. Central to the Republican victories was the crafting of a policy out of the Conservative ideology that supported a strong defense program, strict control of government spending, a more positive attitude about American culture and the Kemp-Roth tax cut.[74] In the words of one observer, Republican control of the Senate introduced into that body a "remarkable degree of political and partisan solidarity . . . [and] a somewhat higher level of partisanship."[75] A high degree of partisanship was important in the passage of Reagan's 1982 budget and continued until Republicans lost control of the Senate in 1984.

One indication of the race-oriented edge of Republican politics may be seen in the 1990 Senate reelection battle between Jesse Helms, icon of North Carolina White Nationalist politics, and Harvey Gantt, a Progressive Black challenger and former mayor of Charlotte. Gantt, supported by a biracial coalition, ran well against Helms, even slightly ahead, until the final days of the campaign, when a negative Helms television advertisement about affirmative action began airing. It implied that Whites would have had more jobs were it not for affirmative action, and it closed with a dramatic shot of a Black hand clamping onto a White one. This striking advertisement doubtless played into the feelings of opponents of both Blacks and affirmative action and helped mobilize them to vote against Gantt. Helms won that election by six percentage points: 53 to 47%. In a rematch between the two in 1996, which Gantt also lost, it could be said, as one observer did, that "conservative Republicans can rely on race-oriented, traditionalist appeals to produce enough votes to match even the strongest white liberal/black coalition."[76]

In the nineties, the sense of a strongly partisan edge hardened in the Senate. When Clinton won election in 1992 with the substantial support of Blacks, his administration proposed a $16.3 billion "stimulus package" as part of a budget that contained over $7 billion in spending for cities. This bill ran into a Republican filibuster in the Senate, which led to its abandonment. Not only would there be no new funding for cities, subsequent negotiations with Republicans forced Clinton to settle for a bill that rescinded $16.5 billion of funding, resulting in severe cuts in many social programs. When the Conference of Mayors met in 1995, its Republican president, William J. Althaus of York, Pennsylvania, remarked: "I have to confess that I must have been a little politically naive at the time because I was surprised at the level of partisan meanness that was to come."[77]

That year Republicans were once again in charge of the Senate, and they began the session by voting down the Simon amendment to the Interior Department appropriation, which proposed allocating $15 million for an African American Museum on the Washington Mall; "we have no money for this project for the foreseeable future," Republicans claimed.[78] Most importantly to Blacks, Senate Republicans initiated measures opposing affirmative action in a manner consistent with their opposition to the 1991 Civil Rights Act.[79] In 1997 they opposed the nomination of Bill Lann Lee, a former civil rights lawyer of Chinese extraction and President Clinton's choice to be the assistant attorney general for civil rights. Sen. Mitch McConnell (R-Ky.) proposed an anti-affirmative action piece of legislation. And the Senate Republican Policy Committee submitted a brief in a Piscataway, New Jersey, case involving affirmative action; as they did so, they expressed once again their opposition to this program, arguing for a "color-blind" interpretation of Title VII of the 1964 Civil Rights Act.[80]

In 1996 Bob Dole of Kansas became Senate Majority Leader. Although the Senate is traditionally less Conservative than the House, it was persuaded by the popularity of House Republicans and by the strength of Gingrichism to follow the House's lead in supporting key tenets of the "Contract with America." Dole, who had previously manifested a positive attitude toward civil rights, began to shift his posture to a more Conservative one when he emerged as the front-runner for the Republican presidential nomination, yielding to the power framework created by the Conservative takeover of Congress and the Republican party. He endorsed the legislative items in the contract and eventually reversed his own position on affirmative action. In the fall of 1997, he introduced the Dole-Canaday bill (H.R. 1909) that would eliminate affirmative action programs.

The extent to which Bob Dole followed the House agenda was evident in the shutdown of the government that accompanied the breakdown of budget negotiations between House and Senate conferees and the White House in December of 1995. The hard line on further concessions to the White House clearly came at the instigation of House Conservatives such as Tom DeLay, a Gingrich loyalist, whose basic attitude was reflected in his assertion that "We just don't trust these people."[81]

However, as leader of the Republican party and as its presidential nominee in 1996, Dole made a speech on the Senate floor in which he defined the social objectives behind a balanced budget. He suggested that a constitutional amendment, a more radical approach than year-to-year balancing activity, was needed because it would make this more difficult for "special interests to drive up the cost of government."[82] In Dole's view, a balanced budget would set a tight fiscal framework that would result in the decimation of social programs in favor of priorities such as defense, the environment and social entitlements oriented toward groups which benefited from Social Security increases, middle-class tax relief and the like. An emphasis on policies to support "the middle class" and Social Security changed the focus of what was commonly meant by social policy: away from Blacks, other minorities and the poor, and toward the White population. Of course, "special interests" who "drive up the cost of government" implied those non-Whites who were the beneficiaries of domestic social spending. Ostensibly, Dole was suggesting that a balanced budget would make the expansion of such spending unlawful, unless it was popular with the White middle-class.[83] When he resigned his seat to become a presidential candidate in 1996, Dole relinquished the Senate leadership to Trent Lott.

Under Lott, Senate Republicans continued to follow the lead of House Republicans in pursuing the "Contract with America" agenda. A balanced budget, welfare reform, term limits, crime control and other issues became their prime objectives. This was evident in the budget cycle of the 105th Congress, when the Senate presented its proposals. One can see in the debate on these proposals the traditional split between Conservative Republican legislators and a Democratic president on the issue of spending.

In his 1998 State of the Union address, Clinton explained that not only would the budget be in balance by the end of 1998, there would be a surplus; he recommended that the primary use of the surplus should be to secure Social Security. Nevertheless, the Senate budget plan deemphasized social spending in favor of significant tax cuts, under the theory that the surplus should be used to pay down the federal debt and give tax relief to "working Americans." John Ashcroft (R-Mo.) used derogatory language in expressing his support of the Senate's proposed budget: "Americans deserve to keep more of what they earn, not have their money wasted on some ill-conceived liberal spending spree."[84] Clinton sent a clear signal that the Senate package would be rejected, thus setting up a scenario of protracted negotiations.

John Kasich's language with respect to the president's approach to spending the budget surplus was similar to Ashcroft's. Asserting that "families, not Washington, deserve more power and money," Kasich (R-Ohio) proposed a ten-year, $743 billion tax cut.[85] Tax cuts of this magnitude followed the Reagan strategy, for they would require radical reductions in programs designed to deliver resources to needy minorities. Thomas and Mary Edsall are correct: the tax cut politics of the Conservative movement have had a disparate racial effect.

SOURCES OF THE 1994 REVOLT

Why the "revolution" of 1994? In chapter 1, I suggested some of the economic factors responsible for the strength of the Conservative movement which found political expression in the election of 1994. The atmosphere surrounding that election is perhaps best described in the congressional testimony of Lee Hamilton (D-Ind.). In January of 1995, immediately after the Republicans recaptured Congress, Hamilton acknowledged: "There is a deep, free-flowing discontent in the country. . . . [It is] difficult to pin down . . . , but it seems to be a fear of the future . . . [an] insecurity about jobs, health care, pensions, and the future of the family."[86] He added that people in Indiana believed government should not try to save everyone, that they did not want their money spent on expanding programs which were already not delivering enough bang for the buck. They wanted less welfare, less taxes, less spending and, most of all, less government. Indeed, Hamilton said, they feel that "government does not benefit them, but benefits somebody else. They want a government that belongs to them."[87]

This attitude manifests a profound sense of alienation from the state. But it also reflects a latent desire for a clear and unambiguous regime for which people feel ownership and which nurtures their sense of personal and group integrity—in other words, a sense of nationalism. The unstated target of the animus clearly appears to be Blacks and other "undeserving" populations. Thus the national vote in 1994 may be interpreted as an act of symbolic racism in that racial animus was likely one motivation of many of those who went to the polls.

The fact that White middle-class anger may have peaked in 1994 is suggested in exit polling data from that election, which revealed the characteristics of voters who supported switching control of Congress from Democrats to Republicans. As shown in table 3.2, this change was favored by a critical group of White male Republican voters, who turned out in greater proportion than White male Democratic voters. About 75 million people voted, but 112.4 million failed to do so. Though this represented only a 2.2 percent increase over the 1990 mid-term election, turnout was up in all regions of the country except New England and the Mid-Atlantic states. In the South, Republican turnout was stronger than 1990 and exceeded Democratic turnout for the first time since Reconstruction (an increase of 15.5% of the southern vote for House Republicans, 13.4% for Democrats).[88]

In the opinion of Thomas Eagleton, head of the Eagleton Institute and formerly a Democratic senator from Missouri, the racial factor was an element in the 1994 congressional election.[89] Doubtless his opinion

| TABLE 3.2 | Key Republican Voting Constituencies in the 1994 Congressional Election (More Than 50% Voting for Republicans) |

Characteristics	*Republicans*	*Democrats*
Men	55%	47%
Whites	56%	44%
Age 30–40	52%	48%
Married	54%	46%
Some college education	53%	47%
Postgraduate degree(s)	57%	43%
Midwestern	55%	45%
Southern	54%	46%
White Protestant	62%	38%
Income over $50,000	57%	43%
"Getting worse"	65%	35%

Sources: Mitovsky International, 1994; Voter Research and Surveys, CBS/New York Times, 1994.

was based on observation of such campaigns as that of Alan Wheat, a popular and noncontroversial five-term African American Congressman who represented a White-majority district in Missouri. Wheat ran for the Senate against John Ashcroft, and lost every one of Missouri's 114 counties, carrying only the city of St. Louis.

Popular themes of the 1994 election included such hot-button issues as crime, debated in terms of the expansion of the death penalty and mandatory sentences for repeat offenders ("three strikes and you're out"); welfare reform, debated in terms of "two years and you're off"; affirmative action, debated in terms of its elimination through such measures as California's Proposition 209; and immigration, debated in terms of imposing strict quotas and cutting resources to new immigrants, as in California's Proposition 187.[90]

It is clear that a leading instigator of the political revolution of 1994 was the White male who was alienated from the political system and demanding from it a new public policy direction that would require political leaders to realign the distribution of government benefits to the detriment of Blacks and other minorities. However, while one must take at face value the fact of White male alienation, it is also important to suggest another underlying reason for the social instability that has turned into political instability with strongly racist undertones.

The Southern Factor

It is obvious that the South has risen again through its critical role within the Republican party, for since the party assumed congressional control the importance of southerners has grown. In the 105th Congress, southerners dominated the Senate's and the party's top posts:

President Pro Tempore: Strom Thurmond, South Carolina
Majority Leader: Trent Lott, Mississippi
Assistant Majority Leader: Don Nickles, Oklahoma
Conference Chairman: Connie Mack, Florida
Conference Secretary: Paul Coverdale, Georgia
Chair, National Senatorial Campaign Committee: Mitch McConnell,
     Kentucky
In the same session, the top three House posts were held by southerners:
Speaker of the House: Newt Gingrich, Georgia
Majority Leader: Dick Armey, Texas
Majority Whip: Tom DeLay, Texas

Southerners from both parties were at the helm of key committees dealing with foreign affairs, intelligence and national security. The impression of southern prominence in American politics deepens when it is considered that the last three Democratic presidents were all southerners—Lyndon Johnson (Texas), Jimmy Carter (Georgia) and Bill Clinton (Arkansas)—and that Al Gore, the former vice president is also from that region (Tennessee).

Thus, very much as at the end of the first Reconstruction, the White South has regained much of its institutional power by nationalizing its attitudes toward race and deflating the power of Blacks.[91] This is especially striking when one considers that the South contains 53% of the Black population and that, not coincidentally, one finds there the starkest poverty in both Black and White communities. Ironically, the politics of the region's representatives now champions pro-business, anti-labor and anti-civil rights interests.

As noted at the outset, political leaders from the South were heavily implicated in the 1998 attempt to eliminate affirmative action. The co-sponsors of H.R. 1909 in the 105th Congress represented the influence of the South in the Republican party coalition: 37% of House Republicans were southerners (from the states of Alabama, Arkansas, Florida, Georgia, Louisiana, Maryland, Mississippi, North Carolina, Oklahoma, South Carolina, Tennessee, Texas and Virginia), and 36% of those who co-sponsored the legislation were from that region. This demonstrates their nearly unanimous support for a policy perceived to harm Blacks.

In addition, it is important to note that despite the fact that ten representatives who co-sponsored the measure had winning margins in 1996 of only 5% or less, they apparently did not fear any political repercussions from their sponsorship. These included Jo Ann Emerson (Missouri, 8th District), Charlie Norwood (Georgia, 10th District), Jon Christensen (Nebraska, 2nd District), Vincent Snowbarger (Kansas, 3rd District), Robert Aderholt (Alabama, 4th District), Bob Riley (Alabama, 3rd District), Kevin Brady (Texas, 8th District), Barbara Cubin (Wyoming, At Large), Merrill Cook (Utah, 2nd District) and Linda Smith (Washington, 3rd District). The other co-sponsors apparently did not fear repercussions either, because their constituents had given them a substantial mandate in the previous election cycle. Moreover, the Conservative orientation in most of the 67 districts the co-sponsors represented is expressed in their constituents' relatively low scores on Liberal issues.[92] And despite the relatively high percentage of Blacks in their districts, another five southern representatives were also co-sponsors (see Table 3.3).[93] Thus in some Deep South congressional districts there was the anomaly that although most Blacks in those districts probably would not want affirmative action eliminated, their congressional representatives co-sponsored legislation that would do so.

White southern leadership in Congress has also contributed to the expansion of state power through the resurrection of the doctrine of "states' rights." "The Southern Manifesto" signed by 90 southern members of Congress in 1956 in opposition to the implementation of the Supreme Court's decision in *Brown v. Board of Education,* established a consensus theory of the Constitution that reappeared in similar resolutions drafted and passed by southern legislatures. The manifesto argued that because the education function is not expressly included in the Constitution, it falls under the reserved powers which are to be exercised by the states. It contained a principle that is almost universally accepted among Whites across America today (though it was written for specific application to the South): "This interpretation, restated time and again, became a part of the life of the people of many of the States and confirmed their habits, customs, traditions, and way of life. It is founded on elemental humanity and common sense, for parents should not be deprived by Government of the right to direct the lives and education of their own children."[94]

It is evident that the policy of devolution has its ideological origin in the attempt on the part of southern states and their sympathizers to

TABLE 3.3	Co-sponsors of H.R. 1909 with Significant Percentages of Blacks in Their Congressional Districts (105th Congress)

Representative and District	% Black
Sonny Callahan (1st Alabama)	28%
Bob Riley (3rd Alabama)	26%
Floyd Spence (2nd South Carolina)	25%
Terry Everett (2nd Alabama)	24%
Roger Wicker (1st Mississippi)	23%

Source: Philip D. Duncan and Christine C. Lawrence, *Politics in America 1998* (Washington, D.C.: Congressional Quarterly, 1998).

avoid the ultimate authority of the federal government for due process at the state level for all citizens. Moreover, changes in the meaning of "state action" with respect to civil rights enable citizens to use state power to privilege private rights, even when the issue is clearly a public one, such as education. The recent constitutionalizing of the doctrine of state action in a direction toward the reestablishment of White privilege is a throwback to the 1896 Supreme Court *Plessy v. Ferguson* decision itself.

CONCLUSION

The main objective of this chapter was to present a picture of the way in which the Conservative revolution captured political power through the electoral process, eventually dominating the White House, the House and the Senate. It illustrated the challenge presented to fundamental interests of Blacks and other dependent groups by the ideological decision to attack and diminish government power by establishing Conservative criteria for government-funded programs and by reducing or eliminating funding for social entitlement programs upon which such groups have traditionally depended.

While I have sought to describe the way in which the White Nationalist movement has affected politics at the national level, its success may also be seen in the adoption of this same politics in state legislatures. Many of these have followed the national trend of depriving cities that contain a substantial proportion of communities of color of badly needed financial resources. For example, in 1994 Christine Todd Whitman, the new Republican governor of New Jersey, announced that she would cut taxes in two stages by 15%, but she shocked the state's urban mayors when she also indicated in her announcement that "we do not plan any significant change in aid to schools and municipalities."[95] Similarly, in 1995 George Pataki, the Republican governor of New York, opposed a $3.5 million budget allotment to the Harlem Urban Development Corporation, which had played a significant role in the revitalization of that section of New York City along 125th Street. In the words of its founder, Rev. William M. James, "the state's action ignores the organization's purpose."[96] A comparable fate befell Los Angeles County in 1996, when the California state legislature refused to extend supplementary financing to its school system—and this after supporting a bail-out of wealthy Orange County.

I suggest that the White Nationalist movement has helped racialize public policy and delivered a rationale to new converts to Conservatism that explains their perception of declining economic return. It is easy to blame Blacks, Hispanics, women, the poor and immigrants for their failure to achieve the American dream or sustain that achievement. To redirect government attention and resources to the middle class, it is convenient to blame the vulnerable and indict them for their failure to exercise personal responsibility. And the most effective means of bringing this about is through the policy system, where political leaders can trade on nationalist sentiments in the public at large and evade personal responsibility for the outcome.

CHAPTER

4

New Democrat Politics and Policy Convergence

INTRODUCTION

I believe what I describe in this chapter is parallel to and in some measure a replication of what happened at the end of the first Reconstruction: the development of race reconciliation and policy consensus among Whites at the expense of Blacks. The emergence of a Conservative political culture in the post-Civil Rights era has had a significant impact, not only on the growth and dominance of the Republican party, but upon the Democratic party as well. And although I will concentrate in this chapter on the Clinton presidency, the trend toward more Conservative politics in the Democratic party began with the administration of Jimmy Carter.

Although the issues that suggest a parallel between the nineteenth-century White rapprochement and today's are dissimilar, in this chapter I argue that, as happened more than a hundred years ago, the White Nationalist ideology of the current Conservative movement has driven the Democratic party to move much closer to positions held by the Republican party. In any case, I will describe what might be called "the politics of convergence" to illustrate the mechanism of racial consensus.[1]

An indication of the strength of that consensus across parties by race may be seen in Table 4.1, which is drawn from the results of a poll

TABLE 4.1 Political Values on Black Issues by Party Identification

Issues	% of All Respondents	% of Republicans	% of Democrats	% of Independents
The position of blacks:				
has improved in recent years	73%	76%	71%	73%
hasn't improved much	23%	2%	26%	23%
Racial discrimination:				
is the reason blacks can't get ahead	31%	25%	37%	32%
is not the reason blacks can't get ahead (blacks responsible for their own condition)	59%	65%	54%	58%
Affirmative action programs to help blacks, women, and other minorities get better jobs and education (surveyed August 1995)				
favor	58%	48%	73%	53%
oppose	36%	45%	22%	43%
Affirmative action programs which give special preferences to qualified blacks, women and other minorities (surveyed August 1995)				
favor	46%	35%	59%	46%
oppose	46%	57%	30%	50%

Source: "Republicans: A Demographic and Attitudinal Profile," Survey, Pew Research Center for the People and the Press, Washington, D.C., August 7, 1996, p. 14. This unusually large sample of 9,652 was surveyed between July 1994 and October 1995. Remaining percentage in each category should be attributed to "don't know" response.

conducted in 1996 by the Pew Research Center. The survey results indicate that questions regarding the position of Blacks and the impact of racial discrimination elicited very similar responses from Democrats and Republicans. One explanation for this similarity may be that although Blacks comprise an estimated 20% of the base of the Democratic party, they constituted only 10% of the sample in this study: 997 Black interviewees of the total 9,652. In effect, the survey highlighted White attitudes and showed close agreement by White Democrats and Republicans with respect to whether the position of Blacks had improved in recent years and whether Blacks (rather than racism) were responsible for their own condition. Notably, Democrats were much more likely to favor affirmative action even when it was defined as "special preferences."

Another Pew survey, this one limited to Democrats, showed that Black and White Democrats held relatively similar positions on questions of government efficiency and regulation (see Table 4.2). However, with

TABLE 4.2   Black/White Responses to Political Values within the Democratic Party

Issue	% Blacks	% Whites
Government efficiency		
government is wasteful, inefficient	55%	58%
government does a better job	41%	39%
Government regulation		
is in the public interest	54%	51%
does more harm than good	40%	43%
Government should		
do more to help the poor	75%	55%
can't afford to do more to help	23%	39%
The position of blacks		
has improved in recent years	52%	71%
hasn't improved much	46%	26%
Racial discrimination		
is the reason blacks can't get ahead	62%	37%
blacks are responsible for their own condition	31%	54%

Source: "Democrats: A Demographic and Attitudinal Profile," Survey, Pew Research Center for the People and the Press, Washington, D.C., August 23, 1996. Survey conducted July 23–July 29, 1995. Remaining percentage in each category should be attributed to "don't know" response.

regard to the question of government's responsibility to the poor, there was a significant divergence of opinion. Similarly, there were significant differences between Black and White Democrats on racial issues: the degree of improvement in the position of Blacks in society and the impact of racial discrimination. To the extent that these responses mirror a racial divide on such questions, they mitigate the perception of an ideologically monolithic Democratic party, show the difficulty of developing a coherent party approach to race and help explain intra-party conflict over racial issues and positions.

Tension within the Legacy

In May of 1977, several months after assuming office, President Jimmy Carter met with the Democratic congressional leadership and other party activists, including Hubert Humphrey, vice president under Lyndon Johnson. Some of these activists were angered by Carter's viewpoint that any new social programs would have to take a back seat to his top priority: balancing the budget.[2] The president explained that the Great Society was financed by the revenues that resulted from a decade of economic growth without significant tax increases. He reasoned that his administration was unable to fund new initiatives because federal revenues had plummeted, cutting the defense budget was not prudent and deficit financing had reached its limits. So, Carter contended, the choice was either high inflation or a balanced budget—a rationale that some who attended the meeting called "pure Republican 'trickle-down theory.'"[3]

As a result of his stance, Carter faced opposition from those sectors of the Democratic coalition that depended upon greater welfare spending and increases in job training programs. His approach to economic policy caused deep concern within Black circles, and Rep. Parren Mitchell (D-Md.), head of the Congressional Black Caucus, had requested a meeting with Carter back in March of 1977, only to be told that the president could find no time in his schedule for such a meeting.

Throughout 1977, the Black Caucus supported the Humphrey-Hawkins bill, a measure which initially included a full employment program, but as Professor Robert Smith makes clear, Carter's support for it was tepid.[4] However, by the following year, the intensity of Black leaders' frustration with Carter's apparent reluctance to make the bill a priority was evident in an angry confrontation they had with Carter and Vice President Walter Mondale in a White House meeting in September of 1978. This led to a walkout by Rep. John Conyers (D-Mich.) and a mass march, led by Coretta Scott King, a week later, during the annual Congressional Black Caucus weekend, to emphasize Black support of the bill.[5]

Tensions subsided during a temporary reconciliation, but they erupted anew when Carter proposed a budget that would cut social programs severely. For example, the Comprehensive Employment and Training Act program would be cut 15%, low-income housing would be cut 18% and further reductions would affect child and family nutrition, health and other social programs. Black mobilization against the cuts was ineffective: the proposed reductions were eventually enacted and constituted the first substantial withdrawal of material resources from federal social programs by a Democratic administration.

As with Conservative Republican leaders, Carter's principal motivation was to balance the budget, and his fiscal Conservatism led directly to a reduction in social spending. Roger Wilkins, a Black journalist and then an urban affairs writer for the *New York Times*, said of Carter, "Domestically, the Southern Populist has turned out to be distressingly conservative"; Wilkins judged that the president's domestic policy warranted "barely a passing grade."[6] Though other observers made similar evaluations of Carter's difficulties with Black political leaders, it had not yet become clear that he was caught in the initial throes of the structural and ideological forces that would come to shape decades of social policy.

Though Carter is widely perceived to have belonged to the populist tradition of other Democratic presidents, there are indications that he was yielding to the growing Conservative trend. In 1993 Steven Shull published an analysis of Reagan's and Bush's civil rights records, based on his examination of their presidential executive orders, legislative initiatives and other actions. He argued that with respect to presidential policy statements, "attention to blacks reached its height in the 1960s under Johnson, Nixon, and particularly, Ford, but that Carter and Reagan distributed their attention much more widely"—presumably away from matters particular to Black interests.[7] This was especially true with respect to presidential calls for legislative action on civil rights. Budget requests for general civil rights agency expenditures decreased 1.8% in Carter's administration; these numbers compare favorably with those of the Reagan administration—a decrease of 4.6%.[8] It should be noted that when Carter was elected president, he ran behind 272 of 292 Democrats vying for House seats that year, and behind all but one of the Democrats elected to the Senate.[9] With the sole exception of the 1964 Johnson landslide, since 1960 a majority of Whites have supported Republican presidential candidates, a fact which made Carter's presidential bid exceedingly weak and inordinately dependent upon votes from the Liberal wing of the party.

Early warning signs of the growing Conservative mood among the electorate were evident in Gallup poll results showing that between 1972 and 1973 there was a 38% increase in voters who felt that "integrity in government" was a problem. This was partly driven by the Watergate affair, and probably some Gallup respondents felt generally alienated.

Other observers began to notice the national trend toward Conservatism. Ben J. Wattenberg argued in his *The Real America* that in the early 1970s, many Americans already felt that "cultural politics" was dead and that the country had capitulated to the demands of the Left. He pointed to a Gallup poll conducted in May of 1974 which indicated that the number of self-identified Conservatives was at an all-time high.[10] A national survey by William Watts and Lloyd Free that same year found that in a listing of attitudinal priorities, Americans rated improving the lives of African Americans through further government spending next to last, largely because they believed that substantial progress had already been made.[11]

The inherent weakness of the Carter candidacy in 1976 was demonstrated by the onset of defections by Catholics and blue-collar workers from the Democratic party. Addressing this issue, John Stewart advised that the future of the party did not rest on a choice between the advocates of the so-called "new politics"—which favored Blacks, women, children and the poor—and broad working-class and middle-class interests. He asserted that "the party cannot win without substantial elements of the traditional New Deal coalition, as Carter's victory proved, but neither can it win unless it moves beyond the coalition's boundaries. This suggests the wisdom of searching for concerns that are common to this broad spectrum of Americans who can be identified as 'Democratic voters.'"[12] The irony of this recommendation, of course, is that it meant the party had to begin to win back the South, which had largely defected to the Republican column in the 1972 election.

The impact of Conservatism was clearly detectable in Walter Mondale's 1984 presidential campaign. Like Carter, Mondale supported a balanced budget. Carter had carried over this approach from the time when he was governor of Georgia, when he was legally bound to balance the state budget, but he also sought to deflate Republican attacks that he was a traditional big-spending Liberal who was wasting taxpayers' money on social programs that did not work. By contrast, Mondale expressed his position on the budget almost as "a positive moral virtue" in order to deflect the demand from his 1984 opponent Ronald Reagan for an across-the-board tax reduction. Here, Aaron Wildavsky noted, "[with] one stroke the Democratic party denied its traditional (and mostly successful) recourse to spending to create employment; it also obligated itself to keep the revenues it can raise from new taxes to reduce the deficit."[13] Wildavsky further suggested that because little was heard from Mondale during the campaign about social welfare or massive spending for employment, Reagan's influence over the course of future domestic policy was strengthened.

Reagan's 1982 budget proposal, which dramatically altered the direction of social services spending, was passed with the assistance of a bipartisan congressional coalition comprised of Republican congressional representatives from the North and Democratic representatives from the south. This coalition was not very influential in the first two decades of its existence, but it became increasingly effective in the 1980s. One analyst points out that while this coalition won passage of only 60% of the measures it supported in 13 of 22 sessions of the Congress in the 1960s and '70s, "in the first year of the Reagan administration, the coalition won 92% of the time it appeared."[14]

Its stability was enhanced as party identification became less important than political ideology. Beginning with the Nixon landslide in 1972, an increasing number of southern Democrats switched to the Republican party. Peter Allen Beck noted the significance of this trend: "Southern conservatism was especially linked to preserving the role of blacks in society [through] strict segregation of the races, as a matter of social custom and law, and the preservation of that practice was central to the political identity of many traditional members of the southern electorate."[15] Beck further remarked that the Democratic party's strength in the South persisted only until northern Democrats began to seriously address the interests of Blacks, at which point southern Democrats veered away from the party. It was assumed that the South would align itself with whichever party subordinated Black interests to those of Whites.

By the mid-1990s, southern Democrats in this Conservative congressional coalition began to refer to themselves as "Blue Dog Democrats," to separate themselves from the more loyal "Yellow Dog Democrats."[16] The "Blue Dogs" number a stable 20–25 in the House and have wielded a disproportionate influence on such issues as the budget, entitlement programs, business regulation, the tax system and the Food and Drug Administration product approval system. The group also includes some northern Democrats, such as Rep. Colin Peterson (D-Minn.), who noted at the end of the 1996 elections that "Centrist" Democrats—actually, those who are right-of-center—had greatly influenced the Democratic party leadership on the budget and other matters.[17] Indeed, between 1994 and 1996 leverage politics exercised by Conservative Republicans in coalition with "Blue Dog Democrats" was a central factor in the implementation of the "Contract with America."

Seeking the Levers of Adjustment: Changing Party Rules

The loss of the 1980 and 1984 presidential elections was traumatic for Democratic party activists, who began to reevaluate basic aspects of the New Deal approach as well as specific party policies that had become unpopular with the public. Analysts offered a variety of opinions regarding the enervation of the Democratic party at the end of the 1970s. Some claimed that the party was disunified, others that Reagan was so far to the right of American national attitudes that the "pendulum would swing back to the Democrats in the 1980s faster." Still others believed that the Republican policy agenda could be implemented if Reagan moved quickly to take advantage of the "rising tide of discontent" in the public as a result of failures of Democratic international and domestic policies.[18]

It should be pointed out that for many Democratic party activists, winning was paramount, especially among the younger generation of activists, and thus they were willing to compete on almost any terrain to alter political realities. To regain the White House, they would drastically change the party's traditional policy commitments and positions. And many of them believed they had to begin with the party nominating process.

In the wake of the loss of the 1980 presidential election, Democratic party professionals became convinced that the party had become too open. They argued that rules governing the selection of the party's presidential nominee should yield a result which produced greater consensus on the eventual winner and put the choice back in the hands of the professionals—in effect recreating the "smoke-filled room." One rule change led to the concept of "super-delegates"—elected party and public officials who automatically receive 25% of the seats at a nominating convention. Another established a 20% "threshold" of votes that a presidential candidate must win in a congressional district to secure a delegate from that district. Still another change gave winners in those districts bonus delegates and the right to approve (or commit) all delegates selected. In addition, a regional primary election day was created in the South that came to be known as "super Tuesday"; this was the result of an effort by southern politicians to achieve parity with important primaries in northern states and possibly produce a presidential candidate who was more Conservative.

Ultimately it was widely acknowledged that these rule changes had not solved the problem. Indeed, they led to the nominations of Walter Mondale in 1984 and Michael Dukakis in 1988, both of whom were repudiated by the electorate. Thus chastened, party activists determined that the only route to regaining power lay in the direction of reshaping party policy to make it more consistent with the Conservative mind-set of the electorate. At a minimum, this meant subordinating the party's emphasis on civil rights and social programs that favored minorities and the poor.

The political realignment of the Democratic party in the South continued throughout the '80s and beyond as even more Democratic elected officials switched to the Republican party. On March 13, 1991, with the presidential election less than eight months away, Governor Charles Roemer of Louisiana changed his political affiliation from Democrat to Republican, bowing to the mood of voters in his state and hoping to bolster his chances for reelection.[19] Democratic pollster Geoff Garin discovered in a Louisiana survey a potent reason for Americans' increasing disaffection with the Democratic party: White voters felt that it was oblivious to their interests. As Garin reported: "They feel ignored by both parties and when they think about the Democratic party, there is a perception that Democrats have really become a special-interest party. The political context for David Duke's success and for the politics of civil rights is a middle class that is very angry and feels very ignored."[20] Garin further suggested that the White middle-class perception that it was in a bind was not necessarily equivalent to racism, but that this perception did underlie its collective responses to the statement: "Qualified whites lose out on jobs and promotions because blacks get special preference due to affirmative action hiring goals."[21] Of all respondents, 39% said this happens "a lot," 41% said "sometimes" and 17% said "not that much." Respondents' belief that they had been deprived of the "balance of attention" is consistent with my thesis regarding the roots of White Nationalism, though it should be noted that voter disaffection was expressed more radically in Louisiana than elsewhere in the South.

Arthur Fletcher, the Black Republican former chairman of the U.S. Civil Rights Commission, recognized that racial tension would be part of the 1992 presidential election campaign. In May of 1991 he noted that the commission had discovered a negative national attitude toward civil rights enforcement and that the "animosity" was spreading: onto college campuses, in the workplace and in the health care industry. He remarked: "The thing that really has me concerned is the fact that the forthcoming 1992 election campaign may be fought, or may be driven, by race."[22]

Indeed, race was a subtext in the 1992 campaign. Many Democratic party professionals were convinced that if the party's posture on affirmative action, crime and the importance of having Blacks in party leadership roles did not change, the party would become even weaker. Christopher Edley, a Harvard Law School professor who served in both the Carter and Clinton administrations, speculated that some key Democratic party activists' adoption of more Conservative views was motivated by the party's crushing defeat in 1984.[23] Edley suggested that while many Democrats emerged from that event—and from the Carter loss in 1980 as well—convinced of the need for "renovation" of the party orthodoxy, others believed that such a change might lead to more objective policies.

Seeking the Levers of Adjustment: Changing Party Positions

Restructuring the Democratic party's policy positions became the task of a new Conservative reform movement within the party that came to be known as the Democratic Leadership Council. Founded in 1985 by Al From, it initially comprised 40 members, largely from the House. In its early years it was headed by Rep. Richard Gephardt of Missouri, Sen. Charles Robb of Virginia and Sen. Sam Nunn of Georgia and from 1990 to 1991 by Bill Clinton, then the governor of Arkansas.

The DLC's intention was to free the Democratic party from the grip of "special interests," such as Blacks and organized labor, and "move the party—both in perception and in substance—back to the mainstream of American political life."[24] Its program proposals tended toward eliminating all race-based programs, watering down the party's opposition to business, promoting free trade and other business interests, eliminating "racial quotas," cutting taxes and emphasizing "family values." The overarching goal was to dismantle or otherwise isolate urban/labor/Liberal advocates within the party and shift its ideology to the Right-leaning "center" of the electorate.

By 1992, the membership of the DLC included 32 Senate Democrats and 140 House members. It also included a number of prominent Black political leaders, such as Willie Brown, Speaker of the California House of Representatives; Roland W. Burris, attorney general of Illinois; former mayor of Atlanta Maynard Jackson; Andrew Young, formerly the mayor of Atlanta, a member of Congress and U.S. representative to the U.N.; former mayor Tom Bradley of Los Angeles; former Rep. Bill Gray III (Pa.); Rep. John Lewis (Ga.); former Rep. Cardiss Collins (Ill.); former Rep. Mike Espy (Miss.); and former Rep. Barbara Jordan (Tex.).[25] For nearly a generation these leaders had followed a strategy of mobilization with the Democratic party, becoming key players in its major structural components both as an offensive strategy—to participate in various power centers—and as a defensive one—to prevent anything deleterious to their interests from happening without their knowledge.

In the late 1980s, it wasn't as clear as it was a decade later that the DLC would become an extension of the Conservative movement within the Democratic party. It cast itself as "Progressive," and indeed this label—which was adopted by its think tank, the Progressive Policy Institute—connoted some of the original meaning of Liberalism: that government should be subordinate to the institutions of the people and the private sector.

Since the inception of the Clinton administration, the DLC has been influential in developing the philosophical direction of the Democratic party. Attempting to craft a political ideology that struck a new course—a "third way"—between the extremes of the political Left and Right, it generated a moderately Conservative doctrine. The following passage from Will Marshall and Martin Schram's *Mandate for Change* illustrates this ideology:

> The new progressives emphasize economic growth generated in free markets as the prerequisite for opportunity for all. They define equality in terms of opportunity, not results. Hence, progressives reject the recent liberal emphasis on redistribution in favor of pro-growth policies that generate broad prosperity. They equally reject the Right's notion that wealthy investors drive the economy, believing that government's role is not to favor the privileged, but to set fair rules of market competition for everyone. At the center of their concern are ordinary working Americans. Progressive economic and social policies seek to unite the interests of Americans who are struggling to get into the middle class and those who are struggling to stay there.[26]

The authors go on to recommend middle course positions in key thematic areas of reciprocal responsibility, community, democracy and entrepreneurial government. The emphasis is squarely on the middle class. People in troubled communities are encouraged to "play by the rules." The goals of moral hegemony abroad and social stability at home are to be accomplished through policies grounded in the moral values of the country's Judeo-Christian heritage. And government should be less bureaucratic, enabling the expression of individual values at the local level.

This vision of the relative roles of government, the private sector and the individual redefined the political constituency of the Democratic party, emphasizing the largely White, suburban majority and employing an almost oppositional tone toward such groups as Blacks and other minorities, labor and the poor. Some parts of the new philosophy, like many concepts in the Conservative movement, are based on highly questionable assumptions regarding the position of minorities in American society. For example, seeking to assert the failure of previous movements for social equity that involved major government expenditures. Marshall and Schram remarked: "Jim Crow was effectively ended, schools were integrated, and . . . a sizeable black middle class emerged. But a large white and black underclass, subject to many social morbidities, remained."[27] Indeed, Neoconservatives in both political parties have labored to create the illusion of the end of widespread racial discrimination as a pretext for eliminating policies that offered Blacks government assistance according to principles of fair treatment and equitable distribution of resources. In this respect, as in so many other areas, the DLC's position is consistent with the prevailing Conservative political ideology.

The Clinton Victory: Demystifying "Change"

Bill Clinton captured the White House in 1992 with 43% of the popular vote to George Bush's 37%; this translated into an Electoral College landslide of 370 to 168. The major impediment to a Bush victory was the third-party candidacy of Ross Perot, a Texas corporate executive who ran as an Independent and captured nearly 20 million votes, 19% of the total. An analysis of the Perot constituency shows that his coalition was predominantly made up of voters who, had he not been in the race, would have voted for Bush rather than Clinton.[28] It also should be acknowledged that Clinton managed to craft a policy appeal which made him more palatable to voters than Bush, and he won back enough "Reagan Democrats" and Catholics to secure his election. Nevertheless, the Perot factor was important as a significant demonstration of the fact that there was a desire for change within the American electorate, although its specific nature was clouded by the melange of reasons voters were attracted to Ross Perot.

The political theme of "change" which Bill Clinton exploited to capture the presidency in 1992 was vague and unstructured. This allowed him to promise a relatively moderate (right of center) version of leadership which gave a critical portion of the electorate confidence in him. But his performance in the initial year of his administration left many White Americans feeling alienated and thinking that he was, after all, a traditional Democrat, symbolic of all the things they had come to abhor.

A generalized demand for change reappeared in the 1994 election cycle. But this time it was clear that rather than "progressive" change, a critical segment of the electorate wanted a far more Conservative shift in public priorities, one that was consistent with some of the themes Clinton initially offered and which the DLC had crafted. For example, in the 1992 campaign, Clinton had proposed to "end welfare as we know it" and adopted a tough stance on crime, and both positions sent the right message to Conservative White voters. Yet two years later, only the crime bill had been signed into law—the welfare system had not been significantly altered.

Clinton saw tax cuts and Social Security issues as a way of courting the middle class. However, his failure to secure tax reductions for the middle class in the early years of his first administration was important because of the underlying economic insecurity that was driving Conservative politics. Moreover, he confused his messages by his initial approaches to governance. He formulated a cabinet with significant minority and female representation and produced executive orders on a series of policies important to White women, but he alienated White male Christians with his positions on fetal tissue research and family leave.

Clinton's first major shift toward Conservative segments of the Democratic coalition came at the expense of Jesse Jackson. The president accepted an invitation to speak at the Rainbow Coalition's annual convention in January of 1992, yet the occasion was marred by the fact that the day before he spoke, he presided over the Arkansas execution of a Black convicted killer, Ricky Ray Rector, who had been evaluated as borderline mentally deficient. A few months later, Jackson extended to Clinton another invitation to speak, and on this occasion he chastised a rap artist known as Sister Souljah, who had suggested that since rap lyrics frequently allude to killing Blacks, perhaps they should also describe killing Whites. Clinton used this opportunity to berate Souljah and, in doing so, to show suburban Whites that he could be tough on Blacks. Columnists Jack Germond and Jules Whitcover contended that this message was a purposeful part of Clinton's political strategy.[29]

A second major move away from the core Democratic base came at the expense of organized labor, with Clinton's support of the North Atlantic Free Trade Agreement initiated by the Bush administration. But even before NAFTA, Clinton had muddied his relations with organized labor. Eager to signal that the Democratic party was now the party of business, Clinton led off his administration with a highly touted economic summit to which he invited many corporate leaders.

Clinton's aggressive championing of business interests in negotiations over NAFTA and the General Agreement on Tariffs and Trade positioned him against the interests of organized labor. The main concern of labor and its allies was that while expanded trade would benefit some sectors of the economy, it might also create additional downward pressure on the working-class wages. Although Blacks and organized labor fought NAFTA, the House passed the treaty in November 1993 (by a vote of 234 to 199), and the Senate did so immediately afterward. In a show of political convergence, Clinton quickly signed it into law, with former Presidents Ford, Carter and Bush in attendance at the ceremony.[30]

For all the signals this sent that Clinton was a pro-business president, cutting the ground from under Republicans on that score, it also increased tensions in the country over the declining wages of workers, Democrats and Republicans alike. In the 1996 primary elections, this issue was raised by the small but noisy far Right wing of the Republican party, led by Patrick Buchanan, and it achieved some prominence as an issue with which Republicans were concerned. It enhanced Buchanan's standing as a serious candidate when other themes he focused on found little salience among the Republican electorate. There was a unique show of unity between Liberals and Conservative Nationalists with regard to the decline in wages. Both sides wanted the focus of the economy to be on "America first," and both wanted an administration that would discourage big business from exporting American jobs and creating only low-wage jobs at home.

Clinton's problems with the electorate were increased by his failure to recognize that for Conservative Nationalists, change meant less government as well as less favoritism on the basis of race, gender and working-class status. As a result of his lack of understanding, a critical portion of the Conservative electorate was energized to turn out for the 1994 congressional election and repudiate Clinton's politics in a unique and powerful landslide in which nearly every Republican candidate won and the Republican party gained control of both the House and Senate. A distinguished expert on political realignments, Professor Walter Dean Burnham, said of the significance of the 1994 election: "the deterioration in conditions of life for The Great White Middle simply crossed a pain threshold . . . and in doing so propelled the political system into a new upheaval phase."[31]

The Democratic Leadership Council quickly pronounced the meaning of the election to be "the death of the New Deal political alignment and the programmatic approaches it spawned."[32] The Liberal wing of the party responded in the person of George McGovern, the 1972 Democratic presidential candidate, who contended that Democrats had given up the fight. Defending government programs initiated by Liberals, McGovern asserted that since Democrats were Liberal and Republicans Conservative, the battle should be fought along those lines. The Rev. Jesse Jackson agreed that there should be a legitimate polar dichotomy in American politics, and he added that Liberals were tired of being scapegoated. He characterized the DLC as the "privatized suburban wing of the Democratic party" and charged that it was set on attracting its own limited constituency rather than supporting the "big tent" philosophy.[33] Several Democrats who were defeated in the election debacle also weighed in. Rep. David McCurdy (D-Tenn.), who lost a bid for the Senate, and Rep. Jim Cooper, a Democrat from Tennessee who lost his House seat, maintained that their identification with the New Deal Democratic party program was the reason for their defeats and that the party must change.[34]

Clinton after 1994: The Politics of Convergence

The 1994 election results made a significant impression on President Clinton, who began to turn more intensively toward Republican-oriented policies. Clinton's far more Conservative direction after the 1994 election appeared to be aimed at repositioning his administration for his reelection bid. He brought David Gergen, a former Republican operative, into the White House to advise him, and he began to listen more closely to the Conservative side of his close coterie of advisers, such as Dick Morris and Erskine Bowles, rather than the more Liberal George Stephanopoulos, Harold Ickes and Leon Panetta. The White House began to distance itself from congressional Democrats, which necessitated the development of a new governing strategy.

This new strategy surfaced in Clinton's State of the Union address on January 24, 1995, when the president asserted that he had "heard America." He said he supported its desire for a smaller, less intrusive government. Declaring that the "era of Big Government is over," he brought Republicans to their feet with his restatement of Republican-leaning themes. His performance led Rep. Martin Hoke (R-Oh.) to wonder aloud the next morning on the floor of the House: "Has the president become a Republican?".[35]

In June of 1995, Clinton suddenly presented his own balanced budget proposals and sought to negotiate with Republicans directly on their plan. His move caught the Democratic congressional leadership by surprise. Previously, both the White House and congressional Democrats had maintained that setting an arbitrary date for balancing the budget would be dangerous, and in any case, it could not be balanced without first overhauling the health care system, a key element in rising federal expenditures.[36] Several Democrats were said to be stunned and outraged. Some used the word "betrayal" to characterize the president's decision to repudiate his Left wing once again. They felt he had ceded their tactical argument that a balanced budget would hurt the poor and the elderly. This was clearly the position of the Congressional Black Caucus, led by Rep. Donald Payne (D-N.J.). Payne charged: "By reacting to everything the Republicans do, it's a sure way to fail. There are many people who are wondering, do we have a partnership going here or is the White House just moving out on its own course? If so, let us know where we stand."[37]

Clinton appeared to be signaling the new political stance he would take in the 1996 campaign. Dick Morris described this as a strategy of "triangulation"—locating the president's position between the two extremes of congressional Democrats and Republicans. Presidential advisers argued that the political tactics that might work for members of a congressional minority would not be effective for a president seeking to build a record of achievement before his reelection bid.[38]

In keeping with the new strategy, later that year Clinton supported several Republican proposals, including the $243 billion defense appropriations bill, which he signed even though it contained $7 billion more in spending than he wanted. The Pentagon declared it did not need the additional funds, but Republicans forced it on the administration because it contained funds for U.S. operations in Bosnia and kept federal workers in the Pentagon from being idled by the looming government shutdown.[39] Clinton also signed the Welfare Reform Act in August of 1996, under what he called "duress." He rationalized this by saying that although it contained measures he would later try to eliminate, it presented a bipartisan opportunity to change welfare. The timing of his signing, however, was clearly designed to affect the fall elections and protect him from vulnerability on this issue. Ironically, however, Republicans achieved more public credit for welfare reform than Clinton did.[40]

After the 1996 election, it appeared that the debate among political scientists, journalists and other observers over the nature and scope of the national political alignment would come to a close: Clinton defeated Dole in a veritable landslide, 49% to 41%, with Ross Perot getting 8% of the vote. As *Time* magazine suggested, Clinton campaigned as "a deficit-cutting, budget-balancing, welfare-reforming President who now believes 16-year-olds should have a drug test before they get a driver's license"; in effect the voters "elected a moderate Democrat President to carry out a moderate Republican agenda."[41] The convergence campaign strategy—moving to the Right after the 1994 election and coopting traditional Republican wedge issues such as affirmative action—resulted in Clinton's leadership of the Conservative national policy agenda.

In 1996 White voters leaned slightly toward Bob Dole, 45% to 44%. (Among all White voters, females supported Clinton by 49% to 42%, and males supported Dole by 48% to 38%, creating a 17-point "gender gap" between the two candidates.[42]) Yet not one analyst in the newspapers of record focused on this evidence of White preference for the more Conservative candidate and his Conservative policies. The Conservative nature of the American electorate in 1996 is underscored when one takes into account the generally Conservative slant of Perot voters.

One reason Clinton was successful was because he captured several suburban Republican strongholds in states such as Pennsylvania and Michigan, evidence that blue-collar Whites were sufficiently attracted to his program to rejoin the coalition.[43] Indeed, Clinton felt he had to take seriously the feelings of Americans who had lost trust in government and who aligned themselves with Republicans, Libertarians or Perot—or who were affiliated with no party. Yet the votes that clinched his victory came from Blacks (84%), Hispanics (73%) and Liberals (78%); these voters constituted 40% of his base. The irony of this is that members of these groups are demonstrably the most loyal part of the Democratic party coalition, and Clinton maintained their support despite the fact that they were poorly served by his convergence policies. The lack of choice—in an election where Ross Perot's candidacy was not credible—made Clinton the only choice for many Americans; in fact, Clinton calculated that this dearth of choice would allow him to pursue convergence policies.

Consolidating Convergence: Clinton II

One week before the official onset of his second term, Clinton met with a group of reporters and told them he believed the issue of government's role had been resolved. With respect to the two philosophies of governance—government as the solution, practiced from the beginning of the twentieth century through the Carter administration, and government as the problem, prevalent since Ronald Reagan—"I think we've found a synthesis," he declared.[44] This simplistic view of history, challengeable on its face but held by many Americans, violates the conception of twentieth-century political change—developed by such distinguished historians as Arthur Schlesinger—that views the relative dominance of Liberalism and Conservatism as cyclical.

Some reporters present at this interview questioned Clinton's notion of achieving a balance between Liberals and Conservatives, citing Schlesinger. In turn, the president challenged Schlesinger's ideas directly: "I think Arthur's problem . . . is this time it doesn't fit the cycle theory. . . . [W]e've been conservative . . . for a generation; we need to come back to being more liberal. What we're doing now is moving to a synthesis, to a new and different approach."[45]

Clinton's 1997 inaugural address developed themes he raised in that interview. In this speech he publicly pronounced the conclusion of the cycle of Democratic party realignment, citing instances where Democratic and Republican views had converged on important questions. With high-sounding rhetoric and the obligatory nod to the issue of the racial divide, Clinton carefully modulated the new language of the Conservative era into his "third way" thesis: "[W]e have finally resolved the great debate over government, and it was not the problem, nor the solution. . . . [Government] should not try to solve all our problems. . . . [It] should give Americans opportunity, not a guarantee." Clinton also emphasized "personal responsibility" as a substitute for government responsibility.[46]

Acknowledging that the negative impact of this change in the role of government would fall disproportionately on the shoulders of those who are dependent on government programs, Clinton included in this second inaugural address the declaration that "we will not succumb" to racism and to hatred, the "dark impulses" that "lurk in the far regions of the soul," and he asserted that diversity was a "godsend in the twenty-first century." Yet regardless of his assurances, Clinton's adoption of the "small government, third way" ideology may have ineluctably enabled the policy of devolution to place disadvantaged Blacks, Hispanics and others in a situation where they will be vulnerable to the "dark impulses" in the souls of politicians he opposed for a considerable period of time.[47]

In another post-election interview, Clinton expressed the opinion that he had not only reformed the role of government, but "rehabilitated" the Democratic party as well. He said that this process was "well under-way," and he supported this assertion by noting that significant portions of the Democratic coalition had supported such issues as deficit reduction, the crime bill, NAFTA and welfare reform.[48] This judgment was repeated by close advisers such as pollster Stan Greenberg, who declared that Democrats "are not going to go back to cultural liberalism"; Greenberg suggested that Clinton may have "created a foundation by resolving a lot of the historic problems of the '60s, '70s and '80s."[49]

With Republicans on the defensive because of the public's perception that they were responsible for the government shutdown during budget negotiations in December of 1995, Clinton was able to resume his initiative on this issue after the 1996 elections. The result was that a five-year budget agreement was negotiated and signed in August of 1997. It provided $85 billion in tax reductions that favored the wealthy, a $500 child credit for children under 16 years of age whose family incomes ranged from $18,000 to $115,000; additions to the welfare reform package for legal immigrants; $24 million in health insurance coverage for 10 million children; $35 billion in tax credits for higher education; and a reduction in the capital gains tax from 28% to 20% for the most wealthy and from 15% to 10% for the middle class.[50]

Though the budget deal added $3 billion to the welfare reform package for welfare-to-work programs, it carefully avoided direct social spending for urban areas—where Blacks are concentrated—in favor of a broad strategy of funding programs for the middle class and the children of the poor. There was little direct spending in the budget for job readiness training or enhanced funding for inner-city schools or similar programs. The Center on Budget and Policy priorities suggested that benefits for the poor would continue to decline not only during the five years covered by this budget, but beyond 2002 as well.[51] While some Blacks would benefit slightly in a budget framework heavily skewed toward the middle class and the wealthy, and others would benefit from increases in welfare funding, targeted spending on Black needs was missing. It was clearly the intention of the budget deal to strengthen the New Democrat strain in the Democratic party and promote its strategy of making the middle class the basis of the party's core constituency.

The Current Crisis for the Liberal Wing

The Conservative movement's influence on the Democratic party has resulted in an uneasy fusion of Neoconservative and traditionally Democratic ideas. A major contradiction now exists between the party establishment and its Black constituency, and tension between them has been increasing. Neither prominent Black Democrats nor other segments of the Black leadership seem willing to address the question of when the contradiction will become critical.

The context of contradiction is palpable. For example, after Clinton signed the welfare reform bill in August of 1996, three officials in the Department of Health and Human Services—Dr. Mary Jo Bane, assistant secretary for children and families, Peter Edelman, assistant secretary for planning and evaluation and his deputy, Wendell Primus—resigned in protest.[52] Yet no Black politician or administration official followed their lead, reflecting both the rather tepid level of opposition to the bill and the high level of support for convergence, led by Clinton.

What appears to be fueling the continuing drive toward convergence is the existence of a political faction that wants to acquire and maintain political power and is willing to abandon traditional positions in favor of reshaping them to compete effectively with political opponents. Shortly after the 1996 Clinton victory, David Kushnet and Ruy Teixeira of the Economic Policy Institute argued that welfare reform represented a "secret" victory for a "winning brand of liberalism."[53] They asserted that "Worker Liberalism," defined as fair play for those who work, was the victor over both "Lifestyle Liberalism," which protected those living at the edge of accepted social norms, and "Welfare Liberalism," which protected those who lived outside the world of work. With respect to another political tendency within the Democratic party in the 1990s, they suggested: "[Worker Liberals] understand something that Lifestyle Liberals don't: Most Americans are tolerant social conservatives. Worker Liberals stand for social inclusion of racial, religious, ethnic and lifestyle minorities on terms that the great majority of Americans can accept: We all want to be productive and responsible citizens."[54] The problem, they argued, is the conflict of identity politics among the least privileged Americans, even as the most privileged continue to prosper.

Kushnet and Teixeira's ideas appear to be a more elegant reformulation of those offered by Morris and other Clinton political advisers. Essentially they reject claims made on behalf of racial groups in favor of generalized claims in the name of undifferentiated "Americans" who are conceived to represent the majority interest. I contend that the notion of "identity politics" is a myth that disguises the ethnic/racial interests of Whites. The political convergence of Conservative White Democrats and Republicans represents the racial consensus of this era. It is a racial consensus because the degree of Black support for the policies of that convergence is generally negligible. The suppression of minority interests has promoted a growing tension within the Democratic party between those who hold traditional views and those—especially among the party leadership—who are pursuing the convergence strategy.

The Liberal wing of the Democratic party has been isolated by these political dynamics. Blacks, Hispanics, Jews, labor, women, gays and others are presented with a strategic choice: whether to accept the present situation and hope for improvement—because Democrats are a little bit better than Republicans—or mount strategies that enable them to drive a harder bargain with party leaders. The first choice was acceptable in the past, when the party was delivering. But what can be the rationale for that now, when both Democrats and Republicans seem committed to spending the $1 trillion budget surplus on programs that yield little benefit to disadvantaged Americans?

Clinton supporters would argue that political convergence is the only course for the future. In a 1994 symposium about the Clinton administration sponsored by the Institute for Policy Studies in Washington, D.C., the dialogue between Stan Greenberg and Roger Wilkins was telling. Greenberg asserted that Clinton won in 1992 by forging a "bottom-up" coalition based on broad themes of change or enhancement in areas such as employment, income growth, social welfare policies, health services and other issues with general appeal rather than "centering our politics around targeted benefits for specific groups." Such a course was particularly justified, Greenberg argued, in light of the fact that Clinton's 1992 election was not a result of political realignment but of shattering "traditional political coalitions and visions that people have associated with the major parties."[55]

By contrast, Wilkins declared that the political effect of this election was to move the Democratic party so far to the Right that "after 1992 it's hard to tell many Democrats apart from Republicans. That's part of our problem. At their leadership level, both the Democratic and Republican parties are almost wholly business-dominated. Both worship . . . the gods of growth, consumerism, and free trade. . . . [N]either is committed to popular organization, [or] willing to do for unions."[56] Wilkins suggested that Greenberg's analysis of the Clinton strategy with respect to race was flawed, inasmuch as the socioeconomic status of Blacks dictated that some targeting was crucial in order to address urgent problems. "So, the whole idea of avoiding targeting leaves that third of Black Americans who are damaged and distressed exactly where they are and growing in numbers because of these world forces we've been talking about."[57]

Greenberg's response to Wilkins implicitly contained a challenge to the effectiveness of the Clinton strategy. He said that the real test is whether the implementation of "universal policies" such as the Earned Income Tax Credit, job-training, college loans and welfare reform will benefit minority communities. In Greenberg's words: "Are these policies in fact broad-based? Are people in the position to take advantage of them? Will all those who are part of this coalition benefit?"[58] The political question is, what happens if the great gamble fails?

Clinton's "New Democrat" strategy of distributing benefits to minorities through a universalistic approach that attempts to raise the socioeconomic status of everyone is reminiscent of the Roosevelt era. The historical myth is that as a result of the development of programs

designed to pull the country out of the Great Depression, the status of
Blacks improved and thus they became beholden to the Democratic
party. There is no question, of course, that Blacks derived benefits from
A. Philip Randolph's protest movement (which included a threatened
march on Washington) and from the establishment of "Negro bureaus"
in every cabinet agency—under the supervision of the so-called "Black
Cabinet"—that facilitated Black participation in New Deal programs.

But before accepting this myth as the basis of a universalist
approach to distributing benefits, one should compare the Great Depression period to the Civil Rights era, when special consideration was given
to Blacks' socioeconomic and political condition. The rationale for this
special treatment was that because of the legacy of slavery and subordination, the nation was indebted to Black Americans and morally obligated to do whatever was necessary to raise them to the status of equality.
This notion of national obligation was actualized through the mobilization of Blacks—with the aid of their White supporters—who challenged
inequality and racism and demanded their elimination.

The "targeted" approach of the Civil Rights era resulted in far more
rapid progress for Blacks than was ever achieved by the Roosevelt
approach. Moreover, a major deficiency in the "New Democrat" strategy
is that the economic system distributes rewards and benefits on the basis
of skill levels, education, globalization, labor force participation and the
like. How will universalist policies shield "vulnerable" populations from
this system's negative selectivity?

CONCLUSION

Toward the end of Clinton's second term, it became clear that the administration had responded to the pressures of divergence by joining the
Republicans on crime, welfare reform, reduction of government, semi-
privatization of Social Security and other issues. Through the use of symbolic politics, it attempted to mollify its Black constituents who were
troubled by this shift. The administration publicly endorsed affirmative
action, the growth of minority businesses, support for Black colleges, great
attention to Africa, a modest increase in funds for civil rights enforcement
and a so-called "race initiative," and it condemned the burning of Black
churches. But it had become evident that the "triangulation" policy meant
that Blacks and their allies in the Liberal wing of the party were perceived
as expendable. For the time being, their only choice was to go along with

the party's more moderate posture, particularly because neither the Right nor the (politically anemic) Left represented a real option.

The quandary became even more serious. Though Blacks strongly opposed the punitive crime and welfare measures proposed by Ronald Reagan, the vast majority of the Black leadership accepted very similar measures promulgated by the Clinton administration because of their feeling that Clinton was forced to meet the Conservative movement half way. Nevertheless, it is striking that increased defense spending, punitive crime measures, more draconian death penalty laws and drug sentencing programs, cuts in social service benefits, adoption of enterprise zones, reductions in welfare spending and in the function of government itself, and the funding of school choice (charter schools, in Clinton's terminology)—policies that were all endorsed by Reagan—were implemented under a Democratic president with little opposition from members of his own party.

Will this state of affairs persist? Clinton's New Democrat strategy was not as sophisticated as "triangulation." Indeed, it amounted to a set of tactical measures designed to coopt the Republican agenda, without radicalizing either its form or its substance, and gain sufficient popularity with the American people to maintain political power. This "tactical strategy" might well become the new orthodoxy of the Democratic party. Yet this strategy subordinates the achievement of the most important goals of its less-advantaged constituents, and therein may lie the long-term danger.

In the short term, though, party unity stifled vigorous critique of the Democratic party's new orthodoxy, particularly because of the pressure on party adherents to support the president during the impeachment process. To some extent, this forceful political dynamic has papered over the party's internal fissures, but it remains to be seen whether unity will hold now that the White House is in Republican hands and the balance of power in Congress is so tenuous.

CHAPTER 5

The Deregulation of Civil Rights

INTRODUCTION

One area that defines the objectives of White Nationalist ideology perhaps more than any other is the attack on the regime of rights that supports Blacks' efforts to achieve equality, both in principle and with respect to the distribution of resources. The Civil Rights movement fostered a set of policies that moved the historical timetable on this project much faster than was perhaps desired by the White majority, as indicated in opinion polls demonstrating that Whites believed the rate of Black upward mobility has been "too fast." This was especially evident with respect to employment, as illustrated in a June 1997 Gallup poll that measured levels of satisfaction and which is summarized in table 5.1. In every case, White respondents expressed a greater level of satisfaction, except with regard to "job or work"—and this at a time when the economy was booming. This response may explain why affirmative action has become a critical concern: Whites are less confident about their employment possibilities than are Blacks.

Interminable debates over affirmative action and other civil rights issues have come to constitute a symbolic discussion of the wider issue of race in America, encompassing all the subtextual issues relating to the rate and nature of the movement of Blacks into the mainstream. I will examine the debate about racial rights in the context of the attack upon civil rights by Nationalist Conservatives and their attempt to reinterpret the Fourteenth Amendment to the Constitution as the basis of all social

TABLE 5.1	Levels of Satisfaction by Race, 1997 (percent satisfied)		
Issue	*Blacks*	*Whites*	*Gap between Blacks and Whites*
Way things are going in the U.S.	44%	50%	6%
Way things are going in personal life	74%	87%	13%
Income	53%	72%	19%
Standard of living	74%	87%	13%
Housing	76%	90%	14%
Job or work	86%	73%	−13%
Education, preparing for job	68%	75%	7%

Source: "Black/White Relations in the United States," Gallup Poll Social Audit, Gallup Organization, June 1997, Executive Summary, p. 22.

policies. This is an integral part of my contention that this dynamic parallels the successful disestablishment of Black legal entitlements that was the defining event of the last years of the first Reconstruction.

Soundings of public opinion in the period of time with which I am concerned indicate that Americans still supported the principle of affirmative action. In a 1991 Hart/Teeter poll for NBC News and the *Wall Street Journal*, 52% of Whites favored the policy and 37% opposed it; similarly, in a 1996 *Wall Street Journal* poll, 51% of Whites were either strongly or somewhat in favor or affirmative action, and 40% opposed it.[1] However, 64% of the 1996 sample opposed remedies defined as "racial preferences," and many equated "goals and timetables" with "quotas."[2]

A national consensus on civil rights emerged in the 1960s, yet measures that were considered as establishing "quotas" were not popular even then. This point of view was expressed by Ed Meese, U.S. attorney general in the Reagan administration:

> This administration is not against affirmative action. It is trying to find a better way. Affirmative action discriminates against a person on behalf of quotas. Two wrongs don't make a right. If you discriminate against a person on behalf of quotas simply because a person was discriminated against before, quotas are wrong whether to keep people out of jobs or to place people unfairly in jobs. People should be placed in jobs because of qualifications. It's a matter of fairness and justice.[3]

One poll found that Blacks were closely divided on the issue of "preferences" (48% to 42%), but strongly supported "quotas" (61% to 29%).[4]

Nevertheless, the idea of weakening affirmative action as it applies to Blacks while using it to benefit Whites has become part of the American judicial system.

Indeed, civil rights laws and philosophy in this era have been shaped by a so-called "color-blind" concept that was never at the core of these laws. In fact, the closest one comes to an official endorsement of "color blindness" is in the *minority* opinion in the 1896 *Plessy v. Ferguson* decision written by Justice John Harlan, who asserted that the aim of American jurisprudence was "color blindness." However, most analysts who cite this opinion ignore its internal contradiction:

> The white race deems itself to be the dominant race in this country. And so it is, in prestige, in achievements, in education, in wealth and in power. So, I doubt not, it will continue to be for all time, if it remains true to its great heritage and holds fast to the principles of constitutional liberty. But in view of the Constitution, in the eye of the law, there is in this country no superior, dominant, ruling class of citizen. There is no caste here. Our Constitution is color-blind.[5]

How can the law ensure equal protection if Whites are to continue to enjoy racial supremacy "for all time"? Harlan does not specifically associate color blindness with excluding race or color as a consideration, as urged by modern Conservative Nationalists. Instead he seems to be saying that given the adoption of post-Civil War amendments, the Constitution is impartial as to allowing advantage or disadvantage on the basis of race. He does not say—and does not appear to mean—that if claims of racial harm are brought before the court they should be dismissed on grounds of the irrelevancy of race. He clearly considers race important, though he does not resolve the issue satisfactorily.

Connie Rice of the NAACP Legal Defense Fund asserted in 1995: "We tried color-blind thirty years ago, and that system is naturally and artificially rigged for white males. If we abandon affirmative action, we return to the old-boy network."[6] Nevertheless, it has been the goal of White Nationalists to move the law in the direction of "color blindness." Clint Bolick, a major opponent of affirmative action, has taken the position, referencing Harlan, that both the Fourteenth Amendment and the Civil Rights Act of 1964 should be "color blind" in their implementation. He cites the concurring opinions of Justices Anthony Kennedy and Antonin Scalia in *Richmond v. Croson* as support for the idea that "the moral imperative of racial neutrality is the driving force of the Equal Protection Clause."[7]

Apparently the justices did not rely on constitutional history, which clearly indicates that the reason these civil rights laws were written in a neutralist language was to promote the equality of Black people. Instead, this neutralist interpretation has become the accepted standard in courts and legislatures. Thus it is important to review at least the bare elements of the profound changes in the Supreme Court's recent decisions in this area.

SEIZING JUDICIAL POWER

One of the ways the White Nationalist movement has attempted to foster a "color-blind" legal regime has been to target and eliminate so-called "Liberal jurisprudence" by what they term "activist judges" who, the movement asserts, rather than strictly construing the legal doctrines of the nation as found in the Constitution, make public policy from the bench. White Nationalists felt the applicability of this jurisprudence led to a permissive attitude toward crime as well as an expansion of civil rights laws for Blacks and women (especially with respect to abortion and workplace laws) and to lax enforcement of the rights of the White majority.

Richard Nixon's attempts to implement a "law and order" policy through the courts were thwarted by the judges of the Warren Court. But Ronald Reagan was able to begin to dismantle this regime by installing Conservative judges on the federal bench at all levels and appointing only a handful of Black judges. Whereas during his single term Jimmy Carter appointed 28 Black judges (out of a total of 206—13.6% of his district judges and 16% of his appellate judges), Reagan appointed just five Blacks, or less than 2%, in his eight years.[8] Reagan instituted a virtual litmus test on social issues for judicial appointees to ensure a Conservative perspective on the bench. And he did this with the cooperation of the Republican-controlled Senate Judiciary Committee. So pliant was Sen. Strom Thurmond, the committee's chair, that some of his colleagues charged he was acting as a "rubber stamp" for the president.[9]

The Making of the Rehnquist Court

The Conservative majority on the Supreme Court emerged during the Bush administration, but it had been slowly building for years. Dwight Eisenhower chose Justice Potter Stewart, who turned out to be the swing vote between the Liberal and Conservative wings of the Court. John Kennedy nominated Byron "Whizzer" White; although White appeared to be a moderate, he issued opinions that were largely Conservative, especially in his later years. Richard Nixon selected Harry Blackmun and, most significantly, William Rehnquist, a strong Conservative who had supported Barry Goldwater's presidential aspirations in 1964.

Rehnquist's impact on the Court was important even before he became Chief Justice. In 1978, a Supreme Court opinion struck down a lower court ruling regarding the University of California-Davis Medical School's rejection of Alan Bakke's application, partially because of the school's race-based admissions program, which set aside 15 places in the class for Black applicants. The Court held that the program was unconstitutional because race was the principal reason for excluding Bakke, but it reaffirmed the use of affirmative action in circumstances where it could pass the test of "strict scrutiny." The *Bakke* case, decided on a five to four vote with Rehnquist among the majority, was an indication of the changing nature of federal court decisions on civil rights. This reflected the growing ideological differences in the country between the Liberal ethos, which had supported a generous interpretation of the Fourteenth Amendment, and more restrictive interpretations of the legality of remedies designed to compensate for the historic subordination of Blacks.

In his dissent in *Bakke,* Justice Blackmun expressed concern about the scarcity of Black doctors; he wrote: "[I]f ways are not found to remedy that situation [including medical school admissions policies], the country can never achieve its professed goal of a society that is not race-conscious. In order to get beyond racism, we must first take into account race."[10] Restrictive interpretations of civil rights laws—which held, in effect, that Blacks had to prove they had been subordinated in specific instances—ignored the fundamental reality of that subordination: a similar subordination has never been applied to ordinary White Americans. In his dissent in *Bakke,* Justice Thurgood Marshall wrote:

> It is unnecessary in twentieth-century America to have individual Negroes demonstrate that they have been victims of racial discrimination; the racism of our society has been so pervasive that none, regardless of wealth or position, has managed to escape its impact. The experience of Negroes in America has been different in kind, not just in degree, from that of other ethnic groups, it is not merely the history of slavery alone but also that a whole people were marked as inferior by the law.[11]

When Reagan elevated Rehnquist to Chief Justice in 1986, Sen. Edward Kennedy said that he was "too extreme on race, too extreme on women's rights, too extreme on freedom of speech and too extreme on separation of church and state, too extreme to be Chief Justice."[12] At the Senate Judiciary Committee's initial hearing on this appointment, it was revealed that as a law clerk in 1953 Rehnquist supported segregated schools, and that during the 1960s he harassed Black voters at polling places in Phoenix, Arizona.[13] Rehnquist later won high marks from Justice Marshall and others for his administration of the Court, but he has also proven to be a mainstay of its Conservative majority.[14]

Gerald Ford nominated John Paul Stevens to the Court in 1975 and Reagan chose Sandra Day O'Connor in 1981, Antonin Scalia in 1986 and Anthony Kennedy in 1988. George Bush selected David Souter in 1990 and Clarence Thomas in 1991. This cast of Republican presidents also chose the majority of the current lower court judges, who are relatively Conservative. Both those judges and the Supreme Court justices will affect public policy for some time to come. Most relevant to our discussion here, these judges have had an immeasurable impact upon the race-related issues which have come before them.

David Kairys has suggested that the Supreme Court has incorporated into its decisions the viewpoint of White Americans who "see the racial problem as a matter of the African-American community's alleged disruptions of an otherwise innocent and orderly white America: from affirmative action to drugs, crime, AIDS, and whatever else upsets them. The corollary set of villains in the Reagan version of the racial problem are the African-Americans and whites who still carry on about racism—liberals—and have supposedly stacked the deck so that African-Americans now have it better than whites."[15] On the basis of this surreal attitude, Kairys alleges, White Conservative policy makers have often proceeded to defend their constituents against government-promulgated policies on civil rights by openly attacking them.

THE OPEN ATTACK ON CIVIL RIGHTS

Reagan's Rights Policy

For decades now, the policy legacy of the 1960s Civil Rights movement has been under serious and concerted attack in every branch of government and at every level. In the executive branch of the federal government, this attack began with the election in 1980 of Ronald Reagan, whose administration opposed the Equal Employment Opportunity Commission's affirmative action program in employment, the Department of Education's Office of Civil Rights affirmative action program in higher

education, and the minority business set-aside program of the Office of
Federal Contract Compliance in the Department of Labor.

Indeed, as Norman Amaker has remarked: "In every area of executive responsibility for enforcement of the civil rights laws, there has been
clear opposition to the national policy of affirmative action expressed in
the laws and accordingly, a concomitant rejection of the means available
to carry out those policies as provided in the laws themselves and the regulations adopted to enforce them."[16] Amaker argues that although Reagan could not reverse the course of history, he was able to substantially
slow the progress of civil rights enforcement.

William Bradford Reynolds, Reagan's assistant attorney general for
civil rights, reflected the administration's ideological direction. With regard
to affirmative action, he asserted that "Using discrimination to end discrimination, using race to get beyond racism—I don't believe that that
technique has proven helpful or useful in moving us down the path that
we all want to go."[17] Reynolds considered that Whites had suffered racial
harm so significant that it violated the "equal protection of the laws" intent
of the Fourteenth Amendment and constituted "discrimination" within the
original framework of that law. This interpretation, however, is not supported by the original definition of "discrimination": for example, when an
employer fails to hire Black job applicants at a disproportionate rate to others. In any case, such a practice had to be proven with respect to both the
act of racial selectivity or distinction (racial testing or other such methods)
and the fact of a statistical discrepancy.

Nowhere was Reynolds's attitude more influential than in the lax
enforcement of affirmative action in education. A 1987 report of the House
of Representatives Committee on Government Operations found that
although the school desegregation plans of ten southern states which were
established by the decision in *Adams v. Richardson* were no longer in effect,
and vestiges of racial discrimination were still in place, the Civil Rights
Division of the Justice Department had not intervened. Furthermore, the
report discerned a pattern of governmental fraud and deception which
amounted to a "nationwide scheme to backdate civil rights documents,
improperly close discrimination investigations, and provide false information to a federal court."[18] This contradicted the Justice Department's claim
that only a small number of Department of Education offices were involved
in what was, in effect, an attempt to thwart the desegregation of higher
education institutions in the South. Beyond the Justice Department's lax
administration of civil rights laws, Reynolds's central objective was to
change the laws themselves.

The Reagan administration also seriously hampered the ability of the
U.S. Commission on Civil Rights to monitor the government's enforce-

ment of civil rights laws by appointing to the commission—and to its leadership—people who were opposed to traditional civil rights enforcement.[19] Funding was sharply reduced, further weakening the commission's enforcement mission. While the major impetus for the Justice Department's failure to enforce civil rights laws came from Reynolds, this pattern continued throughout the administration of George Bush.

Reagan appointed Conservative movement members Clarence Pendleton, Jr., a Black lawyer, and Linda Chavez, a Hispanic and former Republican official, as chair and executive director, respectively, of the Commission on Civil Rights. Other commission appointees included Morris Abrams, a prominent Atlanta lawyer, John Bunzell, a researcher from the Hoover Institution, and Esther Gonzalez-Arroyo, a teacher from Texas. This group proceeded to turn an activist, independent commission into a relatively moribund agency. In fact, so ineffective did it become that its Liberal members such as Dr. Mary Frances Berry proposed that it be abolished.[20]

Pendleton ran the supposedly independent body in close harmony with the views of the White House and Justice Department, opposing such policies as affirmative action and comparable pay for women, and sparking heated disagreements among commission members. He also angered Congress by turning his part-time position into a full-time one and, in the language of a General Accounting Office report, presiding over considerable mismanagement of funds.[21] As a consequence, in 1986 the House Appropriations Committee voted to de-fund the agency. Its staff declined from 150 to 45, and Morris Abrams, Al Latham and others tendered their resignations.

Meanwhile, courts became a major civil rights battleground. This began with affirmative action in higher education and the *Bakke* decision, but the scope soon expanded to include other areas of civil rights.

LEGAL MEASURES

With an increasing number of Conservative judges on the federal bench, the courts were poised to begin a serious reinterpretation of the law with respect to civil rights aspects of housing, employment, minority set-asides, voting rights and education.

Housing

In *Memphis v. Greene* (1981), the Supreme Court sided with White citizens who had asked the Memphis City Council to close a street in Hein

Park, on the border between White and Black communities, because of "undesirable traffic."[22] The Court upheld the city's action, even though the record indicated that one White resident who opposed the street closing testified at a City Council hearing that he was assailed by his neighbors because of his association with "niggers": "That," he testified, "is the issue here."[23] Despite the fact that Justices Marshall, Brennan and Blackmun dissented, saying that the city was seeking to "carve out a racial enclave," Justice Stevens, writing for the majority, said there was no proof of "purposeful discrimination." This concept of "purposeful discrimination," which suggested that an intent to discriminate must be proved, became an important rationale for Conservative jurists hearing civil rights cases.

Employment

In the 1980s, courts began to challenge affirmative action plans in cases where union contracts for city employees abridged seniority rights of longer-serving White employees in favor of more recently hired Blacks when layoffs were instituted for financial reasons. Two such cases were filed in Memphis, one in 1984 concerning firefighters and the other in 1986 concerning public school employees.[24]

Attacks upon equitable employment policies continued with *Watson v. Fort Worth Bank and Trust* (1988), wherein a Black bank teller who had been rejected for promotion four times by four different White supervisors sued the bank, both as an individual plaintiff and as part of a class action. The Supreme Court affirmed the use of disparate impact analysis to challenge employment decisions, but it split on such issues as the plaintiff's burden of proof. As explained in the dissent by Justices Blackmun, Brennan and Marshall, traditionally the burden of proof was borne by the plaintiff, but if the plaintiff proved a discriminatory pattern, the burden shifted to the defendant employer, who then had to prove that the discriminatory act or actions had a sufficient business rationale. Justices O'Connor, Scalia, White and Rehnquist disagreed. They suggested that the plaintiff had the burden of isolating specific employer practices which led to disparate impact, that statistical disparities should be so substantial as to support the inference of discrimination, that disparate impact must be demonstrated on a "case-by-case" basis rather than through class action and that the ultimate burden of proof lay with the plaintiff "at all times" rather than with employers, who were not required to produce formal validation studies defending their employment practices.[25]

The following year, the Court attempted to apply this section of the Watson decision in the *Wards Cove Packing* case, which featured a fish-canning company that maintained a racially stratified workforce of White managers and technical employees and non-White unskilled canners. The non-White employees sued, alleging racial discrimination, and—by a five to four vote, with Conservatives in the majority—the Court followed the disparate impact argument used in *Watson*.[26] In a dissenting opinion, Justice Stevens pointed out that the structure of the Wards Cove Company resembled a "plantation economy." Justice Blackmun expressed his incredulity with respect to the ease with which the majority had reversed settled law based on the reality of racial discrimination: "Sadly, this comes as no surprise. One wonders whether the majority still believes that race discrimination—or, more accurately, race discrimination against nonwhites—is a problem in our society, or even remembers that it ever was."[27] Significantly, the same five to four alignment recurred frequently in the 1990s in decisions that vitiated other aspects of civil rights law as well.

Minority Set-Asides in Contracting

In *Richmond v. Croson*, the Supreme Court decided in favor of more restrictive use of disparate impact analysis, calling for a narrower burden of proof on the plaintiffs and challenging the practice of minority contracting.[28] Handed down on June 9, 1989, this decision had an immediate impact. Professor John Howard found that within six months of the decision, minority and female contracting in Atlanta, Georgia, went from 35% to 15%, and in Philadelphia, minority contracting fell from 35% to 25%; moreover, by 1991, two dozen cities had suspended their minority contracting programs altogether.[29] Howard asserted that "[t]he conservative vision does not recognize the existence of structural discrimination and in a sense, therefore, does not acknowledge that historical facts may have present consequences."[30]

Only the Civil Rights Act of 1991 slowed the Supreme Court somewhat, by temporarily reestablishing the burden of proof standards of Title VII of the 1964 Civil Rights Act. The Bush administration opposed the new Civil Rights Act, which was first proposed and voted on in 1990, on the grounds that it implemented "quotas," and a confrontation ensued with Congress over whether this was indeed a "quota bill." When Bush vetoed the act in October 1990, he became only the second president (Reagan was the first) to veto a civil rights measure.[31] The Bush administration developed a substitute which capped damages on discrimination awards at $150,000 and allowed some discrimination for what it termed "legitimate business objectives."[32] This proposal was ultimately rejected by Congress, and Bush signed the Civil Rights Act of 1991 in November of that year. One reason he did so was to muffle complaints about his veto of the 1990 version. Another was to publicly repudiate the politics of David Duke. (Duke was an avowed racist who formerly served as grand dragon of the Ku Klux Klan. He won 60% of the White vote in the 1990 Louisiana U.S. Senate race and 55% of the White vote in Louisiana's 1991 gubernatorial race—though he lost both elections.[33]) Bush planned to accompany his approval of the bill with an executive order limiting its scope in conformance with some of his original objections; however, he withdrew this order.

The momentum to change minority contracting standards was impeded by decisions in cases such as *Metro Broadcasting v. FCC* (1990) and *Adarand Constructors v. Pena* (1995), which upheld the use of carefully crafted affirmative action plans in minority set-asides. The Court's decision in the *Metro* case upheld the FCC's use of a diversity rationale in awarding licenses to broadcasters, and its decision in *Adarand* upheld set-asides for minority contractors which survived the test of strict scrutiny and where there was a compelling state interest. Interestingly, the Anti-Defamation League, a leading Jewish organization which had fought alongside Blacks during the Civil Rights era, found itself allied with Conservatives in the Mountain States Legal Foundation in opposition to the Court's stand in *Metro Broadcasting*.

In the 1980s, courts were increasingly persuaded by the arguments of Conservative legal scholars and public interest groups against minority set-aside contracting and by the opposition of a majority of White Americans to affirmative action. Conservative legal scholars felt that race- and gender-conscious remedies had outlived their usefulness and now amounted to "reverse discrimination." One commentator characterized affirmative action as "a euphemism for race or sex discrimination. The basic question it presents is whether government should grant preferences to some individuals, and thereby, disadvantage others, because of their race or sex. For most people the answer is not difficult." This commentator also declared: "The prime virtue of a race and sex-neutral system of law—a system that deals only in individuals—is that it makes all issues of group differences irrelevant. Affirmative action makes discussion of them inevitable. In short, it is a prescription for polarization, conflict and ill will."[34]

These statements illustrate an important reason for opposing a race-neutral definition of rights: such a definition would only lead to equity in a society where no subordination had occurred. However, where inequality is embedded in relative group status as a result of past injustices, group-based remedies within moderately prescribed limits of the law are eminently fair. The legal requirement that Blacks prove their subordinate position compounds the unfairness because it complicates the remedies available and makes them subject to an individualized proof that is often not available.

Weakening Voting Rights

In the 1990s, cases dealing with voting rights and education promulgated a similarly restrictive interpretation. Successive decisions of the Supreme Court have now invalidated the use of race as the primary basis for drawing the boundaries of congressional districts or any other political jurisdiction.

The Voting Rights Act of 1965 was intended to eliminate racial discrimination against Blacks seeking to exercise the right to vote, particularly in the South, where they had been excluded from the franchise in large numbers and in many localities since the turn of the century. Section 2 of the act made it unlawful to deny or abridge the right of anyone to vote on account of race or color.

In *Shaw*, five White North Carolina voters challenged the configuration of the majority-Black 12th Congressional District on the grounds that it violated the principle of a "color blind Constitution."[35] The district court dismissed their claim, but on appeal, the Supreme Court—in a five to four decision—declared: "We conclude that a plaintiff challenging a reapportionment statute under the *equal protection clause* may state a claim by alleging that the legislation, though race-neutral on its face, rationally cannot be understood as anything other than an effort to separate voters into different districts on the basis of race, and that the separation lacks sufficient justification"[36] (my emphasis). In effect, the Court created a right for Whites in Black-majority districts to use the Fourteenth Amendment's equal protection clause to object to the racial composition of the district in which they lived merely on the grounds that race was used in its construction. The Court further suggested that if the state could not justify its plan as "narrowly tailored" to achieve a "compelling governmental interest," the plan would be in violation of the equal protection clause.

With its decision in *Shaw*, the Court shifted the weight of the law from the use of race as a principle of amelioration for past racial exclusion to an assertion that the use of race would be a violation of the equal protection standard.[37] This use of the Fourteenth Amendment effectively alters the original intent of the law, ultimately empowering anew the White majority which created the racial imbalances in political representation in the first place.

By 1995, nearly all 13 of the majority-Black congressional districts which had been created as a result of the 1990 census were under attack. Court judgments were rendered against the districts of several members of the Congressional Black Caucus: the 4th Louisiana District (Cleo Fields), the 5th Georgia District (Cynthia McKinney), the 2nd Georgia District (Sanford Bishop), the 18th Texas District (Sheila Jackson Lee), the 30th Texas District (Eddie Bernice Johnson), the 3rd Florida District (Corrine Brown), the 3rd Virginia District (Bobby Scott) and the 12th North Carolina District (Mel Watt). Most of these representatives survived the elections that followed the Court-ordered redistricting and held on to their seats, but the new racial composition of Cleo Fields's district led to his defeat.

It is clear that in light of the decreasing number of majority-Black districts, if Black incumbents do not run for reelection, new Black candidates will face an uphill struggle, and it is very likely that the racial composition of traditionally Black seats will be taken by Whites. To forestall this likelihood, long-serving Black members of Congress have tried to transfer the aura of incumbency by encouraging relatives or close staff members to run for their seats when they retire.

Education

The Conservative majority on the Supreme Court struck a serious blow at racial integration in schools with its decision in *Jenkins v. City of Kansas City.* In yet another five to four decision, it held the Kansas City, Missouri, school district could not allocate funds for enhanced educational programs at majority-Black schools in the city in order to attract more White students.[38] Some observers concluded that *Jenkins* was one of the most important cases in that session, for it effectively vitiated the decision in *Brown* by cutting off resources intended to help implement desegregation decrees, and it hampered the improvement of schools with majority-Black enrollments.[39]

The Supreme Court decision in *Jenkins* and subsequent lower court decisions eliminating integration plans in Boston and San Francisco have produced a ripple effect that will further circumscribe opportunities for many Black youths.[40] The net effect of the invalidation of the Boston Latin School's desegregation plan—on the basis that it did not meet the new equal protection interpretation—is that Blacks lost nearly 210 seats in the school's fourth grade and Whites gained nearly 80 seats.[41]

It is manifestly evident that in the 1990s, the Supreme Court's race-related decisions reduced the number of Black-majority voting districts, hampered federal affirmative action programs and limited racial integration in education. The court effectively "delivered" for the Conservative cause, sending the message to the nation that "it is time to put race aside."[42] Frank Parker, vaunted legal analyst of civil rights issues, concluded: "The court's decisions are seriously damaging minorities' ability to gain equality in the economic and political life of the country."[43]

THE FOURTEENTH AMENDMENT

Whether one is concerned with affirmative action, voting rights, or set-sides, the key issue in the attack on civil rights in this second Reconstruction is the same as in the first: White Nationalist ideology has sought to redefine the Fourteenth Amendment to advantage Whites, and this has meant changing the race-specific intent of the law to neutralize its application under so-called "color-blind" literal interpretations.

The reinterpretation of this amendment in various fields of public policy has meant repositioning race in the context of the amendment's mandate to secure "equal protection of the laws." Its original purpose was to abolish the subordinate status of ex-slaves by establishing a standard of equality for everyone, including Blacks. This intent is evident in the wording of the proposed Civil Rights Act of 1866, the progenitor of the Fourteenth Amendment. That act declared "citizens of every race and color" to be citizens of the United States, regardless of "slavery or involuntary servitude" and said they should have the same right to property in every state and territory as every other citizen.[44]

Although the 1866 act was never passed into law, Republicans sought to enshrine its meaning in constitutional law through enactment of the Fourteenth Amendment. After defining the concept of citizenship for all Americans, including Blacks, Section 1 of the amendment enjoins states from making or enforcing "any law which shall abridge the privileges or immunities of citizens of the United States; nor shall any State deprive any person of life, liberty, or property, without due process of law, nor deny to any person within its jurisdiction the equal protection of the laws." As Richard Bardolph has observed, although the Fourteenth Amendment, like the Fifteenth, "made no mention of race," the reference to the group status of Blacks was implicit.[45] *In effect, embedded in the neutral language of the Fourteenth Amendment was a strong voice speaking to White society on behalf of Blacks, instructing the nation to strive, at long last, to include Blacks within a single standard of equality for everyone.* Indeed, Republicans attempted to institutionalize not only the civil rights of Blacks, but their social rights as well, in the Civil Rights Act of 1875. In nearly every section of that act, access to public accommodations was extended to Blacks by direct reference, through a phrase which held that the law was "applicable alike to citizens of every race and color, regardless of previous condition of servitude."[46]

Beginning in 1883 and ending with *Plessy v. Ferguson* in 1896, a line of Supreme Court decisions nullified the Civil Rights Act of 1875, reinterpreting the Fourteenth Amendment to provide for "separate but equal accommodations." Yet even this pernicious reversal of the intent of the amendment was instituted on the basis of a recognition of group rights held by Blacks and Whites. The majority decision in *Plessy* held, in part: "The object of the [Fourteenth] Amendment was undoubtedly to enforce the absolute equality of the two races before the law, but in the nature of things it could not have been intended to abolish distinctions based upon color, or to enforce social, as distinguished from political, equality, or a commingling of the two races upon terms unsatisfactory to either."[47] The opinion goes on to propound a mythical basis for the thesis that under the Constitution, racial separation is permissible as long as the facilities available to the two races are equal.

In its 1954 ruling in *Brown v. Board of Education,* the Supreme Court reaffirmed the original intent of the Fourteenth Amendment as interpreted by the Civil Rights Acts of 1866 and 1875, vitiating the concept of separate but equal and establishing a general standard of equality which would have the effect of adjusting the status of Blacks before the law. The Court held that "the plaintiffs and others similarly situated for whom the actions have been brought are, by reason of the segregation complained of, deprived of the equal protection of the laws guaranteed by the Fourteenth Amendment."[48]

This new logic guided Congressional elaboration of a series of civil rights acts with strong prohibitions against racial discrimination in 1957, 1960, 1964, 1965 and 1968. Yet nearly 40 years after the establishment of modern legal precedents using the Fourteenth Amendment as the underlying basis of laws protecting the status of Blacks and other disadvantaged social classes, the courts and the Congress have summarily altered the intent of the amendment once again.

The Redirection of "State Action"

The doctrine of "state action" in the field of civil rights was born when the language of the Fourteenth Amendment made the federal government responsible for the protection of citizens' due process rights. But it left unsettled whether this protection applied to the "public" citizenship of Blacks or to private actions of citizens, even where they were arrayed against the interests of Blacks. In *United States v. Cruikshank* (1876), a group of Whites in Louisiana were charged with conspiracy after they broke up a meeting of Blacks who were intending to exercise their right to vote. In its decision in this case, the Supreme Court declared that: "The Fourteenth Amendment prohibits a state from depriving any person of life, liberty or property, without due process of law; but this adds nothing to the rights of one citizen as against another. It simply furnishes an additional guarantee against any encroachment by the States upon the fundamental rights which belong to every citizen as a member of society."[49] The decision was important because it interpreted the Fourteenth Amendment as protecting private citizens against impermissible state actions.

Bardolph explicates the evolution over time of the concept of state action: "The definition of 'state action' was progressively widened until few discriminatory acts, however remotely they depended upon the public process, were ultimately immune to the judicial negative. Indeed, it went almost the whole way to abolishing the distinction between acts of the state and acts of private individuals, so far as the applicability of the Fourteenth Amendment was concerned."[50] The expanded doctrine of state action became the norm and undergirded the civil rights acts of the 1960s. Whenever its applicability became a matter of dispute in Congress, as in the debates over the Voting Rights Act of 1965 and the Fair Housing Act of 1968, southern Conservatives continued to argue that the assumption of federal responsibility for civil rights was an unconstitutional extension of federal authority into state affairs.

There is legitimate confusion over this issue. The definition of the extent of federal powers has been subject to the vagaries of political interpretation and reinterpretation as ideological winds have shifted. This is understandable in light of the fact that "the state" itself is an amorphous entity, with fluctuating degrees of authority. Joseph Tussman observed: "The judicial enforcement of discriminatory private undertaking can be seen in two ways. It can be regarded as simply sustaining and protecting the integrity of the system of private agreements which gives scope to private preference. Or it can be seen as state action which is imbued with the quality of the agreement it enforces and therefore, under the equal protection clause, as prohibited state action."[51] A generation ago, southern politicians may have wanted to preserve Tussman's first meaning of "the private": that the Constitution meant that private action was shielded from federal intrusion, even when it included the practice of racism. More recently, changes in the meaning of state action carry with them the attempt by Nationalists to configure federal protection of private interest in a number of discrete areas. This privatization of public power is a zero-sum game. It de-legitimizes the public arena of rights, where Blacks have the most access to public resources, in favor of the private arena, where Whites have greater access to resources such as private schools, private investments, private housing and so on.

Bending government toward the protection of localized private rights is one part of the Nationalist agenda. Another is enhancing the protection of Whites by legitimizing their status as targets of discrimination, using language which neutralizes—and therefore nullified—the special responsibility of government to protect the rights of Blacks on the public level. House Resolution 1909 in the 105th Congress reads: "[N]either government nor any officer, employee, or agent of the Federal government shall discriminate against, or grant a preference to, any person or group based in whole or in part on race, color, national origin, or sex, and etc."[52] Similar language appears in California's Proposition 209, Washington State's Initiative 200 and many other state legislative proposals intended to eliminate affirmative action.

When Rep. Frank Riggs (R-Calif.) and his congressional colleagues attacked affirmative action in higher education in H.R. 1909, they were careful to identify the state as the agent of the theorized "discrimination"—which they defined as granting a preference—and prohibit it from "discriminating" by such action against "any person or group" in the protected classes established by the Civil Rights Act of 1964. This proposed House resolution was intended to limit the federal government's ability to act in such important areas as contracting, employment and higher education.

This frontal assault on the rights of protected classes intended to change the meaning of state action against disadvantaged minorities and foster a different interpretation of the Fourteenth Amendment. Proposition 209, known as the California Civil Rights Initiative, and Washington State's Initiative 200, as indicated, prohibit these states from "discrimination" or from extending "preferences" to protected classes, thus shielding citizens in these states from the protection of the federal government in delimited areas. This also opens up the question of what is meant by "discrimination," a concept traditionally connoting White bias toward Blacks with an intent to harm. However, recent changes in the definition seem to indicate that the identification or selection of any cultural group, even if for the purpose of taking action to equalize groups' relative status in society, constitutes "discrimination."

Tussman worried that if the public/private distinction was not clarified by the courts, it would be construed too narrowly—that every reference to race or ethnic category might constitute a public offense. Yet by switching the emphasis to private protection from discrimination, the White majority has claimed an important use of state action to shield itself from liability for discriminatory acts.

Employment Discrimination and Affirmative Action

By establishing a federal right to equal opportunity in employment, Title VII of the Civil Rights Act of 1964 required "employers, labor unions and employment agencies . . . to treat all persons without regard to their race, color, religion, sex, or national origin." Everyone who held affective social power was instructed not to participate in racial or other forms of discrimination.

The first implication of a neutralist interpretation of Title VII is that it prohibits discrimination against any individual or group and enhances the protection of Whites against what has been called "reverse discrimination." The second implication is that it places Blacks and other disadvantaged groups in a situation where there is no effective enforcement authority to promote the enhancement of their status within the labor force or other important arenas such as higher education.

Using this neutralist interpretation, some opponents of traditional civil rights have claimed "reverse discrimination" in individual incidents on the basis of anecdotal evidence that rarely proves to be persuasive. The singular act of hiring a qualified Black person rather than a White person or advancing a Black person's employment status may trigger a charge of "reverse racism," even though the authority for such action has been sanctioned by law or company policy. Indeed, it is a clear manifestation of the power of Whites in general that on the basis of such anecdotal evidence the behavior of institutions in dispensing racial values can be changed to favor Whites. The latest reinterpretation of the Fourteenth Amendment is meant to halt the use of measures designed especially to adjust the status of Blacks in society. In that sense, it has the effect of legitimizing the status quo, preserving current racial inequalities and ensuring the continued dominance of Whites in a racial hierarchy.

Weakening the Remedy

The proposal by Nationalists that Title VII should be the only legal instrument for redressing employment discrimination and ensuring that minorities are equally represented in the workplace and other institutions means relying solely upon either mediation or the courts to achieve these ends. Paul Burstein has described this as a system that focuses on voluntary conciliation, case-by-case resolution and heavy reliance on prosecution by individual victims of discrimination. Burstein notes that "It took years for the appellate courts to resolve any substantial number of EEO [Equal Employment Opportunity] cases, especially for women, finding that the law could not have become effective until 1971, seven years after passage, with the first United States Court of Appeals decision that made the threat of such penalties effective."[53] He concludes that "EEO enforcement effort seems slow and uncertain rather than swift and sure."[54] Although the average time for the settlement of EEO cases has improved somewhat in recent years, it is still close to the rate described by Burstein in 1985. The process of resolving discrimination claims is slow in part because the resolution of racial discrimination, especially through the EEOC, has not been a priority of government since the Reagan administration, which successfully stifled the federal government's civil rights machinery.

It is widely acknowledged that the litigation process is heavily weighted against the poor in favor of the rich. Nevertheless, the publicly funded Neighborhood Legal Services Corporation has been attacked severely by Conservative-movement politicians. Its funding was substantially reduced over the years, and it has been prohibited from bringing cases over a variety of civil rights violations involving many kinds of groups. In the context of such impediments, a litigation strategy to achieve fairness is no substitute for affirmative action.

THE EMERGENCE OF WHITE CIVIL RIGHTS

In the late twentieth century, as a result of the Civil Rights movement, there was a growing perception that Blacks had achieved an advantage in their social, economic and political mobility at the expense of some Whites, and because of this, governmental mechanisms which fostered that advantage should be disassembled. This perception arose even as the civil rights laws promulgated in that era first began to address the general issue of racial and other forms of societal disadvantage.

Even in the post-Civil Rights era the problem of group disadvantage and the mechanisms embedded in civil rights laws to correct this problem have been regarded largely as "Black issues," essentially because of the historical American racial drama and because power often insulates Whites from racial concerns. Thus today, even though millions of Whites benefit from affirmative action programs, these programs are pilloried as unnecessary governmental gifts bestowed on racial minorities.

So strong is White animus regarding affirmative action and so widespread its portrayal as a mechanism favoring Blacks alone, that Americans in general are now in denial about the reach of the culture of civil rights and the ways in which it has enriched them.[55] Moreover, in denying the obvious benefits of civil rights to all Americans, they misconstrue the contribution of this culture to the construction of a truly democratic state. It is an unassailable fact that the establishment of the principle of equality of rights and the fashioning of a concrete remedy of recompense for groups which have been disadvantaged has benefited the entire society. Perhaps the major contribution of the principle and the remedy is that they impact such vital issues as the unequal distribution of power that often harms non-Whites, whites who are elderly or disabled, White females and even White males.

The Predominance of White Protected Classes

Indeed, the irony is that *the ultimate beneficiary of the Civil Rights era has been the White population.* Title VII of the 1964 Civil Rights Act prohibited employment discrimination across the board, on the basis of race, color, religion, sex, or national origin. The Age Discrimination in Employment Act (ADEA) was adopted in 1967, prohibiting discrimination against persons age 40 and older; and the Equal Pay Act (EPA) of 1963—protecting women and men against sex-based wage discrimination for performing substantially the same work—was added to the EEOC enforcement mandate in 1979.[56] Moreover, the Rehabilitation Act of 1973 prohibited discrimination against persons with disabilities in federal government employment, and as a result of the Americans with Disabilities Act of 1990, all persons with disabilities are protected from employment discrimination and guaranteed access to reasonable accommodation on the job. Thus even though such categories as the aged and disabled are not included in affirmative action programs, the protected classes of Americans against which employment discrimination is prohibited now covers most significant classes of individuals, extending far beyond the limits of race.[57]

The years 1983 to 1997 represented a critical period of expansion in the scope of discrimination cases handled by the EEOC. Immediately following the inception of Title VII, complaints of race discrimination as the basis for action led all other categories (Title VII, ADEA, EPA, ADA, other) among those which the EEOC was responsible for processing. However, between 1990 and 1994, complaints of racial discrimination under Title VII dropped from 73% of total complaints to 59%.[58]

A major reason for the decline in racial discrimination complaints as a proportion of the EEOC's total caseload was the growth of ADA cases, which went from 1.5% of the total in 1992 to 17.4% of the total in

1993. In addition, complaints of sex discrimination have been growing faster than complaints of race discrimination. As shown in Table 5.2, there is an evident pattern in the distribution of Title VII employment discrimination complaints. The growth categories are sex, EPA, ADA and retaliation. From 1983 to 1994, the gap between race and sex complaints narrowed, from nearly 13,000 in 1983 to nearly 8,000 in 1993, less than 6,000 in 1994 and less than 3,800 by 2001. This suggests that at some time in the future, sex discrimination complaints will outnumber race discrimination complaints in the EEOC caseload.

Indeed, the pattern of litigation has already begun to reflect such a change. As can be seen from the figures set forth in Table 5.3, litigation in Title VII cases increased from 60% in 1983 to 68% in 1993, to 73% by 2001. And this increase is largely accounted for by the growing number of discrimination complaints by women in 1993, as the figures in Table 5.4 indicate. Both the litigation pattern and the complaint pattern reflect the fact that discrimination against women has become a substantial and growing priority among all categories of suits filed pursuant to complaints of discrimination. In 1993 suits charging discrimination against women were double the number for racial discrimination. The same trend held true for the period 1997–2002, with sex discrimination becoming a clear priority of the litigation effort.

TABLE 5.2   Equal Employment Opportunity Commission Charge Receipts by Basis of Complaint and Fiscal Year (FY)

Basis of Complaint	FY 1983	FY 1993	FY 1994	FY 2001	% Change 1983–2001
Race	48,449	31,695	31,656	28,912	−41
Sex	35,729	23,919	25,680	25,140	−30
National origin	10,793	7,454	7,414	8,025	−26
Religion	2,469	1,449	1,546	2,127	−14
Retaliation	8,785	12,627	14,415	——	+14.2 [2]
EPA	3,131	1,334	1,395	1,251	−61
ADEA	27,669	19,884	19,571	17,405	−38
ADA	——	15,274	18,808	16,470	+1.07 [1]

Sources: "18th Annual Report 1983," U.S. Equal Employment Opportunity Commission, April 1984. Equal Employment Opportunity Commission, Fiscal Year 1994 Annual Report, Table 3, p. 10; race generally represents complaints filed by Blacks. (EPA=Equal Pay Act; ADEA=Age Discrimination in Employment Act; ADA=Americans with Disabilities Act of 1990.)
[1]Reflects the difference between FY 1993 and FY 2001.
[2]Reflects the difference between 1983 and 1994.

TABLE 5.3	Pattern of Litigation in Equal Employment Opportunity Cases Filed by Fiscal Year (FY)					

Basis of Complaint	FY 1983	%	FY 1993	%	FY 2001	%
Title VII	82	60	260	68	269	73
ADEA	33	24	115	30	5	1
EPA	21	15	2	.005	62	17
ADA			3	.007	32	8

Sources: "18th Annual Report, 1983," Equal Employment Opportunity Commission, Washington, D.C., April 1984, Table D, p. 26. "Annual Report, Fiscal Year 1993," James R. Neely, Jr., Deputy General Counsel, Office of the General Counsel, U.S. Equal Employment Opportunity Commission, Washington, D.C., September 30, 1994, Table 5, p. 39. EEOC Litigation Statistics, FY 1992 through FY 2001, The U.S. Equal Employment Opportunity Commission, 2002 (http://www.eeoc.gov/stats/litigation.html).

Most significantly, it will be seen from the data in Table 5.5 thant Blacks lodge the largest number of complaints in only one category, "race," among the original groups of the "protected classes in Title VII of the Civil Rights Act of 1964." In other protected classes, such as sex and religion, as well as the newer categories of ADA, EPA and ADEA, Whites have lodged the largest percentage of complaints to the EEOC in each of these categories in the period 1992–2001. The percentage of retaliation complaints by race are about even between blacks and whites, and Hispanics have brought the majority of the national origin complaints to the EEOC.

TABLE 5.4	Bases of Complaints Alleged in Equal Employment Opportunity Commission Litigation				

Basis of claim	1993	%	1997–2002	%
Age (ADEA)	119	23.2	199	11
Disability (ADA)	3	0.6	311	16
Equal pay (EPA)	16	3.1	40	2
National origin	30	5.9	171	9
Race	72	14.1	328	17
Religion	16	3.1	104	6
Sex	(149)	(29.1)	732	39
Female	141	27.5		
Male	8	1.6		

Source: "Annual Report, Fiscal Year 1993," James R. Neely, Jr., Deputy General Counsel, Office of the General Counsel, U.S. Equal Employment Opportunity Commission, September 1993, Table 6, p. 39. Total number of bases of complaints exceeds the number of suits filed because many suits are filed on multiple bases.

TABLE 5.5 Trends in the Racial Composition of EEOC Discrimination Complaints by Title VII and ADA, EPA, ADEA Categories, 1992–2001 (%)

		1992	1993	1994	1995	1996	1997	1998	1999	2000	2001	Avg.
Title VII Race Receipts												
Race												
	Black	87.9%	87.9%	88.0%	86.0%	85.4%	86.1%	86.2%	86.8%	85.0%	84.9%	0.9%
	White	8.9%	9.0%	8.9%	10.2%	10.8%	9.9%	9.4%	9.7%	9.7%	10.2%	9.6%
	Other	1.9%	2.1%	2.0%	2.8%	2.7%	3.0%	4.7%	4.7%	4.5%	4.1%	3.2%
Title VII Sex Receipts												
Race												
	Black	23.9%	24.2%	24.3%	24.1%	23.8%	25.8%	27.2%	28.2%	27.1%	27.3%	25.6%
	White	63.2%	0.6%	65.2%	64.2%	61.6%	60.4%	56.4%	54.4%	55.7%	55.1%	60.0%
	Other	9.7%	9.5%	8.2%	9.8%	12.4%	11.8%	14.1%	15.0%	14.2%	14.7%	12.0%
Title VII Religion Receipts												
Race												
	Black	28.6%	29.6%	30.3%	30.4%	29.0%	31.9%	32.7%	32.4%	34.9%	34.0%	31.6%
	White	52.8%	51.9%	53.0%	52.5%	52.5%	48.1%	43.4%	44.4%	44.3%	44.3%	48.3%
	Other	15.1%	14.8%	12.9%	13.1%	15.0%	16.6%	20.5%	20.9%	16.4%	19.1%	16.7%
Title VII Retaliation Receipts												
Race												
	Black	45.2%	42.6%	42.5%	41.1%	39.1%	40.4%	44.4%	44.7%	42.9%	42.4%	42.5%
	White	41.8%	45.2%	46.0%	46.5%	46.1%	45.1%	39.5%	38.1%	39.9%	41.2%	42.6%
	Other	9.9%	9.7%	8.8%	10.1%	12.7%	12.2%	14.2%	15.2%	14.4%	14.1%	12.5%

Title VII National Origin Receipts

National Origin											
East Indian	3.7%	4.2%	4.0%	3.9%	3.7%	3.8%	3.3%	3.8%	3.2%	3.2%	3.7%
Hispanic	45.7%	46.7%	45.8%	45.3%	43.3%	42.9%	41.4%	41.7%	43.3%	41.9%	43.8%
Mexican	14.9%	15.6%	14.7%	12.9%	12.5%	11.9%	12.4%	13.9%	14.7%	15.2%	13.9%
Other National Origin	46.8%	47.1%	48.4%	49.8%	51.7%	52.6%	53.9%	53.1%	50.7%	51.3%	50.5%

ADA Race Receipts

Race											
Black	19.6%	17.1%	18.4%	18.1%	18.4%	19.6%	20.3%	22.4%	21.8%	21.4%	19.7%
White	70.6%	69.2%	70.8%	69.2%	68.3%	66.6%	64.6%	61.2%	63.4%	64.0%	66.4%
Other	7.3%	10.3%	8.8%	10.9%	11.0%	11.3%	12.4%	13.9%	12.3%	12.1%	11.4%

EPA Race Receipts

Race											
Black	13.9%	13.6%	16.3%	16.5%	14.6%	16.7%	20.6%	19.2%	21.8%	18.6%	17.1%
White	67.0%	74.8%	73.5%	72.8%	71.5%	67.3%	64.5%	64.3%	60.7%	67.5%	68.5%
Other	12.8%	8.9%	8.1%	8.9%	12.4%	9.9%	11.6%	13.7%	14.2%	11.0%	11.1%

ADEA Race Receipts

Race											
Black	12.5%	13.6%	14.1%	14.9%	14.9%	16.9%	18.6%	19.7%	21.4%	18.8%	16.3%
White	67.7%	70.2%	72.9%	72.3%	67.8%	68.3%	64.7%	61.8%	60.2%	65.7%	67.4%
Other	15.2%	12.0%	9.9%	10.5%	15.0%	12.6%	13.5%	15.9%	14.9%	13.1%	13.1%

Source: "EEOC Trends: Title VII and ADA, EPA, and ADEA Receipts," National Aggregate Data, Fiscal Years 1992–2001, EEOC National Data Base, Office of Research, Information and Planning, U.S. Employment Opportunity Commission, September 2002.

In any case, if one applies the percentages of the number of complaints by race in each category to the number of actual complaints received, it is clear that the vast majority of complaints overall are being made by Whites. *Thus the general American public, predominantly White, is using this mechanism of amelioration.* Indeed, now that the law has allowed the disabled and aged to maintain a protected place in the workforce, if it develops that there is a social benefit to expanding their numbers, the law may well be changed to enable them to utilize the mechanism of affirmative action as well.

Another change in the mandate of the EEOC that affects a group other than Blacks has come about with the adoption of greater federal responsibility for ensuring fairness in the workplace for Native Americans. This issue used to be handled exclusively by the Bureau of Indian Affairs in the Department of the Interior, but as part of its strategic planning, the EEOC presented to Congress in 2000 its "Strategic Objective 1.3." This proposal was designed to strengthen partnerships with state and local agencies in the process of enhancing the implementation of employment discrimination statutes. In many states Native Americans have an autonomous profile of responsibility for tribal affairs, and a co-dependent relationship between tribal governments and state government has evolved in many arenas. Through measures outlined in "Strategic Objective 1.3," the EEOC would train 93 Federal Employment Practice Associates (FEPAs) and 61 Tribal Employment Rights Organizations (TEROs) in interactive techniques to enforce local and federal statutes.[59]

Finally, it is an acknowledged fact among researchers on affirmative action that White women have been its major beneficiary.[60] *If one theorizes that most White women marry White men, then it will be understood that the White family has been the major beneficiary of civil rights laws. Moreover, White males are some of the major beneficiaries of the direction that the EEOC has taken in the fields of ADA and ADEA. This marks the EEOC transition as distinctly not a racial preserve, but an American project that any mature society needs as a mechanism to correct social distortions flowing from the misuse of power.*

THE FUTURE OF AFFIRMATIVE ACTION

Continuing the Beneficial Effect

One argument for continuing current equal rights programs, especially affirmative action, is that they have worked. Opponents of affirmative action have suggested that since it has not substantially affected the poverty rate of Blacks and other minorities, it should be eliminated. However, the data show that in 1964, the labor force participation rate for women was 30%, and women's earnings were considerably less than two-thirds of men's. Yet by 1977, women had gained a striking ten million more jobs, and between 1988 and 1993, White women procured two million new professional and managerial jobs. Indeed, between 1970 and 1993, women's labor force participation increased by 15%, twice as much as Blacks, five times as much as Hispanics and twenty times more than White males.[61] By 1993 women had become 46% of the labor force, earning nearly three-quarters of what men earned, and they represented 42% of all managers and professionals.[62]

Though African Americans have not risen in the employment ranks as fast as women, they have made progress. Achievements by both groups were assisted by affirmative action, but it was not the sole cause. In 1960 the Black middle class represented 5% of all Black families, but this number increased to 35% in 1995. This increase was fueled in part by enhanced Black access to higher education. In 1970, 23% of Blacks were enrolled in colleges and universities, and this number increased to 33% by 1993. They comprised 8% of all college and university graduates in 1980 and 13% in 1994. This led to a growth in average Black income between 1979 and 1993 of $3,500. (During that same period, however, income for married couples—Black as well as White—declined.[63])

It should be further underscored that affirmative action has been beneficial for America because it has provided what was intended—a fairer representation of all Americans in the workplace, in ownership and in all occupational categories. The notion that affirmative action is deleterious to employers has no basis in fact. To the contrary: the record shows that firms participating in affirmative action programs have demonstrated stronger economic viability. Perhaps this is why George Bush's support for the elimination of affirmative action ran into vigorous corporate opposition.

CONCLUSION

The Continuing Need for Civil Rights Measures

Affirmative action and other civil rights mechanisms are needed to keep America viable as it faces a future of increased racial diversity and enhanced interaction with the international system. The clock will not turn back. Minorities and women have made substantial progress, yet at the end of the twentieth century, there are barely 1.5 million African Americans in American universities and colleges poised to take their rightful places as qualified professionals at all levels of society.

Substantial racism is still manifest in many areas of American life, whether its targets are African Americans of upper, middle or lower income. A new civil rights movement is required to eliminate racist acts that have the effect of restricting opportunities for Blacks and other members of the protected classes. More attention must be paid to the behavior of corporations—to their employment practices, certainly, but also to their control over image-making, environmental quality and other key features of American life. The struggle for fair access, dignified treatment and fair distribution of corporate products are central elements of the new civil rights movement.

The Moral Argument

Civil rights are still needed because *racial discrimination is still practiced, it is still wrong and it is right to eliminate it.* By any measure, racial discrimination in America is still practiced disproportionately upon Black citizens and with an intensity that begs relief by some effective regime. It is not the moral responsibility of Blacks to eradicate racial discrimination, though it is their responsibility to assist those who have the power to do so.

It has been a project of White Nationalists to rid themselves of responsibility for the continuing modern racial burden that is the legacy of slavery. However, this is a futile project, for the history of slavery in America cannot be expunged, nor its effects ignored forever. Suggesting that Whites bear the burden of eliminating racism throughout society, not just in the economic arena, Thomas McCullough recites the story of Wendell Berry, a White Kentucky farmer whose acknowledgment of the evils of slavery created a "hidden wound of racism" in his spirit.[64] Perhaps the experience of Wendell Berry is not unique.

Opponents of various aspects of civil rights law have misappropriated the words of Martin Luther King, Jr., to declare that special treatment for certain people is in itself immoral. They cite King's expressed hopes for a future when character rather than race would be the predicate upon which Blacks are judged. King's words have been twisted to suggest that he proposed there should be no changes in the social, economic and political environment and the distribution of personal resources. In his speech that was the highlight of the 1963 March on Washington, King specifically noted that the marchers had come together to cash a check—but the check was marked "insufficient funds." He spoke of an unrealized future, and in the view of most Black citizens, that condition continues to prevail.

Study after study shows that Blacks are still socially, economically and politically constrained today, even with respect to employment. For example, in the 1990s Donald Tomaskovic-Devy examined patterns of racial opportunity in manufacturing and found that "black employees seem to be more closely supervised than white employees not only because of the characteristics of the jobs they hold but because they are black."[65] He also pointed out that with respect to employment in general: "Black males and females have very high unemployment rates, reflected in their exclusion from many jobs. This is clearly an important indication of black exclusion and white opportunity."[66] This condition must be remedied, for it is immoral to sustain it.

When the decision in *Brown v. Board of Education* was handed down by the Supreme Court in 1954, most Americans objected to it. When Title VII was passed, most Americans were nervous that this would mean the widespread implementation of quotas. Successive presidents have used executive orders to bring about a regime of equal opportunities for minorities and women in employment and federal contracting, because such measures would not have been supported in a popular referendum. In light of the historical evidence that special measures have been necessary, those who would leave the fortunes of Blacks and other disadvantaged groups to the vagaries of either the impersonal economic market or raw public opinion must ask whether these are likely to produce an equal opportunity structure in America.

In opposing the Civil Rights Act of 1991, Senate Conservatives asked a set of questions regarding the direction of fairness policies:

> What kind of society do we want to establish? Is it one free of bias, that guarantees equal opportunity for all, that penalizes those who discriminate on the basis of race, sex, ethnicity, age, or disability, that ensures equal opportunity so that one is free to rise or fall based on one's own experience, abilities, and merit? Or is it one that has created a convoluted, tortured, and often contradictory legal system which requires every job in America to match perfectly the numerical mix of the surrounding relevant labor pool, one in which one's rights depend on the group to which he belongs, one in which every employment policy is governed by numerical quotas?[67]

It is instructive to note the Conservative emphasis on the provision of "opportunity" as the only responsibility of a program of government rights.

This issue has been confronted in modern times by those who understand that in a society where the targets of racism are minorities severely deprived of resources, the mere provision of an opportunity to compete for public bounty is insufficient. One of the best answers to the question of opportunity that I have found is in a Supreme Court opinion written by Justice Potter Stewart in a 1968 housing discrimination case. Stewart wrote: "At the very least, the freedom that Congress is empowered to secure under the Thirteenth Amendment includes the freedom [for a black person] to buy whatever a white man can buy, the right to live wherever a white man can live. If Congress cannot say that being a free man means at least this much, then the Thirteenth Amendment made a promise the Nation cannot keep."[68]

The Attack on the Black Poor

INTRODUCTION:
WELFARE ELIMINATION

I did not begin this section on welfare with the word "reform" because I have concluded that the objective of the Conservative movement where welfare is concerned has been less reform than elimination. The true intent has not been to remove people from poverty—the real, but ignored issue in the welfare debate—but to end government assistance to them, and this implies a moralistic and racist attitude that is consistent with the overall objectives of the White Nationalist movement.

In the mid-1990s, the values of a majority of the American people, as expressed in their attitude toward "welfare," were being driven by powerful emotions. Emotions, rather than empirical evidence, determined government welfare policy. In the context of declining national economic opportunities, poverty was linked to race, and the result was an attempt at "reform" with a distinctively punitive character. The clamor over the welfare system became a public priority, as illustrated by the fact that Bill Clinton made welfare reform one of the tenets of his 1992 presidential campaign. After he took office, he expressed the view that the failure of the welfare system was "perhaps the most pressing social problem we face in our country."[1] Such remarks by the president of the United States lent important credibility to the heightened priority of this issue on the public agenda.

In the formal sense, the welfare system was established to address the issue of persistent poverty. The 1980 census officially classified 29.6 million people as poor, signifying a national poverty rate of 13.2%; this included 10% of the White population (20 million people), 32% of the Black population (8.5 million) and 26% of the Hispanic population (3.5 million).[2] By 1992, the proportion of people in poverty had grown to 14.5%, or 36 million: 11.6% of Whites (24.5 million) were classified as poor; 33.3% of Blacks (10.6 million); and 29.3% of Hispanics (6.6 million).[3] Over twelve years, 6 million more Americans became part of the poor population, and the national poverty rate grew 1.3%. Though the rates for Blacks and Whites grew proportionally, the Hispanic rate rose 3% beyond its 1980 level. Yet racialization of the explosive growth in the numbers of poor Americans became the basis of "welfare reform" policy, and economic development of the areas in which they live was largely ignored.

Also underlying the notion of "welfare reform" was the view that "work" is not only the antidote to sloth, it is a way of designing a punitive system, the returns from which would be disproportionally distributed to Whites. In the tradition of Southern Conservatism, work is related to the institution of slavery, which existed as a means of exerting social control over Blacks. George Frederickson observed that "field work on plantations and domestic service were slave occupations that no white person could perform, even for wages, without losing caste."[4] As Professor Ira Berlin remarked, such labor was known as "nigger work."[5]

Work has always been an important element in defining social status. In Japan, for instance, the Barakumin were ethnically the same as the rest of the population, but they were assigned a lower status consistent with their occupations. The same might be said for Indian untouchables and similar classes in other societies. In America as well, work is related to caste and, historically, to the status and self-esteem of White southerners, even those who did not own slaves. So the popular stereotype of Blacks as welfare recipients bolstered the self-esteem of those Whites who have always considered themselves better than Blacks, not only because they work but because Blacks worked for their ancestors.

White Nationalists have acted on the presumption that Blacks get a disproportionate share of government resources even as they indulge in immoral behavior—from teenage pregnancy to sloth. White Nationalists also believe there is widespread corruption in the distribution of these resources, and this corruption is symbolized by "the welfare queen."[6] Their goal is to reduce the government's economic support of Blacks and to achieve this through many avenues, including the elimination of job training and urban development programs and, of course, abolishing the welfare system.

This attitude has translated into public policies which have politicized not only the welfare system, but also the very concept of society's collective responsibility to care for the less fortunate among us, regardless of their race. Through this process, White Nationalists have accomplished a historic feat: the elimination of America's responsibility for the poor, a disproportionate number of whom are Black. The central issues in this chapter are the differential ways in which Black and White dependency are managed, and the impact on welfare policy of White Nationalists' hostility toward Black dependency.

POVERTY AND DEPENDENCY

White Dependency

The economy of twentieth-century Britain was devastated by two world wars, and the resulting poverty led the central government to take a strong role in reconstructing society. One manifestation of this was the adoption of recommendations in a report drawn up by the eminent economist William Beveridge, which called on the government to insure a minimum income to every citizen.[7] Thus in Britain, and in other European countries as well, by the middle of the twentieth century support for the poor became accepted as a duty of the state. Yet in the United States this idea continued to be rejected, and negative attitudes toward the poor became institutionalized within the system of public assistance known as "welfare"—particularly within the Aid to Families with Dependent Children program (AFDC), whose rolls have historically been dominated by Whites.

In the 1930s, Franklin Roosevelt sought alternatives to widespread relief spending as a means of pulling the nation out of the Great Depression. Reluctantly, he turned to a series of programs such as the Works Progress Administration and the Civilian Conservation Corps. His cautionary attitude toward state involvement in assisting the poor is evident in a speech he gave in January 1935, in which he said: "continued dependence upon government . . . induces a spiritual and moral disintegration fundamentally destructive to the national fibre. To dole out relief in this way is to administer a narcotic, a subtle destroyer of the human spirit. . . . [The federal government] must quit this business of relief."[8] Even though Roosevelt implicitly acknowledged that the capitalist system could not provide economic security to all classes of Americans, he evinced the traditional upper-class aversion to the idea of the state permanently assuming responsibility for this. Indeed, the assistance programs of this era were developed largely as alternatives to permanent government relief programs.

Nevertheless, by 1935 Roosevelt was moving toward the establishment of a systematic approach to dealing with the problem of public welfare. That year he promulgated the Social Security Act, which promised assistance to the elderly poor, the blind and dependent children. Yet even these limited populations were not fully served. Localities, still operating under the old value system, imposed harsh parameters governing their approach to assisting dependent families. They disallowed aid to the children of mothers with criminal records or with modest amounts of property and set up standards of "suitable homes"; as a result, many poor and minority Americans were disqualified from receiving assistance.

In the 1940s and 1950s, urban Whites became less dependent on government assistance programs. First wartime employment and then the booming postwar economy made many Whites more affluent and thus not in need of welfare assistance. Essentially, their color, ethnicity and skills bestowed on them high preferences in employment and other areas of social life. White immigrants continued to develop separate communities, to which they transferred many social institutions and resources from their countries of origin, and which served as bases of their upward mobility. Their ties to official political power were enhanced as they came to control the politics of their communities through ethnically dominated political machines. And some who were unable to negotiate the legal economy found a substantial income and control over legitimate commercial activity through participation in organized criminal activity.[9]

The combined impact of government war spending and the rising postwar economy appeared to confirm the belief of politicians and Keynesian economists that "full employment" would lower poverty to an "acceptable level." Yet between 1940 and 1962, the welfare caseload rose dramatically, from 700,000 to 3 million.[10] Michael Harrington noted in *The Other America* that the face of poverty had changed.[11] With intact White families becoming more affluent, welfare primarily served such groups as the elderly, female-headed households and minorities. But it was the minorities—especially Blacks—who attracted the most attention, as a debate began over the characteristics of poor inner-city children and their families.[12] Even though 60% of the welfare caseload was White by the 1990s, class bias was not powerful enough to stimulate wholesale welfare reform.

Stereotypical attitudes toward Blacks obscure the problem of poverty, the generator of candidates for welfare. Although job growth in America was relatively strong in the mid-1990s, the record of the previous two decades shows that fewer Americans overall were being lifted out of poverty, for the economy produced fewer higher-wage jobs and a greater number of low-paying jobs. Indeed, as William Gorham suggested, "[m]uch of the decline in poverty since the mid-1960s resulted from increased transfers to the elderly, a pattern that has come to an end."[13] Since the combination of work and welfare now replaces transfer payments, the result will only affect the poverty rate if employment is available for those who need it. However, the fact that the welfare rolls contain a significant number of historically dependent Blacks demonstrates government's abrogation of its responsibility to combat poverty. The attendant consequences of greater social instability loom large, for a substantial portion of the population has not benefited from the economic system.

Throughout the history of the American democratic experiment, systemic aspects of business cycles combined with economic racism have deepened poverty, and the government has attempted to mitigate poverty's most pernicious social impacts. However, in practice, it has often done a better job of creating support for poor White families than for Blacks. Whites have had access to a panoply of preferences, including Social Security, the GI bill, the National Defense Education Act, employment and higher education, and substantial preferences in access to capital for homes and business formation. These have had the effect of lifting millions of Whites out of poverty and into affluence.

Black Dependency

White Nationalists have mythologized the sources of Black poverty, yet it is clear that the enslavement of African Americans established the basis of a dependent population in the United States. Slavery not only impoverished Blacks, it distorted and corrupted the structure of the Black family. In a survey of 612 Black families in rural Georgia in the 1930s, Black sociologist Charles Johnson found vivid evidence of communal disorganization: 29% of all children were illegitimate, and 25% of families were headed by a female; though an additional 37% of families were headed by married couples, the rest were common-law households. Johnson noted that "sex, as such, appears to be a thing apart from marriage."[14] This is comparable to the function of sex in the slave system, where it was mostly "a thing apart from marriage"—a practice permitted by slave masters.

The heritage of slavery—pervasive poverty and family disorganiza-tion—was not confined to the rural South. It also impacted the urban Black community, as demonstrated in W. E. B. Du Bois's study, *The Philadelphia Negro.* Du Bois asserted that traditional African family prac-tices were shattered by the institution of slavery, which fostered a depen-dent family structure.[15] He went even farther back in history, illustrating the attitudes of early eighteenth-century Whites toward Blacks by citing a 1726 Philadelphia ordinance. Declaring that "free Negroes are an idle and slothful people and often prove burdensome to the neighborhood and afford ill examples to other Negroes," the ordinance required slave owners to give £30 to the county for each slave they freed, to indemnify it for their care.[16] The fact that this sum went to the county rather than to individual Blacks created a legacy of social dependency, as Du Bois observed: "Emancipation and pauperism must ever go hand in hand; when a group of persons have been for generations prohibited from self-support and self-initiative in any line, there is bound to be a large num-ber of them who, when thrown upon their own resources, will be found incapable of competing in the race of life."[17]

The rapid influx of rural southern Blacks to the urban North in the twentieth century spread the legacy of slavery into new regions. Demog-rapher Philip Hauser traced this movement through five decades: from 1910 to 1920, 454,300 people; 1920 to 1930, 740,000; 1930 to 1940, 347,500; 1940 to 1950, 1,244,700; and 1950 to 1960, 1,457,000.[18] He argued that this migration "poured so large a Negro population into the . . . large cities over so short a period of time that it made the in-migra-tory Negro stream relatively inassimilable—economically, politically and socially." Moreover, Hauser determined that in 1962, 72% of urban "Negro families" qualified for food assistance programs.[19]

Similarly to Du Bois, Hauser located the problem of endemic poverty in the institution of slavery, which denied many Blacks the oppor-tunity to adopt a middle-class family lifestyle. However, he suggested that its most devastating impact was on the Black male, who, both within the slave system and thereafter, was unable "because of the lack of opportu-nity and discriminatory practices, to assume the role of provider and pro-tector of his family in accordance with prevailing definitions of the role of husband and father."[20] Because of substantial damage to "normative" Blacks and consequently to their families and social structure, they have been relatively more dependent upon the state.

With reference to the Black family, the eminent sociologist E. Franklin Frazier suggested that the reason many observers are puzzled by the persistence of the high Black "illegitimacy" rate is because they do not take into account an elementary fact: "[T]he constant flow of simple peasant folks from rural districts to the poverty and disorganization of city slums constantly re-creates the problem of unmarried motherhood."[21] Frazier identified other factors that contributed to problems in Black urban families, arguing that families became destablized as a result of attempting to cope with racially segregated neighborhoods and discriminatory treatment in accessing social services. He called attention to "pressures on breadwinners to travel long distances to and from work; the necessity of wives to supplement the family wage, leaving children unattended; the diminished influence of religious institutions; and the lack of adequate facilities and services such as housing and education." The result, he held, was "high rates of family disorganization, youth delinquency, crime, ill health, low educational attainment and overcrowded housing."[22]

Blacks found that poverty was substantially more difficult to cope with in northern cities. In the South, Blacks were often able to produce food to sustain themselves, and their familiarity with the relatively simple social structure made it easier to avoid pitfalls. In the North, however, there was a much more complex alignment of social relations. Having to deal with many different ethnic groups and their turf, the unwritten laws of the industrial workplace, a politically complicated city and persistent police surveillance made life exceeding harsh. Poverty and dependency were often the result of a failure to maneuver through this environment successfully.

The notion promulgated by Beveridge and others—that all citizens are entitled to a minimum level of government support—did not take root in America because of the existing racial hierarchy, which imposed upon Blacks an exclusionary "internal colonial" status. Blacks were subject to a variety of local, state and national laws that subordinated the status of their labor and constricted their social lives within strictly segregated boundaries. And where legal segregation was not the rule, informal patterns of segregation separated Black communities from White ones and excluded Blacks from participation in social, economic and political institutions.

The Early Policy Response

As Blacks began to agitate for greater access to services in the 1960s, the notion of a "welfare crisis" evolved, accompanied by an increasingly deprecatory public attitude toward Blacks. In the South, many Blacks were unable to establish a successful claim to public assistance, but the number of northern Blacks receiving public assistance grew significantly. In fact, the increase of Blacks on northern welfare rolls occurred in part because of southern governments' policies designed to keep them off theirs; indeed, the Welfare Advisory Committee of the Department of Health, Education and Welfare observed that "millions legally entitled to benefits were denied them."[23]

In 1960, welfare rolls in Louisiana—which had a 35% Black population—were shown to include a significant number of Blacks. In response, the state legislature ended welfare benefits to 23,500 children—a disproportionate number of whom were Black—whose mothers had given birth to an illegitimate child since entering the program.[24] Such responses became more pervasive as welfare became more and more identified with the Black poor.

This identification was enhanced by the emergence of the National Welfare Rights Organization (NWRO) in the late 1960s. Led by George Wiley, an outspoken, militant Black who had been on the faculty at Syracuse University, NWRO comprised a group of national chapters led by welfare mothers. The organization not only demanded a guaranteed income, it insisted that the current welfare system, far from assisting Black families, maintained Blacks in near-serfdom and had to be changed. Wiley carried his basic demands to the White House Conference on Civil Rights on November 17, 1965,[25] yet many of NWRO's proposals for radical reforms had no chance of success in the face of the growing racial backlash. To White Nationalists, the antidote for dependency has always been sanctions, either elimination from public support or some other form of punishment.

Perhaps the critical point in the nation's changing attitude toward the Black welfare population was reflected in the policy assault upon the system that began in the late 1960s, when the welfare system became linked to militant Black demands for an adequate level of financial support. Although Lyndon Johnson was known as a champion of civil rights, on January 2, 1968, he signed into law a welfare measure supported by Rep. Wilbur Mills (D-Ark.), then head of the House Ways and Means Committee. This legislation froze welfare payments, halted program expansion and required work and job training for mothers with children who were older than 16 years old and no longer in school.[26] On the House floor, Mills referred to Black welfare recipients as "brood mares"— a flagrant example of the new negative bias. Sen. Robert Kennedy (D-N.Y.) described this bill as "the most punitive measure in the history of the country." And though its enactment gave impetus to the "Poor People's Campaign" launched by Martin Luther King, Jr., the Civil Rights movement never developed a strong role in the struggle against poverty, largely because of his assassination.

Rather than encouraging the idea of a welfare system that would be more supportive of Black families, some politicians demanded that mothers be made to work in return for receiving welfare benefits. Indeed, in a 1966 telecast while he was governor of California, Ronald Reagan played upon the theme of the "undeserving poor," arguing for a work requirement for all able-bodied welfare recipients in his state.[27] By the end of the 1960s, the fact that welfare rolls were nearly 40% Black, together with the high visibility of the Civil Rights movement, translated many anti-Black attitudes into anti-welfare attitudes as well.[28] The Black poor became "Nigger bums," welfare mothers became "welfare queens," Blacks' automobiles became "welfare Cadillacs," and so on.

One of the reasons for the persistence of this attitude is that Blacks have been a substantial part of the long-term welfare population. Although historically most recipients utilized welfare assistance for only a few years, Blacks were more likely to use it for longer periods. A 1982 study found that 48% of the welfare population was short-term, 34% medium-term and 18% long-term. Of the long-term users, Blacks were disproportionately represented at 55%.[29] Another study indicated that in 1990, 43% of long-term recipients were Black, a smaller percentage than eight years earlier, yet still a significant one.[30]

Worsening Public Attitudes

Conservatives began to believe in the urgency of welfare reform in the decade between 1965 and 1975, when the number of AFDC recipients mushroomed into what some observers called a "boom": from 4.4 million in 1965 to 11.4 million in 1975.[31] These additions occurred mainly in northern urban areas, where liberal policies of eligibility accompanied an expansion of the Black population and the impact of the Civil Rights movement. In a 1978 publication, Dorothy Newman remarked that "[t]he public perception has been that idle black welfare recipients lived on Easy Street, despite the fact that in the only terms that count— money—welfare took only a little over 10 percent of the black house-holds . . . out of poverty, but two times as many of the whites."[32]

In the minds of many White Americans, welfare faced a "crisis." Yet Professor James Jennings, who evaluated public opinion data from the 1970s, suggested that the notion of a "crisis" in social welfare was created by a few vocal leaders (such as Ronald Reagan and others in the Conservative movement).[33] Jennings also argued that Reagan's concept of "New Federalism" was based on the idea that the existence of poverty was not caused by a flaw in the economic system, nor a flaw in preparing people to become involved in economic activity, but a flaw in people themselves: "cultural and human flaws such as dependency and the lack of motivation."[34]

Indeed, the Reagan administration mounted a major attack on the welfare system. Reagan's welfare recommendations were designed to reduce dependency, decrease errors and abuse in welfare eligibility, eliminate fraud and waste, tighten "workfare" requirements, constrain stepparents to assume more responsibility for children, increase absent fathers' responsibility for child support, and provide benefits to the "truly needy."[35] Whatever else these measures may have accomplished, the conclusion of a credible group of analysts was that they decreased dependency only slightly.[36]

In the course of promoting his new policies, Reagan routinely referred to female recipients of assistance as "welfare queens." Expressions such as these became more widely employed as the Conservative movement became more prominent, and they constituted one of the keys to the modern origin of negative attitudes toward welfare policies.

With the juxtaposition of race and welfare dependency solidified in the public imagination, there was a return to the concept of the "undeserving poor" and to images of laggard, lazy, dull welfare recipients on the "dole" who deserve the punishment visited upon them because they constitute a drag upon the economy and a blot upon the moral image of the nation. Michael Katz's *Undeserving Poor* illustrates how people on welfare whose only crime, in most cases, was being poor, were invested with immorality and attacked accordingly.[37] Moreover, though this concept used to be employed only by the elite, because of its convenient linkage to racial stereotypes it has been generalized into views held by a significant sector of the White population as a whole. Nevertheless, the linkage is specious. Black families in general are not "overly dependent" upon welfare funding. In 1996, public assistance accounted for only 4% of the total annual income of all Black families and only 15% of the total annual income of families headed by Black women.[38]

Indeed, the stereotype that has driven negative attitudes toward Blacks as intergenerationally dependent upon welfare has been essentially manufactured out of the general racial ethos and can be shown to be largely false. Table 6.1 shows that 66.3% of non-Whites living in households receiving at least one dollar from AFDC between 1980 and 1989 were dependent for less than one year. Further, 81.2% of non-Whites living in households receiving at least 50% total household income from AFDC and food stamps during the same period were dependent for less than one year. The report cited in Table 6.1 also noted that

| **TABLE 6.1** | Long-Term Welfare Dependency by Nonwhite Status, 1980 to 1989, by Two Definitions of Dependency |

	Fraction living in households in which head of household or spouse received at least $1 from AFDC	*Fraction living in households in which at least 50% of total household income was from AFDC and food stamps*
Years on Welfare	*1980 to 1989*	*1980 to 1989*
Less than 1 year	66.3%	81.2%
1 to 2 years	13.8%	7.6%
3 to 7 years	12.6%	7.4%
8 to 10 years	7.2%	3.7%

Source: "Overview of Entitlement Programs," 1993 Green Book, Committee on Ways and Means, U.S. House of Representatives, July 7, 1993, Table 44, p. 720.

the majority of women—both Black and White—who became highly dependent on welfare had parents who were never enrolled in government assistance programs.[39] Thus most non-Whites who were welfare dependent did not exhibit a pattern of intergenerational dependency.

In 1992 Thomas and Mary Edsall presented a view which has now become standard: White attitudes toward welfare helped fuse the issues of race and taxes. This was central to the development of the policy logic of the Conservative movement and to the Nationalist element which wanted to limit resources to racial minorities and elevate their own resources through tax cuts. The passage of Proposition 13 in California in 1978 was the leading edge of this sentiment. It was also reflected in public opinion polls taken between July 1977 and November 1979 that expressed emphatic support for reducing public expenditures for welfare and, to a lesser extent, for public housing.[40] Since that time, terms such as "taxpayers" and "hard-working Americans" have become euphemisms for Whites. They serve as code words for the feeling that non-White groups have consumed Whites' taxes unfairly through the largesse of a federal government that has not demanded accountability in return.

The public image of the AFDC recipient is of the Black welfare cheat: "Say the word 'welfare' and immediately the image of the lazy Black welfare queen who breeds for profit surfaces in the minds of those who have come to believe the hideous stereotype. It is a myth that persists despite government figures and authoritative studies showing that Whites overwhelmingly reap the lion's share of the dole."[41] Joe Feagin confirmed the existence of this point of view through a study of racial attitudes and welfare in the mid-1970s. His sample of attitudes of ordinary Whites (whom he called the "Average American") about people on welfare produced the most vitriolic combination of negative racial stereotypes, resembling those held toward Blacks as a whole.[42]

Empirical research on the race-welfare linkage led Gerald C. Wright, Jr. to reason as follows: "If white racism is a major factor accounting for why a disproportionate number of blacks are poor, and therefore on welfare, then racism can also reasonably be expected to influence those policies ostensibly aimed at alleviating that poverty. Where the political climate is more favorable toward blacks whether as a result of successful black demands or from racial liberalism among whites—support for welfare is likely to be greater."[43] Wright's research found high negative correlations among variables such as a state's high AFDC payments and low percent Black population and with its lack of civil rights liberality, thus lending great weight to the presumption of a racial dynamic in welfare policy. And his conclusion that in a favorable political climate support for welfare is likely to be greater supports the burden of my argument in this chapter.

Jill Quadagno's work illustrates the symbiosis between the attempt to eliminate financial assistance to the poor and the way in which the welfare system has become racialized, offering a symbolic target for attacks on poor Blacks and Hispanics and the women and children in these cultural groups.[44] Similarly, Martin Gilens, a Yale University political scientist, found in his study of the factors determining Whites' perspectives on welfare that the negative attitudes they hold are related for the most part to their attitudes toward Blacks.[45] Although statistics clearly showed that most of those on AFDC were White, the ideology of White Nationalism ignored this in favor of retaining the stereotype of a Black-dominated welfare system.

In any case, the locus of racialized attitudes toward welfare comports with the fact that policy leadership on this issue has been provided by southern politicians, consistent with our thesis that this group is the source of much American racial animus. There were much higher average levels of Blacks on welfare rolls in the Deep South in 1989 compared to the regional average, as seen in Table 6.2. By comparison, the average rate of AFDC enrollment for Blacks in all states this same year was 40.1%, for Whites it was 38.4%, and for Hispanics it was 15.9%.[46] By mid-1998, however, Whites were leaving the welfare rolls at such a rate that Blacks and Hispanics outnumbered them by 2 to 1, increasing the racializing effect of the problem.

| TABLE 6.2 | AFDC Families by Race, October 1988–September 1989 by Selected Southern States |

State	% Black
Alabama	79.3%
Arkansas	66.7%
District of Columbia	98.7%
Florida	59.5%
Georgia	79.5%
Louisiana	82.9%
Maryland	69.8%
Mississippi	86.5%
North Carolina	71.9%
South Carolina	82.1%
Tennessee	55.4%
Texas	41.5%
Virginia	66.4%
Average	72.3

Source: "Characteristics and Financial Circumstances of AFDC Recipients," Fiscal Year 1989, Aid to Families with Dependent Children Program, Family Support Administration, Office of Family Assistance, U.S. Department of Health and Human Services, Washington, D.C., 1989, Table 10, p. 28.

WELFARE REFORM IN THE '90S

As argued above, the root of Black dependency is the historical legacy of economic deprivation that, when married to the national economic crisis in the 1930s, created a structural condition which originally lent much credence to the establishment of systematic support for the poor. In the 1990s, the structural problem intensified because of the national transition to a service economy and the loss of jobs requiring physical labor. This trend will likely continue, creating additional unemployment and instability, as poor former welfare recipients compete for low-wage jobs with the poor already in the labor force and wage-depression continues as the result of an increasing number of immigrant workers with marketable skills.

In the early '90s, the intersection of Blacks' objective poverty status, negative attitudes toward the poor and negative racial attitudes made for a combustible situation. The projected out-of-control expansion of the welfare system drove the search to eliminate welfare altogether under the guise of "reform." Bill Clinton's January 15, 1994, State of the Union message carried forward a campaign pledge to "change welfare as we know it." His subsequent proposals called for public assistance for two years, after which time recipients must find a job or enroll in a job training program; resources provided for child day care; and confiscating the drivers' licenses of men who were delinquent on their child support. Moreover, in the name of experimentation, he authorized many waivers from the federal AFDC program at the state level. Indeed, by 1995 the Clinton administration's welfare reform proposals had become very similar to those promulgated by Ronald Reagan. Although Republican proposals were somewhat more radical than Clinton's, the political consensus endorsed the short-term utilization of welfare, after which a work requirement would be imposed.

President Clinton believed that the generation of welfare recipients for which he had responsibility were "different" from those for whom the welfare system was originally constructed. The main difference, he suggested, is that whereas the original recipients were poor Whites who used welfare as a transitory program, over the years recipient caseloads gradually cultivated a hard-core group who maintain their poverty status. He proposed, therefore, to liberate them from welfare status by forcing them from "isolation" and into job training and eventually the workforce, in order that they might gain a sense of economic and social independence.

In a speech delivered in February 1997, Clinton asserted:

> I believe that we never intended to create a class of permanently dependent people in our society. . . . [I]t only happened because the welfare system we set up for people who had genuine misfortune— the typical welfare recipient 60 years ago was a West Virginia miner's widow, with no education and no expectation of being in the work force, and children running around the house that had to be cared for, and a society that did not require high levels of education for success.[47]

He contrasted this model with two current types, which he characterized as "[t]hose who use it when they need a little help" and "members of the permanent underclass." This second group he described as "mostly younger women and their young children with little or no education, little or no job experience, little or no ability to move into the work force on a sustained basis."[48] Yet in this speech, President Clinton left several questions unanswered: How can one assume that forcing the second type of family into the workforce will resolve the issue of their economic and social viability if it does not have the support necessary for upward mobility? And, in light of negative racial attitudes, what incentives will make employers hire and maintain Black welfare recipients on an equal basis with other groups?

The underlying premise of the Reagan, Bush and Clinton administrations was that adequate employment opportunities exist and individuals should exercise "personal responsibility" to locate them. This view clings to the misguided belief that the capitalist system can solve the structural problems of an economy which produces a cyclical supply of viable jobs and thus creates instability for poor people. Yet even though the economy as a whole produced 6.5 million new jobs between January 1993 and January 1999, growth in the service economy placed downward pressure on the average family's wage rate, since the average service job yields only about half the wage rate of an industrial job.

The descent into structural poverty in the '90s was more pronounced for African Americans. Historically, two-parent families have performed much better than female-headed households, and between 1980 and 1990, the percentage of Black two-parent families dropped from 48% to 37%, affecting average family income in the process.[49] And the proportion of poor African American children grew from 41% in 1981 to 48% in 1987.[50] In the 1990s, descent into deeper poverty was reversed by the miraculous performance of the economy, which somewhat favored Blacks: they accounted for 60% of the decline in the general poverty level, with their poverty rate decreasing by nearly 2%, from 28.4% to 26.5%.[51] It is unclear whether the historic shift in welfare policy will address the structural features of Black unemployment and poverty through an enforced work regime.

The principal aim of Republicans with regard to welfare reform was to cut $54 billion from the program over six years. A welfare reform measure initiated by 120 House Republican co-sponsors in January of 1995 was passed by the end of the year; the vote in the House was 245 to 178, with 26 Democratic supporters, and the Senate registered a largely party-line vote, 52 to 47. Clinton vetoed this bill, and months of negotiation followed between Congress and the White House. Clinton signed the compromise measure—the Personal Responsibility and Work Opportunity Reconciliation Act (PRWORA)—in August 1996. At the time, he stated his objection to the deep cuts in the food stamp program and to the provision denying benefits to legal immigrants until they had lived in the country for less than five years or attained citizenship, and he vowed to change these in the future. Clinton's efforts on behalf of PRWORA were widely thought to have helped decrease the voter alienation which led to the Democratic defeat in 1994 and insulate Clinton from charges that he was continuing the Liberal policies of former Democratic administrations.

Under PRWORA there is no individual entitlement to government financial support for indigent people beyond a five-year lifetime limit. Administrative authority is devolved to individual states, which may establish eligibility and mandate how it will be provided. PRWORA gives the secretary of Health and Human Services only modest enforcement power, through the use of a range of financial incentives. Part of the old welfare entitlement program was changed to create the Child Care and Development Fund, which consolidates former low-income assistance programs into a block grant to states, giving them considerable flexibility in designing child care programs.[52]

Several Clinton administration officials reacted strongly when the president signed the welfare revision bill. David Ellwood, a welfare expert and former deputy assistant in Health and Human Services who helped develop the administration's original proposal, described the new version as "welfare reform in name only."[53] He pointed out that the bill as enacted provided little assistance for the transition to work. Wendell Primus, the deputy assistant secretary for planning and evaluation, resigned immediately after Clinton signed the bill, asserting: "To remain would be to disown all of the analysis my office has produced regarding the impact of the bill." Primus concluded that the measure would push one million children into poverty.[54] Peter Edelman, then assistant secretary for planning and evaluation for the Department of Health and Human Services—and the husband of Marion Wright Edelman, a prominent child advocate as head of the Children's Defense Fund and a major critic of the welfare bill—also handed in his resignation. He shared Primus's assessment of the negative impact the bill would have, citing both HHS studies and Children's Defense Fund analyses.

Mary Jo Bane, assistant secretary for children and families, also resigned in protest and set forth her rationale:

> All the political and financial incentives are for states to cut assistance, to impose time limits shorter than five years, to meet the work requirements without spending any money, to shift responsibility to local governments and private contractors, and to use the block grant funds for more politically popular programs.
>
> Politics at the state level are not likely to support adequate spending on the very poor, given the freedom and incentives to use the funds more broadly. Competition among the states, I predict, will continue over who can be tougher on welfare. The for-profit firms

bidding to run welfare systems will be driven by cost considerations. There will be little incentive for states to put money into job development, job training or worker support. Freed from the constraints of the federal law and the waiver process, it would be surprising if state legislatures did not enact further restrictions on cash benefits. And Congress is unlikely to overrule state decisions.[55]

Like the other officials who protested the measure, Bane clearly believed that the bill as enacted would do great harm to children. Even if it is possible to take Clinton's motive at face value—that he wanted to break the cycle of dependency of generations of the poor—the credible opinions of this group of professionals was that it would hurt children.

Although one may assign Clinton a somewhat more benign motivation than Conservative Republicans held, the White Nationalists who mobilized a punitive animus toward the African American community appear to have achieved their policy objective. It is clear that this program, heavily weighted as it is on forcing families from government support in a relatively short period of time, does not fully take into account nor respect the complexity of the roots of Black dependency. It would seem that race sanctions, not the empowerment of Black families, represented White Nationalists' primary reason for pursuing welfare reform.

Sanctions exist in PRWORA as the main instrument through which the program's moral aspects are enforced. A potential recipient who does not comply with the program's provisions is eliminated from it. This is tendentious, however, for the morality of the policy is based on specious assumptions having to do with racial stereotypes. For example, a common charge against the AFDC program is that it destroyed the families of those who participated in it. However, longitudinal research by David Ellwood and Mary Jo Bane established as early as 1987 that "welfare simply does not appear to be the underlying cause of the dramatic changes in family structure of the past few decades."[56] But empirical evidence provided by credible experts could not withstand the tide of ideology which became the basis of policy reform.

CONSEQUENCES

The Harm in Racial Stereotypes

Ultimately, racism reduces *all* blacks to "dependency" because, in varying degrees, it subordinates and controls the images of Blacks and their opportunities. Yet today it is fashionable to discuss the socioeconomic condition and value system of what Professor Andrew Billingsley calls "nonworking poor" Black families as though they exist in a vacuum and have no relationship to larger forces in American society.[57] Welfare recipients are judged to prefer dependency on the welfare system to economic viability and thus must be driven to accept the personal responsibility they have formerly shunned.

The policy response has exhibited impatience with the continuing existence of poverty and a frantic desire to force individuals off welfare rolls and into the ranks of the employed. Here, however, one runs into other value conflicts: the loss of free will and the assumption that anyone on public relief loses the right to self-determination; and the availability of "good" jobs on which one can raise a family, as opposed to the mandate to accept any job at the cost of one's dignity. I agree with Bernard Boxill that with respect to the underclass, "an error in philosophy is that reform must always serve the majority interest. This either misunderstands the nature of justice or depreciates its importance. . . . [This notion] is opposed to the spirit and letter of democracy, is elitist and implies an unjustified contempt for the moral powers of the average person."[58] The underlying assumption is that people on welfare are too lazy to find employment, and therefore government must manage the task.

The elevation of *work*—even forced work—to the primary place over other human values raises certain basic questions of human rights. If an individual or family with very little choice to begin with is forced to accept a certain kind of work or the alternative of non-support, that person has little better status than the slave who does not have the free will to choose non-support by the state.

As early as 1994 there was clear evidence of the harm to poor people that ensues from depriving them of public assistance. In 1991, when the economy was still in the doldrums, Governor John Engler of Michigan eliminated 85,000 people from general assistance, and two years later only 38% of them had found productive jobs.[59] This shows that the notion that able-bodied people can find jobs if they look hard enough is unrealistic in a setting where jobs are scarce and where the skills needed to acquire them are not quickly obtainable.

The employment picture improved in the mid- and late 1990s, but in most cases Blacks continued to fare less well than Whites with respect to both employment access and family viability. Nationally, welfare caseloads fell by 19% in 1997; the White House Council of Economic Advisers traced proportions of this decrease to economic growth (41%), a variety of state welfare initiatives as a result of waivers granted (30.9%)

and various other causes (25%).[60] Data collected by the *Washington Post* for 1997 established that in Indiana more than half of the 14,248 welfare cases closed were the result of sanctions; in Tennessee, 40% of cases were closed as the result of sanctions and 29% because former recipients had found work; and Florida officials reported that one-third of their cases closed in the last half of 1997 were due to sanctions.[61]

Welfare rolls continued to diminish in 1998, to the point that caseloads were only 48% of what they were when PRWORA was enacted. The *Washington Post* reported in March of 1998 that as thousands of families were forced off the rolls, the evidence was mounting that large numbers of them were not finding employment.[62] By June of 2000, 66% of the five million families who were on AFDC in 1994 had left the welfare rolls, a dramatic decline of 3.3 million; and whereas 62% of poor children received benefits in 1994, this figure had fallen to 43% six years later.[63]

Push-offs

No one can say to what extent the working poor will be pushed deeper into poverty by the larger pool of low-wage labor that has become available. What can be said is that poor people are being pushed off of assistance, sometimes into jobs and sometimes into the streets. In 1997, for example, federal data showed that in one three-month period, 38% of recipients who left Temporary Assistance to Needy Families (TANF)—a program spawned by PRWORA, and which replaced the Aid to Families with Dependent Children and Jobs Opportunities and Basic Skills Training programs—did so because of sanctions for such infractions as missing appointments or refusing to search for work.[64] Dr. Manning Marable found that in early 1997, 166,000 people in New York City had been pushed off welfare, but only 11,700 found real jobs through the Work Experience Program, another PRWORA plan.[65]

The harsh and unrealistic expectations of the work-oriented program are evident not only in urban areas with tight job markets but also in rural areas such as Appalachia and the Mississippi Delta, where government transfer payments are a main source of income because regular employment is scarce or nonexistent. Lack of child care and public transportation aggravates the ability of people to easily obtain employment. In Mississippi, where 80% of those on welfare rolls are Black, the state government has utilized an aggressive diversion and "push-off" strategy, resulting in the loss of income for thousands and pressure to obtain low-wage jobs. Professor Frank Howell of Mississippi State University indicated in 1997 that although the Delta's poverty rate was 41%, only one new job was developed for every 254 families leaving the rolls in the five-county area surrounding Greenville.[66] In Mississippi a powerful motivating factor for the "push-off" and diversion strategies resides in the belief that poor people fail to assume "personal responsibility" and in the more racially tinged conviction that Blacks must be forced to work, even when no work is in sight.

The situation calls for more vigorous attention to policies that help subsidize work, such as increasing the minimum wage and improving health benefits, child care and transportation benefits for the working poor.[67] The question of what is happening to those who have been pushed off the welfare rolls has not been adequately answered. However, there are indications that many have joined the ranks of the homeless. In 1999 the U.S. Conference of Mayors reported that families with children made up 38% of the homeless population, and a study by Drexel University for the Welfare Reform Watch Project—a Washington, D.C., coalition of faith-based organizations—indicated that the basic needs of the poor were not being met after their welfare funds had been cut off.[68]

These results were unanticipated, even by critics of PRWORA, who expected that serious problems would occur when many current and former recipients reached the five-year limit set by the law but had not yet found work. However, the situation has been exacerbated because many state welfare plans call for more onerous sanctions; Georgia, for example, mandates that welfare benefits are lost for a lifetime if a recipient receives two sanctions. States are invoking immediate or harsh sanctions when recipients fail to comply with various requirements such as enrolling in job training programs, identifying fathers in paternity cases and finding work.

Race and Ethnic Disparities

There have been other consequences of policies based on the ideology of reducing both individual programs and entire government agencies: the loss of human rights through the creation of additional poverty and the disproportionate impact on Black government employees when their positions were eliminated. Moreover, some cities adopted the practice of diverting people from enrollment in TANF by referring clients to jobs, job training or education programs. New York City adopted an aggressive diversion program; whereas previously 53% of applicants for welfare, food stamps and Medicaid were successful, this figure dropped to 25% in the late 1990s under TANF provisions.[69] Indeed, the New York practice was so aggressive that it invited Justice Department scrutiny in the fall of 1998.[70]

In the current context of the implementation of this new policy, the subject of racial and ethnic disparities has drawn some attention because of the rapid pace at which the welfare rolls are becoming more dominated by the poorest clients, who are "harder to serve," more urban and more often people of color. As of 2001, over 3.5 million people had been moved off welfare rolls in a relatively short period of time, and the remaining welfare caseload has become substantially Black and Brown. Whether this disparity has occurred because Whites possess greater skills than people of color, because there is substantial racial discrimination within the process of administering the new TANF regulations, or because of other factors is important to determine.

Studies of welfare leavers paint a picture of people of color who experience greater difficulties in finding initial employment and remaining in their jobs than Whites.[71] The fact that these individuals comprise racial and ethnic groups of color compounds an observation by Professor William J. Wilson: "we do not know what is happening to these people."[72] And the impact of disproportionate low-wage employment on people of color is clear. The figures in Table 6.3 show that while 84% of Whites are in low-wage jobs, 2% fewer are in the low-wage/low-income population and even fewer of them have children. Although Blacks, Hispanics and immigrants comprise a roughly proportionate share of the low-wage workforce compared to their presence in the general population, they are more likely than low-wage Whites to have low-income status and to have children in their families.

TABLE 6.3 Race, Ethnicity, Citizenship and Immigration Status of Low-wage Workers, 1997

Race/Ethnicity	Low-wage	Low-wage, low-income	Low-wage, low-income, with children	All
White	83.9%	81.6%	75.2%	73.3%
Black	13.8%	20.2%	22.7%	11.5%
Hispanic	15.7%	22.7%	27.9%	10.1%
Foreign born	14.8%	20.6%	23.4%	11.5%
Noncitizens	11.1%	16.7%	19.2%	7.1%

Source: Gregory Acs, "A Profile of Low-Wage Workers," Urban Institute, Table 11. Statistics developed by the Urban Institute from March 1998 Current Population Survey of 1997 data.

Following the enactment of PRWORA, there was an expansion of low-wage employment. And the Economic Policy Institute found that although overall poverty lessened afterward, it "deepened for those who remain poor and has increased among working families"; the institute also determined that families now face greater hardships in moving from welfare to work.[73] In addition, researchers at the Center for Law and Social Policy highlighted the crisis for low-income parents who try to balance the competing demands of jobs and parenting, particularly because when these parents enter the workforce they have less outside support than more affluent citizens.[74] This problem was most critical with respect to health: 41% of mothers who had been on welfare for two years or less had children with chronic health and development conditions that needed attention, compared to 21% of mothers who had never been on welfare.[75]

According to the monitoring project of the Children's Defense Fund, as a result of TANF the problems of the working poor are likely to increase with the reduction in welfare rolls, particularly for people of color, who are disproportionately represented in the "hard to serve" group.[76] Indeed, with respect to health care coverage, the CDF noted that "racial and ethnic disparities in coverage persist: children of color are more likely to be uninsured"; moreover, "children in immigrant families are particularly likely to lack health coverage and access to health care."[77]

One important question is whether barriers to employment and long-term viability for families and individuals of color are related to the traditional barriers they experience because of race or ethnicity—obstacles which challenge Americans of color of every class. In recent history, race and ethnicity have been especially implicated in the dramatic changes in the welfare system.[78] Clearly there is a connection between issues of race and class as they exist traditionally in society and the changes that have occurred in the system of support for low-income Black families.

Without doubt, negative racial stereotypes have played a role in the virulence of the implementation of TANF in various states. Professor Susan Gooden's research on the movement from welfare to work in Virginia revealed that at every step in the transition process—caseworker information, employment training, hiring, firing, employee mentoring and so on—Blacks were treated more negatively than Whites.[79] Her research was confirmed by a survey of W-2 clients in Wisconsin by Dr. Michael Bond, who found that with respect to such factors as the administration of employment pretests, information provided by caseworkers and the provision of readiness skills, there were substantial disparities in the treatment of Blacks and Whites.[80]

A similar study was carried out by Gary Delgado and his associates at the Applied Research Center, who surveyed 1,500 subjects in 14 cities. Along with other negative aspects of TANF implementation, their survey found that aggressive patterns of diversion of people of color existed in a pattern Delgado calls "racializing" the welfare process in the TANF transition phase.[81] Another study, performed by Joe Soss, Sanford Schram, Thomas Vartanian and Erin O'Brien, found that: "As the black percentage of recipients rises from low to high, the probability of strong sanctions increases from .05 to .27, the probability of strict time limits shifts from .14 to .66, and the probability of a family cap climbs from .09 to .75. The estimated effects of having more Latinos on the rolls are similarly large, lifting the probability of strict time limits from .22 to .61 and boosting the probability of a family cap from .19 to .63."[82] While this study does not explore the reasons for the differential, it underscores the existence of a racial effect that calls for a causative explanation. All these studies implicate the dynamic response to race in the administration of TANF, which supports my assertion that race is a primary political motivation of those who initiated the program.

The situation grows increasingly grim with the realization that cities containing heavily Black populations of TANF recipients are among those with a substantial number of people reaching the five-year lifetime limit for government support. For example, officials in Washington, D.C., estimated that beginning in the fall of 2002, 2,700 of the 16,000 households receiving welfare would begin to have a portion of their benefits cut and that an additional 2,300 families would be released from support altogether.[83] Recognition of this led the city to prepare a government employment program for those who would be unable to find jobs in the private sector. Six months later, according to a newspaper account, despite the deployment of private vendors to provide employment training, "the overwhelming majority" of welfare recipients had refused to comply with the accountability aspects of the program and thus faced elimination of their status.[84]

States such as Iowa have found that in order to create the conditions that will make the transition from welfare to work more effective, greater financial resources had to be expended in the early years.[85] In Connecticut and New York, where the transition is swift, some welfare recipients who enrolled in educational programs faced the loss of benefits, thus defeating the long-term aims of reform in order to achieve short-term declines in the welfare rolls. Lawrence Mead, a Conservative expert on welfare reform, analyzed data from the Wisconsin welfare-to-work program and found that "the way to affect such change is not by cutting welfare bureaucracies, but by beefing them up substantially" to deliver the range of required services that promote effective work-related information and skill development.[86]

Two Brookings Institution analysts went even further in proposing how to make welfare reform more effective. John DiIulio and Donald Kettle maintained that "every relevant study indicates that nationally initiated contract-style welfare reforms can be achieved only where significant resource increases are made in government bureaucracies that administer new programs."[87] Two social scientists from opposite sides of the ideological spectrum, Nobel Prize-winning MIT economist Robert M. Solow and James Q. Wilson, a leading political scientist at UCLA, agree with this view. They argue that effective approaches to poverty may well entail devoting more resources to its amelioration, but these resources should be spent more wisely than under previous social programs.[88]

Low-Wage Jobs

There is presently a consensus that people with the highest skill levels have left the welfare rolls. This leaves the "hard-core" welfare recipients, who must obtain employment within two years of first receiving assistance through TANF but have few jobs skills, and lack both orientation to long-term employment and accessibility to areas where there are jobs. William Julius Wilson's research on the dearth of jobs in the inner city indicates that even Black employers recognize the challenge of finding employment for those who have not had consistent employment opportunities or experience.[89] Wilson and other experts suggest that cutting resources devoted to job training and child care will only deepen joblessness and poverty, preventing the transition from welfare to work that is the purported goal of the new TANF system.

The Manpower Research Demonstration Project supports the conclusion that without such resources, the best that can happen to the very poor is that they will be elevated to the ranks of the "working poor."[90] In 1997, the number of new jobs grew by a net 3.2 million, yet data show that wage growth did not match that which occurred between 1985 and 1987, for the majority of these new jobs were in the service sector, and these do not pay as well as jobs in industry.[91]

Moreover, the framework of employment in the inner city lends itself to a low-wage labor force, and this complicates upward mobility for those who already hold entry-level jobs in the public or private sector. In the public sector, many such jobs are unionized, and labor unions are concerned about the impact of the continued entry of large numbers of low-wage employees on the benefit structure of unionized employees. This has led to agreements between labor officials—representing such unions as the American Federation of State County and Municipal Employees Union— and officials in the City of New York to provide for orderly entry of former welfare recipients into the public-sector labor force.

Devolution: More Resources or Less?

A substantive question exists with respect to whether the devolution of resources used to construct a humane version of "welfare reform" that protects vulnerable children and families can be achieved through TANF as it is administered in many states. Devolution may not address serious issues such as whether welfare should support adults, children or families. For example, in 1994, a poll found that 48% of respondents agreed that welfare spending should be cut, with only 13% urging an increase. Yet when the focus shifted to the issue of public assistance for children, 47% advocated an increase in public spending and only 9% advocated cuts.[92] However, most of America's poor children are the responsibility of adults who are ill-equipped to provide for them adequately.

Observers have noted that when the federal government shrinks in size, it becomes increasingly vulnerable to the influence of special interests, thus endangering the interests of the less powerful. The Ford Foundation released a report in 1989 which suggested that the reduction of financial resources in welfare assistance was self-defeating: "Each and every one of us has a stake in providing infants and young children, wherever they may live, the nutrition and emotional nurturing that allows them a decent start in life, both because it is right and because if we don't, they may burden us for decades with the cost of illness, dependency, and crime."[93] Concern for the future deepens when we consider that although many states accumulated considerable financial reserves during the late 1990s, in 2002 the declining economy has challenged their economic viability, complicating the strategy of using "rainy-day funds" to enhance the ability of low-income individuals to enter the workforce and to support themselves.

CONCLUSION

From a historical perspective on social policy, it is clear that the new welfare reform program has accomplished the transformation of a system designed to care for the poor to one that seeks to employ the poor—or, at any rate, to lessen the public responsibility for the poor no matter what the outcome may be. This change has been the chief goal of those who blame the poor for their own problems and urge the necessity of restricting and devolving tax dollars to change their values and behavior. Thus I have argued here that the intention of this new program was to eliminate welfare by eliminating people from the system.

Meanwhile, what remains of the system of care for those who have been eliminated from state financial support? It is divided between those who remain in the old welfare system—struggling to adapt to new requirements for job readiness and often without the means to do so—and those who have adhered to the new "quick-fix" rules and become employed in dead-end jobs with little chance for upward mobility. Some who quickly became employed had skills that made them marketable, and one could argue that they would have become employed with the welfare system structured as it was. However, those who have not done so remain hidden, outside the glow cast by the "success" of the newly employed, and their condition may ultimately become more critical as states become less and less able to cope with the financial requirements of the revised program.

Under this new, more punitive system, many people face greater challenges, without the resources to cope with them. This policy shifts the burden, substantially reducing the role of the federal government and passing responsibility on to the states, which lack adequate resources to assist poor families in achieving viability in the job market. Producing little real change in their condition, the new system of welfare amounts to a new system of social control.

The problems of the poor are complex and interrelated. Poverty generates and is connected to other social factors—including crime, drug abuse, poor education, geographical location, poor health and racism—which a work ethic alone is insufficient to resolve. Yet White Nationalists have utilized this Conservative ideology to enact welfare-to-work laws as the primary solution. The end result could be a disaster in human resource programming that would be the natural result of the blindness of ideologically driven public policy.

CHAPTER 7

The War on Blacks: Criminalizing a Race

INTRODUCTION

The Concern with White Safety

National crime rates have always been a major concern of Americans, who view rate increases and decreases in terms of their personal security. More than a century ago, an inquiry into whether crime was increasing noted the widespread belief that it was.[1] The inquiry was prompted in part by the fact that between 1880 and 1890 incarcerations grew from 58,609 to 82,329, an increase of over 24,000 and more than in any previous decade.[2] David A. Wells noted that increased incarceration in the North was attributed to "the great foreign immigration" and in the South to "the emancipation of the Negroes."[3]

Amos Wilson has observed that because American lower classes, like such classes in other parts of the world, inhabit the spawning ground of criminality, lower-class sectors of the Black community are similarly implicated today. It is ironic that Whites, having kept Blacks in such classes disproportionately, would regard Blacks as the chief threat to their personal safety. As Wilson says, the "chief concern" of the White American criminal justice establishment "is with African American containment and the prevention of White victimization by Black criminals."[4]

In 1980 the White electorate's preoccupation with the issue of crime contributed significantly to the landslide election of Ronald Reagan.[5] Indeed, Professor James Q. Wilson found that this issue was already a primary public concern in 1976.[6] Yet even earlier it was clear that the "law and order" slogan employed in the 1968 and 1972 presidential campaigns resonated with the American people, for it led to two Nixon victories. Political protests and demonstrations of that era undoubtedly induced some of the public unease, but the violent urban rebellions of this period were factors as well. These were characterized as "criminal behavior" and engendered a fear for personal safety, hastening the migration of Whites from the cities to the suburbs.

A significant crackdown on crime began in the 1980s. Between 1980 and 1994, the number of people in prisons increased nearly threefold, from 320,000 to 882,000. In 1990, America's incarceration rate was the second highest in the world, as Table 7.1 shows. Today, Americans are arguably more upset about crime than at any point since the "law and order" period of the late 1960s and more so than people in any other industrialized country. For example, a September 1994 Gallup poll revealed that 55% of Americans believed that crime was the most pressing problem facing the country.[7]

Does America have more crime, and thus more criminals, than other major countries? The answer is no. You are more likely to be robbed in Australia or New Zealand, more likely to be robbed with violence in Spain and more likely to be raped or assaulted in Canada, Australia or Germany.[8] One reason for the difference in incarceration rates may be that these countries, unlike America, are for the most part culturally homogenous, and only recently began to undergo social diversification. Though America began as a culturally and racially heterogenous society,

TABLE 7.1   Persons Incarcerated in Selected Industrialized Countries, 1990

Country	Incarceration per 100,000
Russia	558
U.S.	519
South Africa	368
Canada	116
Mexico	97
Japan	36

Source: "The International Use of Incarceration, 1991–1993," Report of the Sentencing Project, Washington, D. C., 1995.

TABLE 7.2	Citizens' Attitudes toward Punishment by Selected Industrialized Countries

Question: Should a young burglar who has committed more than one offense go to prison?

Country	Percent answering "Yes"
U.S.	53%
England and Wales	37%
Italy	22%
Germany and France	13%

Source: International Crime Survey, Ministry of Justice of the Netherlands; cited in the Economist, July 18, 1996, p. 23.

issues of cultural difference and especially hierarchy have become important contributors to the perception of and response to crime. Interestingly, the Netherlands Ministry of Justice asked a sample of citizens in several different countries what should happen to a young burglar who committed more than one offense. The results showed that Americans' attitude toward repeat offenders was more punitive than that of other countries, as seen in Table 7.2.

The brunt of Americans' punitive approach to repeat offenders falls heavily upon Blacks, suggesting that the U.S. incarceration system is influenced by race.[9] In this punitive era, for instance, some Alabama politicians and policy makers called for the revival of the chain gang. In Mississippi they proposed the restoration of the practice of flogging prisoners, expanded application of the death penalty and treating juvenile offenders as adults, sending far more of them to prison. There was also "talk of restoring fear to prisons, of caning, of making prisoners 'smell like a prisoner,' of burning and frying, of returning executions to the county seat and of making Mississippi 'the capital of punishment.'"[10] It is worth noting that both Alabama and Mississippi have large Black populations.

Dane Archer of the University of California at Santa Cruz wondered why Americans are so violent, yet data would seem to suggest that they are not more violent, they are more afraid.[11] Lawrence M. Friedman suggests that "they are most afraid of sudden violence or theft by strangers; they feel the cities are jungles, they are afraid to walk the streets at night."[12] As early as 1970, Andrew Hacker, an astute observer of race relations, argued that most crime in Black neighborhoods has its roots in economic forces and that Whites' reaction to crime committed anywhere was fear for their own safety.[13]

Fear of crime has risen even more in the past two decades. Friedman links a generalized fear of areas populated by Blacks with Black crime. The association of crime, especially violent crime, with Blacks is prevalent not only in America but in other countries as well. In Britain, "for all practical purposes, the terms mugging and Black crime are now virtually synonymous."[14]

The Disparate Incarceration of Blacks

This view of crime as synonymous with Blacks may explain why the criminal justice system has treated the Black community so harshly. African Americans of all ages are arrested, tried and punished at a greater rate than Whites, but this is especially true for Black youths. In 1995, 7% of Black males were incarcerated, though only 1% of White males were in jail. By 1996, one of every three Black males age 18 to 25 was either awaiting sentencing, imprisoned or on probation.[15] Black males comprised over 51% of the 1.1 million people in American jails in 1997;[16] they also had the highest incarceration rate of any group, as the figures in Table 7.3 attest. Indeed, Justice Department statistics show that during the ten-year period 1984–1994, nearly three-quarters of a million (735,200) Black adults were incarcerated in state and federal institutions, as compared to 725,100 Whites. Though Blacks were only 12% of the national population, they represented more than half of the total prison population, and most were serving hard time for drug-related offenses.[17]

The serious effects of institutional bias are reflected in several studies, including one which shows Blacks are more likely than Whites to be held in jail pending federal trials.[18] In 75 of the most populous U.S. counties, felony defendants are often released prior to trial, including 63% of violent offenders, 37% of murder defendants and 54% of rape defendants.[19] If the only people being denied pretrial release are predominantly Black, this constitutes another form of racial discrimination—though in

---

TABLE 7.3   Rate of Male Incarceration, December 1999

Racial group	Rate per 100,000
Black	3,408
Hispanic	1,335
White	417

Source: Bureau of Justice Prison Statistics, U.S. Department of Justice, December 31,1999.

the pretrial federal incarceration study referred to above, officials claimed this occurs because Blacks charged with crimes were frequently from another jurisdiction and thus considered greater flight risks.

It is important to note that incarceration rates often do not correspond directly to crime rates, either for the U.S. as a whole or for individual states. The Sentencing Project found that in 1992 Louisiana had the highest rate of both crime and incarceration; that Oklahoma had the third highest rate of imprisonment, but only the 21st highest crime rate; and that Mississippi had the 16th highest crime rate yet the fourth highest rate of incarceration.[20] Moreover, it is not clear whether the punishment meted out by the criminal justice system is focused on violent crime or on any kind of Black antisocial behavior. In an assessment of arrest warrants in Duval County, Florida (which includes Jacksonville), Jerome Miller determined that the highest rates of arrest were for such offenses as "breach of the peace," "consumption of alcohol on city property," "drinking in public," "petit theft (mostly shoplifting)," and "possession of alcoholic beverages by person under 21."[21] Miller calls this pattern, which is exhibited in other states as well, "rabble management."[22]

Resource Withdrawal and Community Instability

Little observed in the explanations offered for the astronomical growth in drug-related crimes is a study by Richard Freeman and Harry Holzer on the dynamics of Black youth unemployment. The authors provide a striking picture of the growth of Black youth unemployment in every age cohort between 1954 and 1981. Their data—reported in Table 7.4—suggest in stark terms what the authors describe as the "catastrophic" situation that existed in the early years of the Reagan administration—though it had been in the making for a number of years before then.

TABLE 7.4   Percent of Black Youth Unemployment from 1954 to 1981

Age	1954	1964	1981
16–17	13.4%	25.9%	40.1%
18–19	14.7%	23.1%	36.0%
20–24	16.9%	12.6%	24.4%

Source: Richard B. Freeman and Harry J. Holzer, eds., *The Black Youth Employment Crisis,* National Bureau of Economic Research (Chicago: University of Chicago Press, 1986), Table 2, p. 7.

Freeman and Holzer found the causes of Black youth unemployment included the rise in female labor force participation rates, the rise in low-income poverty and welfare enrollment and discriminatory employment practices. Although they did not find that any single group of immigrants had negatively impacted Black youth employment opportunities, they did determine that Black youths were more vulnerable than their elders to the effects of increasing numbers of immigrants in the labor force.[23] Freeman and Holzer also remarked that in the mid-1980s nearly one-third of Black youths had experience with drugs more potent than marijuana.[24] Thus, just at the time the Reagan administration was cutting back federal assistance to urban areas, a large number of Black youths were at risk of being drawn into the drug trade.

It was no accident that the rise in drug commerce in the mid-1980s occurred about the same time that massive economic resources were being withdrawn from inner-city communities all over the nation. This began with Reagan's 1983 budget, which entailed deep reductions in social programs. The magnitude of these cuts is shown in Table 7.5. Moreover, they impacted Blacks more severely than Whites. Total government jobs dropped by 400,000, and minorities represented one in three persons laid off. Social security (10% of whose recipients were Black) was cut 3%; military pensions (7% Black) were cut 2%; Medicare (9% Black) was cut 5%; and Supplementary Security Income (27% Black) was increased by only 1%. U.S. Office of Management and Budget Director David Stockman was said to "bristle" at the inference that the cuts were related to Black participation in these programs. However, John Jacob, then head of the National Urban League, felt that "a lot of people in this country thought that this thing about government was really all about all of these minorities draining off government resources, particularly blacks."[25]

The Reagan budget cuts, occurring in such critical areas, were responsible for severing the links between Blacks and the legitimate economy, and they promoted substantial urban decline, leading many to turn to a source of illegitimate income to support themselves and their families. Indeed, the economic pressure placed on Black families by these budget cuts and by the recession of the late 1980s devastated many communities, causing Black middle-class flight, weakening community institutions and disassembling families.

As noted in chapter 6, the disintegration of the Black family—manifested in higher divorce and "never married" rates and a resulting increase in poverty rates—has been portrayed as a moral problem instead of being linked to the impact of the withdrawal of economic resources. Yet it is clear that when legitimate work is not available in a community, many males are

TABLE 7.5	Reductions in Federal Spending for Social Programs to State and Local Governments from Fiscal Year 1981 to Fiscal Year 1983 (in millions of dollars)		
Type of aid	*1981*	*1983*	*% Change*
Total	94,762	81,418	−14.1%
Social welfare	65,375	55,431	−15.3%
Social services	27,200	18,094	−33.5%
Community development	4,042	3,350	−17.2%
Employment and education	21,146	12,281	−42.0%
Health	2,012	2,463	+16.4%
Income security	38,174	37,337	−2.2%
Medicaid	16,833	17,006	+2.1%
AFDC	8,462	5,422	−36.0%
Housing	4,035	4,260	+5.3%

Sources: Bureau of the Census, Statistical Abstract: 1985 (Washington, D.C., U.S. Government Printing Office, 1981), Table 490, p. 294. Social Analysis of the Budget of the U.S. Government, Fiscal Year 1982, Special Analysis H., Table H-11, pp. 29, 36; cited in Michael K. Brown, "Gutting the Great Society: Black Economic Progress and the Budget Cuts," *Urban League Review* 7 (Winter 1982–1983): Table 2, p. 18.

considered to be ineligible for marriage because they cannot support a family. This leads in turn to the formation of fewer families, to family instability and to an inability to impart and reinforce strong family values to children, including self-discipline, goal-setting, establishing connections to positive social institutions and the like. The lack of authority, especially in many female-headed households, has enabled Black male youths to participate more aggressively in the drug trade than youths from intact families. Indeed, the predominantly lower-class status of the youths who participate in the drug trade is itself a reflection of their lack of viable economic choices. For two decades, these youths have experienced exceedingly high rates of unemployment, estimated to be between 20 and 50%. Tragically, these Black males are disproportionately vulnerable to being drawn into the maelstrom of gangs, drugs and violence.[26]

Summing up this problem, William Julius Wilson said that social dislocation in cities, caused by factors such as the disappearance of living-wage, low-skill jobs, had created an urban crisis of deepening poverty and an intractable "Urban Underclass."[27] In *When Work Disappears*, Wilson chided Neoconservative politicians and other policy analysts who trace dysfunctional behavior of ghetto residents to personal shortcomings rather than adaptations to chronic subordination and years of limited opportunities.[28] As Wilson suggests: "The presence of high levels of drug activity in a neighborhood is indicative of problems of social organization. High rates of joblessness trigger other problems in the neighborhood that adversely affect social organization, including drug trafficking, crime, and gang violence."[29] He believes that the urban inner-city was desperate for any form of commerce, even illegal ones, and thus ripe for the crack cocaine trade that emerged just as poverty-intensifying factors were having an enormous impact. The result was the explosion of the crack trade, and the violent behavior that attended it took a heavy toll on the lives of Black youth and on the safety and viability of their communities.

A Driving Force: The Drug Epidemic

The violent crime associated with the drug epidemic heightened Whites' fear of Black street crime. The number of Black teenage homicide victims rose from about 38 per 100,000 around 1985 to over 120 per 100,000 by 1991—an increase of 154%.[30] By comparison, the homicide rate among Whites age 15 to 19 grew by only 19 per thousand over the same period, though this still represents a steep rise.

In 1994 public alarm over the rise in violent crime was reflected in a *U.S. News and World Report* feature which included this phrase: "[A]

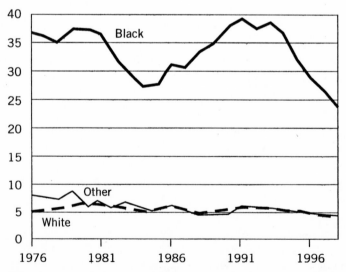

Chart 1 Homicide Rate Per 100,000 Population, 1976–1998

Source: "Violent Victimization and Race, 1993–1998," Special Report, Bureau of Justice Statistics, March 2001, U.S. Department of Justice.

scary orgy of violent crime is fueling another public call to action."[31] Pointing to "killer teens," the explosive anger of White males, workplace killings, carjackings, drive-by shootings and other violent crimes, the exposé focused, as many have done, on the most obvious factor driving the soaring homicide rates: the drug trade.

When the crack epidemic first hit urban communities in the mid-1980s, young Black men were recruited as street dealers, earning from $20 to $100 per day, and soon they were organized into "crews" to protect their selling areas from being taken over by others.[32] Some West Coast gangs, such as the Bloods and the Crips, expanded their operations into the nation's Midwest, while gangs such as the Natural Born Killers, the Red Top Crew and others developed a thriving commerce on the East Coast.[33] Violations of the norms of the drug trade led to almost certain death. The symbiotic relationship between drugs and youthful gangs made the open-air drug markets that sprang up in many Black communities the most dangerous territories in the nation.

The "War on Crime"

The "war on crime" slogan mirrors the way in which the government approached the problem of drugs and violence. Its strategy, compounded in some cases by aggressive tactics utilized by local police, imposed considerable pressure on civil liberties. Citizens began to organize block patrols and "orange hat brigades" to drive out drug dealers who were corrupting their communities with drug sales and whose violence threatened the viability of their neighborhoods.

The federal government developed such countermeasures as the "Weed and Seed" program," which dispensed funds to local police departments for aggressive and punitive operations and for positive programs as well. The rationale behind "Weed and Seed" was to "weed out" violent crime, gang activity, drug use and drug trafficking in targeted communities and then restore affected neighborhoods by "seeding" them with economic activity.[34] The program was supposed to enable communities to take advantage of existing economic development programs in the Department of Housing and Urban Development, but department funding for such initiatives was woefully inadequate. As a result, the program has focused on policing poor Black neighborhoods and neglected the promised economic development.

The Clinton administration, like those of Reagan and Bush, approached the so-called "war on drugs" in a timid fashion. It raised the "drug czar" post to Cabinet level in 1993, and then promptly cut its budget for staff and functions: for fiscal year 1996, funds for the "war" were cut by $1.345 billion, and what was left was devoted to interdiction. The administration's emphasis on the punishment side of the crime elimination task was reflected in Clinton's proposal to put 100,000 policemen on America's streets.

In the mid-1990s, the political volatility of the crime issue led to calls for the revival of the death penalty in states which had not revived it directly after the 1976 Supreme Court decision to lift the ten-year moratorium on capital punishment. Politicians responded eagerly. The death penalty was restored by several state legislatures, and at the federal level a capital penalty statute which had been used for drug kingpins was expanded to cover a multitude of violent crimes, including street crime and "terrorism." The New York Supreme Court upheld Governor George Pataki's removal of Robert Johnson, a Black Brooklyn district attorney, from a case because he would not ask for the death penalty against a Hispanic defendant who had killed a police officer. Johnson's use of prosecutorial discretion to determine whether the death penalty was warranted was overridden by Conservative politicians substituting their judgment for his in order to affect a specific outcome.[35] Judges who were deemed to be "soft on crime" were harassed and, in some instances, driven from the bench because they either did not believe in mandatory minimum sentencing or the death penalty. One Maryland politician remarked: "Politicians asking for prosecutions, and prosecutors acting on those requests—I think you have opened the door to a police state."[36]

BLACK CRIME AND THE CRIMINAL JUSTICE SYSTEM

Black Attitudes toward the Law

The historic antipathy of Blacks toward the police arose because of the nature of White policing during the slavery era.[37] Criminologist Katheryn Russell describes the extensive criminalization of Black behavior under slave codes which regulated the conduct of Blacks toward Whites—especially White women. After slavery ended, this regime was carried on in the form of Black codes and racist statutes in various states, especially in the South.[38]

In twentieth-century urban settings, police were seen as an invading army that had no interest in maintaining the civil context of Black life and that, in fact, promotes the existence of two separate societies with two norms of justice based on race.[39] Evidence of the attitudes Blacks continue to hold about the police may be seen in Table 7.6. Blacks have far less confidence in the police than do Whites, think that charges of police brutality are often justified and believe that Black people are roughed up unnecessarily and not treated the same as Whites. Recognition of these attitudes has prompted the establishment of "community policing" programs in order to improve police relations with Black communities. The goals of such programs are to integrate the police into the community and produce a change in both police and community attitudes.

Negative Black attitudes toward the criminal justice system have additional sources beyond police behavior; they stem as well from the racism Blacks have experienced in other aspects of the criminal justice system. Evidence that police harassment of persons held in custody is pervasive comes from a 1997 Los Angeles Police Department study, which revealed that in 65 out of 2,000 arrests, members of the LAPD inflicted post-arrest injuries serious enough to require hospitalization.[40]

The use of jury nullification to negate racism in the criminal justice system became an issue in the O. J. Simpson trial. Some Whites

---

TABLE 7.6   Attitudes toward the Police by Race, Spring 1991

Attitude	Total	Blacks	Whites
Confidence in local police			
a great deal or quite a lot	55%	30%	59%
very little or some	44%	70%	39%
When charges of brutality are raised			
likely to think they are justified	67%	82%	65%
not likely to think they are justified	24%	11%	27%
Police in respondents' neighborhoods don't			
rough people up when arresting them	27%	42%	25%
rough people up unnecessarily	63%	47%	66%
Police in big cities			
are tougher on blacks than on whites	51%	67%	48%
treat blacks and whites the same	34%	15%	36%
Police in respondents' communities			
are tougher on blacks than on whites	19%	42%	16%
treat blacks and whites the same	66%	45%	69%

Source: New York Times/CBS News Poll, April 1–3, 1991; cited in New York Times, April 5, 1991, p. A16.

charged that when the jury acquitted Simpson of murder, they effectively "nullified" the law by ignoring the "facts" in the case. From this
point of view, the jury's decision was a way to retaliate against the criminal justice system for having prosecuted and convicted other Blacks.
Some Blacks did view Simpson's acquittal as a symbolic community victory of historic proportions.[41]

In the aftermath of the Simpson trial, some lawyers argued that in
many cases involving the potential incarceration of young Black males,
majority-Black juries in urban areas refused to convict. Indeed, Professor Paul Butler, a Black law professor at George Washington University,
openly advocated this practice because Blacks are disproportionately victims of the criminal justice system.[42] However, if jury nullification had
been practiced on a grand scale by Blacks, it would be unlikely that one
in every three young Black inner-city males in America would have some
relationship to the criminal justice system.

Blacks have tried to explain that Whites have practiced "jury nullification" for centuries. In fact, it was part of the reimposition of White
power in the South, a method of regaining social control of Blacks after
slavery. In most southern states Whites created a system of justice in
which Blacks were prohibited from even testifying in court against
Whites and needed the assistance of Whites to obtain anything resembling a fair hearing. White juries routinely refused to convict White
defendants, including the police, of crimes against Blacks, excusing from
punishment even those who had committed the most heinous crimes.
This system continues to this day, as revealed by an analysis of records in
Prince George's County, Maryland, where police officers who killed 46
Blacks between 1990 and 2000 were never charged with a crime.[43] This
exposé indicated that in a thirteen-month period alone between 1999 and
2000, police in this county shot 12 people, killing five, and beat two other
men to death; all of these actions were ruled "justified."[44]

Conservative politicians have aggressively attempted to mitigate the
actions of predominantly Black juries by pressuring Liberal judges and
prosecutors to produce specific outcomes. For example, in December of
1997, Judge Lawrence Zatkoff ordered the release from prison of Larry
Nevers, a White Detroit police officer who in 1993 was convicted of sec-
ond-degree murder in the beating death of Malice Green, a Black man.[45]
Zatkoff ruled that Nevers, who had served four years of a 12-year sentence, should be released because the predominantly Black jury that convicted him had seen the movie *Malcolm X* while they were sequestered;
he maintained that its scenes of racial bigotry and police brutality had
influenced their decision. He also remarked that he believed jurors had

Death penalty policy is important to members of the Congressional Black Caucus because their districts are heavily impacted by the criminal justice system and because Blacks are disproportionately targeted for such sentencing. In White communities, the absence of open-air markets makes drug consumption more difficult to detect, and so Black communities are the targets of drug policing and their inhabitants more likely to receive death sentences.

Even though 75% of persons convicted of participating in a drug enterprise were White and 25% Blacks, 78% of those given the death penalty for drug-related offenses were Black and only 11% White. Moreover, while 75% of those convicted under the "drug kingpin" statute were White, 89% of the defendants who received the death penalty under that statute were either Blacks or Hispanics.[57] In 1996 one observer found that 80% of 61 defendants approved for capital punishment by the U.S. attorney general were members of minority groups; strikingly, 66% of federal death penalty prosecutions have been brought against African Americans.[58] By 1999, the percentage of blacks on death row had grown to 43% of the total, even though they are only 13% of the population.[59]

On April 20, 1994, the House passed the crime bill with the Racial Justice Act attached, defeating an attempt to delete it by 217 to 212, with Democrats accounting for 211 of the 217 votes. Some members of Congress opposed the Racial Justice Act in House-Senate conference negotiations. Like other Republicans, Rep. F. James Sensenbrenner, Jr., referred to it as a "quota" provision, designed to "prevent anybody from being executed in this country." He asserted: "[V]ictims of crimes committed by members of minority groups are members of the same minority group. So we do not have a quota system for victims being discussed here, but we are having a quota system for criminals being discussed here."[60] In his colloquy, he went even further, claiming that the provision would "destroy the structure of justice in America [thus creating] an environment in which considerations of race are central to death penalty cases."[61] House Speaker Newt Gingrich also argued against the provision, maintaining that the deeper problem was that it would prevent the criminal justice system from dealing with criminals as individuals.[62] Orrin Hatch (R-Utah), who took the Senate floor in the spring of 1994 to denounce the Racial Justice Act, declared that the Fourteenth Amendment to the Constitution prohibited the unequal application of the death penalty.[63] This represented yet another attempt to redirect the focus of the equal protection clause of the Fourteenth Amendment, to minimize the social conditions under which Blacks and Whites were given the death sentence and to ignore the disparate application of the

---

to deliberate under the threat that a race riot would ensue if they did not convict Nevers, and he asserted that Mayor Coleman Young had prejudiced potential jurors by saying, shortly after Green's death, that a cold-blooded murder had occurred. Federal courts threw out Nevers's conviction and that of his partner, Walter Budzyn; in a retrial in the spring of 2000, Nevers was convicted of involuntary manslaughter.

One could cite numerous other examples where what amounts to a criminal punishment system is at war with itself as Conservatives attempt to make the system work in conformance with popular perceptions of guilt or innocence and deliver punishment accordingly. Such political pressure can only mean that the system will increasingly become a tool of state repression and punishment rather than a fair dispenser of justice. The racial composition of juries will continue to be disproportionate so long as convicted felons are disqualified from voting. In many communities, jurors are chosen from voter rolls, and even though substantial gains have been made in Black participation in voting, the number of Blacks in jury pools is kept low by the practice of barring convicted felons from voting and thereby becoming eligible to serve on juries.[46]

THE CRIME BILL OF 1993–1994

Background: "Three Strikes" Politics

In the early 1990s, politicians at the national level used "three strikes and you're out" as a slogan to push for a tougher general approach to crime, and candidates for state offices began to view it as a "smart political move" to exploit the theme. Yet this policy was endorsed with little information about its economic costs, the impact it would have on prison conditions or any other rational considerations that usually accompany policy making. Politicians appeared to hold the view that a large proportion of violent crimes are perpetrated by a small number of criminals and that this policy would get repeated violent offenders off the streets for a long time. The idea became so powerful that it was difficult for even a Liberal governor such as Mario Cuomo of New York to reject it; his version of the slogan was "three strikes and you're in."[47]

The policy's effectiveness is questionable. Beyond the cost of incarcerating an inmate—approximately $25,000 per year—it means taxpayers must fund the needs of aging prisoners who require additional health care. Moreover, the "three strikes" law and mandatory minimum sentencing programs have contributed to the explosive growth in prison sentences given to young Blacks and sharply increased their incarceration rates. In 1999 a study of the California prison system by the Justice Institute questioned the effectiveness of "three strikes" in reducing crime.[48] The state attorney general's office argued that the imposition of the law had led to reductions in crime by repeat offenders and saved the state substantial amounts of money.[49] Yet the Justice Institute noted that even though different California counties applied the law disparately, reductions in crime were relatively uniform throughout the state.

The Crime Control Act

In the 1992 election campaign, Bill Clinton, like many other politicians, endorsed the "three strikes and you're out" concept as a solution to the growing problem of crime. In his January 1993 State of the Union address he iterated his commitment to this policy, saying "those who commit repeated, violent crimes should be told, when you commit a third crime, you will be put away, and put away for good. Three strikes, and you are out."

On August 11, 1993, in a White House Rose Garden ceremony, Clinton proposed a crime bill, known as the Crime Control Act, with the following features:

—community policing, with 100,000 more officers on the street;
—the Brady gun control provisions;
—boot camp/state prisons for youthful first-time offenders;
—drug courts and drug treatment programs for addicts;
—safe schools—including metal detectors, additional police, and the establishment of drug-free zones.

Introducing the bill, he said the following: "For too long, crime has been used as a way to divide Americans with rhetoric. It is time—and I thank the Republican members of Congress who are here today—it is time to use crime as a way to unite Americans through action. I call on the Democrats and Republicans together to work with us and with the law enforcement community to craft the best possible crime legislation.[50]

The bill criminalized many acts, subjected offenders to automatic sentencing with mandatory minimums, and expanded by 66 the number of crimes which could incur the death penalty. Two particular provisions of the Crime Control Act had the most grievous impact upon the Black community: the so-called "three strikes and you're out" rule; and crack cocaine sentencing mandates.

In January of 1994, as a conference committee was set to work out the differences between the House and Senate versions of the crime bill, journalist Richard Berke remarked that the winter meeting of the Republican National Committee "resembled a convention of prison builders,"[51] as delegates reasserted their "tough on crime" stance. Rep. Newt Gingrich of Georgia called on the government to erect "as many stockades as necessary" on surplus military bases to incarcerate violent offenders.[52] Sen. Phil Gramm of Texas said, "I want a crime bill that grabs violent criminals by the throat," adding that he was not "looking for rehabilitation, but there reaches a point where you've got to say, 'Enough is Enough.' "[53] Governor George Allen of Virginia attributed his election success in November 1993 to his "no parole" position on violent criminals.

John DiIulio, a Brookings Institution policy analyst, summed u[p] Republican sentiment by saying that "Americans have lost interest in [the] Anglo-Saxon, innocent-until-proven-guilty model of justice. They [want] to get the bad guy."[54] On the floor of the House, Rep. Steve Ho[rn,] Republican from California, characterized the crime bill as "an att[ack on] a multitude of criminal actions that have battered our quality of lif[e: mur]der, drug dealing, armed assault, rape, robbery, kidnaping, ca[rjacking,] child pornography, domestic violence. It contains an arsenal of [weapons] intended to return peace and security to our nation's co[mmunities] through measures that are punitive as well as preventive. [We are under] attack, and the Crime Control Act is a solid weapon to lead th[e battle."]

Death Penalty: The Racial Justice Amendm[ent]

The 1993 debate on the crime bill included reference t[o the fact] that of the 2,356 individuals on death row in 1991, 1,[173 (50%) were] White; 943 (40%) were Black; 24 (1%) were Native A[merican; 44 (2%)] were Asian; and 172 (7.3%) were Hispanic.[56] This f[igure led the Con]gressional Black Caucus to push for a "racial [justice" clause in death] penalty sentencing. The House Judiciary Commit[tee agreed, and brought] to the floor a measure known as the "Racial Justi[ce Amendment," which] allowed legal challenges to the death penalty [on the] basis of statistical racial disparities or a showin[g]

The intent was that when the death per[son was] of African descent, that person had the rig[ht to challenge] the rate at which such punishment was util[ized and the way in which] it was issued. It further holds that if racial d[isparity in the death] penalty was found, this would trigger an i[nquiry, and during the] time as the reasons for the disparity cou[ld]

equal protection clause in the legal process that led to an unequal number of Blacks on death row.

Offering an amendment to instruct the Senate conferees to reject the Racial Justice Act provision, Sen. Alphonse D'Amato (R-N.Y.) cited a *New York Times* opinion piece written by Ed Koch, former mayor of New York City. Koch denied that the application of the death penalty was unfair to Blacks. He argued that while 40% of persons executed since 1977 were Black, "55% of the murders in this country were committed by Black perpetrators," and he denounced the Racial Justice Act as a "quota" for the death penalty.[64]

Opposition to the Racial Justice Act also emerged from such sources as the State of California District Attorneys Association and the National District Attorneys Association. Moreover, when Attorney General Janet Reno testified on the crime bill before the Senate Judiciary Committee in late April of 1994, she indicated that the administration was neutral on the provision.[65] By August of 1994, weak Republican support for the measure led House and Senate conferees to strike the Racial Justice Act from the bill.

Apparently those who opposed the measure did so because they believed race is an inappropriate criterion in the consideration of punishment. Yet the evidence is clear that race is, in fact, a substantial element in both death penalty prosecutions and death row status. Why politicians ignore this is a matter of opinion, but that they deny empirical evidence in favor of promoting punishment which has a racial effect triggers the characterization of such behavior as White Nationalism.

Sentencing Guidelines

Though many Democrats attempted to make crime prevention measures the major focus of the Crime Control Act, its punitive aspects became far more dominant. In the words of Rep. Robert C. "Bobby" Scott (D-Va.), "the Crime Bill was all about more incarceration versus more prevention."[66] Scott went on to say: "In the politics of crime, the right thing and the politically popular thing are totally opposite. The politics of crime involves emotional appeals for mandatory minimum sentences, life in prison without parole, no probation, no rehabilitation, and more death penalty provisions without appeals. While espousing these simple-minded policies appeals to the emotions of a fearful public and helps politicians get elected, they do nothing to reduce crime in the streets."[67]

As suggested above, the high rates of incarceration of young Black males are driven by sentencing guidelines. For example, in the state of

California, with a "three strikes" policy, Blacks constitute only 7% of the population but they account for nearly 18% of those arrested and 32% of the prison population. In fact, nearly 40% of young Black Californians have some connection to the criminal justice system, a situation which is driven by the crack cocaine trade.[68]

In a revealing interview, Marc Mauer, assistant director of the Sentencing Project—a Washington, D.C.–based research organization— substantiated the pattern of disparate sentencing for Blacks and Hispanics in relation to Whites, asserting that this is directly related to cocaine sentencing guidelines. As he pointed out: "At the federal level, possession of five hundred grams of cocaine powder results in a mandatory five years in prison. Possessing crack cocaine, however, only requires five grams to get that same five-year mandatory prison term, so there's a 100:1 discrepancy in the quantity of drugs required to trigger that five-year mandatory sentence."[69]

Mauer noted that Blacks are the targets of use and possession policing because of their participation in the crack cocaine trade, and they receive longer sentences even though Whites use powder cocaine at a much greater rate and crack cocaine at a slightly greater rate, according to data from the National Institute on Drug Abuse.[70] He suggested that despite detailed testimony presented to congressional committees in 1995 about the racial disparity issue, politicians rejected proposals to equalize sentencing guidelines for cocaine because they were "concerned about being perceived as soft on crime" and thus ignored "the facts presented by the Sentencing Commission and others."[71]

Mauer contended that race is an unacknowledged issue in the criminal justice system inasmuch as the decisions made by police and prosecutors are subjective, "made on the streets or behind closed doors, and less subject to public scrutiny and analysis." Even though judicial decisions are also subjective, he argued, because judges must follow mandatory sentencing guidelines, police and prosecutors have more leeway. Decisions about whether to make an arrest, what charge to bring or whether to plea bargain, all heavily define the case before the judge gets it. This is important to keep in mind because of Mauer's finding that at the federal level, sentencing practices allow Whites to plead to charges that do not carry mandatory minimum sentences more often than Blacks and Hispanics.[72]

Furthermore, class is a companion issue with race, not only with respect to the defendant's ability to afford competent legal assistance— as seen in the O. J. Simpson trial—but also with regard to the way in which the criminal justice system treats those found guilty of crimes.

Mauer contends that if two defendants are found guilty of the same drug abuse offense, and one comes to court with his or her high-income parents and agrees to enroll in a legitimate drug treatment program, a judge will be more inclined to accept the treatment option. However, if a low-income person who is found guilty does not have such support or resources, the likely sentence is a prison term.[73] A combination of racism and class disadvantage is responsible for the negative impact of sentencing dynamics upon the Black community.

In 1995 the Congressional Black Caucus and other members of the Black and Hispanic leadership attempted to equalize drug sentencing guidelines. The Federal Sentencing Commission submitted proposals to equalize the crack cocaine sentencing laws, but these were rejected by the Clinton administration and by the Republicans who controlled both the House and Senate. Reasoning that the crack cocaine trade evokes more violence than commerce in powder cocaine, Clinton refused to instruct Attorney General Janet Reno to equalize the sentences for crack and powder cocaine; however, in 1997 the administration recommended moving powder and crack cocaine sentencing guidelines toward a 5:1 ratio rather than 100:1.

CONSEQUENCES

In general, Blacks have been the victims of crime to a disproportionate degree. This has made some Black communities as sensitive to crime as White communities. By slender margins, Blacks approve of tougher measures against crime such as the death penalty, and by larger margins they have supported the "three strikes" approach.[74] Nevertheless, it is clear that in responding to the consequences of violence, the political system has been much more concerned about the safety of the majority population and has worsened the victimization experienced by Blacks.

"De-Citizenization": Felony Voting Rights and Access to Jobs

One of the most destructive aspects of the use of questionable strategies of punishment is criminalization of an entire cohort of the population. One result is that of an estimated 1.46 million Black men who have been incarcerated, 14% have lost the right to vote because they were convicted of a felony; indeed, in 1997 the Sentencing Project determined that one of every seven Black men was ineligible to vote because of a felony conviction.[75] In October of 1998, Human Rights Watch published a report entitled, "Losing the Vote: The Impact of Felony Disenfranchisement in the United States." The report noted that if current trends continued, "in a dozen states as many as 30–40% of the next generation of black men will permanently lose the right to vote."[76] And in 2001, this situation still obtained. Human Rights Watch found that in that year there were 1.4 million ex-felons in some degree of disenfranchisement; and in states such as Florida and Alabama, as many as one in three Black males could not vote because of felony convictions.[77]

Criminal punishment strategies are directly related to the lack of employment opportunities for American Blacks. James Johnson and Walter Farrell have found that in "labor markets with far more job seekers than available jobs, men who had had a brush with the law were 72% less likely to be working than those without a criminal record."[78] They go on to show that race and color are implicated in joblessness because of the disproportionate number of Black job seekers with criminal records.[79] With 41% of Black men not in the labor force and those attempting to access jobs two and a half times as likely to be unemployed as White males, it follows that the effect of criminalization on job-readiness represents a serious problem for the future of the Black community and perhaps for the nation as a whole. The adoption of policies that result in high incarceration rates for one particular group has cost American society dearly in terms of unrealized economic and political contributions from all its citizens.

Death Penalty Rates

Since the mid-1990s, crime has decreased steadily each year, yet the application of the death penalty has increased. Although there is no established correlation between the rate of serious crimes and the use of the death penalty, this has not stopped politicians from exercising their belief that it deters crime. Indeed, some policy makers maintain that regardless of whether the penalty deters crime, if one criminal is executed this means one less person capable of committing a crime in the future. In effect, "deterrence" has taken on a double meaning, and in the 1980s this led many states to restore the death penalty in the wake of the increase in violent crime. It is no coincidence that even though some states north of the Mason-Dixon line—such as New York—have reinstated the death penalty, what has been described as the real "death belt" is in the South, where (coincidentally?) the majority of Blacks still reside.[80]

It is important to note that while the Racial Justice Act was opposed by groups such as the National District Attorneys Association in 1994 because it might make the imposition of the death penalty impossible, by

1997 the American Bar Association, the nation's largest and most influential organization of lawyers, voted to halt the use of the death penalty. They did this because they believed it was administered through "a haphazard maze of unfair practices."[81]

The reference to unfairness likely was a recognition of the persistence of flaws in death penalty trials: a number of persons convicted and sentenced to death were later found to be innocent. Since 1973, 99 prisoners on death row have been released.[82] In 2001, the governor of Illinois declared a moratorium on the use of the death penalty and other states were being pressured to do so. Opinion polls show that from 1994 to 2001, public confidence in the death penalty slid from 80% to 65%.[83] In fact, the American Civil Liberties Union has asserted that the death penalty has historically had a 68% error rate—meaning that two of every three persons convicted and sentenced to die did not commit the offenses for which they were executed.[84]

Race is a major determinant in the application of the death penalty; since 2001, Blacks constituted 35% of those on death row. Moreover, the race of either the victim or the defendant was implicated in death penalty decisions 96% of the time. Indeed, over time the murder of a White person has been the most stable determinant of the institutional use of the death sentence.[85]

Rampant Incarceration

The surest indication that the incarceration edifice constructed by the criminalization strategy of the 1993–1994 Crime Control Act and targeted policing is taking its toll on the Black community may be seen in increasing Black incarceration rates—which bear no relationship to crime rates. In May of 1996, the FBI reported that serious crimes had dropped for the fourth year in a row, led by an 8% decrease in homicides nationally, while major cities throughout the country reported substantial reductions in 1995.[86] This trend continued into 1997, as data reflected a drop in crime for the fifth year in a row—the longest recorded decline in 25 years by the FBI.[87]

Yet between 1984 and 1997, the State of California, which contains the nation's largest prison population, built an additional 21 prisons (though only one college campus), even though violent crime in the state fell from 57% to 42% over that period.[88] A national pattern of increased incarceration, driven by drug laws and their strict enforcement, has heavily impacted young Black males. By 1996, 8.3% of Blacks between the ages of 24 and 29 were prison inmates, compared with 0.8% of White males.[89] In fact, between 1990 and June 2000, incarceration rates rose rapidly, although crime rates slowed considerably during this period, declining each year beginning in 1996.

WHITE NATIONALIST PUNISHMENT THEORY

The necessity for punishment is firmly ingrained in the institutional fabric, at least partly because of Conservative theorists such as Professor James Q. Wilson of Berkeley, who helped destroy the Liberal view that the most socially productive way to reduce crime is to eliminate its "root causes." In 1985 Wilson declared: "It has become increasingly clear to me that what some people who worry about 'root causes' really mean is not that such causes should be found by careful investigation and then remedied by imaginative policies, but rather that these causes are already known and that they can be easily addressed by government programs, provided we have the 'will' to do so."[90] While Wilson did not outright oppose this thesis, he opined that studies were inconclusive, including those which purported to establish a relationship between unemployment and crime. He offered instead a theory of deterrence, using sanctions designed to simultaneously raise the cost of crime and the cost of non-crime; he also argued that "Putting people in prison has been the single most important thing we've done to reduce crime."[91]

Other Conservative scholars, such as Abigail and Stephan Thernstrom, assert that the reason the criminal justice system has visited more punishment upon Blacks is because Blacks have committed most of the crimes, including violent crimes.[92] Yet how can their data show "no greater zeal" for the system to punish Blacks than Whites when they admit that in 1993, 51% of Blacks who were convicted went to jail while only 38% of Whites did so? They attribute this disparity to "legitimate nonracial factors"—for example, Blacks committed more serious crimes, they were more likely to have prior records, or they lived in counties which were tougher on crime in general.[93]

Questions remain about how the Thernstrom interpretation can be correct when other researchers have found that incarceration rates, like other aspects of the criminal justice system, "are the outcome of social processes"?[94] Citing the work of Alfred Blumstein, Professor Katheryn Russell makes the point that there is a disparity between arrest and incarceration rates for Blacks and Whites which is not explained by the disproportionally high number of Black offenders. Blumstein says that as much as 20 to 25% of the Black incarceration rate cannot be explained by disproportionate offending, and Russell suggests this may be traced to racism in the criminal justice system.[95]

For Conservative theorists to deny the contextual framework of the violent drug trade not only ignores root causes, it provides no rational argument for containing crime through a humanistic methodology. What Wilson and others do not admit as yet is that there are severe limits to the use of sanctions to achieve deterrence. The cost of deterrence may be too high, especially if it is not balanced by a robust direction of policy which substantially expands opportunity and thus provides attractive awards for non-criminal behavior to a large enough sector of the low-income population. It is important to note that even Wilson's modestly Conservative theory has been stifled by the Nationalists, who since 1994 have been determined to enact a regime of punishment without concomitant rewards. The imbalance in this equation has not only resulted directly in what may be irreparable damage to a sector of the Black population, but indirectly imperiled the future viability of the nation as well.

Criminalization as Social Control

Put simply—perhaps too simply to make the point—the White Nationalist answer to Whites' fears of violence that may affect their personal safety is to criminalize and punish offending Blacks. This is the ultimate objective of the strategy outlined so elegantly by Professor Wilson, and it amounts to an explicit formulation of social control. As suggested above, the strategy ignores the lack of correlation between crime rates and incarceration rates.

Professor Darnell Hawkins proposes that from a historical perspective, the only concept which explains the relationship—or lack of relationship—between the percent of Blacks in a state population and their incarceration rates is the use, at various times in history, of social control regimes. In his study of the history of the racial composition of the prison population in North Carolina from 1870 to 1980, Hawkins determined that variations in the Black prison population reflected the fact that the penal system was an important source of labor. This resulted in an inordinate bias in the larger socioeconomic structure because the demand for labor directly affected the accumulation and use of Black prisoners.[96]

Professor Hawkins's emphasis on the economic aspects of incarceration rates is akin to a series of studies by Professor Richard Freeman, who noted that although the growth of incarceration rates in the early 1990s should have been accompanied by a decrease in crime rates, it was not.[97] Freeman and William Rodgers found five years later that in a robust economy marked by a tight labor market, young Blacks were experiencing a reduction in incarceration rates and a boost in both earnings and labor force participation.[98] This evidence should support the argument that the availability of legal—and illegal—employment is a central factor in determining the choices made by young Black males.

Hawkins's view has merit in that the variations in incarceration rates he cited are accounted for by "economically based transformations" rather than by "the independent effect" of varying conceptions of race.[99] Nevertheless, the principal impetus behind recent increases in the incarceration of Blacks is racial punishment, even if this is also related to macroeconomic forces. Indeed, Professor Coramae Richey Mann shows impressively that in the construction and use of various Black codes in the colonial period, in the racial focus of the revised southern state constitutions during the Reconstruction period and in urban policing throughout most of the twentieth century, racial victimization has been a persistent motivating force in high rates of Black incarceration.[100] It seems evident that for most of the nation's history, race and economics have each played a significant role in the phenomenon of Black incarceration.

CONCLUSION

Some scholars maintain that Blacks are overrepresented in the criminal justice system because their criminal behavior is disproportionate to other groups in society. Other observers are sensitive to the fact that policing is a subjective process from beginning to end. Unless there are eye witnesses to a crime—and sometimes even then—those who are suspected of having committed it undergo a process of evaluation that is often biased according to indices of color, ethnicity and wealth. Indeed, two analysts note that "minorities may be overrepresented in jails and prisons in part because the primarily white upper classes get a better break each step of the way. Not only are the crimes of the middle and upper classes harder to detect, there is also good reason to question whether society allocates sufficient law enforcement resources to the task."[101]

The impact of this disproportionally negative treatment of Blacks may be summarized thus: Activities in which Blacks are involved have been more closely criminalized and sentencing has been extended for those offenses; that as a result of the targeted policing of Black communities and extended sentencing, incarceration rates have increased dramatically; that the most serious offenses committed by Blacks disproportionately yield a death sentence, and the range of those offenses has been broadened. The end result of this systemic pattern of treatment by society through the instrument of the law is that the breadth and depth of the incarceration rates and application of the death penalty have captured a significant portion of the Black population, rendering it unviable for the common social pursuits of family, community and citizenship for some time to come. The results of imprisonment and death sentencing, both of which are rendered in a manner that is racially tinged, define the ends of the policy of the White Nationalists as racial punishment.

For the present, crime has fallen and Americans are feeling somewhat easier about public safety. Yet ironically, while the crime rate has fallen, including the murder rate, Black additions to prisons and to death row continue. Since there is little correlation between the downward spiral of the crime rate and the continued upward rate of incarceration and the application of the death penalty, Americans must consider whether the economy is the more powerful engine of the decline in crime, and whether a public policy which contains a structure of laws that do not respond to the behavioral changes of most Blacks who are gainfully employed merely exists to placate the punishment motives of the Nationalist movement.

CHAPTER 8

Attacking Black Access
to Education

INTRODUCTION

A critical impact of the White Nationalist movement in the field of education has been the achievement of the goal of massive resistance to racial integration, thus contributing further to the lack of equal educational opportunity for Blacks and other minorities. Through the systematic rejection of court-ordered busing and the elimination of financial resources for targeted school districts, these instruments of integration were severely weakened or eliminated, and the resegregation of American education is occurring.

Moreover, resistance to integration has resulted in the attempted privatization of education through methods such as providing vouchers for children to attend private schools and the rise of charter schools and magnet schools that provide students with specialized educational experiences. The comprehensive ideology of "school choice" has turned public attention away from the challenge of developing excellence in the public school setting, with race as a strong motivating factor. The drive toward choice systems has had the effect of threatening the depletion of resources that public schools need to remain viable.

Higher education has likewise come under attack by the Conservative movement because of the increasing number of Blacks seeking greater access to both selective and less selective institutions. Limiting such access has become the goal of the Nationalist movement, and through reinterpretation of the legal basis of equal educational access, the position of Whites in these institutions has been enhanced. I will outline some of the basic Nationalist policy elements with respect to primary and secondary education in part I and higher education in part II.

PART I: PRIMARY AND SECONDARY EDUCATION

Resegregating K-12

On May 17, 1954, in *Brown v. Board of Education,* the Supreme Court decided that the "state action" which held that separate schools could be equal was wrong. On the basis of a consideration of both tangible and intangible factors, the Court held that separate educational facilities were inherently unequal and that the state's permission of such segregation amounted to a denial of the equal protection of the laws. More recently, however, the Court has, with equanimity, revised the Constitutional underpinnings of the *Brown* decision, and the result has been the preservation of a racially based system of public education.

This was not the product of a benign or objective viewpoint but one rooted in the desire of White racial interests in education to be expressed predominantly in overwhelmingly White social and educational settings, using the instruments of the law and politics to effect this. Social policy designed to increase Black access to better funded, predominantly White public schools has been subverted. Indeed, Professor Gary Orfield has said that "we are going right back to where we were—only worse. Many of the schools in inner-city neighborhoods are isolated in a way they've never been before."[1]

In the mid-1980s, a study by Ira Katznelson and Margaret Weir observed that what they described as "democratic education" had begun to suffer because of changes in American society.[2] They called attention to the role of class issues in the suburbanization of the White middle class and the concomitant loss of interest in inner-city schools. They argued that: "More and more Americans, including members of the working class, have been able to purchase residences in areas protected by defensive zoning to ensure their homogeneity. Housing and schooling markets have displaced educational politics as key forums of decision making. As a result, public education, which had been the repository of egalitarian aspirations and opportunities, has become more and more a force of social division and inequality."[3] One must wonder what kinds of homogeneity Katznelson and Weir were imagining, because the economic and demographic forces they took into account, including race, were the very factors responsible for the structural problems in urban schools.

The belief that the public education system is in crisis was promoted by the publication in 1983 of "A Nation at Risk," a report of the National Commission on Excellence in Education.[4] The report described the crisis as one of educational "standards." Expressing the crisis in this way ignores the persistent effects of race and racism in determining educational access and excellence.

A study by Orfield and Eaton found that following the 1954 Supreme Court decision, public school integration increased dramatically until the late 1980s and then began to decline. In other words, resegregation began to rise in the Bush administration as a result of cumulative policies in the Reagan administration.[5] Several factors contributed to this resegregation.

1. According to Orfield, although White migration to the suburbs was part of the reason for the smaller number of White children in urban schools, another important factor was the lower White birth rate in cities.[6] (By contrast, Black and Hispanic populations in inner cities have grown dramatically.[7]) Although Whites have left the cities or failed to replicate their original portion of the urban population—and thus have less personal interest in urban schools—they maintain most of the power to decide the levels of funding these schools receive.[8]

2. In *Board of Education v. Dowell* (1991), the Supreme Court allowed the Oklahoma City school district to "bail out" of the *Brown v. Board of Education* requirements because of the city's changing demographics. A new order permitted the school board to substantially eliminate busing and return to neighborhood schools.[9]

3. Throughout the Reagan administration, no new desegregation orders were written. The Office of Civil Rights in the Department of Education was closed down in 1981, and that same year the 1972 Emergency School Aid Act, which helped fund desegregation in communities with particular challenges, was turned into a block grant program with no specific instructions to promote school integration. In effect, the Reagan administration gutted the federal enforcement infrastructure established to accomplish school integration. This situation continued through the Bush administration and the first Clinton administration as well, as indicated by the fact that the Justice Department position of assistant attorney general for civil rights was left unfilled until 1997.

4. The Supreme Court delivered a severe blow to the funding of school integration in 1995 with its decision in *Missouri v. Jenkins,* which

eliminated the authority of a district judge to monitor school desegregation in St. Louis and prescribe funding for this purpose.[10] According to Orfield, this decision—together with the Oklahoma City case cited above and a 1992 Atlanta case[11]—effectively vitiated the 1954 *Brown* decision. In addition to eliminating busing, it rescinded the authority of judges to direct districts to provide increased funding to attract White students into educationally enhanced, majority-Black schools.[12]

The NAACP rationale for supporting a policy of school integration was correct: when the majority of public schools were historically White, they were funded by the political system and thus were able to offer students the opportunity to pursue educational excellence. Whatever the NAACP assumed the more mystical benefits of racial integration might be, at least this much is true today: Black-majority schools have fewer resources, fewer facilities and fewer good teachers than do White-majority schools.

Many Black parents who were beneficiaries of the Civil Rights movement agreed with its emphasis on school integration. Yet as it became clear that opposition to housing integration and busing was preventing the goal of school integration from being achieved, they began to focus more on making Black-majority educational institutions a setting for academic excellence. A late 1990s Public Agenda study of 1,600 respondents—with a unique sample of an equal number of Black and White parents—found that nearly 80% of Black parents wanted schools to devote more resources to raising academic standards and achievements, while only 9% wanted to emphasize more diversity and integration.[13]

To be sure, many Black parents were never convinced in the first place that racial integration should be a higher priority than academic excellence. This was especially true where the promotion of busing held the demeaning assumption that Black children had to sit next to White children in order to learn, and where Black children suffered the inconvenience of being bused long distances from their neighborhoods. But when it became clear that school busing and similar measures were essentially transferring Black children from schools in majority-Black communities to majority-Black schools in other communities, recognition of these measures brought the realization of the need to change policies. Indeed, Professor Glen Loury, a prominent Black Conservative economist, spoke for many parents when he questioned the wisdom of pursuing school integration policy and suggested that enhancing integration was the "wrong strategy."[14]

The obvious fact, all but ignored by the NAACP and many Black families, is that no matter how much Blacks desired racial integration, the burden of attaining this has always rested with the White population. White flight from integrated housing and White rejection of the means to achieve integrated schools illustrate that a racially integrated education system is unlikely to develop in the foreseeable future. In the Public Agenda study cited above, 82% of White parents said that they did not care about the racial makeup of their children's schools, yet 61% of them said they feared that a large influx of Black students would result in declining test scores and increased discipline problems.[15] Clearly, such attitudes have constituted a motivation for White migration from urban areas.

The result of the policies of the past three decades is that most Blacks still attend predominantly Black schools (see Table 8.1). The data from Orfield's 1993 study, summarized here, show that although the percentage of Black students in predominantly minority schools decreased by more than 10% between 1968 and 1992, that trend reversed in the period from 1992 to 1999. Latino students experienced a similar integration/resegregation shift: 58.4% were in predominantly minority schools in 1968–1969, 75.6% in 1999. The growth of the Latino population and the steady withdrawal of the White population from urban areas explain why more than one-third of both Black and Latino students currently attend schools that are more than 90% minority.

While stereotypes suggest that segregated schools are predominantly in the South, this was not true in the early 1990s, as Table 8.2 shows. Indeed, racially segregated school systems were actually more common in

TABLE 8.1   Percent of Black Students in Predominantly Minority Schools

Period	Percent
1968–1969	76.6%
1972–1973	63.6%
1980–1981	62.9%
1986–1987	63.3%
1991–1992	66.0%
1994–1995	67.1%
1996–1997	68.8%
1998–1999	70.2%

Sources: Gary Orfield, "The Growth of Segregation in American Schools: Changing Patterns of Separation and Poverty since 1968," Executive Summary, Harvard Project on School Desegregation, December 1993, Table 1, p. 7. Gary Orfield, "Schools More Separate: Consequences of a Decade of Resegregation," Civil Rights Project, Harvard University, July 2001, Table 9, p. 35.

TABLE 8.2	Most Segregated States for Black Students, 1991–1992

State	Blacks enrolled in school systems that are more than 50% Black
New York	84.6%
Illinois	80.2%
California	80.0%
Michigan	79.9%
Mississippi	74.4%
New Jersey	73.5%
Maryland	72.2%
Wisconsin	70.1%
Pennsylvania	69.0%
Louisiana	68.4%

Source: Gary Orfield, "The Growth of Segregation in American Schools: Changing Patterns of Separation and Poverty since 1968," Executive Summary, Harvard Project on School Desegregation, December 1993, Table 6, p. 12.

the Northeast (where 76.2% of systems were more than 50% Black), the Midwest (69.9%) and the West (69.7%), with the lowest percentage of segregated systems in the border states (59.3%).[16] By 1999 racial isolation had increased in all regions. The greatest increase in the numbers of Blacks attending schools with student bodies over 50% minority were registered in the South (7.6%), followed by the border states (5.4%), the West (4.3%), the Midwest (2.9%) and the Northeast (1.3%).[17] At the end of 2000, Orfield found a pattern of increasing isolation of Black and Latino children in public schools, leading him to observe: "We are punishing people who've never been given an equal opportunity."[18]

Black Schooling and Poverty

While one source of the apparent aversion of many Whites to having their children educated with Black children is race, they may also be averse because Black children predominantly attend schools that correlate with high poverty. The most pronounced school segregation is found in large to mid-sized cities in the inner urban core, where concentrated poverty is high. Orfield emphasizes a well-known fact when he notes that: "[Black children] face not only discrimination and stereotypes about minority schools, but schools struggling with the much greater concentration of health, social, and neighborhood problems that are found in high poverty schools."[19] Indeed, Orfield found that in 1998–1999, 88% of minority schools with high segregation existed in neighborhoods with concentrated poverty.[20]

A study released in January 1998 held that 43% of the nation's minority children and 35% of its poor (amounting to 11 million children) attended urban schools which were failing, and two-thirds of these children failed to achieve national norms on standard tests of performance. Gaps in performance were found to have been most pronounced in Maryland, Connecticut, New York, New Jersey and Missouri, states which, as Orfield indicates, also experienced high levels of racial isolation.[21]

What made the failure of school integration in the 1980s and 1990s possible was the formation of a new Conservative movement. Michael Apple and Anita Oliver maintain that White parents became alienated by cultural change and its manifestations in the school curriculum, igniting the mobilization of religious Conservatives.[22] Apple and Oliver also identified another motive: class tension fomented by the declining economic fortunes of the working class, which engendered an antigovernment, religio-authoritarian politics.[23] This grassroots movement, as we suggested in chapters 1 and 2, has become manifest in national politics and public policy.

Funding and Performance

With the emergence of the White Nationalist movement, the notion of alleviating poverty through improvements in education gave way to an emphasis on education funding (or per pupil expenditure) and whether education was cost effective in producing higher achievement levels.

The argument about funding is often presented in an unsophisticated fashion, even by education advocates. For example, a 1997 report in *Education Week* concluded that money was not the central issue in school performance, since spending in underachieving districts was above state averages.[24] Yet one of the study directors suggested that what mattered more was how the available funds were spent, noting that some districts spent more per pupil on administration than other districts spent on instruction.[25] Nevertheless, it cannot be argued that since 70% of Black students attend primarily minority schools which are poorly funded that funding is irrelevant to educational performance. In a recent speech commemorating the *Brown v. Board of Education* decision, Robert Chase, president of the National Education Association, said: "Instead of correcting historical school finance inequities, over the past 46 years regressive political forces have designed new schemes to divert even more public money away from public schools. Many of the more than 500 court-ordered and voluntary school desegregation plans established since *Brown* have been eliminated in less than a decade."[26]

Merely comparing school expenditures to population without asking who is being funded and what are the conditions under which they are being educated begs the question. Middle-class institutions perform better not only because per pupil expenditures are high—because of the property tax funding scheme—but because these sums are complemented by middle-class parents' ability to contribute extra time and money, both to the schools and to their children's enrichment, health and security. The right question to ask is: How much does it cost to educate a child when one adds to the poverty quotient the social disorganization quotient caused by years of oppression and neglect that produced the social milieu in which the education of poor Black children takes place?

Some studies are beginning to use a more sophisticated concept of the "buying power" of the funds assigned to the education of poor children. In such analyses, the dollars applied to the actual cost of providing education are compared to such relative factors as the cost of living and the educational needs of different children. Such adjustments reflect the fact that $5,000 spent for education in New York City may not buy as much education as $5,000 in, for example, Wisconsin.[27] And some studies are beginning to ask the right questions. For example, T. B. Parish, C. S. Matsumoto and W. Fowler found that school districts with more than 50% minority students spend more per pupil on average than those with less than 50%, with the differential in 1996 placed at $431 per student.[28] However, this figure by itself is not instructive, for they found that when the concept of "buying power" is taken into consideration, districts with the highest percentage of minority students have a deficit of $286 per student per year compared with nonminority districts.[29]

CHOICE: THE FINAL SOLUTION

One Conservative strategy to deal with the possibility of racially integrated schools was to localize educational power by challenging and destroying desegregation enforcement programs at both national and local levels. Another was to privatize education and educational resources by dismantling the public school system itself, allowing children to opt out of public school and enroll in private ones by using public resources. Milton Friedman, Nobel Prize-winning economist and Conservative Republican policy maker, first proposed school choice in 1955 in response to the

Supreme Court's decision in *Brown* a year earlier; he argued that competition would inevitably improve the quality of public schools.

Friedman's argument has not been decisively proven. In November of 1998, for example, the Indiana Center for Evaluation at Indiana University, which manages the state's voucher program, released a study of the differences between fourth grade public school students and their counterparts in the voucher scholarship program. The study found that: "In general, scholarship students performed significantly better than public school students in language and less measurably better in science, but otherwise there are no significant differences in reading, mathematics or social studies."[30] In other words, the differential settings yielded only slightly better results in the voucher-driven program. In many cases, evaluation of the use of vouchers is influenced by the ideological orientation of the organization performing or funding the study. However, one assessment derived from an international database of 16 industrialized countries—the International Assessment of Educational Progress—provides evidence that "private schools do not have significantly higher student achievement than public schools after controlling for student background."[31]

Ironically, the idea of using vouchers to achieve school choice was launched by a Black Wisconsin Democratic state legislator, Polly Williams. She crafted her legislative initiative, known as the Milwaukee Parental Choice Program, in 1990 as a "progressive" response to the problem of limited education options available to poor inner-city children, most of whom were Black. For several years, Williams was referred to by leaders of the Conservative movement, such as former Secretary of Education William Bennett, as a leading spokeswoman for school choice, and she was instrumental in legitimizing this policy as a new proposal for urban education, even though those who would actually benefit the most from the legalization of school choice were middle-class Whites.

Middle-class Whites represent the political class which was most alienated by school integration policies such as busing. They wanted to restore neighborhood schools because of the likelihood that they would be majority White. And they wanted to receive a federal or state subsidy for private education that they could use to help defray the costs and thus make private schools affordable. Some poor Black families in Milwaukee have benefited from the voucher program, but most still attend public schools because there is not enough voucher money to enable them to do otherwise. To make a private school education available to every child in America would require building another school system altogether, an unimaginably costly enterprise; presently there are 47 million children in public schools and only 7 million in private ones.

The concept of school vouchers as the instrument to bring about choice is a hotly debated issue. A wide variety of educational officials and politicians of both parties support it, along with Conservative organizations such as the Bradley Foundation and the Washington, D.C.–based legal organization known as the Institute for Justice. Many Republican governors have also championed some version of school vouchers. But vouchers are opposed by the Congressional Black Caucus, the NAACP and the American Civil Liberties Union, with the National Education Association posing the most strenuous objections.

In January of 1999, congressional Republicans sponsored a proposal to fund $7 million in tuition for private schools for 2,000 children in the District of Columbia at $3,200 per child; the measure passed in both the House and the Senate, but it was vetoed by President Clinton. By comparison, the Milwaukee program pays $5,000 for each of 6,200 children to attend 122 private schools, and while it provides an acceptable education for these children, this comes at a cost to the other 100,000 children in the Milwaukee public schools: $25 million in financial resources in 1998 alone.[32] As it became clear that the Milwaukee voucher system was depleting the city's public schools, Polly Williams reflected on her initial support for vouchers and her role as a spokeswoman for the program: "The conservative movement made me their poster girl as long as it appeared I was supporting their cause. And now I am the odd person out. They want the religious schools to be tax-supported. Blacks and poor are being used to help legitimize them as the power group."[33] Rep. Williams had been left behind in the drive for more aggressive support through the voucher system for the real beneficiaries, the White middle class.

Polly Williams is not the only Black person who has seen vouchers as a viable alternative to improving Black schools. Many Black parents, sensitive to the effects of limited educational opportunities in their children's public schools, have recently sought to place their children in private schools in much greater numbers. Moreover, some Black church leaders support a voucher program because it allows them to obtain greater financial resources for their church-based educational institutions. One example is Rev. Floyd Flake, formerly a member of the Congressional Black Caucus, who heads a large religious institution in Brooklyn that operates a considerable number of social outreach programs, including a school. His support for vouchers while he was a Democratic member of the caucus earned him low marks from his colleagues.

Black students' access to parochial schools was enhanced by a decision of the Wisconsin Supreme Court which authorized the use of state funds to support education for children in private educational institutions. The Wisconsin suit, initially litigated by Kenneth Starr, the former independent counsel who investigated President Clinton, ended in a deadlocked court in 1996. However, in June of 1998 the court issued a decision allowing taxpayer money to be utilized to support students in religious schools.[34] Critics of the decision observed that these resources would be diverted from public schools that are overwhelmingly Black in Milwaukee to support overwhelmingly White religious schools outside the city. This shift in resources through the promulgation of policy is undeniably intentional.

The door has been opened wider for those seeking profit under the totally untested theory that competition will improve schools. One participant in the charter school movement decried the fact that the policy of providing more choice options for students has, in many instances, provided additional opportunities to for-profit organizations that operate public schools. The possibility of such opportunities may be part of the increased attention to the charter school concept at both state and local levels.[35] And this may also help explain why in the past decade businesses have become more intensively involved in financing private voucher programs by donating money to organizations set up for this purpose by the publishing magnate Walter Annenberg, by the investment lawyer and chair of Gulfstream Aerospace Theodore J. Forstmann and by John T. Walton, a director of Wal-Mart and son of its founder, Sam Walton.[36]

Clinton Administration Objections to Vouchers

The Clinton administration attempted to "split the difference" on the issue of choice by supporting charter schools but opposing voucher programs because vouchers have a greater potential to seriously damage public schools. The administration's stance can be traced at least in part to its alliance with the National Education Association, which has been a stable and formidable member of the Democratic party coalition and which aggressively opposes vouchers. However, charter schools and magnet schools have been attacked by Whites and Asians who maintain that their children are excluded from them, and with the devaluation of race as a policy criterion, Blacks may eventually lose access to these as well.[37]

The Clinton administration also objected to voucher programs because of their lack of enforceable standards of protection for civil rights. For example, Clint Bolick, litigation director of the Conservative Institute of Justice, was a major instigator of the 1997 congressional legislative plan to greatly expand vouchers within the District of Columbia.

The proposed legislation—which passed Congress but was vetoed by Clinton—excluded the application of Title VI, Title IX and Section 504 of the 1964 Civil Rights Act from the D.C. voucher program. This would have meant that although private schools would be supported by public funds, they would be allowed to discriminate in contravention of Title VI and they would not have to equalize opportunities for female students to participate in school athletics as called for in Title IX. Most important, students would not have access to the full protection of the Individuals with Disabilities Education Act, which ensures that disabled children have a right to education. (On another occasion the Institute of Justice proposed that public funds in Wisconsin be utilized to support private school choice programs.[38])

The Clinton administration offered its own legislation, known as National Educational Goals (or Goals 2000), which reaffirmed the importance of the public schools. It asserted that American education needed to be improved and that the principal mechanism for this should be the development of a set of national standards which would be voluntarily achieved and monitored by standardized testing of both teachers and students. Given fifty different educational systems, the administration argued, it would be difficult to have national accountability and a means of comparing educational quality without such a set of standards and testing. Richard Riley, Clinton's secretary of education, expressed the administration's support for public schools:

> Quality public schools are the foundation of a democracy and a free enterprise economic system. The public school concept is fundamentally American: most of the fifty U.S. states have a provision in their state constitution for free, public education. These statutes reflect a commitment to the idea that all children, regardless of their academic readiness, race, socioeconomic status, language proficiency, or special education needs, have equal access to a quality K–12 education, and a chance to develop to their maximum potential.[39]

Vouchers are antithetical to this position. In the words of Neil Postman, they would signal "the end of education."[40]

The administration's objections to vouchers were based on the likelihood that they would divert attention from the need to improve the public schools; add to the public cost of education; reduce accountability; and force private and parochial schools to become less private and less parochial. Moreover, it was feared that private schools would accept only the best and brightest students, limiting, in particular, the proportion of students with costly physical disabilities who were accepted. It was also pointed out that private schools would be unable to absorb large numbers of students, and that voucher programs possibly violate the U.S. Constitution—and state constitutions as well—with respect to the separation of church and state.

A brief review of the eligibility requirements for the Milwaukee school choice program confirms the validity of the Clinton administration's concerns:

1. Private schools may not use information in the admissions process that pertains to: race, ethnic background, religion, residence, prior test scores, grades, church membership, or agreement to school policies.
2. All eligible choice students must be accepted by lottery.
3. The amount of the voucher is limited to $4,894 and the difference in higher cost schools must be made up by parents or others.
4. Students with special needs have no guarantee of the availability of special services, since no such information can be requested from students.[41]

Furthermore, it is difficult to conceive that more selective institutions would accept an unlimited number of low-income students. Thus, even under a choice system, students are likely to be segregated within a set of existing private institutions by class, or prevented altogether from accessing available institutions in the numbers required to have a serious impact upon minority education.

Minorities: The Shill for Localization

Conservative school choice policies translate into the right of parents to be able to send their children to private schools at government expense. The White Nationalist movement seeks to use school choice to dissipate the power of government. School choice not only localizes decisions about public education, obliterating methodologies such as busing for the purpose of achieving school integration, it also redirects economic resources in the service of this policy.

It is interesting that one of the ameliorative policy directions that appears to have achieved consensus among political moderates and Conservatives in the context of choice programs is education for minorities. Indeed, in the balanced budget agreement between President Clinton and Republicans in 1997, the one area of social policy where significant expansion occurred was in education. Still, it is puzzling that at the same time Conservatives agreed that education is the preferred route to social progress for minorities, they voted to kill a $5 billion White House proposal to fund the rehabilitation of crumbling inner-city schools. This proposal was a derivative of one suggested by Sen. Carol Moseley Braun (D-Ill.), who, on April 21, 1998, proposed an amendment to the 1999 education appropriation bill that contained an increase of $22 billion for school construction funds. Sen. Paul Coverdale (R-Ga.), who managed the main bill—which championed such measures as education savings accounts and education tax credits—led the charge to defeat the Braun proposal. This is a classic case of a policy outcome which moves from being merely Conservative to White Nationalist because of the presumptively positive effect such funding would have on Black students or on inner-city schools that are predominantly Black.

This brings us back to the Clinton administration's objections to a voucher system. The costs of a voucher or choice program would fall disproportionately upon Black children.

—Black children would lose many of their civil rights in a private school
     setting;
—Black children would suffer from diminishing economic resources in
     public schools;
—Black children may be vulnerable to exploitation where they represent
     numbers in a for-profit system that is not subject to accountability;
—Black children will not be accepted into private educational institutions in numbers great enough to affect the general status of Black
     education.

More and Better Teachers

The fiscal year 1998 appropriations bill signed by President Clinton appeared to be generous toward education. It added $3 billion in education spending—not counting increases for Pell grants for college students—more impact aid to communities with a large federal burden and an increase in Title I funds for disadvantaged students.[42] In light of research that relates class size to improved student performance and to greater teacher effectiveness, Clinton also proposed the addition of 100,000 teachers to the nation's classrooms.

Clinton's national educational standards proposals reflected renewed emphasis on testing teachers to improve instructional competence. To many of the Nationalists—and also some NEA members, no doubt—a testing regime for teachers translated into a mechanism for eliminating from the system many highly regarded, older, Black teachers. However, when Massachusetts, a state with a large number of esteemed educational institutions, tested prospective teachers using an instrument based on much higher standards, nearly 60% of prospective teachers failed to obtain a passing grade: about 40% earned a grade of "D" and 20% failed altogether.[43] Subsequently, it was suggested that Massachusetts abandon this examination.

Educational Devolution: The Road Ahead

It should not go unnoticed that as with welfare reform, housing policy and other aspects of social policy, vouchers amount to a robust form of devolution. They represent a style of governance which alters the balance of federalism to favor states by releasing them from federal regulatory mandates and providing them with flexibility in the administration of funding. It is no surprise that in early 1999, Republicans demanded flexibility in the use of federal education funds and tied this to Title I of the Elementary and Secondary Education Act (ESEA), which governs 70 education programs and disburses $14 billion.

The new Speaker of the House, Dennis Hastert (R-Ill.) announced this proposal in January, and the House Education and Workforce Committee soon opened hearings on an expansion of the 12-state pilot program known as "Ed-Flex," under which some states gained specific waivers of federal regulations so they could tailor spending to local initiatives.[44] In his announcement, Hastert typically indicted federal government involvement in education: "While this administration thinks federal control and Washington-based initiatives are the answer, we have faith that the folks back home, those closest to the problem, will come up with common-sense solutions that work."[45] Legislators like Sen. Judd Gregg (R-N.H.) appeared to indict Title I as well, charging that as the flagship of K–12 programs, it had not met its goal of reducing the achievement gap between disadvantaged students and established national norms, although $112 billion had been spent on Title I since it began in 1965.[46] At the same time, the proposal for Ed-Flex was presented in the Senate by Bill Frist (R-Tenn.) and Ron Wyden (D-Ore.)—a signal of bipartisanship in the aftermath of the Clinton impeachment and an indication that the policy had wide support both in Congress and among governors.[47]

Though the waiver authority under Ed-Flex is broad, some regulations cannot be waived, such as those in the Individuals with Disabilities Education Act and in civil rights-related court orders.[48] Nevertheless, some lawmakers critical of Ed-Flex feared that resources devoted to Title I, which are specifically intended for disadvantaged students, would be diverted to other programs. Title I funds several programs pertinent to Black and Hispanic students, including: Helping Disadvantaged Children Meet High Standards; Even Start; Migrant Education; and Neglected, Delinquent, and At-Risk Youth. Also considered vulnerable to diversion were Safe and Drug-Free Schools and Communities programs administered under Title IV, and Emergency Immigrant Education programs administered under Title VI. A valid reason for this concern can be seen in the Texas waiver that was approved by the Department of Education:

> Provision to be Waived: Title I, Part A. Description of Waiver: "The law currently requires school districts to allocate Title I, Part A funds to eligible campuses on the basis of the number of children from low income families. A waiver will allow allocation of funds based upon campus needs and program designs."[49]

The House passed the Ed-Flex bill on March 11, 1999, by a vote of 330 to 90, with 14 representatives not voting. The Senate passed the measure by a vote of 98 to 1, with only Paul Wellstone (D-Minn.) dissenting. In the House, 32 of the 36 voting members of the Congressional Black Caucus voted against it, with Reps. Sanford Bishop (D-Ga.), Harold Ford, Jr. (D-Tenn.) and Albert Wynn (D-Md.) voting for it, and Rep. Chaka Fattah (D-Pa.) not voting.[50] The chairman of the Congressional Black Caucus, Rep. James Clyburn (D-S.C.), said that the reason most of the CBC opposed the bill was the fear that it would dilute Title I, that block grants have historically worked against the interests of minorities, that the House version of Ed-Flex altered the concept as it was conceived by the White House and that it should have been incorporated into the reauthorization of ESEA so that it could be regularly evaluated.[51] As the Clinton administration came to a close, states' "flexibility" with respect to the use of federal Title I funds had become a fixed principle of policy.

CONCLUSION

In general, private schooling does not deliver significantly higher levels of education, especially given its higher cost, so there must be other motivations behind the move to privatize public education. One possible motive comports with the "localization of power" thesis—that many Whites desire to maintain the cultural objective of a predominantly White social system which includes the right of their children to be educated in a predominantly White environment.

One might draw some understanding of this objective from the first modern reference to "school choice," which accompanied the "Massive Resistance" movement that sprang up in the South following the 1954 *Brown v. Board of Education* decision. The function of this slogan was explicated by Professor Hardy Cross Dillard of the University of Virginia Law School in a 1962 article: "According to its proponents freedom of choice is simply a vindication of the right to be free in choosing one's associates. It is asserted that this freedom is invaded if one citizen is compelled to associate with another. Inasmuch as elementary education is compulsory it follows that school 'integration' violates this freedom."[52] Dillard thus attempted to ground southern segregationists' opposition to *Brown* in the Constitutional doctrine of "freedom of association." Even though he admitted that the doctrine was not amenable to such an interpretation, he found that it was, nevertheless, close enough. In effect, Dillard suggested that the motivation of parents who seek to privatize education is that it permits them to escape from the mandates of racial inclusion that exist in the public system based on legitimate state action.

In the contemporary iteration of "school choice," it would appear that the racial exclusionary motive is still present. This time, however, the political power of the majority has shaped policy to change the direction of state action to allow them to evade responsibility for publicly mandated racial inclusion and to exercise private educational choices using public resources that will result in resegregation. For whatever the motivation may be, this is the legacy of White flight and the abandonment of the notion of widespread racially integrated schools. Despite the fact that the public has rejected vouchers by large margins and defeated various referenda, the Supreme Court's 5 to 4 Conservative majority finally approved them in a Cleveland case, *Zelman v. Simmons-Harris,* at the end of its 2001–2002 term.[53]

PART II: HIGHER EDUCATION: THE RETURN OF APARTHEID

The White Nationalist movement has attacked affirmative action in higher education because its institutions have served as the means for many Blacks to enter the mainstream of American society. Thomas M. Smith has expressed this succinctly:

> Minorities in the United States have long suffered lower economic prosperity and social status relative to the white majority. Higher education often serves as the best means of social mobility available to our nation's young people. For example, graduating from college is associated with more stable patterns of employment and higher earnings. As the gap in earnings between high school and college graduates continues to widen, attending college has become even more important for minorities who are trying to enter into a globally competitive labor market.[54]

Data from the 2000 census indicate that while the average income of Black high school graduates is $19,934, Black college graduates earned $37,830.[55] In 1998, an assessment of the median weekly earnings of full-time workers found that Black women showed the highest education effect on their earnings, with a 57% premium for a bachelor's degree and a 100% premium for an advanced degree, compared to a high school diploma.[56] Nevertheless, Black college graduates still earned only $32,062 annually, 77% of what White college graduates earned: $41,439.[57] But in absolute terms, higher education has promoted Black advancement in society whether the comparison is between college-educated and non-college-educated Blacks or between college-educated Blacks and Whites.

Black youths have begun to increase their college enrollment rate, as a consequence of their understanding of the education effect upon future earnings and social standing and with the help of affirmative action programs. Yet at the same time, according to Professor Robert Allen, "because they promise to make significant inroads against the established status quos of racial and patriarchal hierarchy—affirmative action programs are under severe, extensive attack from powerful vested interests."[58]

Thwarting Black Access

Black youths and their families have responded enthusiastically to the greater access to college and universities made possible by the Civil Rights movement of the 1960s. For example, in 1972, 32% of Black high school students said they intended to go to college, but in 1994, 52% expressed the same sentiment. Yet while the percentage of White students who were enrolled in college the year following their graduation from high school went from 50% to 60% between 1972 and 1994, Black enrollment directly after high school showed a different pattern. Black college enrollment was at 50% in 1972, declined in the late 1970s and through about 1987, then reached 50% again in 1994. The decline in the late 1970s to 1987 period illustrates the impact of cuts in education grants in the fiscally depressed late Carter era and the changes in educational financing during the Reagan administration: fewer grants and more loans. This shift was important to Black and Hispanic students, who, because of their families' lower economic status, are more dependent upon grants and scholarships.[59]

More important, equal access to higher education was threatened by the challenge to the legal basis upon which it was founded. The Supreme Court decision in *Adams v. Richardson* (1970) was the rough equivalent of the *Brown* decision in that it established the principle of the desegregation of higher education in law as a national objective.[60] This directly challenged the dual systems of higher education maintained by southern states and set up a protracted legal battle as acrimonious as that experienced in elementary and secondary education. The *Adams* decision was overturned in 1990, after the Reagan administration challenged its continuing applicability in 1987; U.S. District Court Judge John Pratt agreed with the Justice Department that civil rights lawyers no longer had standing in the case.[61] This set the stage for other court battles in the South over desegregation and affirmative action as the principal tool for guaranteeing Black access to colleges and universities.

In other regions of the country, affirmative action in higher education and other arenas was under attack. California's Proposition 209 was voted on in 1996 and passed by 54.6% to 45.4%. It outlawed the use of affirmative action programs in state agencies associated with education, employment and contracting.[62] The measure—which was upheld by a technical decision of the U.S. Supreme Court in September of 1997—called for the elimination of "racial preferences" in language that appears to be a straightforward rendering of the language of the 1964 Civil Rights Act. "The state will not use race, sex, color, ethnicity or national origin as a criterion for either discriminating against, or granting preferential treatment to, any individual or group in the operation of the state's system of public employment, education, or public contracting." This follows Title VII in prohibiting discrimination against the original protected classes. However, the prohibition against "granting preferential treatment" to those same classes was designed to thwart the state's affirmative action programs, which were not the subject of Title VII. Proposition

209 thus directly challenged the finding in *Wygant v. Jackson,* wherein Justice Sandra Day O'Connor wrote on behalf of the majority: "Although its precise contours are uncertain, a state interest in the promotion of racial diversity has been found to be sufficiently 'compelling,' at least in the context of higher education, to support the use of racial considerations in furthering that interest."[63]

In 1998 Rep. Frank Riggs (R-Ca.) introduced an amendment to the higher education appropriation bill in an attempt to eliminate affirmative action in higher education. He couched this action in a clear exposition of his theoretical line of attack: "After 25 years of preference, racial preferences continue to be a powerful source of racism and racial resentment in our society. . . . They have poisoned racial relations at universities and schools across this country. It is time for us to admit to ourselves, to our fellow Americans that race conscious State action is not a cure for racism. It is simply a reinforcement of it."[64] It is clear that like others in the White Nationalist movement, Rep. Riggs reinterpreted affirmative action to make it a *source* of "racism"—substantial proof of the fact that he, as others, perceived that the benefits from what are called "racial preferences" perpetrate a harm upon Whites can be defined as "racism."[65]

Riggs's allegation of racism was based on ideological principle, not on any detailed show of proof that Whites had been harmed—a method which has been adopted by other spokespersons in the Nationalist movement. Moreover, Riggs suggested that his legislation was intended to reestablish "color blindness" in the administration of the law, a goal supported by his colleague Rep. Tom Campbell (R-Ca.), who declared: "The danger is that once the State begins to use race, it is very, very, hard to do it right, to do it in a fair and constitutional way."[66] Campbell's statement illustrates his lack of understanding or appreciation of the manner in which racial disparities are routinely produced in myriad ways by public policy, either purposefully or accidentally.

Congressional Republicans attempted to ground their proposal to eliminate affirmative action on the notion of minority suffering and on the issue of restoring color blindness and merit. But as the following discussion illustrates, they were oblivious to context and perspective, and they linked the issue of Black qualifications with the notion of White harm.

Minority suffering: Riggs suggested that minority groups admitted under lower standards suffered since on the whole they performed less well than White students and often did not complete their course of study. This view was forcefully refuted by the most extensive study to date of the impact of affirmative action on minorities in selective institutions of higher education.[67] William Bowen and Derek Bok, the former presidents of Princeton and Harvard, respectively, marshaled a study of 45,184 cases of Black students who entered 28 highly selective colleges in the fall of 1976 through the fall of 1989. The study found that but for their race, many of these Black students might have been denied access because of lower test scores. It further revealed that although affirmative action programs admitted Black students with somewhat lower scores, these students often went on to achieve *more* than their White counterparts.[68] For example, Black college graduates were more likely than White college graduates to earn post-graduate degrees (40% of Black graduates in the survey earned such degrees compared to 37% of White graduates). Moreover, Black graduates were much more likely to go on to become leaders in their community and in social service as well as other professional occupations. Most important, the authors found in their survey little evidence for the conservative thesis that Blacks regret having obtained educational access through affirmative action or that they feel otherwise harmed by race-sensitive policies. Indeed the survey found Black opinions about affirmative action to be exceedingly positive: 75% felt that colleges should devote a great deal of attention to racial diversity.

Restoring color blindness and merit: Rep. Riggs and his colleagues argued that eliminating affirmative action in public institutions of higher learning would restore color-blind treatment to admissions and reestablish merit as the dominant criterion. Supporters of affirmative action have pointed out, however—as early as *Bakke v. University of California/Davis Medical School*—that race has never been the sole criterion for college and university admissions and that merit has always been part of the evaluation of a minority student's application. Moreover, supporters have argued that a retreat to (presumptive) "color blindness" would likely create selection pools of students who were either White or Asian. Although White Nationalists would apparently be comfortable with the resulting exclusion of Blacks and Hispanics, the question is whether society as a whole is comfortable effectively accomplishing the resegregation of higher education institutions by attempting to achieve an ultimately problematic meritocracy.

It should be pointed out that of the 22,000 applicants turned down for the 8,000 admission slots at University of California/Berkeley for the fall of 1998, 800 were underrepresented minorities with grade point averages of 4.0 and Scholastic Aptitude Test scores of 1100 and over.[69] One of the reasons for this outcome is related to structural racism. These minority students were competing with White and Asian students who had taken advanced placement courses in high school which earned them up to one additional grade point: because of a weighted system, their grade average could be as high as 5.0. Such advanced placement courses are available in many more suburban high schools, to which White students have access, than in urban high schools, where most Black and Hispanic students are enrolled.[70]

Context and perspective: Rep. Charles Canady (R-Fla.), who also had offered a bill generally eliminating affirmative action, spoke on the Riggs amendment. He cited a speech made by Sen. Charles Sumner of Massachusetts in 1871 during congressional debate over a civil rights bill. On that occasion, Sumner asserted that any rule excluding a person on account of his color was "an indignity, an insult and wrong." Canady ignored the context of Sumner's words—a debate about freeing Blacks from bondage—and thus the fact that it was not a neutral formulation of the rights of all citizens. As I have argued elsewhere,[71] the contemporary use of the principle of prohibiting exclusion based on race effectively allows the White majority to utilize its preponderant power in an unchecked fashion to achieve substantial domination.

Black qualifications/White harm: The issue of whether Blacks are qualified to enter more selective colleges and universities was raised long after they had proved themselves capable of meeting rigorous standards in every such institution in America. This issue might be viewed as merely curious, were it not for the fact that increasing numbers of Blacks will be attempting to enter such institutions in the twenty-first century. Much of the anathema toward the idea of using "race" in the higher education application process is the perception that in many cases "race" was the only factor that led to the admission of people of color, and thus a disproportionate number of unqualified individuals were admitted. On the basis of this perception, the law relating to the role of race in higher education admissions has been reversed. Whereas race could once be used as a factor in developing a regime of admissions or access, in the wake of Supreme Court decisions in the late 1990s its use has been seriously undermined. In any case, expressions of concern about "qualifications" often amounts to the resurrection of an objective barrier behind which it may be convenient to hide racial motivations. While this concern has some legitimacy, it must be recognized that "qualifications" is a cultural term that relates not only to the ability of Blacks but also to their right to achieve relative cultural access to a vital instrument of social power.

This issue has been at the heart of such cases as the one brought by Cheryl Hopwood in 1992 when she was denied admission to the University of Texas Law School; her suit alleged that the university practiced "reverse racial discrimination" in that less qualified Blacks were admitted but she was not. In 1994 the Supreme Court held that the "University of

Texas School of Law may not use race as a factor in deciding which applicants to admit [1] in order to achieve a diverse study body, [2] to combat the perceived effects of a hostile environment at the law school, [3] to alleviate the law school's poor reputation in the minority community, or [4] to eliminate any present effect of past discrimination by actors other than the law school."[72] This very broad prohibition of the use of race in admissions was no doubt intended to make it possible for White students, already in the vast majority, to benefit from the elimination of any preferences for Blacks.

The *Hopwood* decision was followed the next year by one that involved the Banneker Scholarship at the University of Maryland, which set aside 40 scholarships for Black students who were fully qualified to enter the university. This decision by the 4th Federal District Court in Richmond—widely understood to be the most Conservative court in the federal system—was effectively upheld by the Supreme Court when, on May 22, 1995, it refused to review an Appeals Court decision affirming the 4th Circuit one. According to one observer, the Court's action "placed in jeopardy an incentive that many colleges have used to increase their minority enrollment."[73] Although the University of Maryland subsequently combined the Banneker program with the Francis Scott Key program, the number of scholarship awards there is presently lower than it was before the 4th Circuit decision.

In 1997 Barbara Grutter sued the University of Michigan Law School, alleging that she was denied admission in favor of less qualified minority students who had been admitted under a quota system. U.S. District Judge Barry Friedman ruled the law school's admission policy unconstitutional in that it used race not as one factor, as university officials claimed, but as the primary factor.[74] This decision was obviously based on the finding in *Hopwood*. However, it was contrary to a positive decision on the use of race in the University of Michigan's undergraduate college the previous December by U.S. District Judge Patrick Duggan. Duggan ruled that the previous policy of set-asides was illegal, but the present policy of using race among other factors was consistent with the *Bakke* decision.

In the Michigan Law School case, as in others, Barbara Grutter and her co-plaintiffs were represented by a coalition of Conservative legal firms such as the Center for Individual Rights, the Institute of Justice—headed by Clint Bolick—the American Civil Rights Institute—headed by prominent Conservative Black activist Ward Connerley—and the Independent Women's Forum. They and others—such as the Center for Equal Opportunity, headed by Linda Chavez—have formulated a strategy of researching application procedures at some of the nation's more selective institutions to determine the basis of admissions methods used when Black students with low SAT scores were accorded entrance. They have matched these students with unsuccessful White applicants in order to create plaintiffs and represent them in actions challenging affirmative action. Their goal is to have one of the cases heard by the Supreme Court—which has shown a tendency to invalidate the use of race in many arenas—and thus destroy affirmative action altogether.

Taxation without Education

Even though Blacks have historically been denied access to higher education systems, their taxes have consistently been used to support them. The result is that they have subsidized services provided to Whites. During the debate over the Riggs amendment, one Hispanic lawmaker pointed this out: "The Riggs amendment would say to black and Latino taxpayers that even though you, because of these very same programs, help to pay for the cost of public education in your state, college administrators cannot design outreach programs to maximize opportunities for your children to attend their institutions. This is wrong."[75] Through court suits in Louisiana, Alabama and Mississippi, Blacks have challenged southern states to provide access to their institutions of higher education to Black taxpaying citizens. Even if it could be argued that many Whites are similarly denied admission to these institutions, the case may be made that for Blacks the denial rate is profoundly disproportional.

The *Ayers v. Musgrove* case in Mississippi reflected attempts to eliminate the vestiges of a racially exclusive system of higher education in the South while preserving the Black institutions, both because of continuing Black exclusion from White ones and because they are vital cultural institutions.[76] In 1992 the Supreme Court ruled that Mississippi must do more to allow Black and White students to attend the state colleges and universities of their choice[77]—in effect ruling that the state's version of "choice" was unconstitutional. In 1998, however, Black parents petitioned to equalize the state funding formulas for Black and White institutions of higher education, claiming the Court had "side-stepped" the question of whether Mississippi had done enough to desegregate its colleges and universities.[78] The *Ayers* saga continued into 2001. In March of that year, a settlement for $500 million was reached by the parties, but Mississippi District Court Judge Neal Biggers challenged the settlement. He felt the it replaced one court-ordered plan with another, but principally he was concerned that the settlement was too costly to Mississippi taxpayers and that the seeming heart of the case, access to White institutions, was only a subsidiary issue in the settlement.[79]

The elimination of Black students from selective White institutions creates a mixed result for Blacks. On the one hand, it keeps Black students from entering White institutions in the numbers to which they are entitled. Yet the fact that Black students are prohibited from entering such institutions forces many to elect to attend Black institutions, and though this outcome is positive for the viability of those institutions[,] it reenforces the concept of separate but equal education. Yet there is certainly no stigma attached to the project of enhancing the ability of students in Black educational institutions to achieve all of which they are capable.

In this chapter we have attempted to answer some of the questions raised by Rep. Corrine Brown (D-Fla.) during the debate on the Riggs amendment. Why is it that attitudes expressed toward Blacks in that debate were so hostile? And why do discussions of affirmative action inevitably lead to attacks on the use of race as an admissions criterion when it is well known that many applicants receive special consideration, for instance if they are outstanding athletes or the children of alumni?[80] The answer is that the presumed racial advantage of Blacks in access to higher education has become the focus of the White Nationalist movement because this process is the key to enhanced racial competition.

Currently there is a foreboding feeling among the Black leadership that affirmative action in higher education is losing ground because of the Conservative campaign against it. The victories of the movement in California and Washington resulted in the adoption of a program of "outreach" rather than set-aside strategies. And Florida Governor Jeb Bush's executive order outlawing affirmative action and creating a "One Florida" plan—which guarantees admission to the state's colleges and universities to the top 20% of graduates from the states' high schools[81]—threatens to become the norm unless the Supreme Court decides otherwise.

CONCLUSION: EDUCATION NOT A PANACEA

As suggested at the outset, education is a key to Black social mobility, offering the opportunity to participate in projects of individual, community and national advancement. White Nationalists, however, prefer education as a solution to the issue of racial amelioration over other measures because it is relatively conflict-free, it represent a long-term process and it fits into the self-development model of "bootstrap-ism." It also comports with the view that impediments to socioeconomic progress lie within the persons affected rather than in the structural racism managed by the dominant group. Indeed, some Whites prefer education as an amelioration strategy because it is the slowest and most precarious route of Black progress and because it admits the fewest to mainstream privileges. For others, it supports the notion that cultural "qualification" is a legitimate standard of admission into majority society.

In a 1995 report, the Economic Policy Institute called attention to the significant gap between Black educational performance and labor market participation; although Blacks have narrowed the higher education gap, this was not reflected in the labor force wage structure. After an exhaustive review of the reasons for this, the institute concluded that Blacks are overrepresented in sectors of the labor market which are particularly vulnerable to economic instability; the decline in union membership and efficacy have hit Blacks hardest; the decline in real wages and the increase in wage inequality favored highly educated workers; and Blacks have been the subject of rampant labor market racial discrimination.[82] So although education is an important factor in Black advancement toward equality, the fact that in 1997 Black college graduates still earned, on average, 77% of the wage their White peers earned suggests that other measures to equalize wages—affirmative action and other programs applicable to private and public sector employers—must be employed. It should also be noted that the exclusion of Blacks from selective institutions through the elimination of affirmative action would depress Black wages and thus exacerbate the wage differential with Whites.

With respect to primary and secondary education, it is all but admitted that school integration policy is dead and that the new frontier is educational quality or "adequacy." Civil rights leaders have begun to encourage Black parents to participate in legal actions designed to force the federal and state governments to fund an adequate educational system where it can be shown that their negligence has resulted in substandard education. If successful, such a policy would have a significant impact upon Black children, because the bulk of substandard schools are in areas with heavy concentrations of Blacks. In 1998 voters in Florida passed a referendum establishing that the state was obligated to provide a "uniform, efficient, safe, secure and high-quality system of free public education." A coalition that included the NAACP, the League of United Latin American Citizens and the Florida Appleseed Center for Law and Justice subsequently sued the state for having failed to meet this obligation.[83] Similar clauses setting out state responsibility to provide an equal and free public education are contained in many state constitutions, and may become the basis of further litigation.

The struggle for racial integration in the schools should continue as a companion policy to the achievement of institutional adequacy. The decision in *United States v. Jefferson County Board of Education* (372 f. 2d 863, 1966) raised this question: "How far have formerly de jure segregated schools progressed in performing their affirmative constitutional duty to furnish equal educational opportunities to all public school children" in the wake of the *Brown* decision?[84] This question still haunts us today, essentially because of the vigor with which Whites have resisted racial integration and erected new impediments to achieving the resources necessary to improve Black educational opportunities.

CHAPTER 9

Black Conservatism: White Interests

BLACK CONSERVATISM

Introduction

One of the most intriguing features of the White Nationalist movement has been the attendant "rise" of Black Conservatism, whose adherents include several highly regarded intellectuals, government officials and civic activists. Among the intellectuals are Professor Thomas Sowell of Stanford University, Professor Walter Williams of George Mason University, Professor Glen Loury of Boston University, Professor Shelby Steele of the University of California/Santa Clara and Professor John McWhorter of the University of California/Berkeley. In the ranks of government officials one finds Supreme Court Justice Clarence Thomas, former Congressman J. C. Watts, Jr. (R-Okla.), former Congressman Gary Franks (R-Conn.), Clarence Pendleton, Jr., former head of the U.S. Civil Rights Commission, and Michael Williams, former assistant secretary of education for civil rights. The social activists include the nominal head of the Congress of Racial Equality, Roy Innis; Robert Woodson, head of the National Center for Neighborhood Enterprise; Jay Parker, head of the Lincoln Institute; and communications professional Armstrong Williams. This group has spawned a series of organizations such as Black America's Political Action Committee and the Center for New Black Politics. In addition, a Conservative television station managed by Armstrong Williams serves as an outlet for Black Conservative viewpoints.

The word "rise" is set in quotation marks in the previous paragraph to call attention to the fact that the evolution of this group owes as much to the White Nationalist movement as to its own members' adroitness in taking advantage of the evolution of a nationwide Conservative movement.

Indeed, the attempt on the part of White Nationalists to cultivate an increased number of Conservative Black leaders began in 1981 when a foundation associated with Ed Meese III, soon to be the U.S. attorney general, sponsored a meeting in California that came to be called the Fairmount Conference. The focus of this meeting was developing a new generation of Black leaders, and the conference's 23 speakers set the tone for the Reagan administration's support of Conservative Blacks. Clarence Thomas was in attendance, and he said of the meeting's intentions: "It was his [Thomas Sowell's] hope, and certainly mine, that this conference would be the beginning of an alternative group—an alternative to the consistently leftist thinking of the civil rights leadership and the general black leadership."[1] Meese contrasted this meeting with one held earlier the same week, in which Reagan met with mainstream Black leaders who sought to protect social programs. Meese asserted that whereas the president's meeting focused on the past, the Fairmount gathering was about the future.[2]

The initiative to develop new Black leadership received support from Newt Gingrich (R-Ga.), who declared: "It is in the interest of the Republican party and Ronald Reagan to invent new black leaders, so to speak. People who have a belief in discipline, hard work and patriotism, the kind of people who applauded Reagan's actions [such as the] . . . [invasion of] Grenada."[3]

Journalists Jack Anderson and Michael Binstein pointed out the parallels between this endeavor to invent new Black leaders and the actions of another Conservative, FBI Director J. Edgar Hoover. Hoover's angst over the activities of Dr. Martin Luther King, Jr., led him to try to discredit King's leadership by placing him under the most rigorous surveillance—a scheme which was first reported by Anderson and Binstein.[4] Indeed, there is a long history of police and domestic intelligence services attempting to manufacture moderate Black leadership and suppress militant, outspoken Black leaders, as the campaigns against Marcus Garvey, Malcolm X, W. E. B. Du Bois, Paul Robeson and others attest. Records from the COINTELPRO surveillance program administered by Hoover document the kind of moderation he sought: virtually every civil rights leader of the era and their organizations were subjected to aggressive tactics designed to weaken the movement's attack on racism.[5]

In order to provide context to this discussion, a brief review of Black Conservatism will outline its essential elements, focusing on the philosophy of earlier Black Conservatives and the public personae of the current leaders of Black Conservatism.

EARLY CONSERVATIVE ACTIVISTS

Origins

The essential nature of Black Conservatism was forged in the slavery era. It is conceivable that the stereotype of Blacks as docile, passive, submissive and extremely deferential to Whites was developed to conform to their actual position of powerlessness. Elderly Black males were often known as and responded to the appellation "uncle," a term used by Whites not to designate a relationship in a family structure but as a derogatory reference to their dependent role in the slave system.

Harriet Beecher Stowe, an adherent of what George Frederickson calls "romantic racialism," popularized the notion of docile and deferential Black males in *Uncle Tom's Cabin*. This confirmed perceptions long held by Whites, but it also introduced the idea of Blacks as a "feminine" race that mirrored the sublime and blameless nature of perfect Christians. Other observers have pointed out that most Whites "knew" Blacks only through popular stereotypes and that these stereotypes were personified in the fictional characters of Uncle Tom and Uncle Remus: "faithful and loyal servants who were kind to children and possessed a certain 'mother wit.' Yet, they presented no threat to the master's power and gave no thought to freedom. Ironically, this stereotype continued to develop long after slavery was over."[6]

This characterization allowed the Christian establishment to set its relationship to slaves within a "heathen"/"Christian" framework that allowed it to condone slavery and seek the liberation of slaves on its own terms. In some instances, slaves who became Christians were freed or treated better than those who did not, but generally Black converts were not treated differently.[7] Whites still clung to the myth of the happy Black person who knew—and was content with—his or her place, and they promoted this view in popular literature and through the opportunity structure which they managed.

Blacks who became leaders in their communities often acted in conformance with this myth, justifying this behavior because it led to productive relationships with Whites and thus benefited their communities. Professor August Meier pointed out that before the Civil War, many Blacks were partial to the Democratic party because, as the prevailing power in the South, it was the most likely place to find opportunities for political expression.[8] And while researching Black political trends in the late 1930s South, Dr. Ralph Bunche noted a strong accommodationist strain among Black leaders seeking political participation.[9]

The leadership paradigm also held that Blacks who stepped outside established roles would be treated as incorrigible rabble-rousers and trouble-makers, courting severe discipline that included the ultimate sanction of death. Black militants and others who have challenged or otherwise operated in ways which contradicted this paradigm have generally been feared, shunned and vilified by Whites.

Blanche Kelso Bruce

Consistent with Meier's thesis of opportunism, Black political Conservatism became more overt when Blacks secured posts in the U.S. Congress in the aftermath of the Civil War. The Reconstruction Congress included many Black members in both the House and Senate, and prominent among these was Blanche Kelso Bruce. Bruce was an educated man, a Mississippi planter whose initial positions on issues were consistent with those of his aspiring Black constituents. However, once he got to Washington, he was often reluctant to "stand up and be counted." Like any other southern planter facing the loss of cheap labor, Bruce vigorously opposed the "Exoduster" movement, when many oppressed southern Blacks migrated to Kansas, and the "Back to Africa" movement, when many took serious steps to emigrate to Liberia. A Bruce biographer relates that he distanced himself from Blacks after marrying a mulatto woman, socializing when he was in Washington almost exclusively with Whites.[10]

Booker T. Washington

Booker T. Washington became the nineteenth century's most notable Black Conservative by also following established prescriptions for Black leaders. His reaction to the Supreme Court's decision in *Plessy v. Ferguson* (1892)—which established the legitimacy of the doctrine of "separate but equal"—was to suggest that it did not matter whether Blacks rode in an inferior railcar or one that was separate from Whites; what was important was whether the passenger in the separate car was a "superior man or beast."[11] In his Atlanta Exposition address in 1895 he pleaded with Blacks to eschew the struggle for racial equality and instead pursue autonomous economic security and self-development.

Washington's brand of Conservatism may well be regarded as logical for a late nineteenth-century Black southern leader who confronted the challenge of dealing with an illiterate population that was substantially without modern industrial skills and under the yoke of White physical and political power. His agenda of self-segregation, self-help through the acquisition of working-class skills and utter deference to Whites was tailored to the circumstances that he faced. However, a problem arose when Washington attempted to *nationalize* this philosophy. He quickly encountered opposition from northern Black elites who had already established the goal of achieving full equality and participation in civic affairs. This often led them to oppose White power and to pressure the government to secure its support—tactics that were antithetical to Washington's.

The impact of Washington's Black Conservatism was most apparent in the economic arena, in particular through a national network of clubs known as the Negro Business League.[12] Economic motives, as well as fealty toward Abraham Lincoln, considered "the Great Emancipator," were the basis of continued Black association with the Republican party. Blacks tried to use the party as a facilitator of their economic interests even as they supported the civil rights aspirations of their communities.

Though Booker T. Washington was not deeply engaged in party politics, William Hooper Council, the Black president of the A & M College in Normal, Alabama, functioned as an extension of his thought. Believing that Blacks had lost the right to vote because they had adhered too closely to the Republican party, Council advised southern Blacks to reconcile with White politicians and split their votes between Republicans and Democrats.[13] This recommendation mirrors the advice of contemporary Black Republicans that Blacks should be adherents of both political parties, because if most of them are loyal to a single party, it will take them for granted.

George S. Schuyler

The bridge between the Washington/Council era and modern-day Black political Conservatism lies in the thinking and writing of George S. Schuyler. Schuyler, who was said to know more about the Black working class than any other intellectual of his day, flirted with socialism during the period of the Harlem Renaissance, and his concern for the economic well-being of Black workers was consistent with the views of Washington's followers.[14] However, he came to eschew notions of an authentic Black culture, effectively aligning himself with mid-twentieth-century White Nationalists, whose view of America did not countenance any legitimate culture among people with African forebears: the only legitimate culture was the one they themselves had constructed.

Jeffrey Leak, editor of a collection of Schuyler's essays, relates Schuyler's point of view to Peter Eisenstadt's characterization of Black Conservatism:

> Perhaps the most basic tenet of black conservatism is a deep-seated respect for the culture and institutions of American society and Western civilization, and the related conviction and insistence that blacks, through their own resources, can make it within American society. This does not mean that black conservatives have either been indifferent to racism, or opposed to government intervention in the social order to make black advancement possible. It is rather that black conservatives placed their focus on individual achievement rather than on government action and redress.[15]

Eisenstadt seemingly agrees with other observers who have defined as an important aspect of Conservatism its opposition to government intervention designed to affect individual effort. Yet Schuyler and other Black Conservatives have overlooked the implications of the strong collective culture their forebears brought with them from Africa and which, to a substantial extent, was kept alive by the necessity of the work routine and living circumstances of the slave culture that nurtured family reconstitution and other survival mechanisms after official slavery ended.

Other aspects of Schuyler's Conservatism included his fidelity to the norms of the state, which led him to emphasize the progress of Blacks to the point of undervaluing their oppression. Moreover, he was often accommodating toward White views and virulently critical of Black leadership. Leak cites, for instance, Schuyler's insensitive remark when Dr. Martin Luther, King, Jr., was awarded the Nobel Peace Prize: "methinks the Lenin Prize would have been more appropriate."[16] In 1964 Schuyler ran on the Conservative party ticket for the congressional seat of the embattled Rep. Adam Clayton Powell (D-N.Y.). Leak associated Schuyler's strong belief in "personal responsibility" with the views of Professor Glen C. Loury. Loury's individualism is rooted in his Progressive belief in the equal ability of all people, but perhaps Schuyler was more realistic in repudiating the notion that a national commitment to equality would become the foundation of public policy.[17]

Summarizing Historic Black Conservatism

Accommodationism: Booker T. Washington's program was designed to legitimize the existing social and political arrangement between the races. It encouraged Black collective development through the adoption of an individualistic philosophy, the acquisition of work skills and the promulgation of the integrity of virtually any kind of effortful work.

Loyalty to national norms: Schuyler believed in the essential framework of the country, in the rightness of the national norms which governed the country and, by extension, the social system as it exists at any given time.

Deference to White power: Both Washington and Schuyler believed in and assented to the authority of Whites in personal as well as professional affairs, acknowledging the validity of the control Whites exercised over society as a whole as well as over Black affairs.

Racial symbiosis: Washington, Bruce and Schuyler appeared to desire interaction with Whites but not full Black/White social integration. To the extent that they deprecated Black norms, standards and associations, they seemingly wished to interact with Whites within the White collective cultural system.

Ideological opposition to America's enemies: Both Washington and Schuyler adopted prevailing attitudes toward America's enemies of the day. Washington toured Europe and exalted the American way of life, comparing Blacks with poor Europeans and proclaiming that in many ways American Blacks were better off. Schuyler was a rabid anticommunist who denounced Blacks as well as Whites who were suspected of being communists.

Denial of the integrity of Black culture: Schuyler deprecated Black culture as a phenomenon with no integrity except that which was accorded it through the prism of the White perspective. He viewed the White cultural construct as the only authentic American culture.

Denial of the capability of Black leadership: In addition to his criticism of Dr. Martin Luther King, Jr.'s having won the Nobel Peace Prize, Schuyler held a less than sanguine view of W. E. B. Du Bois, perhaps because of his ideological persuasions. He criticized with abandon Black leaders of any persuasion for the public positions they took on various issues of the day.

Denial of the integrity of Black interests: Bruce and Schuyler appeared to absent themselves when it came to a vigorous defense of Black interests, either in denial that such interests existed or because these conflicted with their own.

The Stability of Black Ideology

Ironically, the philosophy of integration adopted by northern Black leaders in the late nineteenth and early twentieth century as a freedom strategy required breaking the racial conventions that guard the boundaries of group control. Though Booker T. Washington considered integration, especially in the South, to be an impossible goal, northern civil rights organizations of the day such as the NAACP and the National Urban League considered it entirely plausible. As suggested by Professor Hanes Walton, their strategy was radical to the extent that it challenged the hegemony of Black professionals in an essentially segregated market.[18] Integration was an outward-looking and progressive alternative which offered Blacks the maximum social choice.

Yet by the time the Black Power movement developed in the 1960s, the goal of racial integration seemed conservative to Blacks, for in effect it defined Black worth and integrity in terms of proximity to White individuals, groups and standards. Black Nationalist activists reinstituted collectivism of the captive market and its community environment, opting for political control of their communities and other forms of decision-making which affected their lives. However, although Black Nationalism contained aspects of conservatism, insofar as it wanted to preserve and purify Black culture politically, it fostered the most vigorous form of challenge to White racism.

Disparate Attitudes toward Issues

Many issues important to Blacks are inherently conservative, including school prayer, corporal punishment, capital punishment, disapproval of some forms of abortion and approval of defense spending. Indeed, an August 2000 survey by the Joint Center for Political and Economic Studies found that a majority of Blacks (57%) support school voucher programs. This support among Blacks came from those under 35 (75%); Republicans (69%); members of households with school-age children (74%); and Christian Conservatives (57%).[19]

However, as early as 1978 there was evidence that for Blacks in general, "issue Conservatism" does not translate into political Conservatism.[20]

One might theorize that there is little direct correlation because many Blacks place higher priority on issues such as socioeconomic status equality, fair treatment and the urgent necessity to employ nonconservative methods to attain them. Law suits, protest demonstrations and political mobilization all indicate a strong orientation toward social change rather than toward the stability offered by Conservatism.

Also, the issue Conservatism category must be broken into two substantive parts: social issues and economic ones. According to a statistical analysis by political scientist Charles Hamilton, formerly of Columbia University, Black Americans have consistently been "decidedly in the economically liberal camp"; conversely, his data suggest that socially "blacks are more conservative than they are on economic matters."[21] Yet another category is defined as operational issues, relating to the responsibility of government. Thus a dichotomy of substance and method, or policy and operational issues—not merely the substance of the community's position on issues—shapes Blacks' ideological attitudes and approaches toward the political system.

A closer look at how Black ideology is formulated reveals the critical role played by race differences. One could approach this by suggesting how Black ideology is formed in the absolute sense; however, I choose to do so by comparing Black and White policy values and operational issues. Table 9.1 summarizes data derived from a *Washington Post*/Kaiser Foundation/Harvard University racial attitude survey released in July 2001. These survey figures show that the greatest difference between Blacks and Whites on issues is related to operational attitudes involving the extent to which the federal government should intervene to provide assistance in achieving equality for Blacks in several issue categories—indeed, there is a significant difference of 30.5%.[22] Blacks do not appear substantially different from Whites in their attitudes in section A of policy value measures; in fact, the racial difference was only 9.5%. However, there was a more substantial difference—20.4%—in section B. Lastly, responses to the perception of racial status measures exhibit a difference score which approximates that of responses to operational issues.

In each of the three areas, the critical differences appear to be related to the extent to which they deal either directly or indirectly with the issue of race. The operational issues and perception of racial status measures yield relatively equal distances between the attitudes of Blacks and Whites because the first group deals directly with operationalizing racial advantage and the second with racial status. But while policy values exhibit less racial distance, there is still a marked difference between sections A and B, with responses in section A relating indirectly to racial

TABLE 9.1 Black/White Responses on Operational Issues, Policy Values and Perception of Racial Status

1. *Operational issues*

Agree: "It is the responsibility of the federal government to insure equality with whites, even if you have to pay more taxes."

Issue	Black	White	Difference
Jobs	73%	40%	33%
Schools	89%	65%	24%
Health care	90%	55%	45%
Courts and police	89%	69%	20%

Average difference = 30.5%

2. *Policy values*

	Black	White	Difference
A. Favor school vouchers	46%	44%	2%
Accept same-sex marriages	29%	35%	6%
Accept having a child outside marriage	73%	60%	7%
Accept felons' voting rights	76%	58%	18%
Religion most/very important	80%	57%	23%

Average difference = 9.5%

	Black	White	Difference
B. Favor trans-racial adoption	84%	80%	4%
Race should not be a factor for minorities in securing jobs, education, and so on	86%	94%	8%
Favor extra effort to reach out to qualified minorities	77%	49%	28%
Favor more minorities in Congress	75%	32%	43%
Oppose using race in redistricting	70%	90%	20%

Average difference = 20.4%
Total average difference A and B = 14.4%

Perceptions of racial status

	Black	White	Difference
Blacks have less opportunity than whites	74%	27%	47%
Lots/some discrimination against African Americans	86%	71%	15%
Still major problems facing racial minorities	88%	63%	25%

Average difference = 29%

Source: Washington Post/Kaiser Family Foundation/Harvard University poll; data collected March 8–April 22, 2001, released July 11, 2001. Sample: Whites = 779, Blacks = 323.

issues and section B relating more directly. (This survey confirms others which indicate that Black consciousness is primarily shaped by real life or symbolic experiences—the Rodney King beating, the O. J. Simpson trial and the James Byrd killing, for example—that are salient for group identity, and this governs the differences in issue perception between Blacks and other groups.[23])

Racial difference scores in the *Washington Post*/Kaiser Foundation/Harvard University survey manifest a consistent distance which suggests that no matter how issues are defined vis-à-vis Conservatism, Blacks are more Liberal than Whites on nearly every measure which relates to the responsibility of government to insure equality. With respect to policy values, Blacks are more Liberal except for same-sex marriages, abortion and religious adherence. This is consistent with survey responses which revealed that while 26% of Whites described themselves as Conservative, only 11% of Blacks did so. Contemporary Black Conservatives manifest views that are seemingly consistent with those of Whites who espouse an orthodox Conservatism that affects operational, economic and social issues either directly or indirectly connected to race.[24] Thus while only 11% of Blacks consider themselves Conservative by the measures used in this survey, orthodox Black Conservatives constitute an even smaller portion of the Black population.

It is clear that Blacks' and Whites' attitudes on issues of race have constituted an important axis of Conservatism, especially in the 1960s and 1970s. However, in the 1980s, the basis of social Conservatism shifted to secondary issues which presumably support racial advantage or otherwise threaten the status of Whites, including government intervention, crime, welfare and affirmative action.

CHALLENGING THE LIBERAL CONSENSUS IN THE BLACK COMMUNITY

It is important to understand the function of Black Conservatives in a social system where Blacks do not control society's rewards. The Whites who control that system have always utilized their power to create a subclass of Blacks who are especially attentive to their political needs, for these Blacks act to protect those needs as if they were their own. Martin Luther King, Jr., was particularly astute when he observed:

> The white establishment is skilled in flattering and cultivating emerging leaders. It presses its own image on them and finally, from

imitation of manners, dress and style of living, a deeper strain of corruption develops. This kind of Negro leader acquires the white
man's contempt for the ordinary Negro. He is often more at home
with the middle-class white than he is among his own people. His
language changes, his location changes, his income changes, and
ultimately he changes from the representative of the Negro to the
white man into the white man's representative to the Negro.[25]

In this statement, King was not singling out Black leaders of any
particular party or ideological persuasion. Yet his words describe the way
in which White Neoconservative intellectuals influenced such Blacks as
Bayard Rustin, who was a stalwart of the Civil Rights movement. In his
later years, Rustin teamed with Carl Gershman to attack White Liberals'
support of more radical aspects of the campaign for social justice, such
as the antiwar movement, the Black Nationalist movement and the
movement for Black studies in American universities.[26]

But whereas Rustin's conversion had a philosophical basis, the
emergence of the group of Black Conservatives in the post-Civil Rights
era was more politically partisan. Indeed, it harked back to the period
before the Civil War and the first decades of the twentieth century, when
the Democratic party, which was then very conservative on racial issues,
dominated the South. As indicated above, southern Blacks with any hope
of participating in the political system became involved in Democratic
party politics, whether because they agreed with the party's Conservative
ideas, they saw political opportunities there, or both.

An analogous circumstance prevailed between 1968 and 1992, a
period with only one Democratic presidential administration. Blacks who
came to professional maturity during that period had to manipulate a
political opportunity structure that was controlled on the national level
by Republicans and Conservative Democrats. This period also saw the
repositioning of the southern vote from the Democratic party to the
Republican party and the concomitant shift in what one observer called
the "racist vote"[27]—the expression of southerners' preference for candidates and issues perceived to be oppositional to Black interests—from
Democrats to Republicans. This transition helped solidify the political
identity of the Republican party over time, changing the basic ideological predisposition of Republicanism from moderation to Conservatism.
Civil rights issues of busing, affirmative action and others attracted such
negative treatment by the reformulated Republican party that this over-
shadowed the congruence between Republicans and Blacks on other

issues, repelling the majority of Blacks and anchoring them more firmly within the Democratic party.

The New Black Conservatives

This transition period prepared the ground for the emergence of the new Black Conservatives, who are very different from their Black Republican predecessors. They have moved beyond the older economic utilitarianism that prompted their precursors to become associated with the Republican party and adopted the more comprehensive and orthodox Conservative ideological framework, which encompasses a strongly Conservative economic and social orientation together with an anti-civil rights posture. With regard to their inclusion in the Conservative ranks, Professor Robert Smith has said: "Apart from using the White House to confer publicity and prestige, the Reagan administration recruited their appointees from a new generation of young, highly educated blacks whose backgrounds show little identification with traditional black institutions. Frequently educated at white institutions, they have aggressively defended the Goldwater-Reagan approach to race and social policy, both publicly and in internal administration deliberations."[28] The new visage of Black Republican activists cannot be overemphasized. Richard Nixon appointed a number of Black politicians, professionals and business persons to important government posts, including Edwin Sexton, Samuel Cornelius, Samuel Jackson, Arthur Fletcher and James Haley, but Ronald Reagan considered these men not Conservative enough when it came to staffing his administration.

In an attempt to illustrate further the function of Black Conservatism in the White Nationalist movement, I will briefly profile the activities of five Black Conservatives who have, in the past 20 years, exercised the most significant public policy influence: Clarence Pendleton, Jr., Robert Woodson, Sr., Clarence Thomas, Ward Connerly and J. C. Watts, Jr.

Clarence Pendleton, Jr.

One of the earliest members of what would come to comprise the cadre of new Black Conservative government operatives was Clarence Pendleton, Jr., a Republican businessman from San Diego and friend of Ed Meese III. In 1982, in an action similar to Richard Nixon's firing of Rev. Theodore Hesburgh from the same post exactly a decade earlier, Ronald Reagan fired moderate White Republican Arthur Fleming as chair of the

U.S. Civil Rights Commission and installed Pendleton in his place, an event which many said diminished the independence of that body. From that position, and with the appointment of other Conservatives to the commission, Pendleton proceeded to align his views with those of the White House. He defended Reagan's Conservative approach to civil rights by declaring: "I don't equate conservatism with racism. I think a lot of people are using that as a straw man."[29]

Pendleton immediately began criticizing the commission's own reports showing persistent high unemployment among minorities by countering that there was no need for the government to enforce affirmative action and other civil rights laws to address such inequities. He characterized affirmative action as "a bankrupt policy" and likened efforts to advance the status of Blacks to a "new racism." He also denigrated the idea of comparable worth as a "the looniest idea since Looney Tunes."[30] Routinely denigrating Black civil rights leaders and their tactics in a blunt and derisive style, he used media debates with prominent Liberals to aggressively forge a public role as a defender of Conservative values.

From time to time Pendleton's mode was unorthodox and inconsistent. He founded an organization known as the New Coalition for Economic and Social Change, a Black Conservative group associated with the Heritage Foundation, but he also sent a letter to the White House suggesting that he would "never knowingly attend any meeting you [President Reagan] or members of your administration convene exclusively with black appointees,"[31] Pendleton also chastised the administration for what turned out to be a temporary reelection strategy: wooing unlikely adherents, arranging special briefings for Blacks, or doing minor favors for Blacks, Hasidic Jews and minority contractors. Pendleton also dissented from the administration when it granted tax exemptions to private schools which practiced racial discrimination and for its dilatory endorsement of the extension of the Voting Rights Act.[32]

Two things stand out about Clarence Pendleton. First, the general faithfulness with which he supported the Reagan administration's philosophical position. Those who had known him when he was the president of the San Diego Urban League found him so changed that Vernon Jordan, for one, observed that this was not the man he knew. The head of the Urban League in Rochester, New York, even suggested that in comparison to the attitudes Pendleton had expressed in the past, "it sounds like he is a man from Mars."[33]

Second, the occasional congruence of his views with those of Black Power advocates was surprising. Journalist Juan Williams interviewed

Pendleton and elicited the strong sentiments of a person who grew up in segregated Washington, D.C., and was bitter about the dissolution of the Black community there that the government had fostered: the abandonment of Black schools, businesses and other services.[34] Pendleton's cultural and economic Conservatism mirrors a feature of the Nationalist ideology that is attractive to both Black and White Conservatives alike, since it comports with racial separatism. It does not contain the militant self-determination described in Stokely Carmichael and Charles Hamilton's *Black Power*[35]—that is, even a segregated Black community can be utilized as a base from which to fight racism and oppose regressive racial accommodation.

Robert Woodson, Sr.

A strong supporter of Republican administrations and a member of the inner circle of prominent Black conservatives, Robert Woodson, Sr., is a former official at the National Urban League. He became a research fellow at the American Enterprise Institute, and in the late 1980s he founded the National Center for Neighborhood Enterprise, a Conservative organization which focuses on grassroots empowerment projects. Woodson's empowerment approach gained the support of Jack Kemp, secretary of the Department of Housing and Urban Development in George Bush's administration. Kemp's own "micro-enterprise" approach to capitalizing housing ownership among the poor motivated him to support several of Woodson's initiatives. During the Reagan administration Woodson utilized his prominence to develop a moderately bipartisan entity known as the Council for a Black Economic Agenda, which supported the transfer of Reagan administration resources to projects mounted by grassroots organizations. The council was dedicated to bypassing elite Black leadership and putting project management in the hands of those who were directly affected by poverty.

Although many of Woodson's projects have been positive—admirable in scope and actually empowering to local housing residents—he gained considerable prominence within the Black Republican establishment and among Republicans at large for the ferocity of his attacks upon Black leaders. He criticized them for their dependence upon government funding, despite the fact that many of his own organizations depended on the same source. He charged that Black leaders were merely "bitching" about their condition and exploiting the Black condition to further their own interests.[36] Woodson has often been featured in the media as a spokesman for

Black Conservative interests, usually in opposition to Liberal Black analysts and heads of Black organizations.

Clarence Thomas

As head of the federal government's Equal Employment Opportunity Commission, Clarence Thomas brought an antigovernment philosophy into an agency that was responsible for the enforcement of Title VII of the 1964 Civil Rights Act and of affirmative action laws. On one occasion Thomas said that it was "insane" for Blacks to expect relief from the federal government for past discrimination—despite the fact that Title VII was predicated on that assumption. His reasoning was that "ultimately the burden of your being mugged falls on you. Now, you don't want it that way, and I don't want it that way. But that's the way it happens. . . . Before affirmative action, how did I make it?"[37] There was obviously a deep divide between the attitude of the commission's chairman and his mandate, which was clearly established in the law as well as in past practice.

Before becoming a Supreme Court justice, Clarence Thomas went through a high-profile confirmation process in October of 1991. During the Senate Judiciary Committee's hearings, he momentarily garnered the support of Blacks by undergoing what they perceived to be—in Thomas's words—a "high-tech lynching" at the hands of the Democrat-dominated committee.[38] This support eroded, however, after he became a member of the Court in late October, because of a series of votes he cast during his first years in opposition to the consensus position of the Black community.

Thomas's fidelity to the Conservative Nationalist movement became evident in the positions he took in several decisions, including those focusing on congressional redistricting, the rights of convicts to be free of cruel and unusual punishment, financing school integration and minority contracting. By far the most contentious of his early decisions was in *Shaw v. Reno* (1993), in which the Supreme Court invalidated using race as a major consideration in drawing congressional district boundaries; in the five-to-four decision, Thomas sided with the majority.

During his first year on the Court, Justice Thomas decided cases in a way that confirmed the most dire predictions of his opponents (including this author), who reasoned that his record as assistant secretary for civil rights in the Department of Education and director of the Equal Employment Opportunity Commission clearly signaled that he was likely to render decisions that would negate gains made in the field of civil rights. In *Hudson v. McMillian* (1992), the question of the subjection of prisoners to cruel and usual punishment was decided against the interests of the prisoner.[39] Perhaps Justice Thomas's soft spot is with respect to Black higher education, for in *United States v. Fordice* (1992), he supported Black access to the predominantly White southern flagship institutions—although he counseled that there should be an emphasis on the "policies that produced the racial imbalance rather than the imbalance itself."[40] In 1993, Royce Esters, president of the Compton, California branch of the NAACP—who had broken with the national NAACP in 1991 and supported Thomas's nomination to the Supreme Court—called him a "house Negro."[41]

The following year the Court rendered a decision in *Holder v. Hall* (1994), a case brought by Black plaintiffs who had attempted to apply section 2 of the Voting Rights Act to the governance system in Bleckley County, Georgia—a 218-square-mile jurisdiction controlled by a one-person commission that exercised legislative and executive power over a broad array of county services. Justices Thomas and Antonin Scalia wrote the 59-page decision which held that the commission's size did not violate section 2 and which overturned the lower court's ruling in their favor. Not only would acceptance of their logic invalidate the Court's decision in *Thornburg v. Gingles* (1968), which activated section 2, it would also overturn the ruling in *Gomillion v. Lightfoot* (1960), which allowed legal challenges to racial gerrymandering and governed nearly 40 years of voting rights jurisprudence. In an often overlooked case that was described as Thomas's "favorite," the decision in *Norfolk & Western Railway Co. v. Hailes* (1996) reduced protection of worker safety in the railway industry, thus affecting a significant number of African Americans.[42]

Thomas's siding with the majority in the five-to-four decision in *Al Gore v. George Bush* (2000), which effectively awarded the presidency to the Republican candidate, was consistent with his usual adherence to the Conservative wing of the Court. He frequently votes with Conservative Justices William Rehnquist, Sandra Day O'Connor and Anthony Kennedy, and nearly 90% of the time with Antonin Scalia, the Court's most Conservative member.[43]

On the evidence of his judicial record, most Blacks have roundly rejected Clarence Thomas. The most strident public expression of this occurred in 1996, when Thomas was invited to speak at an awards ceremony at the Thomas Pullen Middle School in Prince George's County, Maryland. Kenneth Johnson, a school board member who represented the district where the Pullen School is located, opposed Thomas's appearance.[44] Johnson was quoted as saying: "There's no place for

Clarence Thomas anywhere in my district, . . . He has done everything he can to undermine the things that are important to the people in my district. There is nothing he has to say that I would want to hear. . . . He certainly hasn't represented us in Prince George's County on the Supreme Court."[45] Johnson threatened to lead a protest demonstration if Thomas appeared at the awards ceremony. His opposition was widely shared by Blacks in Prince George's County, an area that had attracted a rapidly growing Black, largely middle-class population from Washington, D.C.; at the time, over 50% of the county's population was Black.

Reacting to the controversy, Prince George's County School Superintendent Jerome Clark rescinded the invitation to Thomas, but this sparked another round of protests. The County Council, majority-White at that time, denounced the withdrawal of the invitation, going on record to assure the judge he was welcome in Prince George's County and calling for a new invitation to be issued. The president of the Pullen School PTA also urged that the judge be re-invited. When it appeared that the invitation to Thomas would be renewed, Johnson said: "The people in my district don't want him here. That is the bottom line."[46]

In response to these different voices, Superintendent Clark issued a new invitation to Thomas. Following the ceremony on June 10, a front-page picture appeared in the *Washington Post* showing Justice Thomas seated on the Pullen Middle School stage along with four other people—all of them White and all apparently triumphant over his appearance. The *Post* also reproduced photos taken outside the school, where Johnson and a group of protestors, mostly Black, demonstrated their objection to his presence.

This incident achieved national notice and prompted a robust discussion of Judge Thomas's record and the basis of his rejection by most Blacks. His advocates cited the First Amendment's guarantee of freedom of speech and chided Blacks for being afraid of a Black person who held opinions outside the Black mainstream.[47]

In January 1997, Dr. Benjamin Carson, a Baltimore surgeon, invited Judge Thomas to speak at a youth festival in Delaware. The Delaware branch of the NAACP threatened to picket the speech, and Hanley Norman, president of the Maryland branch, said: "If white folks want to have Justice Thomas serve as a role model for their kids, that's their business"; moreover, Norman referred to Thomas as a "colored lawn jockey for conservative white interests."[48] Soon afterward, Kweisi Mfume, newly elected president of the NAACP, surprised many observers by declaring that the Maryland chapter's action would have a "chilling effect" upon Thomas's First Amendment Rights.[49] Sen. Patrick Leahy (D-Vt.) also expressed concern about the infringement of Judge Thomas's First Amendment Rights; Leahy introduced a *Wall Street Journal* article about the controversy into the Senate record and declared that "McCarthyism of the left [is] as bad as McCarthyism of the right."[50]

The depth of the disaffection with Judge Thomas within the Black community is evident in a survey by the Joint Center for Political and Economic Studies, a Black think tank. Conducted in February 1996, this poll revealed that Justice Thomas's support among Blacks was extremely low. Survey respondents were presented with a list that included Bill Clinton, Bob Dole, Newt Gingrich, Jesse Jackson, H. Ross Perot, Colin Powell, Louis Farrakhan and Clarence Thomas, and asked to rank them in descending levels of support. Black respondents ranked Thomas the least favorable, and his unfavorable rating (44.5%) was greater than his favorable rating (32.5%).[51]

Two years after this survey was taken, the convention chair of the National Bar Association, America's oldest Black legal organization, invited Justice Thomas to be the main speaker at its annual meeting in July 1998. The controversy that erupted within the organization was so severe that its members considered whether the invitation should be withdrawn.[52] Opposing views split the organization. Leon Higginbotham, a former federal judge and at the time a professor at Harvard's Kennedy School of Government, launched an aggressive challenge to have the invitation rescinded. Another prominent Black jurist, Federal Circuit Court Judge Damon Keith of Detroit, took the position that "lawyers and judges, above all, should not be afraid to hear people speak."[53]

Thomas did indeed speak at the convention, and his right to do so was vigorously defended in a *Washington Post* editorial piece:

> It is time for Justice Thomas's critics to engage him in a debate on the merits and flaws of his work, instead of on the specious question of whether he is an adequately authentic black justice. It is time to stop judging him on the basis of a standard—the political outcomes of his votes and opinions—so disconnected from the proper motivation of a justice. It is time also to stop assuming that Justice Thomas must be a mere lackey of the court's white conservatives and allow that he represents cogently a worldview in which he believes deeply and has arrived at honestly.[54]

With this statement, the *Post* set a curious standard: that evaluations of judges' performances ought to be disconnected from the impact of their decisions. Blacks' evaluations of whether Justice Thomas is "an adequately authentic black" proceed precisely from consideration of the negative impact his decisions have had upon Black interests. And many Whites protect Thomas from such criticism precisely because the impact of his decisions accords with their racial views and policy objectives.

At the time of the Pullen Middle School incident, journalist Joseph Mianowany staunchly supported Clarence Thomas against the criticism of Rep. Albert Wynn (D-Md.), a Black congressman whose district includes Prince George's County. Mianowany said: "Strange, but I don't recall specific exceptions being written into the First Amendment. More to the point, why do Wynn and others in the traditional black leadership treat Thomas this way? What are they afraid of? If Thomas's views are so obviously wrong won't that become clear as soon as he opens his mouth? Or do they perhaps see Thomas and his views as a threat they cannot effectively counter?"[55] Mianowany is correct, of course, in that as Conservative ideology became supported by the White majority, Black leadership found it difficult to counter. The real issue, however, is that such a defense has become a standard feature of White Conservative attitudes toward Black Conservatives.

Ward Connerly

In 1993, Ward Connerly, a Black businessman from Sacramento, was appointed by Republican Governor Pete Wilson to a 12-year term on the University of California Board of Regents. Wilson also asked him to lead the campaign to eliminate affirmative action in California by serving as head of the California Civil Rights ballot proposition designated as 209. Some considered this a blatant misuse of Connerly's position as a regent, since Article 9, Section 9(F) of the California Constitution says: "The University shall be entirely independent of all political or sectarian influence, and kept free therefrom . . . in the administration of its affairs." Nevertheless, to pursue this cause, Connerly formed the American Civil Rights Institute, which was launched by a group of Conservative organizations at a dinner in Washington, D.C., on February 12, 1997.

This co-opting of the term "civil rights" and the goal of the campaign provoked strong negative reaction from mainstream civil rights leaders. Disregarding this reaction, Connerly proceeded to emphasize what he called the "fairness" of eliminating affirmative action:

> For every wrong that I have endured because of skin color, there are several demonstrable examples of fairness, America's passion for fairness, to which I could point.

America is caught in the grip of a profound clash of values. [There] are those of us who believe . . . that race has no place in American life and law. We believe that the Fourteenth Amendment protects the rights of *individuals*, that government derives power and authority from the American people, that there is a moral force from which we can draw our strength and guidance, and that certain principles are inviolate.

There are those who believe that race matters, that we have to use race to get beyond race, that the Fourteenth Amendment is intended to protect the rights of groups, to ensure that groups have equal opportunity and parity. They believe in a more *intrusive* government, which defines how long a leash the American people will be allowed, that nothing is inviolate and everything is up for grabs.

Eliminating preferences is the only way that we can have an America in which its people are one.[56]

Connerly has artfully adapted the language of the Civil Rights movement with respect to fairness and justice to make it applicable to Whites rather than Blacks. When he says "I feel we should treat everybody the same and I don't see why that is so difficult for people to accept," or "I do not believe that my government should be allowed to discriminate," this replicates then distorts the message traditional Black leaders wanted to send to Whites. Connerly implies that Blacks do not accept his rationale for eliminating affirmative action: "we should treat everybody the same." Moreover, by "discriminate" he does not mean to suggest governmental or White discrimination against Blacks, Hispanics, women and other disadvantaged groups, but the government's discrimination against Whites on behalf of these groups, thus making Whites the victims.[57]

With this conceptual basis, Connerly's Proposition 209 campaign attracted substantial contributions from Conservative organizations and the Republican party, leading to its passage in 1996. Connerly then joined the campaign against President Clinton's "Race Initiative," sending him a letter demanding that affirmative action be eliminated from the agenda of the initiative's advisory committee.[58] He also began to coordinate funding for Initiative 200 in Washington State, a proposal to eliminate affirmative action much like California's Proposition 209. In 1997 Connerly campaigned in Washington State vigorously, leading a high-profile protest against US Bank, which opposed I-200, and withdrawing $600,000 from a US Bank branch in Sacramento.[59] Affirmative action was eliminated in Washington State when I-200 passed by a vote of 57% to 42%.

Connerly's role as protector of the majority interest from attempts by the disadvantaged to gain equality through the law has led individuals such as Rev. Jesse Jackson to characterize him as a "house slave" and "a puppet of the white man." But prominent White leaders have stoutly defended Connerly's actions. Speaker of the House Newt Gingrich entered into the *Congressional Record* an article by Ben Wattenberg supporting Connerly's role in the passage of Proposition 209 in California.[60] Gingrich agreed with other congressional representatives who characterized affirmative action as "affirmative racism," and he set forth a political rationale for Conservatives' attempt to divide Black leaders: "[T]his is the race-neutral side of the civil-rights argument. As, and if it gains further currency, it can shatter the monopoly of the racial politics now seen in the Democratic party."[61]

By contrast, Ward Connerly is viewed with disdain by many Black leaders not primarily involved with civil rights. When the Associated General Contractors of America (AGC) invited him to speak at their 1998 annual convention in New Orleans, the National Association of Minority Contractors (NAMC) protested. In a letter dated March 4, 1998, Nigel Parkinson, president of NAMC, wrote: "Mr. Connerly does not speak for minorities. He does not speak for African Americans. He speaks for himself, and I deeply resent the fact that AGC would parade him around and promote him as a spokesperson on the subject of special preferences."[62] The AGC rejected the NAMC proposal that someone be invited to present a view contrary to Connerly's: "[O]ur position is that we are committed to equal opportunity in our industry and across America. But we're not in agreement with the unequal opportunity that special preference creates."[63] The upshot was that Connerly's appearance at the AGC convention was picketed by the Coalition of Minority Contractors of Louisiana.

J. C. Watts, Jr.

It is noteworthy that J. C. Watts, Jr., a former University of Oklahoma football star, businessman and an ordained Baptist minister, was elected to the U.S. House of Representatives in 1994—the year of the Republican landslide—from a district that was only 7% black. That year he won with just 52% of the vote, but he steadily increased his margin of victory in subsequent campaigns. He was elected to the leadership of the House Republican Conference in 1998 and became a spokesperson for Republican party and Conservative issues.

In 1994 Watts supported the "Contract with America," the platform of his entering class of congresspersons. He campaigned on issues such as welfare reform and aid to minority businesses but took a softer position on affirmative action than his colleagues. He maintained that although affirmative action had generally failed the poor, it had helped females.[64] By 1995 he had developed what he called "A New Civil Rights Agenda," which consisted of revitalizing the family through welfare reform and support of churches; seeking academic excellence through school choice; fighting crime by increasing law enforcement resources in the inner cities and emphasizing punishment by imposing longer sentences; improving access to capital by removing restrictive regulatory barriers and repealing the Davis-Bacon Act; emphasizing outreach as the basis of traditional "affirmative action"; and enforcing antidiscrimination laws.[65]

In 1996 Rep. Watts added a legislative focus on inner-city economic development to his concern for minority business development, calling it the "Renewal Community Project." Watts and the project's co-sponsor, Rep. Jim Talent (R-Mo.) argued that the Republican party should have an approach to the issue that employed the traditional party methodology of offering tax incentives, capital gains relief for small businesses and reduced regulations.[66] Providing for 100 "renewal communities," this bill was eventually passed in 2000 on a bipartisan basis, drawing the support of some leading members of the Congressional Black Caucus. Bipartisan support increased after the bill was merged with the Clinton administration's "New Markets" initiative, which used the enterprise zone tax incentive method to stimulate urban growth in a manner similar to that of the Talent-Watts bill.

Watts's attitude toward affirmative action has been problematic for Republicans. He has not joined radical Conservatives in his party seeking its complete elimination. Noting that after affirmative action was removed at the University of California/Berkeley and at the University of Texas Law School Black enrollments there decreased, he has maintained that the Republican party should not attempt to eliminate this program until it has developed a better alternative—and this has not yet happened.

The strength of Watts's convictions was tested in a May 1997 meeting in the office of Speaker Newt Gingrich with Ward Connerly, who was lobbying the Speaker to support Rep. Charles T. Canady's (R-Fla.) bill to eliminate affirmative action. Connerly argued that the anti-affirmative action vote in California was a mandate for congressional action, but Watts disputed this. He restated his position that since there was no good alternative, the time was not right to do away with it, and he asserted that passage of the Canady bill would diminish the Republican party's chances of making inroads in Black and Hispanic communities.[67]

Watts's position on affirmative action has won him significant legitimacy with other Black members of Congress. They were grateful when he kept the 1996 Republican National Convention from taking a strong negative position on affirmative action. (In this effort, Watts was joined by General Colin Powell, who announced at the convention that he was in favor of affirmative action.) During Rep. James Clyburn's (D-S.C.) term as head of the Congressional Black Caucus, he suggested to Rep. Bennie Thompson (D-Miss.): "We have not done right by J. C. Watts. When you read what he has to say, he was exactly where we were on the end result."[68]

After he became Republican Conference leader in 1998, Rep. Watts's positions shifted somewhat, as the party's agenda became his agenda. Indeed, in 2001 the NAACP awarded him a grade of "F" with respect to his voting record in the 107th Congress.[69]

Throughout his tenure in Congress, Rep. Watts refused to join the Congressional Black Caucus on the grounds that it was biased toward the Democratic party.[70] (By contrast, Rep. Gary Franks [R-Conn.], who also represented a minority Black Congressional district and was the only Black Republican in Congress during the late 1980s, did join the caucus.) Watts followed the pattern of other Black Conservatives in disapproving of the adherence of mainstream Black civic and political leaders to civil rights themes and tactics. In fact, on one occasion he referred to Rev. Jesse Jackson as a "race-hustling poverty pimp," which drew general condemnation from other Black leaders.[71] Because of his ideology, Watts gained the acceptance of White Nationalists within his party, even as he pursued a more moderate, compassionate/conservative, economics oriented legislative agenda than they endorsed. In July 2002, Watts announced his decision to retire from Congress that December, and while he said he wanted to spend more time with his family, others felt that his frustration at not having a more significant impact on party decision-making was the real motivation.[72]

CONCLUSION

From this brief review of some major Black Conservatives, it would appear that contemporary Black Conservatism has much in common with White Nationalism, including an ideological commitment to destroy the edifice constructed by the 1960s Civil Rights movement along with the leadership of that movement. But because the Civil Rights movement and its Black leaders have enabled Blacks to compete, even modestly, with Whites, the majority of Blacks oppose Black Conservatism.

Whites support Black Conservatives because they share the same value system and language—an oppositional language to traditional civil rights policies and to the demands of Black leaders for government redress for past subordination—as well as a denial of the existence and impact of racism. A vivid expression of this symbiosis occurred when Dennis Praeger, a Conservative talk show host on a CBS radio station in Los Angeles, interviewed Black comedian Jimmy Walker; Walker proceeded to lecture the listening audience on individualism and personal responsibility, to which Praeger replied: "He certainly spoke for me. I didn't need to say anything. I felt that I was talking but that there was a black face out of which it was coming."[73] Because they serve a similar function, Black Conservatives have acquired uncommon access to the media and the political system, and support from a network of Conservative organizations and individuals.

Observers have largely been mystified about why Blacks adhere to Liberal ideology when the country's political center of gravity has clearly shifted to Conservatism. The way to understand the mainstream Black perspective on Black Conservatism is to look beyond the distance between Blacks and Conservatives on the great issues of the day. What is important is the degree to which the Conservative position affirms or denies the integrity of the Black community's consensus on their condition and goals, and the accountability of Conservative leaders to this paradigm in relation to the White community. From the Black perspective, radical Conservatism evokes a sense of the *intent to harm* through public policy and a sense of *betrayal* by Blacks who adhere to that philosophy.

The prominent features of the new Black Conservatism are: (1) acceptance of accommodation as the mode for achieving self-development and self-advancement; (2) adoption of the White community's values, goals and leadership; (3) the negation and distortion of the validity of Black values, including the struggle against White racism, and acceptance of the view that Blacks themselves are the major cause of their arrested development; (4) support for issues that are often incompatible with the Black agenda as initiated by Black leaders in Congress and in civil society; (5) compatibility with established Conservative views on policy values and operational issues; and (6) a deep hostility toward traditional methods of achieving Black progress, such as those developed by the Civil Rights movement, and toward the leadership that has attempted to actualize them. These characteristics illustrate why Black Conservatives' views are often vigorously and forcefully rejected by the Black community.

Yet perhaps the most salient explanation for Blacks' rejection of Conservatism begins with the Black Conservative phenomenon itself.

The emotional content of Black opposition may be a more powerful barrier to a bond between Blacks and Conservatism than any theoretical
bridge between Blacks and Whites constructed on the basis of shared
support for some issues. That is to say, it may be that Blacks do not evaluate Conservatism in terms of its support of issues that matter to them—
whether processual or socioeconomic, substantive or operational—but
on more powerful emotional factors associated with their analysis of the
threat posed by White Nationalism.

Black Conservatives may be viewed as representatives of the collective harm fostered by radical White Conservatives, a role they maintain because it promotes personal advance and political mobility. The
close proximity of Black Conservatives and White Nationalists is more
explanatory in limiting Black membership in the Conservative movement
than any issue congruence there may be between Conservatives and their
Black "brothers and sisters."

Conclusion:
The Integrity of Black Interests

Embedded in the White Nationalists' ideology is the goal of achieving as much "freedom" from government intervention as possible. For people of African descent, this has meant White Nationalists are free to inflict considerable damage upon them through the unbridled use of their group's power. The morality of such a one-sided notion of freedom must be challenged, for ultimately it is destructive to civil society. It contravenes inclusiveness of both groups and individuals on a plane of equality in social relations, and it fosters the denial of collective responsibility. This denial is significant because, as a sector of the majority, White Nationalists who share social power with other Whites also share the corporate mandate to use it within the framework of a democratic legacy.

The concept of a political covenant between members of society stems from the earliest days of the American democratic experiment. In 1630, aboard the *Arbella* as it sailed from England to the New World, the Puritan leader John Winthrop addressed his fellow passengers on the duty that members of a community owe each other. His sermon, entitled "A Model of Christian Charity," includes a warning that the Massachusetts experiment would be closely scrutinized: "[W]e shall be as a city upon a hill. The eyes of all people are upon us. So that if we shall deal falsely with our God in this work we have undertaken, . . . we shall be made a story and a by-word throughout the world."[1] Fifteen years later, in the course of a lawsuit brought against him for overstepping his powers as governor of the Massachusetts Bay Colony, he spoke of two kinds of law—"natural" law and the law which he called "civil or federal: it may also be termed moral, in reference to the covenant between God and man, in the moral law, and the politic covenants and constitutions, amongst men themselves. This liberty is the proper end and object of authority, and cannot subsist without it; and it is a liberty to that only which is good, just, and honest."[2] Winthrop's formulation suggests that he considered "civil or federal" law to be more responsible than natural law—even conservative—and useful to the productive ends of society because the moral covenant regulated the activity of official institutions. Unhappily, Ronald Reagan's frequent use of the metaphor of a "shining city set on a hill" was ironic, for it echoed Winthrop but implied nothing of the Puritan leader's reminder of the responsibilities all persons in a society hold for each of its members.

AGENCY AND POLICY RACISM

I have asserted above, with considerable supporting documentation, that there exists a kind of racism which has operated through the public policy system to produce outcomes deleterious to the interests of Black people in the United States during the height of a period of political nationalism in which Whites were the primary actors. I have suggested that White Nationalism has produced "policy racism"—that is, the White Nationalist movement created an ideology which has had a decisive impact upon the political system, producing elected and appointed officials as policy makers who utilized this ideology to foment institutional racism within the courts, the Congress and the executive branch. Policies were designed to punish Blacks, change their behavior and otherwise produce racially disparate outcomes to comply with selective standards developed by those policy makers.

This analysis adds to the theory of institutional racism by examining the factor of agency. Historically, this theory assumes that racism is an inadvertent attitude held by well-meaning people, or that it is an accidental holdover from a time when Blacks were intentionally disadvantaged by governmental actions. For instance, Michael Lipsky maintained that groups who provide services to large numbers of people, such as blue-collar workers, teachers and policemen, often use racial stereotypes as a shorthand tool "under conditions of enormous stress and little information." These stereotypes then become incorporated into institutional decision-making, thus distributing racially disparate outcomes.[3] Yet Carter Wilson says that "ideological racism functions more directly to legitimize a racially oppressive order."[4] This, in effect, constitutes the category of racism of which White Nationalism is one manifestation.

Journalists and academics have had difficulty locating and analyzing the racist component in the activities of radical Conservative policy makers, even where it was rather obvious that the White Nationalist movement had deliberately intended to use its control of public policy to disempower Blacks. When Sen. Jesse Helms (R-N.C.) announced in August 2001 that he would not run for reelection, prominent journalist David Broder of the *Washington Post* observed that most of the coverage of Helm's career had been "circumspect to the point of pussyfooting," concealing his 30-year record of racism in American politics. Broder also noted that the major papers of record typically characterized Helms as a "conservative stalwart" or "archenemy of liberals."[5] He asserted that Helms's racism was generally allowed to remain hidden under the banner of mainstream Conservatism—even when he used racial politics in the 1984 race against former Governor Jim Hunt, and in the 1990 and 1996 races against Harvey Gantt, an African American former mayor of Charlotte—although one observer did point out that "the ugly politics of race are alive and well. Helms is their master."[6] Remarking that Helms had been a strong and consistent opponent of civil rights and other Liberal and humanitarian causes, Broder drew a distinction between Helms and Sen. Strom Thurmond (R-S.C.), who openly recanted his racist past and worked with Blacks locally in South Carolina, and Rep. Henry Hyde (R-Ill.), who became chairman of the House Judiciary Committee when Republicans took over the House as a result of the 1994 "revolution."

The irony, however, is that Broder's forthright assessment assigns much more significance to policy makers' individual views than their impact upon the institutions in which they serve. For example, Hyde was Judiciary Committee chair in 1997 when Rep. Charles Canady (D-Fla.) introduced legislation in Congress to eliminate affirmative action in federal contracting. The bill was ultimately tabled because a co-sponsor, Rep. Elton Gallegly (R-Pa.), urged that the bill not be passed during the final moments of the congressional session. Yet Hyde—also a co-sponsor of the measure—used his power to help bring the measure to a floor vote, claiming that Rep. Canady "deserved" to have it voted upon.[7] Sen. Thurmond was one of eight co-sponsors of S. 950, the companion bill in the Senate to Canady's proposed legislation. In addition, Thurmond co-sponsored a bill in the 106th Congress, S. 2266, that attempted to strengthen the states' rights doctrine and limit prisoners' civil rights by exempting state and local prisons from all regulations governing the delivery of public services and from complying with the federal Americans with Disabilities Act and the Rehabilitation Act. Although none of these measures was passed into law, the attempts to do so give evidence of the ideology at the center of institutional activities.

Given the fact that so much of the emotional content underlying the ideology of White Nationalism is predicated upon the view that the Black community has lost the moral capital to make further demands upon the political system, I close this exploration with a discussion in keeping with the focus on policy: reasserting the legitimacy of Black interests in the political system. I choose to advance the integrity of Black interests not only as an integral aspect of the collective interests of American culture, but as a legitimate set of demands within American *political* culture, both as a basis for seeking the resources with which to accomplish the Black community's self-determination and as a corrective to the anti-democratic trend of imposing policy upon that community with no consideration of the impact. To begin with, I argue that Black interests are coherent, a fact which informs the profile of those interests and which, in turn, leads to an appraisal of how to pursue them. The point is that not only are these interests legitimate but they refute the claims of White Nationalists in the political arena.

THE COHERENCE OF BLACK GROUP INTERESTS

White Nationalists have inferred that relative progress in the class and race position of the Black community makes it unnecessary to continue to protect it legally or construct public policy that would compensate for racism. The White Nationalist movement has asserted its interests over those of Blacks forcefully and without regard to the morality of the rationales for this. As a result, affirming a claim for public policy based upon mainstream Black group interests has become nearly invalid, both politically and legally. The challenge to the moral right of Blacks to demand public policy agendas which reflect the racial condition in America necessitates an examination of the validity of the Black perspective.

The Black Perspective on Issues

Despite the fact that the deprecatory term "identity politics" is used with reference to the discourse and activities which flow from minority group mobilization, the underlying White racial interests in objective majoritarian politics has drawn little attention from analysts, except in the case of defensive references to "reverse racism." Yet Black identity is functional in the sense that Blacks—similarly to Whites, Hispanics and other racial and ethnic groups in America—operate out of an identity conceived from a relatively cohesive culture and a history in this country which has given them a roughly coherent outlook on American life. I do not mean to suggest here that "all Blacks think alike," but there does exist a Black mainstream opinion on most important issues that constitutes the dominant consensus of the group.

As wielders of authoritative power, the majority group is not conditioned to think that legitimate opinion exists outside the realm of its own mainstream attitudes toward issues. However, there is more than one American "mainstream." The collective "American mainstream" is comprised of White majority opinion plus those of various racial and ethnic groups. Although the latter are often considered less legitimate because they have been subordinated, nevertheless they constitute the unique lenses through which such groups evaluate their needs, their relationship to the larger society and the world, and the significance of public events.

One example of this distinctive perspective finds Hugh B. Price, president of the National Urban League, commenting on a *New York Times* article which was headlined, "Americans Reject Means but Not Ends of Racial Diversity."[8] Price remarked: "[T]he headline is wrong. Americans do not 'reject' the means to achieve diversity: White Americans oppose those means, generally speaking, by significant margins. Black Americans support them, generally speaking, by even more significant margins."[9] This acknowledgment of at least two distinct perspectives on such issues suggests that groups mobilize on the basis of often different agendas, depending upon how their perspectives influence their interpretation of the "facts." This raises the question of whose perspective is legitimate, the targets' of policy or the policy makers' themselves.

Evaluation of racial attitudes is important in determining whether there is a consensus among Blacks with respect to consistently shared values in the general context of social advancement and specific issues such as housing, education and employment. Table 10.1 presents evidence from the pioneering work of Howard Schuman, Charlotte Steeh, Lawrence Bobo and Maria Krysan that indicates the existence of a consensus among Blacks with regard to a wide variety of issues dealing with race relations.[10] The stability of responses over time on a set of admittedly selected issues in the Schuman et al. study clearly demonstrates this consistent perspective.[11]

TABLE 10.1 Black Responses to Questions on Race Relations that Exhibit a High Degree of Consensus (by year beginning and ending, and by percent)

			Percentages	
Issue	Year begin	Year end	Year begin	Year end
"Do you think that black and white students should go to the same schools?" (Yes)	1972	1995	96%	99%
"White people have a right to keep blacks out of their neighborhoods if they want to." (Disagree)	1966	1986	80%	96%
"If your party nominated a well-qualified black man for president would you vote for him?" (Yes)	1958	1997	92%	94%
"Do you think that there should be laws against marriages between blacks and whites?" (No)	1980	1996	82%	95%
"Generations of slavery/discrimination have created conditions that make it harder for blacks to work their way out of the lower class." (Agree strongly/somewhat)	1972	1994	85%	68%
"These days, police treat black people as fairly as they treat whites." (Disagree)	1981	1992	69%	88%
"Government is spending too little on blacks" (Yes)	1973	1996	83%	84%
"Blacks favor preferential treatment in:				
admissions	1980	1976	86%	92%
hiring and promotion"	1968	1969	86%	96%

Source: Howard Schuman, Charlotte Steeh, Lawrence Bobo and Maria Krysan, *Racial Attitudes in America: Trends and Interpretations,* rev. ed. (Cambridge, Mass.: Harvard University Press, 1997), pp. 238–78.

Political Behavior

The coherence of Black political behavior is an indication of the fact that there a consensus exists within the Black community about which party best represents its interests. Some have attempted to suggest, without evidence to the contrary, that factors other than an assessment of Black interests is involved in the selection of party identification. Yet Blacks have functioned as a consistent coalition within the Democratic party in presidential elections since 1932—with the exception of the Eisenhower victories in 1952 and 1956—and the high degree of Black allegiance to the Democratic party continues.

As can be seen in Table 10.2, in presidential elections from 1972 to 2000 Blacks voted for the Democratic candidate at an average rate of 85%. This pattern has also held firm at congressional and local levels: at this writing all but one of the 39 Black members of Congress are Democrats, and over 90% of Black local level officials are Democrats as well. No other factor accounts for this substantial degree of uniformity in political choice than the calculation that the Democratic party has served as an adequate representative of the political interests of the Black community over time.

In an important study of the 1984 presidential campaign of Rev. Jesse Jackson, researchers at the University of Michigan found that Black group solidarity was the central factor that led Black voters to support him. More importantly, it established that this expression of Black political solidarity reflected a broader phenomenon of African American life consistent with Black identity: the rejection of an exclusively individualistic ideology. The majority of those surveyed indicated that "collective political solutions" were required to successfully attack problems of political subordination. The researchers did find that Black group identity was

TABLE 10.2 Stability of Black Voting for Democratic Presidential Candidates, 1972–2000

1972	1976	1980	1984	1988	1992	1996	2000	
82%	83%	85%	90%	86%	83%	84%	90%	Average = 85%

Sources: Lucius J. Barker and Jesse J. McCorry, Jr., *Black Americans and the Political System* (Cambridge: Winthrop Publishers, 1980), p. 223; Gerald Pomper, *The Election of 1984* (Chatham, N.J.: Chatham House, 1985), p. 67; Gerald Pomper, *The Election of 1992* (Chatham, N.J.: Chatham House, 1993), p. 139; Gerald Pomper, *The Election of 1996* (Chatham, N.J.: Chatham House, 1997), p. 181; Gerald Pomper, *The Election of 2000* (Chatham, N.J.: Chatham House, 2001), p. 138.

more variable than political solidarity, even though "virtually everyone felt close to other blacks." (This variability related to such issues as the strength of their identity with Africa, or the extent to which the Civil Rights movement would benefit them personally, and constant consciousness of their commonality with other Blacks.) The researchers also found that race-centered identity alone was extremely rare and that most African Americans embraced a dual identity both African and American.[12]

Group solidarity was also a central feature of the "Million Man March" in October 1995, when approximately one million Black males gathered on the Mall in Washington, D.C. Howard University researchers determined that strong group interest was responsible for the impressive size of the assemblage. Professor Joseph McCormick, a member of the research team, surveyed the reasons that were most important in drawing Black men to the march, and the results are recorded in Table 10.3. McCormick judged that a combination of these factors constituted a powerful motivation for attending the march and provided evidence of strong group racial solidarity in the Black community.[13]

I suggest that the origin of these patterns of coherence in Black thought and action resides in traditional interest-group theory—that socio-structural and attitudinal factors help contextualize Black interests in a way that makes them distinct from others.[14] As I examine some of these structural and attitudinal factors and related Black interests in public policy, I will be guided by a simple thesis: *The consistency and pattern of Black perspectives on social and political issues suggest a coherence formed by America's racial history, a fact which also defines the way in which Black interests are pursued within the political system.*

TABLE 10.3   Issues Motivating Black Males to Attend the "Million Man March"

Calls for improving and affirming moral values in the black community	88.2%
Encourages building broad-based black unity	85.1%
Calls for self-determination by the black community	85.0%
Calls for atonement and reconciliation among blacks	77.0%
Supports independent black economic programs	74.9%

Source: Joseph McCormick, "The Messages and the Messengers," a survey of subjects at the "Million Man March," Howard University, October 15, 1995, Table 2.

A PROFILE OF BLACK POLICY INTERESTS

Black Socioeconomic Status

Modern Black issue coherence is related to such important factors as the socioeconomic status of Blacks, which, as suggested in chapter 6, may be traced to the fact that poverty has been endemic to the Black experience. In 1865, when 3.5 million of the four million Blacks in America were released from slavery, most entered society virtually penniless. As they migrated to various parts of the country, they transported this characteristic with them, along with an incomplete assimilation to the dominant European culture. So profound was the poverty that it continued to be strongly manifested well after World War II, regardless of the rate of Black employment. In 1959, when 55% of Blacks fell under the official poverty level, 80% of Blacks (and 90% of Black males) were in the labor force. At the same time, only 39% of Black males and 45% of Black females had completed four years of high school or more, though 65% of White males and 68% of White females had done so.[15] Black families essentially comprised a community of the working poor, where cyclically high unemployment rates, low wages and low-level occupations were the norm.

The poverty that typified Black families, even in the midst of relatively full employment, meant that public housing and various other forms of governmental assistance were critical to their viability. The high levels of Blacks on welfare by 1972 discussed in chapter 6 were a product of the poverty that was characteristic of their families as well as of active efforts to keep them from gaining upward social mobility through greater access to better jobs and education. Housing, employment and education have been at the top of the Black agenda, but employment is critical to the other two.

Low employment and income instability have been the rule. Data from companies reporting to the Equal Employment Opportunity Commission show that during the recession of the late 1980s and early 1990s, the only group to suffer a net decline in employment was Blacks. EEOC records indicate that Asians and Hispanics both gained thousands of jobs despite the downsizing that was characteristic of the profit-building strategies of private companies during that period. Managers of firms that were downsizing added Whites, Asians and Hispanics to their workforce, denying that the exclusion of Blacks was the result of racial discrimination in the face of evidence that Blacks were excluded from the workforce at a much greater rate than other groups.[16] Black job loss at selected firms in 1990–1991 is reflected in the figures in Table 10.4. Though there was a

slight silver lining because some firms increased the number of Blacks in
management and other white-collar positions, this increase did not compensate for the purging of blue-collar Black workers. And with respect to
clerical workers, as a *Wall Street Journal* report indicated, "Blacks who held
jobs involving public contact had an especially rough time during the recession."[17] Why this was so may be at least partly explained by the tendency
in a conservative era to placate the racial sensitivities of the White public
arranging for the delivery of various business services.

Even in the late 1990s, with high levels of economic growth, Blacks
did not fare as well as Whites, though they did better than in the recession of the early 1990s. In February 1998, the White House Council of
Economic Advisers indicated that the income gap between Blacks and
Whites narrowed only slightly between 1993 and 1996: average White
family income was nearly $47,000 in 1996, while Black average family
income that year was $26,000, and the Black household net worth of

TABLE 10.4   Black Job Losses in the 1990–1991 Recession

Firm	Black % of 1990 workforce	Black % of 1991 workforce decline	Black job-loss index
BankAmerica	7.90%	28.11%	3.56%
Sears	15.32%	54.32%	3.43%
W. R. Grace	13.09%	32.16%	2.46%
Coca-Cola Enterprises	17.89%	42.06%	2.35%
ITT	11.81%	27.40%	2.32%
American Cyanamid	11.17%	25.19%	2.26%
Safeway	8.62%	15.66%	1.82%
Campbell Soup	16.40%	29.62%	1.81%
J. P. Morgan	16.59%	27.66%	1.67%
Dial	26.29%	43.56%	1.66%
John Deere	4.23%	6.90%	1.63%
Digital Equipment	6.84%	11.04%	1.61%
Schering-Plough	17.80%	28.55%	1.60%
Fluor	11.67%	18.64%	1.60%
General Electric	7.86%	12.55%	1.57%
McDonald's	23.19%	36.52%	1.57%
USX	12.55%	19.72%	1.57%
TRW	8.94%	13.88%	1.55%
Emerson Electric	6.88%	10.51%	1.53%

Source: Rochelle Sharpe, "Losing Ground: In Latest Recession, Only Blacks Suffered Net
Employment Loss," *Wall Street Journal*, September 14, 1993, p. A13.

$4,500 was only one-tenth that of White families. The wealth gap is expressed in the fact that in 1996, 95% of Black families owned no stock or pension funds.

Though the overall Black poverty rate fell in 1997, poverty among Black children in 1998 was at 40% and unemployment stood at 9.4%, twice the rate of Whites.[18]

In other words, the relatively good economic times of the late 1990s made for a better quality of life for Blacks in absolute terms, yet it did not alter the structural distance between the economic fortunes of Blacks and Whites. For a minority group, this comparative measure is critical, since it is the condition of the majority that sets the price and nature of the quality of life.

Revisiting the 1960s Model

I do not propose that the '60s policy framework should be replicated. Rather I suggest that the characterization of the policies of the 1960s as "failed" for Blacks is demonstrably false. Key issues of the Black agenda— including enhanced status in employment, education, housing and social welfare—were addressed by the policies of the 1960s, which became the targets of Conservative social policy in the 1980s and 1990s. If the policies of the 1960s failed, one must ask: against what measure did they fail? If the yardstick is that these policies were intended to eliminate poverty and discrimination, then Conservatives are correct: government policies could not accomplish this in a country where the essential social and economic viability of citizens is dependent upon the private sector for jobs and economic development. However, in the five years between 1963 and 1968 Black average income grew by 36% and official poverty decreased substantially—from 55% in 1959 to 37% by 1969—suggesting that the public assistance available during that period was essential in raising the economic standard of the Black community.[19]

Michael Brown has concluded that not only were Black gains after 1964 extensive, "recent research attributes them to the tight labor markets induced by the rapid economic growth of the late 1960s and to a decline in racial discrimination in the labor market. The latter is usually accorded the most significance, and is thought to be a consequence of the impact of Title VII of the 1964 Civil Rights Act and a 1964 Executive Order issued by Lyndon Johnson that required nondiscriminatory employment practices of federal contractors."[20]

The Great Society program, initiated in 1964, was an instrument of social investment in neighborhoods which were characterized by poverty and distance from major labor markets. It was buttressed by the Elementary and Secondary Act of 1965, the Model Cities administration (with its focus on housing and urban development), and the Manpower Development and Training program (which focused on enhancing labor force skills and providing health and social service programs). The stream of spending resulted in an increase in federal grants-in-aid to state and local governments for social welfare programs from $4 billion in 1960 to nearly $60 billion in 1980; disbursements for social service programs went from $1.5 billion to $30 billion by the end of the 1970s.[21]

As a result, Brown determined, employment increased by two million net new jobs; 90% of these were in state and local government, and Black participation in public sector employment increased from 15% to 27% between 1960 and 1976. Clearly the thrust of the public sector into the Black community in the 1960s was responsible for stimulating solid socioeconomic progress, and this was especially important in building the Black middle class.[22] However, none of this would have worked if Blacks themselves had not exercised a phenomenal degree of "individual responsibility" by taking advantage of the opportunities created by government measures.

Policy Priorities: Thirty Years Later

In 1996 and 2000, pursuant to the presidential elections in those years, national surveys by the Joint Center for Political and Economic Studies—a nationally recognized Black think tank—canvassed the policy priorities of Blacks and Whites. Respondents were asked to name their "most important" policy priorities, and the profiles that emerged are summarized in Table 10.5. In 1996 the most important priorities for Blacks were the economy and jobs, crime and associated issues, the budget crisis and education. In the 2000 survey, there was a shift, with health care and drugs among the top Black priorities, together with education, crime and the economy or jobs.

Whites' top three priority interests were similar to Blacks' in the 1996 survey, and in 2000 both ranked education as the first priority and health care as the second. But the other principal interests of Whites in the 2000 survey included family values and morality, and crime. Although Blacks in the 2000 survey gave the specific issue of race relations a relatively low priority, many of the issues they ranked as important have a racial context.

Even though the substance of Black priority issues would appear to require government programs to address them, Black support of govern-

TABLE 10.5   Policy Priorities of Blacks and Whites, 1996 and 2000,
by Ranking

Blacks	1996	2000	Whites	1996	2000
Economy, unemployment	1	4	Balance budget, national debt	1	—
Crime, violence, gangs	2	3	Crime, violence, gangs	2	5
Balance budget, national debt	3	—	Economy, unemployment	3	6, 7
Education	4	1	Family values, morality	4	3
Drugs	5	3	Government waste, inefficiency	5	—
Health care	6	2	Health care	6	2
Poverty, homelessness	7	5	Education	7	1
Family values, morality	8	7	Government gridlock/ shutdown	8	—
Government waste, inefficiency	9	—	Poverty, homelessness	9	8
Race relations	6	9	Race relations	10	—

Sources: "The Country's Most Important Problems," *1996 National Opinion Poll: Political Attitudes,* Joint Center for Political and Economic Studies, Washington, D.C., October 1996, Table 1. "What Do You Think Is the Single Most Important Problem Facing the Country Today?" *2000 National Opinion Poll-Politics,* Joint Center for Political and Economic Studies, Washington D.C., October 2000, Table 1, p. 3. The 1996 survey featured 27 categories; the 2000 survey featured 11.

ment intervention has declined markedly from the 1960s. Schuman, Steeh, Bobo and Krysan suggest that one reason for this may be the rise in White disaffection with such measures as economic aid to Blacks and busing to promote school desegregation.[23] Black approval of government support of various programs to implement social well-being rose in the late 1960s when social protests were common, but declined in the mid-1970s as protests also declined. Schuman et al. assert: "The decline in black support for federal intervention to desegregate schools could be largely a reaction to white intractability on this issue. Evidence for this interpretation can be drawn from the association between the decline in black support for federal intervention in this area and black objections to busing specifically."[24] Additional evidence for this argument lies in statistics which show a decline in the number of Blacks seeking admission to higher education in Texas and California in 1996 and 1997, following negative court decisions and public referenda on affirmative action.

Perhaps another reason for the decline in Black support for government intervention is that most Blacks have consistently accepted a share of the responsibility for their own situation—despite the ideology of the present Conservative movement. In an April 1992 Gallup poll, Black respondents tended to accept the majority of the blame for such problems as teenage pregnancy (54%) and broken families (46%), but they expressed the belief that government is responsible for unemployment (62%), inferior education (48%) and other social problems.[25] Five years later, another Gallup poll found that while Blacks believed that government should make every effort to improve their condition, they felt responsible for focusing on self-improvement.

Although this response appears to parallel White views that Blacks are substantially responsible for their plight, a smaller percentage of Blacks than Whites held this view.[26]

THE VALIDITY OF BLACK INTERESTS

The Black Perspective on the Black Experience

Now that I have illustrated that there is a substantially coherent objective Black interest, I am prepared to assert that this constitutes the legitimacy of Black interests and is the basis of the presentation of Black group interests in the political system. Since one of the objectives of White Nationalism has been to impose its prescriptions on various problems faced by the Black community, the validity of the Black perspective is often ignored altogether or distorted in the competition for public credibility. In fact, the conflict between the Black agenda and policy racism strongly suggests that the agenda that is activated by the policy system purportedly to address issues related to the Black community often does not involve the Black perspective. Operational issues—such as whose perspective on policy questions should be taken into consideration in formulating policy—determine the nature of policy and its impact upon the Black community.

The Empirical Element

In the Joint Center for Political and Economic Studies' polls referred to above, the response of Blacks and Whites likely reflected their different

TABLE 10.6   How Are Blacks Treated in Your Community?

	Blacks	Whites
Blacks treated same as whites	49%	76%
Blacks treated not as well	38%	15%
Blacks treated badly	7%	2%

Source: "Black/White Relations in the United States," Executive Summary; Expanded Summary, "The Racial Situation in America's Local Communities," Gallup Poll Social Audit, July 1997, p. 6.

experiences. The Black perspective arises from the experience of living as a minority in a social system dominated by Whites and in which there is racial isolation and hostility. Though some Whites have relationships with Blacks, this does not allow them to experience the intensity of racism and thus develop similar perspectives. For example, a 1997 Gallup poll questioned both Blacks and Whites with respect to their experience of unfair treatment in their communities (see Table 10.6). Although they have significantly less experience with racial discrimination, 76% of Whites said that Blacks are treated the same as they are. By contrast, only 49% of Blacks agreed with this statement. When the question of the treatment of Blacks arises, one would logically expect that the responses of Blacks have more basis in experience. Moreover, the experience of Whites seemingly places them in the role of spectator with regard to treatment of Blacks, and their perceptions would be tempered by their attitudes. The dissonance between experience and attitude is relatively consistent: in the same poll Whites expressed more optimism about Black opportunities than did Blacks, as seen in Table 10.7.

TABLE 10.7   Comparative Attitudes about Equal Opportunities for Blacks

Percentage agreeing with the statement
"Blacks in my community have as good a chance as whites with respect to":

	Blacks	Whites	Gap
Getting any kind of job	46%	79%	33%
Education	71%	93%	22%
Housing	58%	86%	28%

Source: "Black/White Relations in the United States," Gallup Poll Social Audit, June 1997, Executive Summary, p. 5.

This 1997 Gallup poll showed an average gap of 28% between the more experience-based attitudes of Blacks and the less experience-based opinions of Whites with respect to such critical issues as jobs, education and housing. Yet White decision makers routinely rely solely on their non-experiential opinions to pass laws that determine the quality of life in the Black community. This raises the question of whether policy is formulated from a sense of the general "national interest" or from a perceived fear of harm to White self-interest—whether this fear is experiential, theoretical, or based on the likelihood of a threat. Since the experience of harm has not occurred, I suggest that perceived threats to White interests constitute the most powerful factor in these responses.

The question of the integrity of Black interests is comprised of a set of factors. The first of these is taken for granted in this work: the right of Blacks to assert their interests within the political system. The second is the coherence of black interests as a legitimate "mainstream" perspective on American life. And third is the morality of the position of Blacks as the recipients of treatment that constructs an empirical experience with racism, producing a perspective on racism that is more immediate and experiential than the detached perspective of its perpetrators.

BLACK AGENDA SETTING

Given that harming Black interests is the objective of White Nationalism, the question arises as to what kinds of actions are effective in carrying out the Black agenda. I follow a traditional course in suggesting that the answer lies in a variety of political mobilizations.

Civic Action Demonstrations

A number of tactics and strategies which have proven effective in influencing public policy belong to the activists' legacy. An example from one end of the civic action spectrum is the NAACP's report card on hotels for Black consumers. Published in 1997, it rated hiring practices and racial representation among franchisees and members of boards of directors.[27] Within one year of this report, the hotel industry improved Black access in all these areas.[28] At the other pole of civic action tactics are more militant actions, such as protest demonstrations. In November 2000, for example, protests effectively brought to the attention of the American public the charge that Black voters in Florida had been disenfranchised in the 2000 presidential election.[29] Black leaders mounted protest demonstrations in Florida because they saw this as a way to support Al Gore's chances of becoming president and thus enhance the possibilities that their agenda would be implemented.

Of course, electoral politics at every level has this function for all citizens, but for Blacks it is a more critical motivation because of the dimension of their needs.

Electoral Politics

The presidential campaigns of Rev. Jesse Jackson in 1984 and 1988 may represent the most effective tactics of Black agenda setting to date, for in those years the Democratic party's ability to establish an agenda was directly related to the political salience of Jackson forces within the party and among elected officials who benefited from his campaigns. Since that time, "clientage politics" as an appendage of Bill Clinton's campaigns and governance was far less effective on behalf of Blacks.[30] However, as noted earlier, this was partly due to the impact of radical Conservatism on the Clinton governing agenda.

Access Politics

Mobilization of the Black community in periods between elections is a function of Black politicians and their allies who have been elected to office, including a range of Liberal and Progressive nongovernmental interest groups. Access to key decision makers is crucial to having an agenda item considered and acted upon, and thus securing the attention of the White House and agency heads has been most vital.

Access to key decision makers in Congress has been difficult for Blacks, since both the House and Senate have frequently been controlled by interests hostile to the Black agenda. This has meant that Black policy makers often have no choice but to opt for bipartisanship, foregoing the implementation of their policy expectations in hopes of achieving something of value for their constituents.

Legal Challenges

Lawsuits on behalf of Blacks have challenged race-based exclusion and maltreatment of Black customers in the private sector; high-profile cases have involved Denny's restaurants, Eddie Bauer clothing stores and Nissan Motor Company, among others. Doubtless, egregious discrimination effected by government agencies and suffered by Black farmers, Black

U.S. Marshals and Black Foreign Service officers would not have been brought to light nor rectified without legal action; linking individual suits within a class-action case has proven to be particularly effective, calling attention to and redressing patterns of discriminatory behavior.

POLICY MOBILIZATION IN THE BLACK COMMUNITY

Without attempting to evaluate in depth the relative merits of the various methods of implementing the Black agenda outlined above, it can be observed that such activity has served effectively as a means of promoting civic participation. Much of that activity has focused on increasing voter turnout. Encouragement of civic mobilization in non-electoral contexts has not been as successful. The irony of this is that participation in the broader civic arena supports the electoral process, supplying the resources to engage and influence the policy-making system. Thus heightened participation in such activities as strengthening the development and dissemination of policy-oriented information is critical. I will comment briefly on the substantial subject of policy mobilization in order to suggest areas for further research and analysis that would strengthen the capability of the Black community to assert its interests in the political system.

Policy Analysis: The policy research infrastructure of the Black community is sorely underdeveloped, with only a small number of institutions concentrating on the production of policy-relevant information. Few policy research centers are controlled by Black scholars either at historically Black colleges and universities or at independent research institutions. One of the most significant is the Center for the Study of African American Life at the University of Michigan's Institute for Social Research. It has conducted original research yielding significant data on a range of issues affecting the Black community. However, little of this research has found its way into the policy arena, since there is not an equivalent unit to "translate" the information into policy language and disseminate it to the relevant actors.

The tasks of developing policy-oriented research, shaping it so that it can be consumed by lay citizens, policy makers and the media, and disseminating it widely have largely been the preserve of non-university-based organizations. This places a great burden on the nonprofit, private sector in helping Black Americans achieve higher levels of policy mobilization. One such private sector organization is the Joint Center for Political and Economic Studies, the longest-serving policy research institution in the Black community. Yet its output is anemic in comparison to the enormous productivity of Conservative institutions such as the Heritage Foundation, the American Enterprise Institute, the Cato Institute and others. These organizations maintain a steady stream of information to legislators all over the nation and thus have been influential in policy circles to a greater degree than more moderate researchers, such as those at the Brookings Institution and similar organizations. The National Urban League maintains a research institute, and the Congressional Black Caucus has intermittently established such a vehicle for its legislative work. Nevertheless, even collectively, these poorly funded institutions are insufficient to support the broad agenda of 40 million people.

The Media: Research shows that the role of the media is central to the process of "framing" policy issues for lawmakers. The problem for African Americans is that as members of a subordinate community, they have not been able to convince the media to accept the way they frame issues. So-called "Liberal" media sources rarely use Black analysts and published reports involving issues of interest to the Black community. Black policy makers, even those who have attained significant responsibilities in Congress or the executive branch, are interviewed far less often than White policy makers. Moreover, few Black media professionals are frequently interviewed or serve as regular members on panels of news analysts.

As a result of limited Black access to the White mainstream media, these media have devoted an inordinate amount of attention to a relatively small number of Black political leaders. Though media coverage of Black leaders' reactions to events is important, it is less effective than consistent, comprehensive and substantive coverage of Blacks and their agenda. The struggle for media attention, often through mass mobilization, is difficult, costly and ultimately an ineffective strategy. Issue positions have routinely been distorted, poorly covered or ignored. Moreover, Black leadership does not capitalize on natural media opportunities provided by such events as the "Million Man March" because it lacks effective media strategies. In the 2000 election campaign, Black newspapers and radio stations proved to be significant resources for Black communication, but these media have not yet achieved a meaningful influence with regard to national issues that become the substance of policy making.

Policy Mediators: Several nonprofit organizations encourage voter turnout on a nonpartisan basis, and once elections are over they participate in policy formation and mobilization. Traditionally, however, they devote far fewer resources to this second effort. Nevertheless, Black organizations such as the National Association for the Advancement of Colored

People and the National Urban League serve as leaders in this respect. From offices in Washington, D.C., their staffs maintain regular contact with decision makers and explicate the views of the African American community on various legislative initiatives. They are complemented by other organizations, such as the National Rainbow Coalition, the Black Leadership Forum, the National Coalition on Black Civic Participation, the Congress of National Black Churches and the National Council of Negro Women, as well as a host of professional associations. Yet these organizations maintain no formal framework through which a collective approach to policy mobilization may be continually achieved. They prefer to work in strategic groups on specific issues, bringing these issues to public attention at specialized events, their annual conferences and fund-raising events.

Policy Makers: At the national level, the Congressional Black Caucus (CBC) is the most active policy-making body of elected officials. The CBC establishes its priority of issues through consensus and frequently publishes the results of its deliberations. The priorities set forth by the CBC for special action in the 105th Congress (1997–1998) are listed here, together with issues that have continuing priority.

Priorities for the 105th Congress
free our families and communities from drugs
strengthen HIV/AIDS education, prevention and research
support and protect grandparents and other family caregivers
rehabilitate our schools and improve access to education
increase access to information technology
increase training and job creation
create capital to assist minority business development
improve access to resources for Black farmers
revitalize our nation's capital and secure voting rights in Congress
expand assistance and support for Africa and the Caribbean

Ongoing Priorities
redefine and improve security for all Americans
ensure equal access to full voter participation
end toxic racism in the environment
eliminate disparities in drug sentencing
maintain an adequate safety net for the poor
provide education about and help prevent teenage pregnancy
provide alternatives for our youth involved in the juvenile justice system
protect our seniors' Social Security and Medicare

improve access to health care for poor communities
ensure equal opportunity through affirmative action
build strong communities through urban and rural economic
    development
expand affordable housing[31]

The relative priority of these ongoing issues changes with the opportunities of each legislative session and the specific interests of Black members' constituents. In the 106th Congress (1999–2000), the CBC added some issues to its list of immediate priorities, including:

monitor the 2000 census for undercounting
close health gaps by supporting "Healthy People 2000"
reject vouchers and support inner-city school rehabilitation and the
    "E-rate" program (which authorizes discounted access to the
    Internet and other telecommunications services)
eliminate mandatory minimum sentences for nonviolent offenders and
    restore voting rights to convicted felons
oppose racial profiling and police use of deadly force

After analyzing legislative initiatives proposed by members of the CBC in the 106th Congress, I determined that CBC members collectively offered 250 measures—an average of 6.5 per member.[32] CBC members most active in this regard are listed in Table 10.8. A listing such as this is only suggestive, since bills, resolutions and joint resolutions have different significance and represent different levels of effort. Moreover, any comparison with the efforts of White members of Congress would have to take into consideration relative length of service and, more

TABLE 10.8   Congressional Black Caucus Members with Ten or More Sponsored Pieces of Legislation, 1999

Member	Number of pieces
Sheila Jackson Lee (D-Tex.)	21
Charles B. Rangel (D-N.Y.)	20
Eleanor Holmes Norton (D-D.C.)	17
John Conyers (D-Mich.)	16
Maxine Waters (D-Calif.)	13
Alcee L. Hastings (D-Fla.)	10
Carrie Meek (D-Fla.)	10

important, their place in the legislative hierarchy, including proximity to congressional leadership.

The nature of the issue agenda the CBC has pursued is illustrated in the overview of themes that were the subjects of members' proposed legislation (see Table 10.9). It is not unusual that private bills represent the highest priority, for constituent service is a principal service of congressional representatives, and the others are clearly important to the general welfare of citizens in every political jurisdiction. Yet more significant than the mere number of legislative measures initiated by its individual members is the CBC's focus on a combination of continuing issues and new ones that reflect current challenges. The CBC represents the interests of a large group in American society which has a substantial investment in the policy system because of the Black community's peculiar history.

Many of the items represented in the CBC listings in Table 10.9 have not been passed into law. This is an indication of the substantial effort facing that group, which supports my observation that the policy mobilization capacity of the Black community needs to be strengthened considerably. I agree with Professor Robert Singh of the University of Edinburgh that improved capacity of the CBC to enact legislation favorable to the interests of African Americans depends upon the correctives they take as an

TABLE 10.9 Legislative Themes as Reflected in Proposals Sponsored by Members of the Congressional Black Caucus, 1999

Themes	Number of Proposals
Private bills	22
Criminal justice	15
Education	14
Health	13
Immigration	10
Africa	8
Guns	6
Consumer issues	5
Housing	4
Minority business	4
Social Security	3
Y2K	3
Youth	3
Voting rights	2
Labor	2

organization.[33] But I disagree with his singular finding that the strategies and tactics of the caucus are questionable: in this determination, he overlooks the impact of contextual factors. The White Nationalist movement is one such contextual factor. It has intensified political polarization in the House under Republican leadership and, through ruthless tactics of control such as government-by-caucus, prevented much of the legislation of the Democratic party from being considered.

CONCLUSION:
WHITE NATIONALISM AND AMERICAN NATIONALISM

As I close this discussion of White Nationalism—in which I have attempted to illustrate that race has been a central determinant in shaping important public policies—I suggest that this work may contribute to the settled proposition in the field of political science that ideology has an impact upon public policy. This impact may often be heightened because politicians who perceive a public consensus on a set of values adopt these as "screening" factors in both election campaigns and governance.[34] Since the force of White majority public opinion most often influences the way Americans think on a given question, it is obvious that whatever effort Blacks can exert may not be sufficient to impact public policy. Therefore, anti-White Nationalists' values must become centered in the general body politic on the basis of traditional notions of fairness and democracy.

In a study conducted in the early 1980s, Robert Entman compared the avowed political positions of members of Congress from Connecticut and North Carolina with their role-call votes, determining that members from North Carolina were more ideological than those from Connecticut.[35] Another observer found that from 1980 to 1993 there was increasing consistency between national public opinion and policy outcomes on 500 issue measures.[36] Yet despite these and other indications of the effect of ideology on public policy, the view that racial ideology has been translated into race-oriented public policy has not been popularly accepted.

In an essay on Conservatism in the context of post-World War II McCarthyism, Professor Samuel Huntington—correctly, in my view—suggested that "neoconservatism" is situational, that it is a response to certain historical factors:

> The conservative ideology is the product of intense ideological and social conflict. It appears only when the challengers to the established institutions reject the fundamentals of the ideational theory

in terms of which those institutions have been molded and created. If the challengers do not question the basic values of the prevailing philosophy, the controversy between those for and against institutional change is carried on with reference to the commonly accepted ideational philosophy.[37]

The circumstances under which the Conservative reaction to the Civil Rights movement occurred match Huntington's thesis, as does my analysis of White Nationalism as a crusade to reserve justice for Whites.

As previously indicated, studies of American voters suggest that they have become more ideological, and that the relationship between their ideology and political behavior has become more coherent.[38] If race is an alienating factor and a stimulus to certain kinds of political behavior, such as political representation and policy making, then it is correct to ask how the political system will react as the racial and ethnic composition of the citizenry—and thus the electorate—changes. I believe it is urgent to begin a discussion of the implications of American nationalism, evaluating whether the dividends and liabilities will accrue to citizens equally, or whether society becomes a "justice preserve" of the dominant group.

American Nationalism

Michael Lind argues that one of the reasons "American nationalism is almost never represented in public discussions of American identity" is the instability of its basis.[39] He suggests that a major reason for this is that many cultural minorities mistakenly relate their racial identity to an external nationality rather than an internal one.

Lind raises an important question when he points out that Newt Gingrich asked Americans to eschew the racial exceptionalism of multiculturalism in favor of a new American exceptionalism. But what, in fact, is the content of that exceptionalism? Is it an authentically inclusive American nationalism—as suggested in chapter 2—or a White Nationalism that exercises a hegemonic role over the terms and content of the expression of America's subcultures? Whether or not one agrees with Lind's conception of racial and ethnic exceptionalism, his discussion raises the possibility that a real antithesis exists between American nationalism and White Nationalism.

One difficulty with Lind's thesis is that it assumes a high degree of not only cultural but political assimilation. American subcultures have not achieved this in relation to the dominant White majority because of the failure to complete the project of integration. The majority group's cultural sheriffs refuse to give equal status to the contributions of sub-cultures to American nationality. Indeed, Lind refers to the tension between the present culture and the continuing grand project of producing American democracy out of diversity. However, especially given the fact that radical Conservatives have elaborated their own narrow forms of multiculturalism, it matters that diversity have a broadly humane and truly democratic character.

A second problem with Lind's thesis is that it requires a substantial degree of democratic practice. It is possible to objectively question the basis on which White Nationalists use their power in a manner contrary to the known interests of the Black community. Yet their use of power is legitimate in the constitutional sense, since it was acquired through legal political processes, asserted its control over political institutions, and enacted legislation. Nonetheless, the act of making laws represents an imposition of will: the construction of an agenda and a strategy for moving society in a certain direction to achieve certain ends. So what is the moral responsibility of that imposition when it encounters the legitimate interests of a subordinate community or group of people which has its own mainstream consensus and a leadership that accurately represents those interests? Conflict often ensues, and rather than judging that this conflict has been resolved fairly only because it reflects the position of the party wielding power, one can take the perspective of the subordinate group whose interests have been violated and conclude that they have suffered an oppressive act. In fact, one might conclude that this use of power by White Nationalists is morally corrupt because it violates the consensus of the community it has targeted. A greater substantive legitimacy would be derived if policy makers follow democratic practices, such as providing an opportunity for the target community to express its views and then include such views in policy formation.

One might also conclude that the majority has a right to suppress a group's interests if the nature of its agenda runs contrary to the professed philosophical or constitutional foundations of the nation. However, the struggle for Black civil rights and social justice has always been conducted within the context of those foundations, as noted by Dr. Martin Luther King, Jr., in his seminal 1963 speech during the "March on Washington," when he declared that his own dream was rooted in "the American dream." By contrast, the "Contract with America" implied no such democratic vision, either in its formulation or the manner in which politicians sought to execute it. In that case, policy making proceeded through a closed system that excluded participants who represented the interests of the Black community.

The essence of the modern struggle for civil rights and social equality—as expressed in legislation dealing with such issues as education, employment and housing, among others—has yet to be fully implemented. At least two tasks clearly remain. One is to preserve both the social progress that has been achieved and the means by which it was achieved. The other is to broaden opportunities. The pursuit of these goals will be increasingly difficult and their achievement in the policy arena tenuous unless the influence of the White Nationalist movement subsides. If this does not happen, it can be predicted that racial tension in America will likely increase, perhaps to levels which will challenge the American experiment with democracy itself.

Notes

Introduction

1. Anne Schneider and Helen Ingram, "The Social Construction of Target Populations: Implications for Politics and Policy," *American Political Science Review* 87:2 (June 1993): 334. The authors also suggest that the "social construction of target populations has a powerful influence on public officials and shapes both the policy agenda and the actual design of policy." They additionally deduce that "public officials often devise punitive, punishment-oriented policies for negatively constructed groups," which they say helps explain why the policy system advantages some groups more than others.

2. George M. Frederickson, *The Black Image in the White Mind: The Debate on Afro-American Character and Destiny, 1817–1914* (New York: Harper and Row, 1971), p. 130.

3. Ibid., p. 133.

4. Frederickson cites Rev. Atticus Haygood, president of Emory College in Atlanta, Georgia, as representative of many moderate southern Whites; *Black Image in the White Mind*, p. 204.

5. John W. Cell, *The Highest Stage of White Supremacy: The Origins of Segregation in South Africa and the American South* (New York: Cambridge University Press, 1982), p. 178.

6. Clarence Y. H. Lo, "Countermovements and Conservative Movements in the Contemporary U.S.," *Annual Review of Sociology* 8 (1982): 117.

7. Christopher Bagley, "Race Relations and Theories of Status Consistency," *Race* (London: Institute of Race Relations, 1970), p. 267.

8. Cited in ibid., 269.

9. Faye V. Harrison, "The Persistent Power of 'Race' in the Cultural and Political Economy of Racism," *Annual Review of Anthropology* 24 (1995): 63.

10. *Congressional Record*, House, May 1, 1997, p. H2124.

11. Ibid., p. H2129.

12. Ibid., p. H2133.

13. Ibid., p. H2137.

14. Ibid., p. H2139.

15. Ibid., p. H2143.

16. Ibid., p. H2144.

Chapter 1

1. See, for example, Sidney Tarrow, *Power in Movement: Social Movements and Contentious Politics* (Cambridge: Cambridge University Press, 1998), which carries forward insights in the cyclical processing of movements formulated in Mayer N. Zald and Roberta Ash, "Social Movement Organizations: Growth, Decay and Change," *Social Forces* 44 (March 1966): 327–41; See also, Mayer N. Zald and John D. McCarthy, eds., *Social Movements in an Organizational Society* (New Brunswick, N.J.: Transaction Books, 1987. Doug McAdam has done some of the best work in theorizing that the opportunity structure in society helps provide an opening for social movements, if other motivational factors are in place. Doug McAdam, *Political Process and the Development of Black Insurgency* (Chicago: University of Chicago Press, 1982).

2. Paulo Freire, *Pedagogy of the Oppressed* (New York: Continuum, 1997), p. 39.

3. Mancur Olson, Jr., "The Relationship between Economic and Other Social Sciences: The Province of a 'Social Report,'" in Seymour Martin Lipset, ed., *Politics and the Social Sciences* (New York: Oxford University Press, 1969), p. 144.

4. Arthur Miller, "Trust in Government," *American Political Science Review* 68:3 (September 1974): 953.

5. Just how much of the lack of trust was related to race was not indicated, but the 1968 survey utilized a new "social issue" measure which found strong correlations to exist on the issues of civil rights and Vietnam with the direction of trust in government. Miller, "Trust in Government," pp. 960–61.

6. Ibid., p. 957.

7. "National Poll Finds Strong Belief in Government's Potential: Better Leadership and Management Critical to Effectiveness," Council for Excellence in Government, Washington, D.C., March 21, 1997, press release. Also see http://www.exclgov.org/hart.htm.

8. Richard J. Herrnstein and Charles Murray, *The Bell Curve: Intelligence and Class Structure in American Life* (New York: Free Press, 1994).

9. Oscar Janowsky, *Nationalities and National Minorities with Special Reference to East-Central Europe* (New York: Macmillan, 1945), p. 17.

10. Rogers Brubaker, *Citizenship and Nationhood in France and Germany* (Cambridge: Harvard University Press, 1992), p. 102.

11. Ibid., p. 3.

12. Tom Nairn, *Faces of Nationalism* (London: Verso Press, 1997), p. 87.

13. Seyom Brown, *New Forces in World Politics* (Washington, D.C.: Brookings Institution, 1974), p. 171.

14. Michael Omi and Howard Winant, *Racial Formation in the United States: From the 1960s to the 1980s* (New York: Routledge and Kegan Paul, 1986), pp. 79–80.

15. Kurt H. Wolff, ed., *From Karl Mannheim* (New York: Oxford University Press, 1971), p. 161.

16. Robert Pois, ed., *Race and Race History and Other Essays by Alfred Rosenberg* (New York, HarperTorch Book, 1970), p. 192.

17. Raymond Hall, *Black Separatism in the United States* (Hanover, N.H.: University Press of New England, 1978), p. 254.

18. In a useful essay, Barrington attempts to clarify the various meanings of "nation" and "nationalism" by considering the leading scholarly definitions from individuals such as Ernest Gellner, Ernst Haas, Roy Mellor, Anthony Smith and others, suggesting both proper and improper uses of the concepts. See Lowell W. Barrington, "'Nation' and 'Nationalism': The Misuse of Key Concepts in Political Science," *PS: Political Science and Politics* 30:4 (December 1997): 713.

19. Cited in ibid., p. 714.

20. One assumes, then, that since White Nationalists' perception is that they are involved in a "zero-sum game" that the logical course of action would be to visit punishment upon their adversaries in an attempt to change the terms of advantage.

21. Anthony Richmond, "Ethnic Nationalism: Social Science Paradigms," *International Social Science Journal* 111 (February 1987): 4–5. Cited in Barrington, "'Nation' and 'Nationalism,'" p. 714.

22. Barrington, "'Nation' and 'Nationalism,'" p. 715.

23. Ruth Frankenberg, *The Social Construction of Whiteness: White Women, Race Matters* (Minneapolis: University of Minnesota Press, 1993), p. 1.

24. A formidable literature has emerged on the subject of "Whiteness," a sample of which may be found in a summary by Faye V. Harrison, "The Persistent Power of 'Race' in the Cultural and Political Economy of Racism," *Annual Review of Anthropology* 24 (1995): 47–74. See also, for example: David Roediger, *The Wages of Whiteness: Race and the Making of the American Working Class* (New York: Verso Press, 1999); David Stowe, "Uncolored People: The Rise of Whiteness Studies," *Lingua Franca*, September–October 1996, pp. 68–77; Peter A. Chvany, "What We Talk about When We Talk about Whiteness," *Minnesota Review* 47 (1996): 49–55.

25. Quoted in Perry L. Weed, *The White Ethnic Movement and Ethnic Politics* (New York: Praeger, 1973), p. 206.

26. David Blight, *Race and Reunion* (Cambridge, Mass.: Harvard University Press, 2000).

27. Cited in George M. Frederickson, *White Supremacy: A Comparative Study in American and South African History* (New York: Oxford University Press, 1981), p. 191.

28. Daniel Bell, "Ethnicity and Social Change," in Nathan Glazer and Daniel P. Moynihan, eds., *Ethnicity: Theory and Experience* (Cambridge, Mass.: Harvard University Press, 1975), p. 161.

29. Hall, *Black Separatism in the United States*, pp. 1, 2, 3.

30. Leslie Roman calls this "white defensive racism" in his article, "White Is a Color," in Cameron McCarthy and Warren Crichlow, eds., *Race Identity and Representation In Education* (New York: Routledge, 1993), p. 74. See also, D.

Dworkin and L. G. Rowman, eds., *Views Beyond the Border Country: Raymond Williams and Cultural Politics* (New York: Routledge, 1993), pp. 1–17.

31. Faustine Childress Jones defines Conservatism as "the attitude and practice of stressing established institutions and social practices and preferring gradual development to swift and/or pervasive change; a nostalgia for the past (status quo ante), which is perceived to be superior to the present in terms of prevailing conditions contributing to social order"; Jones, *The Changing Mood in America: Eroding Commitment?* (Washington, D.C.: Howard University Press, 1977), p. x. Here, however, this definition may be useful in making the distinction between Conservatism and Nationalism in that the motivation of Nationalism is to overturn or radically change the status quo social order in ways that would benefit those involved in the movement to do so.

32. Cited in Frederickson, *White Supremacy,* p. 155.

33. John Cell, *The Highest Stage of White Supremacy* (New York: Cambridge University Press, 1982), pp. 24–25.

34. Alphonso Pinkney, *Lest We Forget: White Hate Crimes* (Chicago: Third World Press, 1994), p. 29.

35. Mary C. Brennan, *Turning Right in the '60s: The Conservative Capture of the GOP* (Chapel Hill: University of North Carolina Press, 1995), p. 47.

36. Cell, *Highest Stage of White Supremacy,* p. 180.

37. Howard Rabinowitz, *Race Relations in the Urban South, 1865–1890* (New York: Oxford University Press, 1978); cited in Cell, *Highest Stage of White Supremacy,* p. 180.

38. Wilson Carey McWilliams, *The Politics of Disappointment: American Elections 1976–1994* (Chatham, N.J.: Chatham House, 1995), pp. 17.

39. Ira Katznelson, Kim Geiger and Daniel Kryder, "Limiting Liberalism: The Southern Veto in Congress, 1933–1950," *Political Science Quarterly* 108:2 (Summer 1993): 283–304.

40. George Washington Cable, *The Negro Question,* ed. Arlin Turner (New York: W. W. Norton, 1968), pp. 12–13, 30.

41. Ruth Sheehan, "South Rises Again on Nostalgia Wave: Confederate Is Cool," *Commercial Appeal* (Memphis, Tenn.), May 5, 1996, p. A8.

42. Ibid.

43. Ibid.

44. Peter Applebome, "Dueling With the Heirs of Jeff Davis," *New York Times,* December 27, 198, Section 4, p. 1.

45. Gary Robertson, "War's Lost, but the Fight Endures," *Richmond Times-Dispatch,* September 29, 1997, p. 1.

46. For a summary of this opinion, see Michael W. Giles and Kaenan Hertz, "Racial Threat and Partisan Identification," *American Political Science Review* 88:2 (June 1994): 317–26.

47. Cited in ibid., p. 318.

48. Ibid., p. 317.

49. Jean V. Hardisty, "Why Now?: The Resurgent Right," *Public Eye* 9:3–4 (Fall/Winter 1995): 12.

50. A report of what were perhaps the earliest such attempts can be found in an article by Ben Wattenberg, "Black Progress and Liberal Rhetoric," *Commentary*, April 1973, pp. 35–44.

51. Stephan Thernstrom and Abigail Thernstrom, *America in Black and White: One Nation, Indivisible* (New York: Simon and Schuster, 1997), p. 183.

52. Ibid., p. 188.

53. Ibid., pp. 188–89.

54. Andrew Hacker, *Two Nations: Black and White, Separate, Hostile, Unequal* (New York: Charles Scribner's Sons, 1992), p. 112.

55. See, for example, Peter Truell, "A Black Joins Merrill Lynch's Top Ranks," *New York Times*, March 22, 1997, p. 29. This article discuss the rise of a single Black professional in the ranks of Merrill Lynch, but it also indicates how rare a phenomenon it is to have a financial manger at one of the top Wall Street brokerages.

56. Hacker, *Two Nations*, p. 114.

57. Ibid., p. 115.

58. Tom Wicker, *Tragic Failure: Racial Integration in America* (New York: William Morrow, 1996), p. 75.

59. Robert B. Reich, "The Revolt of the Anxious Class," Remarks before the Democratic Leadership Council, Washington, D.C., November 22, 1994.

60. Robert B. Reich, "As The World Turns," *New Republic* 200:18 (May 1, 1989): 23.

61. "The Downsizing of America," Special Report (New York: Random House/Times Books, 1996), p. 5.

62. Ibid., p. 6.

63. "Downsizing: And Now, Upsizing," *Economist*, June 8, 1996, p. 72.

64. Louis Uchitelle, "Strong Economic Signals Lift Dow to a Record," *New York Times*, February 5, 1993, p. D1.

65. Richard B. Freeman and Remco Oostendorp, "Wages around the World," NBER Working Paper no. W8058, National Bureau of Economic Research, Cambridge, Mass., December 2000.

66. Ibid.

67. A simple cross-tabulation of the data was provided by Mike Kagay, News Surveys, the New York Times Company, January 10, 1997, in response to a telephone request.

68. Lynne Duke, "White Men Becoming Anxious as Growing Diversity Threatens Their Dominance," *Washington Post*, January 1, 1991, p. A14.

69. Ibid.

Chapter 2

1. Seymour Martin Lipset, *American Exceptionalism: A Double-Edged Sword* (New York: W. W. Norton, 1996), p. 63.

2. Irving Kristol, *Neoconservatism: The Autobiography of an Idea* (Chicago: Ivan R. Dee, 1995), pp. 377–86.

3. George Frederickson felt that the attitude of the more radical Whites who rejected Black domicile in America was also connected to their view of proper racial territoriality. "The full white-nationalist position, the logical outcome of the desire for racial and institutional homogeneity, was more radical: it pointed ahead to the elimination of the Negro as an element in the population"; *The Black Image in the White Mind: The Debate on Afro-American Character and Destiny, 1817–1914* (New York: Harper and Row, 1971), p. 145.

4. Lipset, *American Exceptionalism*, p. 63.

5. John Ehrman, *The Rise of Neoconservatism: Intellectuals and Foreign Affairs 1945–1995* (New Haven: Yale University Press, 1995), p. 37.

6. Shadia B. Drury, *Leo Strauss and the American Right* (New York: St. Martin's Press, 1997), p. 153.

7. Ibid., p. 161.

8. Ehrman, *Rise of Neoconservatism*, pp. 43–49.

9. Cited in John S. Saloma, III, *Ominous Politics: The New Conservative Labyrinth* (New York: Hill and Wang, 1984), p. 65.

10. James Q. Wilson, *Moral Judgment* (New York: Basic Books/Harper-Collins, 1997), p. 1.

11. Ibid.

12. An example is the priority given to this issue by *Newsweek* magazine, which placed the face of rap artist Snoop Doggy Dogg on the cover of an issue that featured an article, "When Is Rap Too Violent?" See John Leland, "Criminal Records: Gangsta Rap and the Culture of Violence," *Newsweek*, November 29, 1993, pp. 60–66.

13. "Bible Backed Slavery, Says a Lawmaker," *New York Times*, May 10, 1996, p. A20.

14. Ibid.

15. Michael Johnson, "The 'New Christian Right' in American Politics," in Stephen D. Johnson and Joseph B. Tamney, eds., *The Political Role of Religion in the United States* (Boulder: Westview Press, 1986), pp. 125–45.

16. James L. Guth, "The New Christian Right," in Robert C. Liebman and Robert Wuthnow, eds., *The New Christian Right: Mobilization and Legitimation* (New York: Aldine, 1983), pp. 34–35.

17. Ibid., p. 36.

18. Philip Selznick, *The Moral Community* (Berkeley: University of California Press, 1992), p. 385.

19. Ibid., p. 447.

20. Thomas D. Boston, *Race, Class and Conservatism* (Boston: Unwin Hyman, 1988), p. 80–81.

21. Thernstrom and Thernstrom, *America in Black and White*, pp. 240–41.

22. My emphasis; see Oscar Underwood, "The Negro Problem in the South, *Forum* (New York) 30 (September 1900–February 1901): 217.

23. George Gilder, *Wealth and Poverty* (New York: Basic Books, 1981).

24. Ibid., p. 68.

25. Charles Murray, *Losing Ground* (New York: HarperCollins/Basic Books, 1984).

26. Murray argues that the elimination of affirmative action would result in productivity benefits because employers would make hiring decisions on the basis of merit and would not have to consider applicants who scored lower on employment test instruments or on other measures of "intelligence" or job performance; this would boost job performance and consequently productivity. He makes this argument with no analysis of the benefits and without considering the counter thesis that affirmative action has actually boosted productivity, since firms that do business with the government have higher wages and productivity than those who do not. Richard J. Herrnstein and Charles Murray, *The Bell Curve: Intelligence and Class Structure in American Life* (New York: Free Press, 1994), pp. 498–508.

27. Newt Gingrich and Ward Connerly, "Face the Failure of Racial Preferences," *New York Times*, June 15, 1997, p. E15.

28. Marvin Olasky, *The Tragedy of American Compassion* (Washington, D.C.: Regenery Gateway, 1992).

29. Tom Wicker, *Tragic Failure: Racial Integration in America* (New York: William Morrow, 1996).

30. Cited in Selznick, *The Moral Community.* See Alan Lewis, *The Psychology of Taxation* (New York: St. Martin's Press, 1982).

31. Robert W. Whitaker, ed., *The New Right Papers: The Nature and Goals of the Movement, Explained by Its Most Prominent Voices* (New York: St. Martin's Press, 1982), p. 67.

32. Thomas Byrne Edsall and Mary D. Edsall, *Chain Reaction: The Impact of Race, Rights, and Taxes on American Politics* (New York: Norton, 1991).

33. Ibid., p. 152.

34. Ibid., p. 182.

35. Ibid., p. 183.

36. Cited in "A Distorted Image of Minorities in America," *Washington Post*/Kaiser Family Foundation/Harvard University survey, *Washington Post*, October 8, 1995, p. A27.

37. Juliet Eilperin, "FBI Probes 80–100 Threats to Members," *Roll Call* 41:87 (May 27, 1996): 1.

38. Willard Gaylin, Ira Glasser, Steven Marcus and David J. Rothman, *Doing Good: The Limits of Benevolence* (New York: Pantheon, 1978).

39. Ibid., p.74.

40. Ibid., pp. 106–15.

41. Martha Derthic, "Whither Federalism?" Series on the Future of the Public Sector, the Urban Institute, no. 2, June 1996, Washington, D.C.

42. John DiIulio, Jr., and Donald F. Kettl, *Fine Print: The Contract with America, Devolution, and the Administrative Realities of American Federalism* (Washington, D.C.: Brookings Institution, 1995).

43. Ibid.

44. "The New Newest Federalism for Welfare: Where Are We Now and Where Are We Headed?" Rockefeller Report, The Nelson Rockefeller Institute of Government, October 30, 1997.

45. Lawrence Mead, "The Politics of Welfare Reform in Wisconsin," *Polity* 32, no. 4 (2000).

46. Kevin Merida, "Gingrich Offers Provocative Views on Racial Issues," *Washington Post*, June 16, 1995, p. A9.

47. Ibid.

48. William Bennett, *The Book of Virtue: A Treasury of Great Moral Stories* (New York: Simon and Schuster, 1993).

49. Newt Gingrich, *To Renew America* (New York: HarperCollins, 1995), p. 34.

50. Ibid., p. 187.

51. Ibid., p. 41.

52. Ibid., p. 80.

53. Andrew F. Brimmer, "Economic Prospects for African Americans, 2001–2010: Politics and Promises," Joint Center for Political and Economic Studies, October, 2000, Chart II, p. 12.

54. ABC News poll, conducted April 30–May 6, 1996, published June 1996.

55. Ibid.

56. Richard Berke,"Congress's New G.O.P. Majority Makes Lobbyists' Life Difficult," *New York Times*, March 20, 1995.

57. Bob Herbert, "What Special Interest?," *New York Times*, March 22, 1995, p. A19.

58. For a useful discussion of this subject, see: Carter A. Wilson, *Racism: From Slavery to Advanced Capitalism* (Thousand Oaks, Calif.: Sage Publications, 1996).

59. Stokeley Carmichael and Charles V. Hamilton, *Black Power: The Politics of Liberation in America* (New York: Random House, 1967), pp. 3–4.

60. Joe Feagin, *Social Problems: A Critical Power-Conflict Perspective* (Englewood Cliffs, N.J.: Prentice-Hall, 1982), p. 125.

61. Ibid.

62. Andrew Hacker, *Two Nations: Black and White, Separate, Hostile, Unequal* (New York: Charles Scribner's Sons, 1992), pp. 20–23.

63. Joe Feagin and Herman Vera, *White Racism: The Basics* (New York: Routledge, 1995), p. 7.

64. Byron M. Roth, *Prescription for Failure: Race Relations in the Age of Social Science* (New Brunswick. N.J.: Transaction, 1994), p. 11.

65. Dan Barry, "Prominent Harlem Minister Calls Giuliani a Racist," *New York Times*, May 21, 1998, p. A33.

Chapter 3

1. Alphonso Pinkney, for example, says: "The ascendancy of conservatism inspired by Ronald Reagan's Presidency has brought about drastic changes in American life, not the least of which has been the resurgence of prejudice and violence against minorities"; Pinkney, *Lest we Forget: White Hate Crimes* (New York: Cambridge University Press, 1982), p. viii.

2. Garry Wills, *Reagan's America: Innocents at Home* (New York: Doubleday, 1987), p. 286.

3. Anthony King and David Sanders, "The View From Europe," in Charles O. Jones, ed., *The Reagan Legacy: Promise and Performrance* (Chatham, N.J.: Chatham House, 1988), pp. 265–88.

4. William Raspberry, "Critical Time for Blacks," *Washington Post,* November 8, 1972, p. 1.

5. Ellis Sandoz and Cecil V. Crabb, Jr., "Conclusion: Electoral Land Policy Realignment or Aberration?" in Ellis Sandoz and Cecil V. Crabb, Jr., eds., *A Tide of Discontent: The 1980 Elections and Their Meaning* (Washington, D.C.: Congressional Quarterly Press, 1981), p. 195.

6. Wills, *Reagan's America,* pp. 371–77.

7. Howell Raines, "Blacks Shift to Sharper Criticism on Civil Rights," *New York Times,* July 26, 1981, p. A17.

8. Ibid.

9. Herbert H. Denton, "Rights Groups Threatened by U.S. Fund Cuts," *Washington Post,* April 12, 1981, p. A1.

10. Ibid.

11. Sheila Rule, "Reagan Greeted Politely but Coolly by N.A.A.C.P." *New York Times,* June 30, 1981, p. D21.

12. Raines, "Blacks Shift to Sharper Criticism."

13. "Reagan Working Hard to Reach Blacks," *Washington Afro-American,* May 18, 1982, p. 1.

14. Paul Delaney, "Differences Widen between Blacks and the White House," *New York Times,* March 24, 1985, p. A23.

15. Quoted in Don Wycliff, "Black Leaders, Black Goals," *New York Times,* March 25, 1985, p. A22.

16. Quoted in ibid.

17. Quoted in "No More Nice Guy: NAACP Calls Ron a 'Racist,'" *Philadelphia Daily News,* May 18, 1985, p. 1.

18. Quoted in ibid.

19. Quoted in Delaney, "Differences Widen."

20. Alfreda L. Madison, "Ed Meese on Black Power," Interview, *City Paper* (Washington, D.C.), April 1–9, 1983.

21. "Excerpts from Final Report on EEOC Prepared by Transition Team of Reagan Administration," Text, Development Group Report, 15, E-1, January 23, 1981.

22. Howard Kurtz, "Groups Challenge Draft Plan to Void Numerical Hiring Goals," *Washington Post,* August 16, 1985, p. A3.

23. See Howard Kurtz, "Set-Aside for Blacks Challenged," *Washington Post,* March 8, 1984, p. A1. Also, "Justice Department Moves to Overturn Indianapolis Plan for Job Quotas," *New York Times,* April 30, 1985, p. A1.

24. Quoted in ibid.

25. Robert Pear, "Rights Unit Chief Urging Parties to Scrap Caucuses for Minorities," *New York Times,* July 15, 1986, p. A21.

26. "Population by Metropolitan and Nonmetropolitan Residence, Sex and Race, March 2000," U.S. Department of Commerce Bureau of the Census, Internet release date, February 22, 2001, Table 21.

27. Ibid., p. 51.

28. Karen De Witt, "Wave of Suburban Growth Is Being Fed by Minorities," *New York Times,* August, 15, 1994, p. 1.

29. George Peterson, ed., *Big-City Politics, Governance, and Fiscal Constraints* (Washington, D.C.: Urban Institute Press, 1994), p. 10–11.

30. Ibid.

31. Martin Carnoy, Derek Shearer and Russell Rumberger, *A New Social Contract: The Economy and Government after Reagan* (New York: Harper and Row, 1983), p. 16.

32. Wills, *Reagan's America,* p. 364.

33. Paul E. Peterson and Mark Rom, "Lower Taxes, More Spending, and Budget Deficits," in Charles O. Jones, ed., *The Reagan Legacy: Promise and Performance* (Chatham, N.J.: Chatham House, 1988), p. 226.

34. Richard McKenzie, *What Went Right in the 1980s?* (San Francisco: Pacific Research Institute for Public Policy, 1994), p. 256.

35. Ibid., p. 269.

36. Howard Kurtz, "Federal Funds for Summer Jobs Slashed for Several Major Cities," *Washington Post,* April 24, 1984, p. A4.

37. Ibid.

38. "Administration Budget Contains Large Cuts in Programs for the Poor," Center on Budget and Policy Priorities, Washington, D.C., 1986.

39. Isabel V. Sawhill, "Young Children and Families," in Henry J. Aron and Charles L. Schultze, eds., *Setting Domestic Priorities: What Can Government Do?* (Washington, D.C.: Brookings Institution, 1992), p. 165.

40. Billy J. Tidwell, Karen V. Hill and Lisa Bland Malone, "Black Economic Development: Still on the Margin," Black Americans and Public Policy: Perspectives of the National Urban League, National Urban League, April 1988, pp. 75–76.

41. *Youth Record* 4:17 (September 14, 1992): 1.

42. "Report of the 1988 Commission on the Cities: Race and Poverty in the United States Today," National Conference: "The Kerner Report Twenty Years Later," 1988 Commission on the Cities, Fred R. Harris and Roger Wilkins, Co-Chairs, March 1, 1988.

43. Ibid.

44. David Stockman, *The Triumph of Politics: How the Reagan Revolution Failed* (New York: Harper and Row, 1986), p. 9; cited in Jones, ed., *Reagan Legacy*, p. 226.

45. Ibid., p. 222.

46. "America's Cities," *Economist*, May 9, 1992, p. 21–22.

47. Steven Shull, *A Kinder Gentler Racism?: The Reagan-Bush Civil Rights Legacy* (New York: M. E. Sharpe, 1992), p. 96.

48. Quoted in Jeffrey A. Frank, "Stuart Butler Had a Great Idea: This Is What Happened to It." *Washington Post*, October 24, 1992, p. D7.

49. "Secretary Jack Kemp Addresses the U.S. Conference of Mayors," Houston, Texas, June 22, 1992.

50. Ibid.

51. Quoted in Michael deCourcy Hinds, "The Cities Are Scraping by, but at a Cost," *New York Times*, July 9, 1993, p. A8.

52. Michael Barone and Grant Ujifusa, eds., *The Almanac of American Politics 1996* (Washington, D.C.: National Journal, 1996), p. xxvi.

53. See Nicole Weisensee, "He's Conservative, Young, Energetic," *Philadelphia Daily News*, November 9, 1994, p. 14, and November 10, 1994, p. 6.

54. Howard Fineman, "The Revenge of the Right," *Newsweek*, November 21, 1994, pp. 36–40.

55. Newt Gingrich, Speech, Washington Research Group, November 11, 1994. See also Charles Krauthammer, "Republican Mandate," *Washington Post*, November 11, 1994, p. A31.

56. Quoted in Guy Gugliotta, "The Federal Page: Capital Notebook—Portraits Change as Hill Picture Shifts," *Washington Post*, January 24, 1995, p. A15.

57. Guy Gugliotta, "The Federal Page: Capital Notebook—The Picture of Conciliation," *Washington Post*, January 14, 1997, p. A13.

58. Seymour Martin Lipset, *American Exceptionalism: A Double-edged Sword* (New York: W. W. Norton, 1996), p. 121.

59. *Congressional Record*, House, September 221, 1994, p. H9526.

60. Ed Gillespie and Bob Shellhas, eds., *Contract with America* (New York: Random House, 1994).

61. "Who Speaks for the Poor?" *U.S. News and World Report*, November 6, 1995, p. 42.

62. See Clay Chandler, "Senate GOP Tax Plan: Less Luxury, Easier to Sell Proposal Keeps Most Major Features of House Proposal but Scrimps on Key Components," *Washington Post*, October 17, 1995, p. B1. Also, Clay Chandler, "GOP Strikes Back in Tax Bill Fight: Roth Lashes out at Analysts for 'Bogus Claims' about Plan," *Washington Post*, October 26, 1995, p. D11.

63. John Charles Boger, "Afterword: A Debate over the National Future," in John Charles Boger and Judith Welch Wegner, eds., *Race, Poverty and American Cities* (Chapel Hill: University of North Carolina Press, 1996), p. 559.

64. Ibid.

65. *Congressional Record*, January 26, 1995, p. H716.

66. Quoted in Eric Pianin, "GOP Budget Approved by House, Plan to Reduce Taxes, Erase Deficit by 2002 Passes on 238–193 Vote," *Washington Post,* May 19, 1995, p. A1.

67. See David Osborne, "Resurrecting Government," *Washington Post Magazine,* January 8, 1995, p. 14.

68. Michael Barone and Grant Ujifusa, "Contract With America," in Barone and Ujifusa, eds., *Almanac of American Politics 1996,* p. xix.

69. Quoted in Marcia Coyle, "EEOC Plans to Try out Workplace Bias Testers," *National Law Journal,* January 19, 1998, p. A10.

70. Ibid.

71. Testimony of House Speaker Newt Gingrich before the House Subcommittee on Employer-Employee Relations on "The Future Direction of the Equal Employment Opportunity Commission," U.S. House of Representatives, March 3, 1998.

72. Ibid.

73. "EEOC Backs away From Race-Bias Suit," Bloomberg Financial Market Commodities News, *Columbus Post,* July 9–15, 1998, p. 5.

74. Michael Barone and Grant Ujifusa, eds., *The Almanac of American Politics 1982* (Washington, D.C.: Barone, 1982), p. xxix.

75. See Ross K. Baker, *House and Senate* (New York: W. W. Norton, 1989), p. 182.

76. See "Action Play: The North Carolina Senate Race," *Economist,* June 1, 1996, p. 25.

77. Quoted in William Claiborne, "Big-City Mayors Voice Frustration over Failure of Stimulus Package," *Washington Post,* May 26, 1993, p. A6.

78. Senate Record Vote Analysis, 104th Congress, 1st Session, August 9, 1995, Vote no. 375.

79. See their opposing position in Senate Record Vote Analysis, 101st Congress, 2nd Session, October 16, 1990, Vote no. 276.

80. "Senate Leadership Files Supreme Court Brief in Piscataway, N.J. Racial Preference Case," Republican Policy Committee, United States Senate, October 21, 1997. Brief attached. This case featured a conflict between the Piscataway, New Jersey, School Board and Sharon Taxman, a White female employee of the school district who had been released in favor of retaining a Black female, Debra Williams, with equal seniority and credentials, because of the desire for diversity. The federal district court ruled, in effect, that no jurisprudence of "diversity" existed as the basis of an affirmative action claim, and thus the firing of Williams was in error. The case was appealed to the U.S. Supreme Court by the school district, but was settled by the plaintiff and defendants when the Black Leadership Forum raised over $400,000 for Taxman, fearing that the Supreme Court's decision, in view of its decision in the Wygant case, would likely severely cripple, if not eliminate, affirmative action.

81. Quoted in "The Republicans Choose," *Washington Post,* December 21, 1995, p. A22.

82. *Congressional Record,* June 6, 1996, p. S5903.

83. Cited in Bob Herbert, "What Special Interest?" *New York Times,* March 22, 1995, p. A19.

84. Quoted in John F. Harris, "Clinton Criticizes Senate GOP Budget Plan," *Washington Post,* April 4, 1998, p. A6.

85. Quoted in Alan Fram, "GOP Offended by Clinton 2000 Budget," the Associated Press, February 2, 1999.

86. *Congressional Record,* January 5, 1995, p. E9.

87. Ibid.

88. Curtis Gans, Committee for the Study of the Electorate, 1994.

89. Tomas Eagleton, "Race Is a Factor in Our Politics," *St. Louis Post-Dispatch,* November 20, 1994, p. 3B.

90. William Raspberry, "The Growing Incivility of the Political Right," *Atlanta Journal-Constitution,* October 14, 1994, p. A12.

91. Peter Applebome, *Dixie Rising: How the South Is Shaping American Values, Politics and Culture* (New York: Times Books, 1996).

92. Philip Duncan and Christine Lawrence, *Politics in America 1998: The 105th Congress* (Washington, D.C.: Congressional Quarterly, 1998), ADA Ratings.

93. This analysis was based on 58% Black and 58% ADA ratings of the 67 cosponsors, because in some cases the data included in the member profile were incomplete.

94. *Congressional Record,* no. 43, 3948, 4004, March 12, 1956, p. 102.

95. Quoted in Joseph F. Sullivan, "Mayors, Feeling Effects of Tax Cuts, Are Cool to Whitman," *New York Times,* November 18, 1994, p. B7.

96. Quoted in Brett Pulley, "End of Urban Agency Draws Fears of Neglect," *New York Times,* March 30, 1995, p. B1.

Chapter 4

1. Here I depart from the meaning of "convergence" used by Cheryl M. Miller and Hanes Walter, Jr., who analyzed the support of Democrats and Republicans in the House and Senate for civil rights legislation between 1957 and 1991. I have instead sought to estimate the policy similarities between the stated agenda of Republicans in the White House and Congress with the positions taken by Democrats in both branches of government. See Cheryl M. Miller and Hanes Walton, Jr., "Congressional Support of Civil Rights Public Policy: From Bipartisan to Partisan Convergence," *Congress and the Presidency* 21:1 (Spring, 1994): 11–27.

2. "Jimmy vs. the Liberals," *Newsweek,* May 16, 1977, p. 44.

3. Ibid.

4. Robert Smith, *We Have No Leaders: African Americans in the Post-Civil Rights Era* (Albany: State University of New York Press, 1996), pp. 187–210.

5. Warren Brown, "Carter, Black Caucus Are Reconciled," *Washington Post,* September 30, 1978, p. A8.

6. Roger Wilkins, "Jimmy Carter's First Year," *Black Enterprise,* March 1978, p. 24.

7. Steven A. Shull, *A Kinder Gentler Racism?: The Reagan-Bush Civil Rights Legacy* (New York: M. E. Sharpe, 1993), p. 67.

8. Ibid., p. 93. See also, Table 4.1, page 78.

9. Ellis Sandoz and Cecil V. Crabb, Jr., *A Tide of Discontent: The 1980 Elections and Their Meaning* (Washington, D.C.: Congressional Quarterly Press, 1981), p. 69.

10. Ben J. Wattenberg, *The Real America: A Surprising Examination of the State of the Union* (New York: G. P. Putnam's Sons/Capricorn, 1974), p. 294.

11. William Watts and Lloyd A. Free, *State of the Nation, 1974: How Do We Look at Ourselves and Our Country?* (Washington, D.C.: Potomac Associates, 1974), p. 274–81.

12. John Stewart, "The Democratic Party in American Politics," in Jeff Fishel, ed., *Parties and Elections in an Anti-Party Age: American Politics and the Crisis of Confidence* (Bloomington: Indiana University Press, 1978), p. 67.

13. Aaron Wildavsky, "President Reagan as a Political Strategist," in Charles O. Jones, ed., *The Reagan Legacy: Promise and Performance* (Chatham, N.J.: Chatham House, 1988), p. 290.

14. William Keefe made an analysis of roll call votes in the period 1961–1982. See William J. Keefe, *Parties, Politics, and Public Policy in America,* 4th ed. (New York: Holt, Reinhart and Winston, 1984), p. 145.

15. Paul Allen Beck, "Incomplete Realignment," in Jones, ed., *Reagan Legacy,* p. 158.

16. Blue Dogs were regarded as Democrats who would rather turn blue than give in to leadership pressures to conform to party positions on, especially, liberal issues.

17. "'Blue Dog' Democrats May Have Their Day in a Kinder, Gentler Congress," *Washington Post,* November 24, 1996, p. A8.

18. These factors are resident in the critiques of both Liberal—or "progressive"—thinkers as well as more Conservative writers. For progressives, see James MacGregor Burns, William Crotty, Lois Lovelace Duke and Lawrence D. Longley, eds., *The Democrats Must Lead: The Case for a Progressive Democratic Party* (Boulder: Westview Press, 1992). For a Conservative presentation, see Ronald Radosh, *Divided They Fell: The Demise of the Democratic Party, 1964–1996* (New York: Free Press, 1996).

19. "Roemer Decides 'tis Nobler in GOP: Louisiana's Maverick Governor Abandons Democratic Party," *Washington Post,* March 12, 1991, p. A1.

20. Quoted in Thomas B. Edsall, "In Louisiana, Whites Often Feel Ignored," *Washington Post,* March 12, 1991, p. A5.

21. Quoted in ibid.

22. Quoted in "Rights Chief Sees Race as Factor in Election," *New York Times,* May 1, 1991, p. A18.

23. Christopher Edley, Jr., *Not All Black and White: Affirmative Action and American Values* (New York: Hill and Wang, 1996), p. 12.

24. William Crotty, "Who Needs Two Republican Parties?," in Burns et al., *Democrats Must Lead*, pp. 66–70.

25. Ibid., pp. 68–69.

26. Will Marshall and Martin Schram, eds., *Mandate for Change* (New York: Berkeley Books, 1993), pp. xvi–xvii.

27. Ibid., p. xxvi.

28. Gerald Pomper, ed., *The Election of 1992* (Chatham, N.J.: Chatham House, 1993), p. 141.

29. Jack Germond and Jules Witcover, *Mad As Hell: Revolt at the Ballot Box, 1992* (New York: Warner Books, 1993).

30. Geoffrey Faux, *The Party's Not Over: A New Vision for the Democrats* (New York: HarperCollins/Basic Books, 1996), pp. 146–52.

31. Walter Dean Burnham, "Realignment Lives: The 1994 Earthquake and Its Implications," in Colin Campbell and Bert A. Rockman, eds., *The Clinton Presidency: First Appraisals* (Chatham, N.J.: Chatham House, 1996), p. 380.

32. Kevin Merida, "Last Rites for Liberalism? Democrats' Legacy Now Symbolizes Their Woes," *Washington Post*, December 28, 1994, p. A1.

33. Cited in ibid.

34. Ibid.

35. *Congressional Record*, House, January 25, 2995, p. H599.

36. Michael Wines, "Clinton Team, and G.O.P. Debate Deficit," *New York Times*, June 15, 1995, p. B12.

37. Quoted in ibid.

38. Ibid.

39. John F. Harris and Eric Pianin, "Clinton Accepts Hill's Defense Spending Bill," *Washington Post*, December 1, 1995, p. A1.

40. Hart-Teeter, NBC News/*Wall Street Journal* Poll, Study no. 4071, Washington, D.C., August 9, 1996.

41. "Clinton Is Not Done," *Time*, November 18, 1996, pp. 34–35.

42. "A Closer Look at the Voters," Washington Post Exit Poll, *Washington Post*, November 6, 1996, P. B7.

43. Dan Balz, "Clinton Broke Republican Grip on Some Suburban County Strongholds," *Washington Post*, November 10, 1996, p. A24.

44. Quoted in "The Second Inauguration of Bill Clinton: An Interview With the President," *Washington Post*, January 19, 1997, p. A25.

45. Quoted in ibid.

46. Quoted in "President Sees Accord on Government's Role," *Washington Post*, January 19, 1997, p. A1.

47. Ronald Walters, "Federalism, Civil Rights and Black Progress," *Black Law Journal* 8:2 (Fall 1983): 220–34. Elsewhere I have attempted to demonstrate that Blacks have made more progress when there was a strong central government than in eras when a decentralized administration of power favored states rights.

48. "Second Inauguration of Bill Clinton," p. A25.

49. Quoted in Dan Balz, "The Democratic Party in Clinton's Image: How Long Will It Endure?" *Washington Post*, January 19, p. A22.

50. Nancy Gibbs, "The Budget Deal: A Conspiracy of Celebration," *Time*, August 11, 1997. Internet. www.cnn.com/Allpolitics/1997/08/04/Time/Budget.htm.

51. Iris J. Lav, "Did Congress Approve Tax Measures Favoring the Well-Off?" Center on Budget and Policy Priorities, Washington, D.C., July 24, 1997. Internet. www.cbpp.org/roth723.htm.

52. Alison Mitchell, "Two Clinton Aides Resign to Protest New Welfare Law," *New York Times*, September 12, 1996, p. A1.

53. David Kushnet and Ruy Teixeira, "Tuesday's Secret Result: A Winning Brand of Liberalism," *Washington Post*, November 10, 1996, p. C4.

54. Ibid.

55. Heather Booth, Stan Greenberg, Saul Landau, Joel Rogers and Roger Wilkins, "Roundtable: Progressive Reform and the 'Clinton Moment,'" in Richard Caplan and John Feffer, eds., *State of the Union 1994: The Clinton Administration and the Nation in Profile* (Boulder: Westview Press, 1994), p. 254.

56. Ibid., p. 255.

57. Ibid., p. 265.

58. Ibid., p. 264.

Chapter 5

1. "The Politics of Race," polling report, Peter Hart/Robert Teeter, for NBC News and the *Wall Street Journal*, May 27, 1991, p. 2.; Hart/Teeter, *Wall Street Journal*, August 1996, p. 15.

2. Ibid. There are considerable data from a wide variety of polls that indicate a more favorable view of the public (both Whites and Blacks) toward the term "affirmative action" and a more negative view of the term "racial preferences" or "preferences" and "quotas." See, for example, Louis Harris, "Affirmative Action and the Voter," *New York Times*, July 31, 1995, p. A13. This aversion, especially of the White population, to racial preferences was part of the combustible material that led to the election of Ronald Reagan. A *Washington Post*/ABC News poll in 1981, for example, included the question: "Because of past discrimination, Blacks who need it should get some help from the government that white people in similar economic circumstances don't get." Response rate: 41% of Blacks agreed, 49% disagreed; 23% of Whites agreed, 71% disagreed. *Washington Post*, March 24, 1981, p. A2.

3. Quoted in Alfreda L. Madison, "Ed Meese on Black Power," Interview, *City Paper* (Washington, D.C.), April 1, 1983, p. 9.

4. *Washington Post*, March 24, 1981, p. A2.

5. *Plessy v. Ferguson*, 163 U.S. 537 [1986].

6. Quoted in Steve Roberts, et al., "Affirmative Action on the Edge," *U.S. News and World Report*, February 13, 1995. http://www.usnews.com/usnews/issue/archive.htm.

7. Clint Bolick, *The Affirmative Action Fraud* (Washington, D.C.: CATO Institute, 1996), p. 59.

8. David O'Brien, "The Reagan Judges: His Most Enduring Legacy?" in Charles O. Jones, ed., *The Reagan Legacy: Promise and Performance* (Chatham, N.J.: Chatham House, 1988), p. 66.

9. Ibid., p. 73.

10. *University of California v. Alan Bakke*, 438 U.S. 265 [1978].

11. Ibid.

12. Quoted in O'Brien, "Reagan Judges, pp. 87–88.

13. Al Kamen, "For Rehnquist, Aftermath of Confirmation Is Routine: Ready to Take Office after Long 3 Months of Scrutiny," *Washington Post*, September 19, 1986, p. A1.

14. O'Brien, "Reagan Judges," p. 88.

15. David Kairys, *With Liberty and Justice for Some* (New York: New Press, 1993), p. 129.

16. Norman C. Amaker, *Civil Rights and the Reagan Administration* (Washington, D.C.: Urban Institute Press, 1988), pp. 108–30.

17. Quoted in Milton Coleman, "Reagan Administration Wants Blacks to Make It on Their Own," *Washington Post*, December 5, 1983, pp. A1, A8.

18. "Failure and Fraud in Civil Rights Enforcement by the Department of Education," 22nd Report, Committee on Government Operations, House of Representatives, October 2, 1987, p. 37.

19. Ibid., p. 169–80.

20. Howard Kurtz, "Rights Panel's Critics Try to Put It out of Business," *Washington Post*, July 11, 1986, p. A15.

21. See Howard Kurtz, "Civil Rights Commission Loses Its Staff Director," *Washington Post*, November 1, 1986, p. A1.

22. Amaker, *Civil Rights and the Reagan Administration*, p. 130.

23. Ibid., p. 134.

24. *Firefighters Union, Local No. 1784 v. Stotts*, 467 U.S. 561, S. Ct. 2576, 81 L. ED.2d 483 [12 June 1984]; *Wygant v. Jackson Board of Education*, 476 U.S. 267, 106 S. Ct. 1842, 90 L. ED.2d 260 [1986].

25. *Watson v. Fort Worth Bank and Trust*, no. 86–6139, 487 U.S. 977, 108 S. Ct. 277; June 29, 1988.

26. *Wards Cove Packing Co., Inc., et al. v. Antonio et Al.*, no. 87–1387, 490 U.S. 642; 109 S. Ct. 2115, 1989 [June 5, 1989].

27. Ibid.

28. *Richmond v. J. A. Croson Co.*, 488 U.S. 469 [1989].

29. John R. Howard, *The Shifting Wind: The Supreme Court and Civil Rights, from Reconstruction to Brown* (Albany: State University of New York Press, 1998), p. 348.

30. Ibid., p. 345.

31. Steven A. Holmes, "President Vetoes Bill on Jobs Rights; Showdown Is Set," *New York Times*, October 23, 1990, p. A1.

32. Steven Holmes, "Rights Leaders Reject Bush Proposal," *New York Times*, October 22, 1990, p. A15.

33. Julia C. Ross, "New Civil Rights Act: Law Reverses Several Recent

High Court Decisions," *ABA Journal,* January 1992. Lexis/Nexus. Also see: Gerald Caplan, "Republican Party Racism Comes Home to Roost," *Toronto Star,* November 24, 1991, p. B3; Derrick Z. Jackson, "Rekindling the Fire That Burns Minorities," *Boston Globe,* November 24, 1991, p. A27; and Anthony Lewis, "Code Words Convey the Politics of Hatred," *St. Louis Post-Dispatch,* November 15, 1991, p. C3.

34. Lino Graglia, "Have Race and Gender-conscious Remedies Outlived Their Usefulness? — Yes: Reverse Discrimination Serves No One," *ABA Journal,* May 1995. Lexis/Nexus.

35. Frank R. Parker, Analysis of *Shaw v. Reno,* Lawyers Committee for Civil Rights under Law, July 6, 1993.

36. Quoted in ibid.

37. Joan Biskupic, "The Mysterious Mr. Rehnquist: Where Is the Chief Justice Going and Who Will Follow?" *Washington Post,* September 25, 1994, p. C1. This article summarizes the impact of Rehnquist's movement of the Supreme Court to the right in a number of areas.

38. *Missouri v. Jenkins et al.,* no. 93–1823 [June 12, 1995].

39. Juan Williams, "The Court's Other Bombshell," *Washington Post,* July 2, 1995, p. C1.

40. "San Francisco Schools Abolish Racial Quotas," Reuters, *Washington Post,* February 19, 1999, p. A10.

41. Beth Daley, "Race-Neutral Policy Urged on Prep Classes," *Boston Globe,* January 28, 1999, p. B7.

42. Joan Biskupic, "Court's Conservatives Make Presence Felt," *Washington Post,* July 2, 1995, p. A1.

43. Quoted in ibid.

44. U.S. Statutes at Large, XVI, 27, April 9, 1866.

45. Richard Bardolph, ed., *The Civil Rights Record: Black Americans and the Law, 1849–1970* (New York: Thomas Y. Crowell, 1970), p. 57.

46. U.S. Statutes at Large, XVII, March 1, 1875.

47. *Plessy v. Ferguson,* 1 163 U.S. Statutes 537 [1896].

48. *Brown v. Board of Education of Topeka,* 347 U.S. 485 [1954].

49. *United States v. Cruikshank,* 92 U.S. 542 [1876].

50. Bardolph, *Civil Rights Record,* p. 428. Also, Steve Gifis says: "Factors to be considered in determining whether the state is significantly involved in a statutorily authorized private conduct for purposes of constituting 'state action' include the source of authority for private action, whether the state is so entwined with the regulation of private conduct as to constitute state activity, whether there is meaningful state participation in the activity, and whether there has been delegation of what has traditionally been state function to private persons"; Steve Gifis, ed., *Law Dictionary* (Hauppauge, N. Y.: Barron's Legal Guides, 1996), p. 484.

51. Joseph Tussman, ed., *The Supreme Court on Racial Discrimination* (New York: Oxford University Press, 1963), p. 3.

52. "The Civil Rights Act of 1997," H.R. 1909, June 17, 1997. See also, the language of Proposition 209, State of California, passed November 1996, and the language of Initiative 200, State of Washington, passed 1998.

53. Paul Burstein, *Discrimination, Jobs, and Politics: The Struggle for Equal Employment Opportunity in the United States Since the New Deal* (Chicago: University of Chicago Press, 1985), p. 144.

54. Ibid.

55. Many surveys of the public opinion of Whites might support this observation. But see a Gallup survey released in June 1997 that contained a sample of 1,269 Blacks and 1,680 Whites. On the question of whether the government should increase, decrease or keep affirmative action the same, Blacks wanted an increase (53%); Whites supported a decrease (37%); and the proportion of each group which wanted it to remain the same was identical (29%). "The Gallup Poll Social Audit on Black/White Relations in the United States," Gallup Organization, June 1997, Executive Summary, p. 12.

56. EEOC: United States Equal Employment Opportunity Commission, Annual Report, Fiscal Year 1994, p. 1.

57. EEOC: United States Equal Employment Opportunity Commission, Annual Report, Fiscal Year 1993, p. 1.

58. "FY 1994 Annual Report," Office of Program Operations, U.S. Equal Employment Opportunity Commission, 1994, p. 29.

59. "FY 2000 Annual Performance Report," Appendix, "Compilation of Fiscal Years 1999 and 2000 Measures," U.S. Equal Employment Opportunity Commission, April 2000.

60. "Job Patterns for Minorities and Women in Private Industry, 1995," U.S. Equal Employment Opportunity Commission, 1996, p. 1.

61. "Household Data Annual Averages," U.S. Bureau of Labor Statistics, Division of Labor Force Statistics, 1993.

62. For data concerning the advance of women in the labor force, see "Household Data Annual Averages," U.S. Bureau of Labor Statistics, Division of Labor Force Statistics, 1993. The data indicate that between 1988 and 1993, White women gained two million new professional jobs, and that between 1970 and 1993, their participation in the labor force increased by 15%, a rate that was twice that of Blacks, five times greater than Hispanics and twenty times greater than White males.

63. *African Americans Today: A Statistical Profile* (Washington, D.C.: Joint Center for Political and Economic Studies, 1996), Figs. 10 and 11, p. 22. Whereas the Black marriage rate was 56% in 1980, it declined to 47% by 1994.

64. Thomas McCullough, *The Moral Imagination in Public Life: Raising the Ethical Question* (Chatham, N.J.: Chatham House, 1991), p. 131.

65. Donald Tomaskovic-Devy, *Gender and Racial Inequality at Work: The Sources and Consequences of Job Segregation* (Ithaca, N.Y.: ILR Press, 1993), p. 17.

66. Ibid., p. 140.

67. "Civil Rights Bill Conference Report/Final Passage," S. 2104, 101st Congress, 1st Session, October 16, 1990, Vote no. 176, p. 8.

68. *Jones v. Mayer,* 392 U.S. 409 [1968].

Chapter 6

1. Quoted in "Progress Is Reported on Welfare Overhaul," *New York Times,* January 29, 1995, p. 20.

2. "Money Income and Poverty Status of Families and Persons in the United States: 1981," Bureau of the Census, U.S. Dept. of Commerce, July 1982, pp. 20–21.

3. "Poverty in the United States: 1992," Bureau of the Census, U.S. Dept. of Commerce, September 1993, p. 23.

4. George M. Frederickson, *White Supremacy: A Comparative Study in American and South African History* (New York: Oxford University Press, 1981), p. 207.

5. Quoted in ibid.

6. This term was re-popularized by President Ronald Reagan. But a reporter who reflected on his experience of spending six months with many welfare women in Philadelphia—a city which has a disproportionate number of Black welfare families—observed: "If there were any Cadillac-driving, champagne-sipping, penthouse living welfare queens in North Philadelphia, I didn't find any." See David Zuchinno, *The Myth of the Welfare Queen* (New York: Scribner's Sons, 1997), p. 13.

7. James T. Patterson, *America's Struggle against Poverty, 1900–1985* (Cambridge: Harvard University Press, 1986), p. 83.

8. Quoted in ibid., p. 59.

9. Edwin Harwood, "Urbanism as a Way of Negro Life," in William McCord, John Howard, Bernard Friedberg and Edwin Harwood, eds., *Life Styles in the Black Ghetto* (New York: W. W. Norton, 1965), p. 23. Harwood uses the example of the Irish.

10. Patterson, *America's Struggle against Poverty,* p. 81.

11. Michael Harrington, *The Other America: Poverty in the United States* (New York: Macmillan, 1969; 2nd ed., 1974).

12. Ibid., p. 88.

13. William Gorham, "The Social Welfare Objectives of the Reagan Administration," in D. Lee Bauden, ed., *The Social Contract Revisited* (Washington, D.C.: The Urban Institute, 1984), p. 12.

14. Cited in Nicholas Lemann, *The Promised Land: The Great Black Migration and How It Changed America* (New York: Knopf, 1991), p. 29.

15. W. E. B. Du Bois, *The Philadelphia Negro* (New York: Schocken Books, 1967), pp. 66–82.

16. Ibid.

17. Ibid., p. 269.

18. Philip Hauser, "Demographic Factors in the Integration of the Negro," in Kenneth Clark and Talcott Parsons, eds., *The Negro American* (Boston: Beacon Press, 1966), p. 76.

19. Ibid.

20. Ibid., p. 78. Harwood also agrees with this assessment; "Urbanism," p. 22.

21. E. Franklin Frazier, *The Negro Family in the United States* (Chicago: University of Chicago Press, 1966), p. 260.

22. Cited in "Research on the African American Family: A Holistic Perspective," Assessment of the Status of Africa-Americans, vol. II (Boston: William Monroe Trotter Institute, University of Massachusetts at Boston, 1989), p. 34.

23. Nick Kotz and Mary Lynn Kotz, *A Passion for Equality* (New York: W. W. Norton, 1977), p. 196.

24. Patterson, *America's Struggle against Poverty*, p. 88.

25. Kotz and Kotz, *Passion for Equality*, pp. 165–66.

26. Kotz and Kotz, *Passion for Equality*, p. 249.

27. Joe Feagin, *Social Problems: A Critical Power-Conflict Perspective* (Englewood Cliffs, N.J.: Prentice-Hall, 1982), p. 6.

28. Ibid., p. 9.

29. Richard D. Coe, "Welfare Dependency: Fact or Myth?" *Challenge* 25:4 (September/October 1982): 43–49.

30. Data from the Bureau of Social Services, U.S. Department of Health and Human Services, January 1995.

31. Lawrence Mead, *The New Politics of Poverty* (New York: Basic Books, 1992), p. 28.

32. Dorothy K. Newman, ed., *Protest, Politics, and Prosperity: Black Americans and White Institutions 1940–1975* (New York: Pantheon Books, 1978), p. 255.

33. James Jennings, *Understanding the Nature of Poverty in Urban America* (Westport, Conn.: Praeger, 1994), p. 42.

34. Ibid.

35. William Gorham, "The Social Welfare Objectives of the Reagan Administration," in D. Lee Bauden, ed., *The Social Contract Revisited* (Washington, D.C.: Urban Institute, 1984), p. 6.

36. Ibid.

37. Michael Katz, *The Undeserving Poor: From the War on Poverty to the War on Welfare* (New York: Pantheon Books, 1990).

38. "Research on the African-America Family," p. 12.

39. "Overview of Entitlement Programs," 1993 Green Book, Committee on Ways and Means, U.S. House of Representatives, July 7, 1993, p. 722.

40. Thomas Byrne Edsall and Mary D. Edsall, *Chain Reaction: The Impact of Race Rights and Taxes on American Politics* (New York: W. W. Norton, 1992), p. 130.

41. "Who Gets Welfare?" *Ebony* 58:2 (December 1992): 55.

42. Joe Feagin, *Subordinating the Poor: Welfare and American Beliefs* (New York: Prentice-Hall, 1975), pp. 5–11.

43. Gerald C. Wright, Jr., "Racism and Welfare Policy in America," *Social Science Quarterly* 57:4 (March 1977): 719.

44. Jill S. Quadagno, *The Color of Welfare: How Racism Undermined The War on Poverty* (New York: Oxford University Press, 1994).

45. See Martin Gilens, "'Race Coding' and White Opposition to Welfare," *American Political Science Review* 90:3 (September 1996): 593–604.

46. See source of Table 6.2.

47. William Clinton, speech, "The Sixth Annual Business Enterprise Awards Luncheon," New York Public Library, February 18, 1997.

48. Ibid.

49. Michael Fabricant and Steve Burghardt, *The Welfare State Crisis and the Transformation of Social Service Work* (New York: M. E. Sharpe, 1992), p. 16.

50. Ibid., p. 19.

51. "Number of African Americans in Poverty Declines while Income Rises, Census Bureau Reports," U.S. Census Bureau, Economic and Statistics Administration, U.S. Department of Commerce News, Press Release, September 24, 1998.

52. H. R. 4, 1995, Rep. Shaw, Rep. Talent, Rep. La Tourette, January 4, 1995. Conference Report, H. Rept. 104–430, December 20, 1995.

53. Quoted in David Ellwood, "Welfare Reform in Name Only," *New York Times,* July 22, 1996, p. A19.

54. Quoted in Alison Mitchell, "Two Clinton Aides Resign to Protest New Welfare Law," *Washington Post,* September 12, 1996, p. A1.

55. "Welfare As We Might Know It," *American Prospect,* January/February 1997, p. 49.

56. Cited in William Julius Williams, *The Truly Disadvantaged* (Chicago: University of Chicago Press, 1987), p. 81.

57. Andrew Billingsley, *Climbing Jacob's Ladder: The Enduring Legacy of African-American Families* (New York: Simon and Schuster, 1992), pp. 46, 47–48.

58. Bernard Boxill, "The Underclass and the Race/Class Issue," in Bill E. Lawson, ed., *The Underclass Question* (Philadelphia: Temple University Press, 1992), pp. 30–31.

59. Sandra K. Danziger and Sherrie A. Kossoudji, "What Happened to Former GA Recipients?" School of Social Work, University of Michigan, 1994.

60. Jason DeParle, "Varied Reasons Found for Welfare Rolls' Drop," *New York Times,* May 10, 1997, p. 9. In this same article, Wendell Primus, former research director at the Department of Health and Human Services—who resigned in protest over the passage of the welfare reform law—said it was more probable that the reduction stemmed from job growth, combined with the incentives of wage subsidies and health insurance, which made entry-level jobs more attractive.

61. Barbara Vobejda and Judith Havemann, "Sanctions Fuel Drop in Welfare Rolls," *Washington Post*, March 23, 1998, p. A1.

62. Ibid.

63. Isabell Sawhill, "From Welfare to Work," *Brookings Review* 19:3 (Summer 2001): 17.

64. Vobejda and Havemann, "Sanctions Fuel Drop in Welfare Rolls."

65. Manning Marable, "The Plight of the Working Poor," *Prince George's Post*, March 6, 1997, p. A4.

66. Cited in Jason DeParle, "Welfare Law Weighs Heavy in Delta, Where Jobs Are Few," *New Times*, October 16, 1997, p. 1.

67. Robyn Meredith, "Jobs out of Reach for Detroiters without Wheels," *New York Times*, May 26, 1998, p. A12. This article details the impediments to employment faced by many low-income, inner-city people living in Detroit; most of the significant job growth in the region has been in the suburbs, beyond the reach of Detroiters who lack adequate transportation, either of a public or private nature.

68. Barbara Reynolds, "So, You Think Welfare Reform Is Working?" *Columbus Post*, February 18–24, 1999, p. A4.

69. Rachel L. Swarns, "Welfare Policies of the City Face Federal Scrutiny," *New York Times*, November 8, 1998, p. 39.

70. Ibid.

71. Katherine Allen, "The State of Welfare Caseloads in American Cities; 1999," Center on Urban and Metropolitan Studies, Survey Series, Brookings Institution, February 1999. Also, Jocelyn Frye, "The Forgotten Question: Exploring the Impact of Welfare Reform on Civil Rights," National Partnership for Women and Families, September 15, 2000, Washington, D.C.

72. Hearing, Congressional Black Caucus Panel on Welfare Reform, September 15, 2000.

73. Heather Boushey and Betheny Gundersen, "When Work Just Isn't Enough: Measuring Hardships Faced by Families after Moving from Welfare to Work," Briefing Paper, Economic Policy Institute, Washington, D.C., 2000.

74. S. Jody Heymann, "Work and Parenting: The Widening Gap," CLASP Update, Center for Law and Social Policy, Washington, D.C., April 2001.

75. Ibid.

76. "Welfare to What: Early Findings on Family Hardship and Well-being," Children's Defense Fund and National Coalition for the Homeless, Washington, D.C., November 1998.

77. *The State of America's Children 2001*, Yearbook, Children's Defense Fund, Washington, D.C., p. 23.

78. Martin Gilens, *Why Americans Hate Welfare: Race, Media and the Politics of Antipoverty Policy* (Chicago: University of Chicago Press, 1999).

79. Susan Gooden, "Race and Welfare: Examining Employment Outcomes of White and Black Welfare Recipients," *Journal of Poverty* 4:3 (2000): 21–41. See also Susan Gooden, "All Things Not Being Equal: Differences in Caseworker

Support toward Black and White Welfare Clients," *Harvard Journal of African American Public Policy* 4 (1997): 23–33.

80. Michael Bond, "Racial Disparities and Welfare Reform in Milwaukee," paper prepared for the Scholar Practitioner Program, W. K. Kellogg Devolution Initiative, Annual Conference, Washington, D.C., June 2001.

81. Gary Delgado, "Racing the Welfare Debate," *Colorlines,* 3:3 (Fall 2000). http://www.arc.org/c_lines/CLArchive/story3_3_04.html. See also, Rebecca Gordon et al., "Cruel and Usual: How Welfare 'Reform' Punishes Poor People," Applied Research Center, Oakland, Calif., 2001.

82. Joe Soss, Sanford F. Schram, Thomas P. Vartanian and Erin O'Brien, "Setting the Terms of Relief: Explaining State Policy Choices in the Devolution Revolution," *American Journal of Political Science* 45:2 (April 2001): 378–95.

83. Sewell Chan, "D.C. Plans City Jobs for Welfare Recipients," *Washington Post,* January 30, 2001, p. B2.

84. Sewell Chan, "Welfare-to-Work Program Fizzling," *Washington Post,* June 24, 2001, p. C1.

85. Johnathan Rabinovitz, "Welfare Fallout Traps Mothers," *New York Times,* May 19, 1995, p. B1.

86. Lawrence M. Mead, *The New Paternalism in Action: Welfare Reform in Wisconsin* (Milwaukee: Wisconsin Policy Institute, 1995), p. 1.

87. John J. DiIulio, Jr. and Donald F. Kettle, *Fine Print: The Contract with American Devolution and the Administrative Realities of American Federalism* (Washington, D.C.: Brookings Institution, 1995), p. 19.

88. Glenn C. Loury, "Welfare Pair," *New Republic,* January 5 and 12, 1998, p. 9.

89. William Julius Wilson, *When Work Disappears: The World of the New Urban Poor* (New York: Alfred Knopf, 1996), pp. 55–64.

90. Thomas Corbett, "Child Poverty and Welfare Reform," *Focus,* no. 15, Spring 1993, Institute on Research and Poverty, University of Wisconsin.

91. Michael Calabrese, "U.S. Job Creation in 1997: Higher Pay, Lower Benefits," *Policywire,* February 5, 1998 (Center for National Policy, Washington, D.C).

92. CBS/*New York Times* poll, December 1994.

93. Neve Gordon, "As Government Shrinks, People Lose Rights: Devolution of Power Is a Great Way to Increase Tyranny," *Philadelphia Inquirer,* July 6, 1998, p. A9. In March of 1997, the Ohio Association of Non-Profit Associations sponsored a state-wide dialogue on the impact of devolution on social programs. One theme that was raised frequently was expresed this way by one of the participants in the dialogue: "[W]e are losing important minimum standards and guarantees of services and care for some of the most vulnerable individuals in our society. It seems to me that one of the most important functions of the Federal government is to provide this protection for all of our children—particularly those who are most vulnerable." Barry Wolson, March 24, 1997. http:/www.rtk.net/ E16777T923.

Chapter 7

1. Roland P. Faulkner, "Is Crime Increasing?" *Forum*, March 1900, p. 596.

2. Ibid., p. 598.

3. Quoted in ibid., p. 597.

4. Amos N. Wilson, *Black-on-Black Violence: The Psychodynamics of Black Self-Annihilation in Service of White Domination* (New York: African World Infosystems, 1990), pp. 1–10, 180.

5. Ellis Sandoz and Cecil V. Crabb, Jr., eds., *The Tide of Discontent: The 1980 Elections and Their Meaning* (Washington, D.C.: Congressional Quarterly, 1981).

6. William J. Wilson, *Power, Racism, and Privilege: Race Relations in Theoretical and Sociopolitical Perspectives* (New York: Macmillan, 1976).

7. The Gallup Poll, January 16–18, 1995. Reported in Michael Golay and Carl Rollyson, eds., *Where America Stands 1996* (New York: John Wiley and Sons, 1996), p. 91.

8. Cross National Comparative Crime Victimization Research, Netherlands Institute for the Study of Criminality and Law Enforcement, Leiden, Netherlands.

9. Michael Tonry, *Malign Neglect: Race, Crime and Punishment in America* (New York: Oxford University Press, 1995), pp. 1–31.

10. Jerome Miller, *Search and Destroy: African American Males in the Criminal Justice System* (New York: Cambridge University Press, 1996), pp. 218–19.

11. Cited in Fox Butterfield, "U.S. Extends Its Lead in the Rate of Imprisonment," *New York Times*, February 11, 1992, p. A16.

12. Quoted in Lawrence Friedman, *Crime and Punishment in American History* (New York: Basic Books, 1993), p. x.

13. Andrew Hacker, *The End of The American Era* (New York: Athenaeum, 1970); quoted in Bertram Gross, *Friendly Fascism: The New Face of Power in America* (New York: M. Evans, 1980), p. 309.

14. Dee Cook and Barbara Hudson, *Racism and Criminology* (Thousand Oaks, Calif.: Sage Publications, 1993), p. 124.

15. See Michael J. Sniffen, "US Inmate Population Soars in '95," *Boston Globe*, December 4, 1995, p. 3; and Charles Sennott, "Big Rise Recorded in Black Men in Criminal System," *Boston Globe*, October 5, 1995, p. 3.

16. Sennott, "Big Rise Recorded," p. 3.

17. Data from the Department of Justice, reported in *Washington Afro-American*, December 9, 1995, p. A15.

18. Associated Press, "Study Finds Blacks More Likely to Be Jailed before Federal Trials," *Washington Afro-American*, May 17, 1997, p. A11.

19. John DiIulio, "The Question of Black Crime," *Public Interest* 117 (Fall 1994), pp. 3–32.

20. Marc Mauer, "Americans behind Bars: The International Use of Incarceration," Report, the Sentencing Project, Washington, D.C., September 1994.

21. Miller, *Search and Destroy,* Table 1, pp. 11–12.

22. Ibid., p. 13.

23. Richard B. Freeman and Harry J. Holzer, eds., *The Black Youth Unemployment Crisis,* National Bureau of Economic Research (Chicago: University of Chicago Press, 1986), p. 207.

24. Ibid.

25. Quoted in Milton Coleman, "More Reliant on Aid Than Whites, Blacks Hit Harder by Cuts," *Washington Post,* December 4, 1983, pp. A1, A18.

26. This pattern has existed for a long time and has been experienced by other than Black children. See Richard A. Cloward and Lloyd E. Ohlin, *Delinquency and Opportunity: A Theory of Delinquent Gangs* (New York: Free Press, 1960), pp. 152–54.

27. William Julius Wilson, *The Black Underclass,* cited in Rob Gurwitt, "Neighborhoods and the Urban Crisis," *Governing,* 5 (September 1992): 57.

28. William Julius Wilson, *When Work Disappears: The World of the New Urban Poor* (New York: Alfred Knopf, 1996), p. 55.

29. Ibid., p. 59.

30. Fox Butterfield, "Teen-Age Homicide Rate Has Soared," *New York Times,* October 14, 1994, p. A22. Chart, "A Rise in Teen-Age Homicide Victims," Centers for Disease Control and Prevention, October 1994.

31. "Violence in America," *U.S. News and World Report,* January 17, 1994, p. 22.

32. Deborah Prothrow-Stith, *Deadly Consequences: How Violence Is Destroying Our Teenage Population and a Plan to Begin Solving the Problem* (New York: HarperCollins, 1991), pp. 113–21.

33. James C. McKinley, Jr., "3 Charged in Killing over Cocaine Dealings," *New York Times,* June 15, 1995.

34. Circular, "National Weed and Seed Program," Executive Office of Weed and Seed, Office of Justice Programs, U.S. Department of Justice.

35. Rachel L. Swarns, "Governor Removes Bronx Prosecutor from Murder Case: Clash on Death Penalty," *New York Times,* March 22, 1996, p. A1.

36. This statement was made by Maryland House Republican whip Robert L. Flanagan, regarding the pressure exerted by Democrats on the County States Attorney, Marna L. McLendon, to prosecute Linda Tripp for having taped her conversations with Monica Lewinsky, a central figure in an alleged sex scandal involving President Clinton. Daniel LeDuc, "Maryland House Erupts over Non-Prosecution of Tripp," *Washington Post,* February 4, 1998, p. A13.

37. Robert C. Trojanowicz and Bonnie Bucqueroux, "Community Policing and the Challenge of Diversity," National Center for Community Policing, School of Criminal Justice, Michigan State University, p. 7.

38. Katheryn K. Russell, *The Color of Crime* (New York: New York University Press, 1997), pp. 14–25. Russell also sets out six principles of fairness for a criminal justice system, all of which have been and are currently repeatedly violated.

39. See Darnell F. Hawkins and Richard Thomas, "White Policing of Black Populations: A History of Race and Social Control in America," in Eugene Cash-

more and E. Ellis McCaughlin, eds., *Out of Order? Policing Black People* (London: Routledge and Keegan Paul, 1991).

40. *Los Angeles Sentinel,* December 11, 1997, p. A12.

41. Teresa Moore, Thaai Walker and Torri Minton, "Aberration or Advance? What Verdict Means for Blacks," *San Francisco Chronicle,* October 6, 1995, p. A1.

42. Patricia Cohen, "One Angry Man: Paul Butler Wants Black Jurors to Put Loyalty to Race above Loyalty to the Law," *Washington Post,* May 30, 1997, p. B1.

43. Craig Whitlock and David S. Fallis, "Police Shot Minorities in Greater Numbers: Blacks, Latinos Make Up 90% of Cases," *Washington Post,* July 5, 2001, p. T3.

44. Editorial, "Mr. Curry and the Police," *Washington Post,* July 7, 2001, p. A22.

45. David Ashenfelter, "Panel to Probe How Judge Got Nevers' Case," *Detroit Free Press,* July 1, 1998, p. 1A.

46. *Chicago Sun-Times* report, May 1996.

47. Ian Fisher, "Why '3-strikes' Sentencing Is a Solid Hit This Season," *New York Times,* January 25, 1994, p. B1.

48. Mike Males, Dan Macallair and Khaled Taqui-eddin, "Striking out: The Failure of California's 'Three Strikes and You're Out' Law," Justice Policy Institute, Center on Juvenile and Criminal Justice, Los Angeles, California, February 1999. http://www.cjcj.org/jpi/strikingout.html.

49. "'Three Strikes and You're Out'—Its Impact on the California Criminal Justice System After Four Years," California Attorney General's Office, 2001. The attorney general's report claims that the savings from "three strikes" enforcement has been between $5.8 and $15.5 billion. However, this has been offset by the most aggressive prison-building program in the country, under which the state of California built nearly twice as many prisons since 1985 as before.

50. "Remarks Announcing the Anticrime Initiative and an Exchange with Reporters," August 11, 1993, Administration of William J. Clinton, Public Papers of the Presidents of the United States, Book II—August 1 to December 31, 1993, p. 1361.

51. Richard L. Berke, "G.O.P. Leaders Attack Democrats on Crime Issue," *New York Times,* January 22, 1994, p. 9.

52. Quoted in ibid.

53. Quoted in ibid.

54. "Violent and Irrational—and That's Just the Policy," *Economist,* June 8, 1996, p. 24.

55. Floor Statement, House of Representatives, *Congressional Record,* August 4, 1994.

56. "40% on Death Row Are Black, New Figures Show," *New York Times,* September 30, 1991, p. A15. The total exceeds 2,356 because Hispanics can be any race.

57. Floor Statement, Congresswoman Cardiss Collins (D-Ill.), U.S. House of Representatives, *Congressional Record,* April 21, 1994.

58. William Matthewman, "The Racial Disparity on Federal Death Row," *Washington Post*, March 15, 1996, p. A29.

59. Bureau of Justice Statistics, "Death Row Inmates," U.S. Department of Justice, mid-2000 report.

60. *Congressional Record*, June 16, 1994, p. H4620.

61. Ibid., p. H4621.

62. Ibid.

63. Floor Statement, Orrin Hatch (R-Utah), U.S. Senate, *Congressional Record*, April 26, 1994.

64. Floor Statement, Alphonse D'Amato (R-N.Y.), U.S. Senate, *Congressional Record*, July 22, 1994.

65. Cited in Floor Statement, Orrin Hatch (R-Utah), U.S. Senate, *Congressional Record*, April 26, 1994.

66. Quoted in "The Crime Bill—Good Politics, Bad Policy," *Focus* (Joint Center for Political and Economic Studies, Washington, D.C.), February 1995, p. 5.

67. Quoted in ibid.

68. Fox Butterfield, "Study Finds a Disparity In Justice for Blacks," *New York Times*, February 13, 1996, p. A12.

69. See "Race and Class in Sentencing: An Interview with Marc Mauer," *Long Term View* 4:1 (Summer 1997): 61.

70. Ibid., p. 62.

71. Ibid.

72. Ibid.

73. Ibid., p. 64.

74. In a poll by the Joint Center for Political and Economic Studies, the degree of support for "three-strikes-and-you're-out" was 73%; Michael Fletcher, *Washington Post*, April 21, 1996, p. A11.

75. "Race and Class in Sentencing," p. 60.

76. Press release, "Felon Laws Bar 3.9 Million Americans from Voting," October 22, 1998.

77. "Federal Legislation to Support Improvements in Voting Procedures Ignores the Disenfranchisement of Million Ex-Felons," Human Rights News, Human Rights Watch, May 2001.

78. James H. Johnson, Jr. and Walter Farrell, "Race Still Matters," *Chronicle of Higher Education*, July 7, 1995, p. A48.

79. Ibid.

80. This term might be attributed to David Von Drehle, "Cranking up the Killing Machine: New York Restores the Penalty, but Will Anyone Be Executed?" *Washington Post*, February 26, 1995, p. C1.

81. Saundra Torry, "ABA Endorses Moratorium on Capital Punishment," *Washington Post*, February 4, 1997, p. A4.

82. Vickie Chachere, "Florida Death Row Inmate to Be released after 17 Years," Associated Press, January 3, 2002.

83. Laurie Goodstein, "Death Penalty Falls from Favor as Some Lose Confidence in Its Fairness," *New York Times,* June 17, 2001, http:/www.moratorium2000.org.

84. "Briefing Paper: The Death Penalty," American Civil Liberties Union, no. 14, Spring 1999.

85. Fox Butterfield, "Victim's Race Affects Decisions on Killer's Sentence, Study Finds," *New York Times,* April 20, 2001. http://www.moratorium2000.org/index. Also, "Briefing Paper: The Death Penalty," American Civil Liberties Union, no. 14, Spring 1999.

86. Fox Butterfield, "Major Crimes Fell in '95, Early Data by F.B.I. Indicate," *New York Times,* May 6, 1996, p. 1.

87. *New York Times,* January 5, 1997, p. 1.

88. Special, "The Nation's War against Crack Retreats, Still Taking Prisoners," *New York Times,* February 28, 1999, p. 20.

89. Ibid.

90. James Q. Wilson, *Thinking About Crime* (New York: Vintage/Random House, 1985), p. 6.

91. James Q. Wilson, quoted in "The Nation's War against Crack Retreats."

92. Stephan Thernstrom and Abigail Thernstrom, *America in Black and White: One Nation Indivisible* (New York: Simon and Schuster, 1997), pp. 258–85.

93. Ibid., p. 274.

94. See Cook and Hudson, *Racism and Criminology,* p. 6.

95. Russell, *Color of Crime,* p. 31.

96. Darnell F. Hawkins, "Racism in U.S. Criminal Justice," *Crime and Social Justice* 24 (1985): 187–209.

97. Richard B. Freeman, "Crime and the Job Market," NBER Working Paper no. W4910, National Bureau of Economic Research, Cambridge, Mass., October 1994.

98. Richard B. Freeman and William M. Rodgers, III, "Area Economic Conditions and the Labor Market Outcomes of Young Men in the 1990s Expansion," NBER Working Paper no. W7073, National Bureau of Economic Research, Cambridge, Mass., April 1999.

99. Darnell F. Hawkins, "Trends in Black-White Imprisonment: Changing Conceptions of Race or Changing Patterns of Social Control," *Crime and Social Justice,* no. 24 (1985), pp. 196–97.

100. Coramae Richey Mann, *Unequal Justice: A Question of Color* (Bloomington: Indiana University Press, 1993), pp. 115–28.

101. Trojanowicz and Bucqueroux, "Community Policing."

Chapter 8

1. Cited in Caroline Hendrie, "Pressure for Community Schools Grows as Court Oversight Wanes," *Teacher Magazine,* June 17, 1998. http:/www.teacher-

mag.org/ew/vol17/40side.h17. Hendrie provides an impressive picture of the many cities around the country where busing has been eliminated and where "walk-to-school" programs or other manifestations of the pressure for neighborhood schooling exist. Yet it is important to note that in some areas neighborhood schooling is impractical, that some candidates who ran on the issue of neighborhood schools in Buffalo, N.Y., in 1996 were defeated and that court-ordered busing in Delaware has not been eliminated.

2. Ira Katznelson and Margaret Weir, *Schooling for All: Class, Race, and the Decline of the Democratic Ideal* (New York: Basic Books, 1985), p. 27.

3. Ibid., p. 27.

4. "A Nation at Risk: The Imperative for Educational Reform," National Commission of Excellence in Education (Washington, D.C.: U.S. Government Printing Office, 1983).

5. See also Gary Orfield, Susan Eaton and the Harvard Project on School Desegregation, *Dismantling Desegregation: The Quiet Reversal of Brown v. Board of Education* (New York: New Press, 1998).

6. Ibid., p. 6.

7. Bill Dedman, "Segregation Persists despite Fair Housing Act, Chicago Study Finds," *New York Times,* February 13, 1999, p. A1. This article reports the striking findings of a study by the Woodstock Institute, a nonprofit organization that studies community development: of 110 communities that were 10–50% Black in the early 1990s, six years later only 27 of the 110 were still integrated; the rest had become overwhelmingly Black.

8. 1990 U.S. Census data independently confirm this finding. See Margery Austin Turner, "A Look at . . . Segregation and Poverty: Segregation by the Numbers," *Washington Post,* May 18, 1997, p. C3.

9. *Board of Education of Oklahoma City Public Schools, Independent School District No. 80, Oklahoma County, Oklahoma v. Dowell et al.,* no. 89–1080 [January 15, 1991].

10. *Missouri et al. v. Jenkins,* no. 93–1823 [June 12, 1995].

11. *Freeman et al. v. Pitts et al.,* no. 89–1290 [March 31, 1992].

12. Juan Williams, "Schools, Not Voting Rights, Was the Key Racial Ruling," *Washington Post,* July 2, 1996, p. C1.

13. Richard Jones, "African-American Parents Want Emphasis Placed on Academics Rather than Integration," *Buffalo News,* July 29, 1998, p. A7; "Black Parents Put School Quality over Diversity," *Challenger* (Buffalo, N.Y.), August 5, 1998, p. 10.

14. Glen C. Loury, "Integration Has Had Its Day," *New York Times,* April 23, 1997, p. A31.

15. Jones, "African-American Parents."

16. Orfield et al., *Dismantling Desegregation,* p. 9.

17. Gary Orfield, "Schools More Separate: Consequences of a Decade of Resegregation," Civil Rights Project, Harvard University, July 2001, Table 14, p. 41.

18. Quoted in Darryl Fears, "Schools' Racial Isolation Growing," *Washington Post,* July 18, 2001, p. A3.

19. Quoted in ibid., p. A1.

20. Orfield, "Schools More Separate."

21. Ethan Bronner, "Report Shows Urban Pupils Fall Far Short in Basic Skills," *New York Times,* January 8, 1998, p. A12.

22. Michael W. Apple, *Cultural Politics and Education* (New York: Teachers College Press, 1996), pp. 42–67.

23. Ibid.

24. "Quality Counts: The State of the States," Executive Summary Special Report, *Education Week,* January 1997. http://www.edweek.org/sreports/qc97/intros/summary.htm.

25. See ibid.

26. Quoted in Darryl Fears, "Schools' Racial Isolation Growing," *Washington Post,* July 18, 2001, p. A3.

27. "Do Districts Enrolling High Percentages of Minority Students Spend Less?" Issue Brief, National Center for Educational Statistics, December 1996, IB-2–96.

28. See T. B. Parish, C. S. Matsumoto and W. Fowler, Jr., "Disparities in Public School District Spending: 1989–90," U.S. Department of Education, National Center for Educational Statistics, Report no. 95–300, 1995.

29. Ibid.

30. Quoted in "Voucher Students Have Slight Edge, Study Says," *Cincinnati Enquirer,* November 25, 1998, p. 25.

31. Quoted in ibid., p. 4.

32. Tamara Henry, "The Voucher Drive: Education Issue Is in States' Hands," *USA Today,* January 5, 1999, p. D1.

33. Quoted in Tamara Henry, "'Rosa Parks' of Choice Sits out Voucher Fight," *USA Today,* January 5, 1999, p. 6D.

34. Pam Belluck, "School Ruling Shakes Milwaukee," *New York Times,* June 15, 1998, p. A12. See also the statement of Governor Tommy Thompson praising the decision of the court and indicating that eligibility for the expanded program, which includes an additional 15,000 low-income students, would be for children whose family income is 175% of the poverty level ($26,000) per year or less. "Governor Praises Historic School Choice Decision," Tommy G. Thompson, Governor, State of Wisconsin, press release, June 10, 1998.

35. Marvin Hoffman, "Charter Schools Are Not a Threat," *New York Times,* January 6, 1999, p. A27.

36. Jacques Steinberg, "Voucher Program for Inner-City Children," *New York Times,* June 10, 1998, p. A28.

37. Caroline Hendrie, "Net Magnet Schools Policies Sidestep an Old Issue: Race," *Teacher Magazine,* June 30, 1998. http://www.teachermag.org/ew/vol17/39magnet.h17.

38. See René Sanchez, "In Wisconsin, Vouchers for Religious Schools

Handed Legal Setback," *Washington Post,* January 16, 1997, p. A3. Also, Rene Sanchez, "Wisconsin Appeals Court Bars School Vouchers," *Washington Post,* August 23, 1997, p. A7.

39. "What Really Matters in American Education," White Paper on Education prepared for U.S. Secretary of Education Richard W. Riley, Speech, National Press Club, Washington, D.C., September 23, 1997.

40. Neil Postman, *The End of Education: Redefining the Value of Schools* (New York: Knopf, 1996).

41. "Milwaukee Parental School Choice Program: Frequently Asked Questions," Department of Public Instruction, State of Wisconsin. http://www.dpi.state.wi.dpi/sms/mpscfaq.html.

42. Eric Pianin, "Budget Pact's 1st Bottom Line: A Surge in Domestic Spending," *Washington Post,* November 26, 1997, p. A1.

43. Carey Goldberg, "Massachusetts Retreats on Threshold for Teacher Test, Flunking Nearly 60%," *New York Times,* July 2, 1998, p. A12.

44. Robert Johnson, "Flexibility the Theme during ESEA Hearings," *Education Week,* February 3, 1999. http://www.edweek.org/eq/vol18/.

45. Quoted in Joetta L. Slack, "Riley: ESEA Plan Will Push Teacher Quality," *Education Week,* February 17, 1999. http://www.edweek.org/eq/vol18/.

46. Ibid.

47. Senate Bill, S.280, "Education Flexibility Partnership Act of 1999." The bill proposed that: "In general—The Secretary [of Education] may carry out an education flexibility program under which the Secretary authorizes a State educational agency that serves an eligible State to waive statutory or regulatory requirements applicable to 1 or more programs or Acts described in subsection (b), other than requirements described in subsection (c), for the State educational agency or any local educational agency or school within the State." Sec. 4.

48. "ED-FLEX FACT SHEET," U.S. Department of Education, September 19, 1996. Known as the Education Flexibility Partnership Demonstration Program, it was established by the Clinton administration as a part of the "Goals 2000" program and initially included the states of Colorado, Kansas, Maryland, Massachusetts, New Mexico, Ohio, Oregon, Texas and Vermont.

49. "Descriptions of Approved Statewide Programmatic Education Flexibility Partnership Demonstration Program (Ed-Flex) Waivers," Texas Education Agency. http://www.tea.state.tx.us/edflex/approg.html.

50. "Education Flexibility Partnership Act of 1999," House of Representatives, March 11, 1999. Recorded Vote, "Noes-90." http://thomas.loc.gov/cg-bin/query/D?r106:7:./temp/~r106hNpswG:e13601:.

51. See "Congressional Roundup," *Washington Afro-American,* March 20–March 26, 1999, p. A2.

52. Hardy Cross Dillard, "Freedom of Choice and Democratic Values," in Hubert H. Humphrey, ed., *School Desegregation: Documents and Commentaries* (New York: Thomas Y. Crowell, 1964), p. 296. This essay was first published in the *Virginia Quarterly Review,* Summer 1962.

53. See "Divided High Court Upholds Ohio Case on Vouchers," Associated Press, June 20, 2002. Also, Brigid Schulte, "Voters Protective of Public Schools, Wary of Vouchers," *Washington Post*, June 28, 2002, p. A11.

54. Thomas M. Smith, "Minorities in Higher Education," Report, The Condition of Education 1996. http://nces.ed.gov/.

55. "Income in 1999 by Educational Attainment for People 18 Years Old and Over, by Age, Sex, Race, and Hispanic Origin," U.S. Census Bureau, Table 8, March 2000.

56. "Black Women Report Highest Earnings Premium for Additional Education," *Monthly Labor Review*, Editor's Desk, U.S. Department of Labor, February 3, 1999.

57. Ibid.

58. Robert Allen, "The Struggle Continues: Race, Equity and Affirmative Action in Higher Education," in Lee Daniels, *The State of Black America 2001* (New York: National Urban League, 2001), p. 88.

59. Ibid.

60. *Adams v. Richardson* 356 F. Supp. 92 [D.D.C. 1973], modified, 480 F. 2d 1159 [D.C. Cir. 1973].

61. Eileen M. O'Brien, "Dismissal of Adams Marks End of an Era," *Black Issues in Higher Education* 7:11 (August 2, 1990), p. 8.

62. California Secretary of State webpage: http://vote96.ss.ca.gov/vote96/htm.

63. *Wygant v. Jackson Board of Education*, 476 U.S. 267 [1986].

64. *Congressional Record*, May 6, 1998, p. H2908.

65. Racism, however, is the expression of a racial animus toward a group or individual with the intention of harming an individual or group on that basis. While the expression of such an animus may be a source of harm, racism has generally resulted in more substantial forms of social harm.

66. *Congressional Record*, May 6, 1998, p. H2905.

67. William G. Bowen and Derek Bok, *The Shape of the River: Long-Term Consequences of Considering Race in College and University Admissions* (Princeton: Princeton University Press, 1998).

68. Cited in Ben Gose, "A Sweeping New Defense of Affirmative Action," *Chronicle of Higher Education*, September 18, 1998, p. A46.

69. Michelle Locke, "California's Proposition 209 Takes Effect: Minority Admissions Plummet," Associated Press, April 1, 1998.

70. Michael A. Fletcher, "Civil Rights Groups File Suit over California Admissions Policy," *Washington Post*, February 3, 1999, p. A2.

71. See Ronald Walters, "Affirmative Action and the Politics of Concept Appropriation," *Howard Law Journal* 38:3 (Summer 1995): 587–609.

72. *Hopwood v. Texas*, no. Civ. A-92–CA-563–SS, 1994 WL 242362 W. D. Tex. [January 20, 1994]. Also, *Hopwood*, 78 F. 3d at 962.

73. Charles Babington, "Court Leaves Intact Ban on Blacks-only Scholarship at U-MD," *Washington Post*, May 23, 1995, p. A1.

74. Maryanne George and Erik Lords, "U-M Law School's Race Policy Rejected," *Detroit Free Press*, March 28, 2001, p. A1.

75. *Congressional Record*, May 6, 198, p. H2914.

76. "Redeeming the American Promise," Report of the Panel on Educational Opportunity and Post Secondary Desegregation, Southern Education Foundation, Atlanta, Georgia, 1995, p. xviii.

77. Ibid.

78. "Supreme Court Rejects Desegregation Case Appeal," *Atlanta Journal/Atlanta Constitution*, Associated Press, January 21, 1998, p. A10.

79. *Jake Ayers, Jr., et al. v. Ronnie Musgrove, Governor State of Mississippi, et al.*, Civil Action no. 4:75cv9–B-D, U.S. District Court of Northern District of Mississippi [May 8, 2001].

80. *Congressional Record*, May 6, 1998, p. H2907.

81. Stuart Taylor, Jr., "Seeking Diversity without Racial Preferences," *National Journal*, November 22, 1999. http://www.nationaljournal.com/taylor.htm.

82. Jared Bernstein, "Where's the Payoff? The Gap between Black Academic Progress and Economic Gains," Economic Policy Institute, Washington, D.C., 1995.

83. Ethan Bronner, "Rights Groups Suing Florida for Failure to Educate Pupils," *New York Times*, January 9, 1999, p. A8.

84. Richard Bardolph, ed., *The Civil Rights Record: Black Americans and the Law, 1849–1970* (New York: Thomas Y. Crowell, 1970), p. 453.

Chapter 9

1. Quoted in Stan Faryna, Brad Stetson and Joseph Conti, eds., *Black and Right: The Bold New Voice of Black Conservatives in America* (Westport, Conn.: Praeger, 1997), p. 5.

2. Charles Hamilton, "Measuring Black Conservatism," in *The State of Black America 1982* (New York: National Urban League, 1983). Professor Hamilton was an invited guest at the Fairmount meeting.

3. Quoted in Jack Anderson and Michael Binstein, "The Republicans' Racial Rhetoric," *Washington Post*, January 16, 1995, p. D9.

4. Ibid.

5. An impressive collection of such documentation exists in Kenneth O'Reilly, *Racial Matters: The FBI's Secret File on Black America, 1960–1972* (New York: Macmillan/Free Press, 1989).

6. Carl E. Jackson and Emory J. Tolbert, eds., *Race and Culture in America: Readings in Racial and Ethnic Relations*, 3rd ed. (Bellweather Press/Burgess International Group, 1989), p. 118.

7. George M. Frederickson, *The Black Image in the White Mind: the Debate over Afro-American Character and Destiny, 1817–1914* (New York: HarperTorch Books, 1972), pp. 97–129.

8. August Meier, *Negro Thought in America* (Ann Arbor: University of Michigan Press, 1963), pp. 25–27.

9. See Dewy Grantham, ed., *Ralph J. Bunch: The Political Status of the Negro in the Age of FDR* (Chicago: University of Chicago Press, 1973), p. 84.

10. See Howard Rabinowitz, ed., *Southern Black Leaders of the Reconstruction Era* (Chicago: University of Illinois Press, 1982), pp. 15–26.

11. See John Hope Franklin and August Meier, eds., *Black Leaders of the Twentieth Century* (Chicago: University of Illinois Press, 1982), p. 7.

12. Booker T. Washington, *The Negro In Business* (1902; reprint, Wichita: Devore and Sons, 1992).

13. Alexander Charles, "Professor Council's Position Ours," *Alexander's Magazine* 2 (May 1906): 23–24.

14. Jeffrey B. Leak, ed., *Rac[e]ing to The Right: Selected Essays of George S. Schuyler* (Knoxville: University of Tennessee Press, 2001), p. xxxiv.

15. Ibid.

16. Ibid., pp. xxxviii–xxxix.

17. Ibid., p. xli.

18. Hanes Walton, "Blacks and Conservative Political Movements," in Lenneal J. Henderson, ed., *Black Political Life in the United States* (San Francisco: Chandler, 1972), p. 221.

19. David Bositis, "2000 National Opinion Poll," Joint Center for Political and Economic Studies, Washington, D.C., p. 9.

20. This unpublished collection of papers was organized by Dr. Robert Smith, San Francisco State University, and is known as "Studies in Black Conservatism."

21. Hamilton, "Measuring Black Conservatism," p. 138.

22. See Richard Rubin, *Party Dynamics* (New York: Oxford University Press, 1976), p. 41; Rubin provides support for the notion that Liberals and Conservatives could be separated along operational lines.

23. Andrea Y. Simpson, "In Search of African-American Conservatives: A Study of Middle-Class Political Attitudes," paper delivered at the 1994 Annual Meeting of the American Political Science Association, New York, September 1–4, 1994.

24. Survey numbers on Black Conservatives are difficult to find, however, because of the paucity of their numbers nationally.

25. See James M. Washington, *Testament of Hope: The Essential Writings of Martin Luther King, Jr.* (New York: Harper and Row, 1986), p. 307.

26. John Ehrman, *The Rise of Neoconservatism: Intellectuals and Foreign Affairs 1945–1994* (New Haven: Yale University Press, 1995), pp. 110–11.

27. In an unpublished paper, "Liberalism Is the Deck, All Else is the Sea: The Structure of Political Belief in Black America," Howard University, 1982, Professor Robert Smith comments on the assertions of Edward Carmines and James Stimson ("The Racial Orientation of the American Electorate," in John Pierce and John Sullivan, eds., *The Electorate Reconsidered* [Beverly Hills, Calif.:

Sage, 1980], pp. 199–218). Smith argues that even though "it is not accurate to describe one party as racist and the other as anti-racist," Carmines and Stimson's data do suggest that "racial attitudes are not only performing the structuring functions associated with the liberalism-conservatism dimension but that much of the meaning of this ideological dimension is also racial in nature" (p. 16).

28. Robert Smith, *We Have No Leaders: African Americans in the Post-Civil Rights Era* (Albany: State University of New York Press, 1996), p. 135.

29. Quoted in Kathy Sawyer, "President to Push Flemming off Civil Rights Commission," *Washington Post,* November 17, 1981, p. A1.

30. Quoted in Jacqueline Trescott and Eve Ferguson, "Chairman Clarence Pendleton, Jr.: The 'Wild Card' of the Civil Rights Commission," *Washington Post,* November 14, 1982, p. HI. Also, Jacqueline Trescott, "Issues amid Festivities: At the Parties, a Debate among Black Republicans," *Washington Post,* January 21, 1985, p. C3.

31. Quoted in Mary Thornton, "Pendleton Complains to Reagan: Rights Chief Raps Favors to Minorities," *Washington Post,* July 3, 1984, p. A1.

32. Trescott, "Chairman Clarence Pendleton, Jr."

33. Quoted in ibid.

34. Juan Williams, "The Harsh Message for Blacks from Clarence Pendleton," *Washington Post,* June 12, 1988, p. C7.

35. *Black Power: The Politics of Liberation in America* (New York: Random House, 1967).

36. Trescott, "Issus amid Festivities," p. C3.

37. Quoted in Milton Coleman, "Administration Asks Blacks to Fend for Themselves," *Washington Post,* December 5, 1983, pp. A1, A18.

38. See Jane Mayer and Jill Abramson, *Strange Justice: The Selling of Clarence Thomas* (New York: Houghton Mifflin, 1994), p. 299.

39. Rudolph Alexander Jr., "Justice Clarence Thomas' First Year on the Supreme Court: A Reason for Blacks to Be Concerned," *Journal of Black Studies* 27:3 (January 1997): 381–82.

40. Quoted in ibid.

41. Quoted in ibid., p. 359.

42. Tony Mauro, "The Education of Clarence Thomas," *American Lawyer,* August 2001, p. 79.

43. Ibid., p. 80.

44. "The Case against Clarence Thomas," *Washington Post,* Outlook, June 9, 1996, p. C2.

45. Ibid.

46. Ibid.

47. Ibid. Mr. Williams is a confidant of Judge Thomas. A not-so-vigorous defense was offered in Thomas's behalf by the *Washington Afro-American,* a Black newspaper that also put forth a First Amendment rationale for its support. Also, the *Washington Afro-American* supported Thomas's right to speak. See "Clarence Thomas," Editorials, *Washington Afro-American,* June 8, 1996, p. A4.

48. Quoted in Edward Felsenthal, "Black Leaders Try to Deny Thomas Status as Role Model," *Wall Street Journal,* January 31, 1997, p. 1.

49. "Mfume Criticizes Action by Md. NAACP," Associated Press, *Washington Post,* January 16, 1997, p. D2.

50. *Congressional Record,* February 1997, p. S1254.

51. David A. Bositis, "Joint Center for Political and Economic Studies' 1996 National Opinion Poll: Political Attitudes," February 1996, p. 5.

52. Joan Biskupic, "For Clarence Thomas, Another Invitation and Another Flap," *Washington Post,* June 18, 1998, p. A6.

53. Quoted in ibid.

54. Opinion Editorial, "Justice Thomas Speaks," *Washington Post,* July 31, 1998, p. A24.

55. Joseph Mianowany, Special to AOL (America Online), June 13, 1996.

56. These excerpts are Connerly's speech printed in the newsletter of an organization dedicated to "the preservation of the free enterprise system and America's Constitutional system": "Behind the Headlines," Newsletter, America's Future, St. Louis, Mo., May 4, 1997.

57. Connerly frequently makes such statements to explain his opposition to affirmative action. The author had direct experience with these views in a debate with Connerly at the University of Tennessee at Knoxville, spring 1998.

58. "Connerly Calls on Clinton to Remove Affirmative Action from Race Panel's Work," *ACRI News,* American Civil Rights Institute, December 19, 1997.

59. "Initiative 200 Backers Picket US Bank to Protest Its Opposition to Measure," Associated Press, August 10, 1998.

60. *Congressional Record,* March 3, 1997, p. E360.

61. Ibid.

62. Quoted in Alan Sayre, "Ward Connerly's Appearance at Contractors Meeting Protested," *Los Angeles Sentinel,* March 19, 1998, p. A-13.

63. Quoted in ibid.

64. Frank McCoy, "Thanks, but No Thanks," *Black Enterprise* (New York, July 1995), p. 22.

65. Bob Dole and J. C. Watts, Jr., "A New Civil Rights Agenda," *Wall Street Journal,* July 27, 1995, p. A10.

66. Kate Walsh O'Beirne, "Bread and Circuses: J. Talent and J. C. Watts Fight for Passage of the American Renewal Communities Act," *National Review,* V. 49, April 21, 1997, p. 21.

67. Paul A. Gigot, "Ward v. Watts: GOP Debates Racial Politics," *Wall Street Journal,* May 23, 1997, p. A18.

68. Quoted in Juliet Eilperin, "Watts Walks a Tightrope on Affirmative Action, and the House GOP Follows," *Washington Post,* May 12, 1998, p. A17.

69. NAACP "Legislative Report Card," 107th Congress, First Session, Midterm Convention Edition, NAACP Washington Bureau, July 2001. This report card was based on the NAACP's position on five issues which came before the House of Representatives: (1) opposition to the president's tax cut; (2) support for

education reform and removal of the provision for reading and math tests for students in grades 3 through 8; (3) support for school construction funds; (4) support for school accountability measures; and (5) support for Sudan human rights sanctions and report by companies doing business there.

70. McCoy, "Thanks, but No Thanks."

71. Quoted in John F. Dickerson, "The Watts Solution," *Time,* November 30, 1998, p. 44.

72. Juliet Zilperin, "Rep. Watts of Oklahoma Set to Retire," *Washington Post,* July 2, 2002, p. A2.

73. The Dennis Praeger Show, CBS Television, March 5, 1995.

Chapter 10

1. Robert C. Winthrop, *Life and Letters of John Winthrop,* vol. 2 (New York: Da Capo Press, 1971), p. 19.

2. Quoted in William Safire, ed., *Lend Me Your Ears: Great Speeches In History* (New York, W. W. Norton, 1992), p. 713.

3. See Michael Lipsky, *Street Level Bureaucracy: Dilemmas of the Individual in Public Service* (Thousand Oaks, Calif.: Russell Sage, 1980).

4. Carter A. Wilson, *Racism: From Slavery to Advanced Capitalism* (Thousand Oaks, Calif.: Sage Publications, 1996), p. 226.

5. David S. Broder, "Jesse Helms, White Racist," *Washington Post,* August 29, 2001, p. A21.

6. Ibid.

7. Robert D. Novak, "Playing the Color Card," *Washington Post,* November 10, 1997, p. A21.

8. Hugh B. Price, "Who Is an American," *Columbus Post,* January 1–7, 1998, p. A6.

9. Ibid.

10. Howard Schuman, Charlotte Steeh, Lawrence Bobo and Maria Krysan, *Racial Attitudes in America: Trends and Interpretations,* rev. ed. (Cambridge, Mass.: Harvard University Press, 1997), pp. 238–78.

11. Ibid., p. 264.

12. Patricia Gurin, Shirley Hatchett and James S. Jackson, *Hope and Independence: Blacks' Response to Electoral and Party Politics* (New York: Russell Sage Foundation, 1989), p. 232.

13. Joseph P. McCormick II, "The Messages and the Messengers: Opinions from the Million Men Who Marched," Political Science Department, Howard University, June 1996.

14. See Lee Sigelman and Susan Welch, *Black Americans' View of Racial Inequality: The Dream Deferred* (New York: Cambridge University Press, 1991).

15. "The Social and Economic Status of the Black Population in the United States 1973," Current Population Report, Bureau of the Census, U.S. Department of Commerce, 1974, pp. 29, 42, 68.

16. Rochelle Sharpe, "Losing Ground: In Latest Recession, Only Blacks Suffered Net Employment Loss," *Wall Street Journal*, September 14, 1993, p. A1.

17. Ibid., p. A13.

18. Editorial, *New York Times*, February 17, 1998, p. A22.

19. "Social and Economic Status of the Black Population in the United States, 1973," pp. 29–30.

20. Michael K. Brown, "Gutting the Great Society: Black Economic Progress and the Budget Cuts," *Urban League Review* 7 (Winter 1982–1983): 13. Here Brown cites Richard R. Freeman, "Changes in Labor Market Activity for Black Americans, 1948–1972," *Brookings Paper on Economic Activity*, 1973, pp. 67–120. Also, Bernard E. Anderson and Phyllis A. Wallace, "Public and Black Economic Progress: A Review of the Evidence," *American Economic Review* 65:2 (May 1975): 47–52.

21. Brown, "Gutting the Great Society," p. 13.

22. Ibid., pp. 14–15.

23. Schuman, Steeh and Bobo, *Racial Attitudes in America*, p. 159.

24. Ibid., p. 161.

25. Larry Hugick, "Blacks See Their Lives Worsening," *Gallup Poll Monthly*, April 1992, p. 26.

26. "Black/White Relations in the United States," *Gallup Poll, Social Audit*, July 1997, p. 15.

27. "Hotel Industry Progress," NAACP Online, 1998. www.naacp.org/programs/econrep/hotelnow.html.

28. See Ronald Walters and Robert Smith, *African American Leadership* (Albany: State University of New York Press, 1999), ch. 9.

29. Shari Rudavsky, Brad Bennett and Andrea Robinson, "Black Voters Protest Alleged Improprieties," *Miami Herald*, November 10, 2000, p. A16. Also, David Montgomery, "Simmering Election Anger Incites Rights Leaders," *Washington Post*, January 5, 2001, p. A10.

30. This is a general conclusion reached in my *Black Presidential Politics in America* (Albany: State University of New York Press, 1988). However, notions of "clientage" in African American politics were first described by Dr. Ralph Bunche, and the word was coined by Professor Matthew Holden in his *The Politics of the Black Nation* (New York: Chandler, 1973).

31. "The Agenda," Congressional Black Caucus, 105th Congress of the United States, 1997–1999.

32. Using the legislative search tool, thomas.gov, I accumulated the record of legislation for each member of the Congressional Black Caucus in the 106th Congress.

33. Robert Singh, *The Congressional Black Caucus* (Thousand Oaks, Calif.: Sage Publications, 1998), pp. 8–10.

34. See Fred I. Greenstein, *Personality and Politics* (Chicago: Markham, 1969), p. 7.

35. Robert M. Entman, "The Impact of Ideology on Legislative Behavior and Public Policy in the States," *Journal of Politics* 45:1 (February 1983): 163–82.

36. Alan D. Monroe, "Public Opinion and Public Policy, 1980–1993," *Public Opinion Quarterly* 62 (Spring 1998): 6–28.

37. Samuel P. Huntington, "Conservatism as an Ideology," *American Political Science Review* 51:2 (June 1957): 458.

38. See, for example, Norman H. Nie, Sidney Verba and John R. Petrocik, *The Changing American Voter* (1976; 2nd ed., Cambridge, Mass.: Harvard University Press, 1979).

39. Michael Lind, "Are We a Nation?" *Dissent,* Summer 1995, p. 357.

Index

Books in the African American Life Series

Coleman Young and Detroit Politics: From Social Activist to Power Broker, by Wilbur Rich, 1988

Great Black Russian: A Novel on the Life and Times of Alexander Pushkin, by John Oliver Killens, 1989

Indignant Heart: A Black Worker's Journal, by Charles Denby, 1989 (reprint)

The Spook Who Sat by the Door, by Sam Greenlee, 1989 (reprint)

Roots of African American Drama: An Anthology of Early Plays, 1858–1938, edited by Leo Hamalian and James V. Hatch, 1990

Walls: Essays, 1985–1990, by Kenneth McClane, 1991

Voices of the Self: A Study of Language Competence, by Keith Gilyard, 1991

Say Amen, Brother! Old-Time Negro Preaching: A Study in American Frustration, by William H. Pipes, 1991 (reprint)

The Politics of Black Empowerment: The Transformation of Black Activism in Urban America, by James Jennings, 1992

Pan Africanism in the African Diaspora: An Analysis of Modern Afrocentric Political Movements, by Ronald Walters, 1993

Three Plays: The Broken Calabash, Parables for a Season, and The Reign of Wazobia, by Tess Akaeke Onwueme, 1993

Untold Tales, Unsung Heroes: An Oral History of Detroit's African American Community, 1918–1967, by Elaine Latzman Moon, Detroit Urban League, Inc., 1994

Discarded Legacy: Politics and Poetics in the Life of Frances E.W. Harper, 1825–1911, by Melba Joyce Boyd, 1994

African American Women Speak Out on Anita Hill–Clarence Thomas, edited by Geneva Smitherman, 1995

Lost Plays of the Harlem Renaissance, 1920–1940, edited by James V. Hatch and Leo Hamalian, 1996

Let's Flip the Script: An African American Discourse on Language, Literature, and Learning, by Keith Gilyard, 1996

A History of the African American People: The History, Traditions, and Culture of African Americans, edited by James Oliver Horton and Lois E. Horton, 1997 (reprint)

Tell It to Women: An Epic Drama for Women, by Osonye Tess Onwueme, 1997

Ed Bullins: A Literary Biography, by Samuel Hay, 1997

Walkin' over Medicine, by Loudelle F. Snow, 1998 (reprint)

Negroes with Guns, by Robert F. Williams, 1998 (reprint)

A Study of Walter Rodney's Intellectual and Political Thought, by Rupert Lewis, 1998

Ideology and Change: The Transformation of the Caribbean Left, by Perry Mars, 1998

"Winds Can Wake Up the Dead": An Eric Walrond Reader, edited by Louis Parascandola, 1998

Race & Ideology: Language, Symbolism, and Popular Culture, edited by Arthur Spears, 1999

Without Hatreds or Fears: Jorge Artel and the Struggle for Black Literary Expression in Colombia, by Laurence E. Prescott, 2000

African Americans, Labor, and Society: Organizing for a New Agenda, edited by Patrick L. Mason, 2001

The Concept of Self: A Study of Black Identity and Self-Esteem, by Richard L. Allen, 2001

What the Wine-Sellers Buy Plus Three: Four Plays by Ron Milner, 2001

Looking Within/Mirar adentro: Selected Poems, 1954–2000, by Nancy Morejón, edited and with an introduction by Juanamaría Cordones-Cook, 2003

Liberation Memories: The Rhetoric and Poetics of John Oliver Killens, by Keith Gilyard, 2003

What Mama Said: An Epic Drama, by Osonye Tess Onwueme, 2003

White Nationalism, Black Interests: Conservative Public Policy and the Black Community, by Ronald W. Walters, 2003

For an updated listing of books in this series, please visit our Web site at http://wsupress.wayne.edu

Printed in the United States
17634LVS00003B/43-102